ROMANS

WITHOUT LAURELS

INDRO MONTANELLI

Translated from the Italian by Arthur Oliver

PANTHEON BOOKS

TO

Susina Moizzi

Contents

To the Reader

WHEN THIS HISTORY OF ROME FIRST APPEARED IN ITALY, I RECEIVED numerous indignant letters. Some accused me of levity, triviality, and pessimism, and others of outright irreverence in the way I treated a subject considered sacred.

I was not surprised at this. In fact, up to now, only the academic apologetic style has been used in writing about Rome. I am sure this is the very reason why precious little of it remains in the reader's head, and why, after finishing school, very few of us are tempted to take a refresher course. Nothing is more boring than to follow a story in which all the characters are monuments. I myself had quite a struggle at first to keep from yawning when, realizing some years ago that I had forgotten everything, I decided to study it all over again. But my boredom disappeared when I came across Suetonius and Dion Cassius who, being contemporaries of those monuments, showed no such reverent and awed respect for them.

Following their lead, I went through the other Roman historians and chroniclers. It was like bringing a stone to life. All at once the famous personages, who at school had been presented to us as mere mummies or as inhuman abstract symbols, lost their immobility and assumed vices, weaknesses, mannerisms, and manias. In a word, they became alive and real.

Why should we respect these personages more than the Romans themselves did? Are we doing them a favor to leave them on pedestals in chilly museum halls where only children, haunted by the examination bogey, are sent by their teachers? I know of Jesuits who, committing no breach of orthodoxy, have written impartial hagiographies in which the saints appear as they actually were, men among men with all their obstinacies and vagaries. The fact that many of them erred and that every one of them was tempted takes nothing away from their holiness. Quite the opposite. Jesus Christ made an Apostle of Saint Peter, who had denied him.

What makes the history of Rome great is not that it was made by men different from us, but that it was made by men like ourselves. There was nothing supernatural about them. If there had been, there would be less reason for us to admire them. Cicero and Carnelutti, the famous jurist, have a lot in common. Caesar as a young man was an utter blackguard, and all his life remained the woman-chaser who used to comb his hair over the top from the back and sides because he was ashamed of being bald. Augustus did not spend all his time like an automaton organizing the empire, but also having trouble with his colitis and rheumatism, and he very nearly lost his first battle against Brutus and Cassius owing to an attack of diarrhea.

I believe the greatest wrong one can do these men is to hush up the truth about them as human beings, as though one feared they might be belittled by it. No. Rome was Rome not because its heroes did not commit crimes and extravagances, but because those crimes and extravagances, however great—and some of them were enormous—could not deprive them of their right to eminence.

I have discovered nothing new in writing this book. Everything narrated here has been narrated before. I hope I have told it in a simpler and more understanding manner, in a straightforward and more readily acceptable style, by a series of portraits which reveal the principal players in a truer light, and by stripping from them the disguise of their stately vestments.

To some this may seem a modest ambition, but not to me. Far from it. I consider it a noble undertaking. If I have made the history of Rome attractive to thousands who hitherto have been put off by the pomposity of my predecessors, I shall count myself, with all due respect to those who accuse me of levity, triviality, defeatism, or even of irreverence, a useful, fortunate, and highly successful author.

INDRO MONTANELLI

Romans Without Laurels

I

Ab Urbe Condita

NOBODY KNOWS EXACTLY WHEN THE FIRST SCHOOLS WERE OPENED in Rome. Plutarch puts it at about 250 B.C., or some five hundred years after the founding of the city. Until then Roman boys were educated at home, the poorer ones by their parents, the richer ones by *magistri*, that is by masters or tutors, usually chosen from among the *liberti*, freed slaves. They in their turn were chosen from prisoners of war, preferably those of Greek origin, who were the most cultured.

We do know with certainty however that boys of ancient Rome had to cram less than those of today. Luckily, they already knew Latin. As the German poet Heine said, if they had had to learn it they would never have had the time to conquer the world.

As for their history lessons, they used to go something like this: When the Greeks of Menelaus, Ulysses, and Achilles conquered Troy in Asia Minor and put it to fire and sword, one of the few surviving defenders was Aeneas. He was strongly "recommended" by his mother, none other than the goddess Venus-Aphrodite. (Nepotism was widespread even in those days.) With his little traveling bag, full of images of his celestial protectors—among whom, naturally, his dear mother had pride of place—but without a penny in his pocket, the poor fellow began to wander aimlessly about the world. After heaven knows how many adventures and misadventures, he landed in Italy and began to travel north. On reaching Latium he married the daughter of King Latinus, a girl called Lavinia, founded a city which he named after his wife, and they lived there happily for the rest of their days.

His son Ascanius founded Alba Longa which became the new capital. After another eight generations, which means roughly two hundred years after the arrival of Aeneas, two of his descendants, Numitor and Amulius, were on the throne of Latium. Unfortunately it's rather tight for two on a throne, so one day Amulius drove out Numitor to reign on his own and killed all his brother's children except one: Rea Silvia. To keep her from bringing any child into the world who, when he grew up, might get the wild idea of avenging his grandfather, he forced her to become a priestess of the goddess Vesta, that is, a nun.

One day Rea, who was probably longing for a husband and did not at all relish the idea of eternal maidenhood, was taking the air on the river bank. It was an infernally hot summer, and she fell asleep there. Just then the god Mars happened to be visiting the district, partly to stir up a little strife, which was his normal job, and partly in quest of girls, who were his favorite pastime. He saw Rea Silvia, took a fancy to her, and without even waking her up got her pregnant.

When Amulius heard about this, he was very angry. But he did not have her killed. He waited until she gave birth not to one but to twin boys. He had these put on a tiny raft and pushed out into the river so that they would be carried down to the sea and drowned. But he had reckoned without the wind. It was pretty strong that day and it stranded the fragile craft in the open country not far away. Here the two waifs, who were bawling their heads off, attracted the attention of a she-wolf who ran to suckle them. Thus that animal became the symbol of Rome, later founded by the twins.

The uncharitable say that this she-wolf was no animal, but a woman, a certain Acca Larentia, nicknamed "She-wolf" on account of her savage character and her many infidelities to her husband, a poor shepherd. They say that she was always skipping off to the woods to make love with the local lads.

The twins suckled milk, and grew their first teeth. One was named Romulus and the other Remus. They grew up and finally found out who they were. So back they went to Alba Longa, stirred up a revolution, killed Amulius, and put Numitor back on the throne. Then like all enterprising young men, instead of waiting patiently for a ready-made kingdom from their grand-father, who would certainly have left it to them, they hastened to found one for themselves a little farther down the road. They chose the very place where their raft had run aground, among the hills through which the Tiber winds just before it flows into the sea. Here, as often happens between brothers, they quar-reled over what name to give the city. So they decided that the one who saw the most birds would win the chance to choose. Remus, on the Aventine, saw six; Romulus on the Palatine saw twelve. The city was therefore to be called Rome. They yoked two white oxen, traced a furrow, and built the walls, swearing to kill anyone who passed through them. Remus, who was a bad loser, said that they were weak walls and broke off a chunk with a kick, whereupon Romulus, faithful to his oath, killed him with one blow of his mattock.

All this, they say, took place 753 years before the birth of Christ, to be exact on the twenty-first of April. This day is still celebrated as the birthday of the city, born as we have seen of fratricide. Its inhabitants dated the beginning of the history of the world from that day, and this went on until the advent of the Redeemer laid down another system.

Perhaps the neighboring peoples did the same: each of them dated the history of the world from the founding of their own capitals, whether it was Alba Longa, Rieti, Tarquinia, or Arezzo. They never succeeded in getting the others to recognize this because they made the slight mistake of losing the war—or rather, the wars. Rome on the other hand won them, all of them. The small holding of a few acres which Romulus and Remus cut out for themselves with a plow among the hills of the Tiber became, in the course of a few centuries, the center of Latium, then of Italy, and then of the whole world. And in all that known world its language was spoken, its laws obeyed, and the years were counted *ab urbe condita*, that is, from that famous twenty-first of April, 753 B.C., the beginning of the story of Rome and its civilization.

Naturally things did not happen exactly like that, but that was how Roman fathers for many centuries wished it to be taught to their children, partly because they believed it them-

selves and partly because, as great patriots, they were very flattered at being able to drop the names of influential gods such as
Venus and Mars and V.I.P.s like Aeneas in connection with the
founding of their city. They had a vague feeling that it was important to bring up their children in the conviction that they
belonged to a country which had been founded with the aid
of supernatural beings, who certainly would not have gone to
the trouble unless they had a great destiny in store for it. This
conviction gave a religious basis to the whole life of Rome,
which in fact collapsed as soon as that basis was undermined.
The city was *caput mundi,* the capital of the world for just as
long as its inhabitants knew comparatively little and were in-
genuous enough to believe the legends which their fathers and
magistri had taught them, and for as long as they were convinced that they were descendants of Aeneas, that they had
divine blood in their veins, and were the "anointed of the Lord,"
even if at that time he was called Jove. It was when they began
to doubt these things that their empire went to pieces and the
caput mundi became a colony. But let's not rush.

Of the charming fable of Romulus and Remus perhaps not
all is fantasy. Let us try to get to the bottom of it in the light of
the few fairly definite facts given to us by archaeologists and
ethnologists.

It appears that thirty thousand years before the founding of
Rome, Italy was already inhabited by man. The experts say they
can tell what sort of man since they have reconstructed his
skeleton from various odds and ends of bones found here and
there that go back to the Stone Age. Not having much faith in
these deductions, let us take a jump forward in time to a much
more recent period. The Neolithic Age of something like eight
thousand years ago was five thousand before Rome. It seems
that at that time the peninsula was populated by certain Ligurians in the north and by Siculians in the south. These people
had pear-shaped heads, lived in caves or round huts made of
dung and mud, kept domestic animals, and subsisted by hunting
and fishing.

Now let us skip another four thousand years. In 2000 B.C.
other tribes were arriving from the north, that is from the Alps.
Who can say how long they had been on the move from their
country of origin, central Europe? These people were not much
less primitive than the natives with pear-shaped heads, but they

used to make their dwellings, not in caves, but on piles sunk in the water. They came, obviously, from marshy country. In fact, as soon as they got to Italy they made straight for the region of the lakes, Maggiore, Como, and Garda, thus anticipating the tastes of modern tourists by several thousand years. And they did introduce to Italy one or two great innovations such as grazing of flocks, cultivating the soil, weaving of cloth, and fortifying villages with earthworks against attack by man and beast.

Gradually they moved south and began to build their huts on dry ground, though they were still perched on poles. Furthermore, they had learned from certain cousins of theirs, who had apparently settled in Germany, the use of iron with which they made themselves a whole lot of new tools, axes, knives, razors, and the like. They were also the founders of what could be called a real city, Villanova, which must have been somewhere near the present-day Bologna. It was the center of a civilization known as Villanovan that slowly spread over the entire peninsula. The Umbrians, Sabines, and Latins are believed to have originated from this civilization—race, language, and customs.

Nobody knows what these Villanovans did with the native Ligurians and Siculians when they occupied the lands on either side of the Tiber. Perhaps they exterminated them as was the habit in those "barbaric" times, so called to distinguished them from our "civilized" times in which we do exactly the same thing. Perhaps they subdued and then absorbed them. The fact remains that by about 1000 B.C. the newcomers had founded a good many villages between the mouth of the Tiber and the Bay of Naples, and that, although they were all of the same race, they were always at war with one another and only got together in the face of a common enemy or on the occasion of some religious feast.

The biggest and most powerful of these little towns was Alba Longa, the capital of Latium, which lay at the foot of Monte Albano and was probably on the same site as the town of Castel Gandolfo. The handful of adventurous young fellows who one day migrated some ten miles further north and founded Rome are believed to have been Albalongans. Perhaps they were farm laborers looking for a piece of land to settle on, or perhaps they were shady types wanted by the police and magistrates of their city. Perhaps, even, they were emissaries sent by

their government to keep an eye on that point of the border
with Tuscany on whose coasts a new population, the Etruscans, had just landed. It is not known what part of the world
these new people came from. In any case, nobody had a good
word to say for them.

Perhaps among those Albalongan pioneers there really was
one called Romulus and another called Remus. At all events
they could not have been more than a hundred strong. The site
they chose had many advantages and many drawbacks. It lay
about fifteen miles inland from the sea, and this was admirable
for it afforded protection against pirates, and at the same time
it had a port as the river was easily navigable by the boats of
that day right down to its mouth. The surrounding swamps and
marshes made it malarial, and malaria is an enemy that has sat
on Rome's doorstep until only a few years ago. However, there
were the hills which to a certain extent protected the inhabitants from the mosquitoes, and it was on one of these, the Palatine, that they first settled themselves, with the intention of
populating the other six in due course.

But to populate them they needed children, and to have
children these settlers, all bachelors, needed wives.

History does not tell us how Romulus, or whatever the
leader of the gang was called, got women for himself and his
crew, and so we have to fall back on the legend. This says that
he organized a big feast, maybe with the excuse of celebrating
the birth of his new city, and invited the Sabine (or Quirite)
neighbors to come with their king, Titus Tatius, telling them to
be sure to bring their daughters along. And while these Sabines
were busily engaged in running and horse-racing, their favorite
sports, their hosts kicked them off the premises and very un-
sportingly stole their girls.

The ancients were touchy on the matter of women. Not long
before, the kidnapping of one named Helen had given rise to
a ten-year war and ended in the destruction of a kingdom:
Troy. Since the Romans had kidnapped the Sabine girls by the
dozens, it was only natural that the next day they should have to
square accounts with the fathers and brothers who came back
armed to retrieve them. The Romans barricaded themselves in
the Capitol, but committed the unpardonable mistake of trust-
ing one of their newly recruited wives with the keys of the
fortress. This Tarpeia, who was evidently none too satisfied with

the husband who had fallen to her lot, opened a gate to the besiegers. They, being a chivalrous people and all against treachery even if it was perpetrated in their favor, rewarded her by crushing her under their shields. The Romans later gave her name to the rock off which they used to push condemned traitors.

The whole thing ended up in a Pantagruelic nuptial banquet because the women who were the cause of the battle placed themselves between the two armies and said they had no intention of becoming widows, which would be the case if their Sabine fathers won, or orphans, if their Roman husbands won. It was high time to call off the quarrel because they were getting along very well with their Roman consorts even if they were a bit wild and wooly. Much better to regularize their marriage than to go on slaughtering each other.

So that is what they did. Romulus and Tatius decided, since each had the title of king, to reign together over this new people born of the fusion of the two tribes, who bore the double name *Romani-quiriti*. Since Tatius obligingly died not too long afterwards, the experiment in double rule went off well this time.

Who can tell what lies beneath this story? Could it be just a version of a conquest of Rome by the Sabines put forth out of pride and patriotism? It is quite possible, however, that the two peoples really did intermingle voluntarily and that the famous rape was just the normal marriage ceremony as celebrated in those times, that is, theft of the bride on the part of the groom, but with the consent of the father, as is still the practice among certain primitive peoples.

If this was really the case, it is probable that the fusion was induced by the presence of a common enemy: those Etruscans who in the meanwhile had spread all over Tuscany and Umbria from the Tyrrhenian coast and who, with all sorts of modern methods, were now pressing south. Rome and Sabina were on the route of this march and directly threatened by it. In fact they did not escape it.

Hence the city which had only just come into being had to deal with some of the most dangerous and insidious rivals she was to meet in all her history. She overthrew them, first by prodigious diplomacy, then with courage and tenacity. But it took her centuries.

II

The Poor Etruscans

UNLIKE THE ROMANS OF TODAY, WHO TREAT EVERYTHING AS A JOKE, the Romans of antiquity took everything seriously. Especially once they had made up their minds to destroy an enemy. Not content with waging war on him and giving him no respite until they had defeated him, even at the cost of throwing away entire armies and untold gold, they did not leave one stone on top of another when they invaded his country.

They reserved particularly harsh treatment for the Etruscans when, after suffering countless humiliations at their hands, they felt strong enough to challenge them. It was a long struggle, with no holds barred, and they did not even leave the losers their eyes to weep with. Rarely has history seen one people vanish so completely from the face of the earth or another cancel all traces of its enemy with such obstinate ferocity. There is practically nothing left of Etruscan civilization—only a few works of art and some thousands of inscriptions of which only a few words have been deciphered. On the strength of these scanty remains, all and sundry have had their little say about this bygone world.

To start with, nobody knows exactly where these people came from. Judging by the way they pictured themselves in bronzes and on terracotta vases, they were stockier and had more massive skulls than the Villanovans. Their features are reminiscent of the people of Asia Minor. Indeed many historians maintain that they arrived from those parts by sea. This would seem to be confirmed by the fact that they were the first of all the inhabitants of Italy to possess a fleet. Certainly they gave the name Tyrrhenian—which means Etruscan—to the sea which washes the coast of Tuscany. Perhaps they arrived in droves and swamped the indigenous population, or perhaps small numbers landed and subdued the natives with their more advanced armament and technique. The superiority of their civilization to the Villanovan was proved by the discovery in their tombs of skulls displaying quite refined samples of bridgework. Teeth are a good indication of the life of a people. They decay in proportion to the advance of progress, hence the more pressing need for better dentistry. The Etruscans already knew about bridges for reinforcing their molars, and the metals needed to make them. In fact, they not only knew how to work iron, which they sought and found on the island of Elba and transformed into steel, but also copper, tin, and amber.

The cities which they immediately set about building in the interior (Tarquinia, Arezzo, Perugia, and Veii) were much more modern than the villages founded by the Latins, Sabines, and other Villanovan peoples. They all had bastions for defense, streets, and as a crowning glory, sewers. They actually followed what today is called a town plan, leaving to engineers, who were excellent for those times, what others left to chance or the whims of individuals. Their ability to organize collective public utility enterprises can be seen in the drainage canals they used for the reclaiming of malaria-infested land. They were, however, formidable traders and money-grubbers, ready to do anything for a profit. At a time when the Romans did not even know what lay behind Soracte, a small mountain not far from their city, the Etruscans had already reached Piedmont, Lombardy, and Venice, had scaled the Alps on foot and following the valleys of the Rhône and the Rhine had taken their products to the French, Swiss, and German markets and bartered them for local goods. It was the Etruscans who brought coinage to Italy as a means of exchange. The Romans then copied this, as is proved by the fact that they engraved the prow of a ship on their coins before they had ever even built one.

The Etruscans were a cheerful people, always looking on the bright side. This is probably why, in the end, they lost the war to the dismal Romans who always looked on the gloomy side. The scenes reproduced on their vases and tombs show well-dressed men wearing the toga, later adopted by the imitative Romans as their national costume. The Etruscans, richly bejewelled at the wrists, neck, and fingers, had long hair and curly beards and always seemed to be busily drinking, eating, or conversing when not engaged in one of their sports.

These were mainly boxing, throwing the discus or javelin, and wrestling, along with two other activities which we think of as being quite modern: polo and bullfighting. Naturally the rules of these games were different from those followed nowa-

days, but ever since that time the sight of a duel between a
man and a bull in the ring has drawn its aficionados. In fact the
Etruscans liked it so much that those who died had souvenirs of
the scene painted on vases and put in their tombs so that they
could continue to enjoy the sport in the other world.

The position of Etruscan women, when you consider the
archaic and patriarchal customs of the Romans and the other
natives, was very advanced. They enjoyed much liberty; in fact
they are depicted as sharing their amusements with men. It
would appear that they were women of great beauty and correspondingly loose morality. In the paintings they are shown
wearing jewels; embellished with cosmetics and untrammelled
by excessive prudery, they gorge themselves with food and sop
up drink like sponges, reclining on ample sofas with their menfolk, or dancing, or playing the flute. One of them, Tanaquilla,
who later became very important in Rome, was an intellectual,
well versed in mathematics and medicine. This means that,
unlike their Latin counterparts who were condemned to abys-
mal ignorance, they went to school and studied. The Romans,
who were great moralists, used to call all ladies of easy virtue
Tuscans, that is to say Etruscans, and in one of the comedies of
Plautus a girl who is a prostitute is accused of having "Tuscan
habits."

Their religion, and a religion is always the moral projection
of a people, centered around a god named Tinia who wielded
power with thunder and lightning. He did not hold sway over
mankind directly, but transmitted his orders to a kind of executive cabinet composed of twelve great gods, so great that it was
sacrilege even to utter their names. So we shall also refrain, in
order not to confuse the reader. Collectively, these twelve
formed a supreme court of justice in the next world, whither the
"genii," a species of usher or policeman, escorted the souls of
the departed as soon as they had abandoned their respective
bodies. A regular trial was then held. Those who did not succeed in demonstrating that they had lived in accordance with
the precepts of the judges were condemned to hell, unless their
surviving friends and relations offered up enough prayers and
sacrifices to obtain their absolution. In this case they were admitted to paradise, where they continued to enjoy earthly
pleasures such as tippling, free-for-alls, and folk songs, cheery
reproductions of which they had had carved on their sepulchers.

It appears however that the Etruscans rarely mentioned paradise, preferring to leave things vague. Perhaps too few went there for them to have much inside information. What they were really well informed about was hell. They knew all the individual torments suffered there. Evidently their priests were of the opinion that to get people to toe the line, threats of damnation were more effective than hopes of salvation. This point of view seems to have survived to more recent times. Dante, who was born in Etruria, also had much more to say about the Inferno than Paradise.

Nevertheless the Etruscans were far from gentle little lambs. They had few scruples about killing, especially with the laudable intention of sacrificing the victim for the salvation of some dear one. Prisoners of war above all were earmarked for this purpose. Some three hundred Romans captured in one of the numerous battles fought between the two people were stoned to death at Tarquinia and from their still palpitating livers augurs tried to foresee the outcome of the war. (Evidently they did not succeed, or they would have called it off immediately.) But such was common practice, though they usually used the entrails of either a sheep or a bull. This, too, the Romans copied.

Politically, the Etruscans' scattered cities never managed to unite. Unfortunately no one of them was strong enough to get the upper hand, as Rome did over her Latin and Sabine rivals. There was a federation dominated by Tarquinia, but it never overcame its separatist tendencies. Instead of uniting against the common enemy, the twelve little states allowed themselves to be gobbled up one by one. Their diplomacy was rather like that of certain modern European nations, who prefer perishing alone to living together.

The foregoing is all sheer deduction from those relics of Etruscan art which have come down to us and are the only heritage left us by that people. Their bronzes are very beautiful, especially the Apollo of Veii, also called the "walking Apollo." The vases are almost always imitations of the Greek, and apart from certain rare examples like the "black jar," are not very striking.

Scarce as these relics may be, they are enough to show us that the Romans, once they had overcome the Etruscans, for so long their mentors and superiors in the fields of technology and organization, not only massacred them, but tried to wipe out every trace of their civilization. The Romans considered it tainted and corrupt, yet they copied from it everything that suited them. They sent their boys to the schools of Veii and Tarquinia to study medicine and engineering. They imitated the toga. They adopted the use of money. They probably even borrowed their political system, though this was common to all other peoples of antiquity. But the Etruscans had also developed the monarchial regime into a republican one, and one governed by a *lucumo* or elected magistrate, and finally into a form of democracy dominated by the wealthy classes. Rome, however, was determined to "protect from" Etruscan laxity her own sound and stoic customs based on self-sacrifice and social discipline. She felt instinctively that it was not enough to conquer the enemy in war and occupy his land if the vanquished slaves were then going to turn around and contaminate the households of their masters. So she exterminated the Etruscans and furthermore insisted that all their documents and monuments be buried.

But all this happened a long time after the two peoples first came in contact with each other. They actually met in Rome itself for when the Albalongans arrived there they found that a small Etruscan colony had already settled in and given the place a name. In fact it appears that Rome comes from *Rumon,* which means river in Etruscan. If this is true, the first population of the city must have been composed not only of Latins and Sabines, peoples of the same stock, as the story of the famous rape would lead us to believe, but also of Etruscans, who were of quite a different race, language, and religion. Some historians claim that Romulus himself was Etruscan. In any case the rite he used to found the city, tracing a furrow with a plow drawn by a white bull and a white heifer after twelve birds of good omen had hovered over his head, was most certainly Etruscan.

Without wishing to compete with the scholars who have been wrangling inconclusively over this topic for centuries, the following is put forward as the most probable version.

The Etruscans, passionate tourists and businessmen, had already founded a small village on the Tiber when the Latins and Sabines arrived. This village was used as a transit and supply base for their shipping route to the south where, especially in Campania, they had already founded rich colonies such as Capua, Nola, Pompeii, and Herculaneum. The local population, called Samites and also of Villanovan origin, came to barter their agricultural produce for the manufactured goods from Tuscany. It was difficult to get down there by land from Arezzo and Tarquinia: there were no roads and the region was infested by wild beasts and bandits. So it was much easier for the Etruscans, the only ones to have a fleet, to go there by sea. The voyage was long and took weeks. The nutshell ships could not carry enough supplies for the crew, and needed ports on the way where they could take on flour and water for the rest of the voyage. The mouth of the Tiber, just halfway along the route, was a convenient bay where they could refill their empty holds. Moreover, navigable as it was at that time, it offered an easy means of reaching the interior and putting through some deals with the local Latins and Sabines. The countryside was dotted with from thirty to seventy settlements (the exact number is not known), each of which represented a small barter market. Not that much business could be done there, since Latium in those days was rich only in timber, thanks to its wonderful, now-vanished woods. Nor did it even produce grain but only a little buckwheat and wine and a few olives. The Etruscans, however, were content with little as long as they could make some money, a vice which persists to this day.

Indeed this was why they founded Rome, calling it by that or some other name, without attaching too much importance to it. Who knows how many Romes there were scattered along the Tyrrhenian coast between Leghorn and Naples? To guard it, they stationed a garrison of sailors and merchants who perhaps considered this new post a punishment. Their main duty was to keep in order the shipyard for repairing ships damaged by storms, and the warehouses for supplying them.

Then one fine day, small groups of Latins and Sabines began to arrive, partly because their own neighborhood was getting a bit crowded, and partly because they wanted to trade with the Etruscans, whose products they needed. To believe that in those days they already had a strategic plan for the conquest first of Italy and then of the world, and that they considered the position of Rome vital for this purpose, is pure fancy on the part of modern historians. These Latins and Sabines were

simply yokels whose ideas of geography hardly extended beyond the limits of their own cabbage patches.

It is probable that these newcomers may have come to
blows among themselves. But it is just as likely that instead of
slaying each other, they united to oppose the Etruscans, who
must have regarded them in much the same way that the English once regarded the natives in their colonies. In the presence
of this foreign people, who treated them with haughtiness and
spoke a language incomprehensible to them, Latins and Sabines
must have realized they were brothers bound together by the
same blood, language, and poverty. The famous rape is probably
nothing but the symbol of this accord from which the Etruscans, of their own free will, were excluded. Considering themselves superior, they had no desire to mix with the riffraff.

This racial division lasted for at least a hundred years,
during which time the Latins and Sabines, by now interbred
into the Roman type, must have had quite a few grievances to
nurse. When, after the reign of Tarquin the Proud, the Romans
got the upper hand, their vengeance was indiscriminate. Perhaps the savagery with which they set about to destroy Etruria,
not only as a state but as a civilization, was the direct consequence of the humiliations which they had had to endure under
the Etruscans in their own country. They wanted to purge away
everything Etruscan, including history itself, even to the point
of giving Romulus a Latin birth certificate and of dating the
origin of the city from the time of their union with the Sabines.

III

The Farmer Kings

WHEN ROMULUS DIED, MANY YEARS AFTER HE HAD BURIED TITUS
Tatius his co-king, the Romans said that Mars had stolen him,
carried him to heaven and made him the god Quirinus. From
then on they venerated him just as the Neapolitans do Saint
Januarius today.

Numa Pompilius succeeded Romulus as third king of Rome.

Tradition makes him half-philosopher and half-saint, like Marcus Aurelius several centuries later.

Numa was mainly interested in religious questions. There must have been an unholy confusion in that field, since all three peoples venerated a different set of gods. As nobody could make out which were the most important, Numa decided to straighten matters out. So as to impose some order on his quarrelsome subjects, he circulated the story that every night while he slept the nymph Egeria used to visit him in his dreams to present instructions direct from Olympus. Anybody who disobeyed would have to reckon not only with the king, a man among men, but also with the Almighty Himself.

This stratagem may seem childish yet there may be a grain of truth in the legend, or at least an indication which enables us to reconstruct the truth. Whatever the names and origins of the kings of early Rome may have been, they must have been more like popes than real kings, just as after all the "Archon Basileus" was at Athens.

All authority at that time was heavily backed up by religion. Even the power of the *paterfamilias* over his wife, his younger brothers, his children and his servants, resembled more or less that of a high priest to whom the Creator has delegated certain functions. In that lay his strength. That is why Roman families were so disciplined and why everybody had, in both peace and war, such a strong sense of duty.

Numa, by establishing an order of precedence for the various gods brought to Rome by each of the three peoples, probably did a job of fundamental political importance. It enabled his successors, Tullus Hostilius and Ancus Martius, to lead a united people in their victorious wars against the rival cities of the region. However, he could not have had much real political power himself, because when all was said and done the final decision remained in the hands of the people. They had elected him, and it was to them he was responsible.

This by itself does not mean much because in every age and regime whoever gives the orders says that he does so in the name of the people. In Rome, however, this was not just idle chatter—at least until the dynasty of the Tarquins who lost the throne because they wanted to sit there as autocrats and not as "delegates."

The chain of command was roughly as follows: the city was

divided into three "tribes," the Latins, the Sabines, and the Etruscans. Each tribe was divided into ten *curiae*, or companies; each *curia* into ten *gentes* or family groups, and each family group into families. The *curiae* usually met twice a year. On these occasions they formed the *comitia curiata*, which among other things elected a new king when one died. Everybody had an equal vote and the majority decided. The king carried out instructions.

It was an absolute democracy without social classes. It worked well as long as Rome remained a small peaceful village inhabited by a few people who rarely stuck their heads outside the walls. As the number of inhabitants increased, so did their needs. The king, who at first, apart from offering sacrifices and performing the other rites of the liturgy, had to enforce the laws and act as judge, no longer had time for all these duties himself and so he began handing them over to officials. This was the beginning of what we call bureaucracy. The erstwhile priest became a bishop and delegated parish priests and curates to help him with his religious functions. Then he needed somebody to look after roads, the census, land surveys, and public health, and nominated specialists to take care of these affairs. Thus the first ministry came into being: the so-called council of elders, or senate, made up of about a hundred members, descendants by right of primogeniture of the pioneers who had founded the city with Romulus. Their only duty at first was to advise the sovereign, but later they became more and more influential.

Finally the army was created as a stable organization, also based on the *curiae*, each of which had to supply a *centuria*, or one hundred foot soldiers, and a *decuria*, or ten cavalrymen with horses. The thirty *centuriae* and the thirty *decuriae*, that is, 3,300 men, made up the "legion." This was early Rome's first and only army corps. The king as commander in chief had power of life and death over the soldiers, but he could not exercise absolute military power without control. He directed operations only after consultation with the *comitia centuriata*, or the legion in arms. From them he had to get approval for the appointment of officers who in those times were called *praetori*.

In short, the Romans had taken all due precautions that their king should not become a tyrant. He was to remain the trustee of the popular will. When a flight of birds passed over or a tree was struck by lightning, his job was to summon the priests and study the portents with them. If the signs seemed to bode ill, he decided what sacrifices were necessary to placate the gods, who were evidently offended at something or other. When two private citizens quarreled or one robbed or killed the other, it was none of his business. But if a person committed a crime against the state or the collectivity, the king would have a policeman bring him in and might well sentence him to death. He could not make decisions in any other matters. In peace time he had to refer to the *comitiae curiatae,* in time of war to the *centuriatae.* If crafty, he might succeed in passing off his opinions as the will of the people. Otherwise he had to submit to it. In any case, before taking action he invariably had to reckon with the senate.

This was the system given to the city by the first king of Rome, whether he was Romulus or not and to whichever of the three races he belonged. Such it remained when the wise Numa handed it on to his successor, Tullus Hostilius, a much livelier character.

He was a man who had politics, adventure, and greed in his blood. The fact that the *comitia* picked him for king means that after forty years of peace under Numa, all Rome was spoiling for a fight. Alba Longa was the richest and most important of all the settlements and cities which surrounded her. We do not know what excuse Tullus thought up for declaring war on her. Perhaps none. The fact remains that one fine day he attacked Alba Longa and razed the city to the ground, even though legend has transformed this act of aggression into a chivalrous and almost gentlemanly tourney. It is said that the two armies decided to leave the outcome of the battle to a duel between three Roman Horatii and three Albalongan Curatii. The latter slew two Horatii but the survivor in his turn killed all three Curatii and won the war. This in no way alters the fact that Alba Longa was destroyed and its king tied by the legs to two chariots which, rushing in two directions, tore him in half. Such was the way Rome treated her motherland, the land she claimed her founders had come from.

Naturally this deed must have caused considerable alarm in the other villages in the vicinity that had not undergone Etruscan influence, were behind the times, and realized they were weaker and not as well armed as the Romans. Tullus

Hostilius and his successor, Ancus Martius, harassed them so much that the day Tarquin Priscus came to the throne as the fifth king, Rome was already the prime object of concern to a territory which must have reached roughly to Civitavecchia in the north, toward Rieti in the east, and as far as Frosinone in the south.

Now it is highly probable that this policy of conquest, which was to become even more aggressive under the last three kings of the Tarquin family, was mainly of Etruscan inspiration, for this very simple reason: while the Latins and Sabines were farmers, the Etruscans were manufacturers and merchants, and every time a new war broke out the former had to let their farms go by the board and join the legion. Furthermore, they risked losing their farms if the enemy happened to win. The latter, on the other hand, had everything to gain by war. Consumption increased, government orders poured in, and in the event of victory new markets were opened up. This has been the way in all times and nations: city dwellers, capitalists, intellectuals, and businessmen want wars against the will of the peasants, who have to supply the manpower for them. The more a state becomes industrialized, the more the city gets the upper hand over the country, the more aggressive and adventurous state policy becomes.

Until the fourth king, Rome's peasant element prevailed and its economy was mainly agricultural. The 3,300 men who formed the army show that the total population must have amounted to some 300,000, the majority of whom were perhaps scattered around the countryside. In the city itself roughly a half of the population had by now spread from the Palatine to the other hills. Most of them lived in mud huts which sprang up higgledy-piggledy, with an entrance but no windows, and only one room in which father, mother, children, daughters-in-law, sons-in-law, grandchildren, slaves (if any), chickens, donkeys, cows, and pigs all ate, drank, and slept together. In the morning the men, senators included, went down to the plain to plow the land, yoke the oxen, sow and reap. The boys helped in the fields because this work was their only real school and their only real sport. Their fathers took advantage of the occasion to teach them that the seed only brought forth good fruit when heaven sent rain and sunshine on the soil in the right amounts;

that the heaven only sent rain and sunshine in the right amounts when the gods so wished; that the gods so wished only when men had performed all their duties to them, and that the first of these duties was for the young to obey their elders.

This was how Roman citizens were brought up, at least those of Latin and Sabine origin, who must have comprised the majority. Hygiene and personal cleanliness must have been reduced to a bare minimum, even for women. No cosmetics, no coquetries, little or no water. The women had to draw this in the valley and carry it uphill in amphoras on their heads. There were no lavatories or sewers; they just went outside the door. Their hair and beards were long and uncombed. As for their clothes, one should not be deceived by the statues, which belong to a much later time when Rome had a proper weaving industry and a class of specialized tailors, mostly of Greek origin and training. In those far-off days the toga which later became so imposing either had not yet been invented or else was still in its most primitive form. Perhaps it resembled the sort of garment the Abyssinians wear today—a tattered length of white material, woven at home by the wife or daughters, and with a hole in the middle to put one's head through. Not many had a spare one. They usually wore the same, summer and winter, day and night, with consequences that can well be imagined.

They indulged in no pleasures, not even that of gluttony. Contrary to the modern theory that the strength of a people is conditioned by their intake of calories and vitamins, which in turn is conditioned by the variety of their diet, the Romans demonstrated that you can conquer the world even if you eat only a badly cooked mixture of kneaded flour and water, a couple of olives, and a piece of cheese washed down on feast days only by a glass of wine. Oil, it appears, came later and was at first used only to anoint them against frostbite and sunburn. This must have done quite a bit to increase the general stench.

Even the kings did not fare any better. Not until the Tarquin dynasty did they get a uniform, a helmet, and special insignia. Up to the time of Ancus Martius the king was an equal among equals; he, too, plowed the land behind the yoked oxen; like everyone else he sowed the seed and harvested the grain. There is nothing to show that he had an office, let alone a court. He used to mix with the people without an escort, because if he had had one everyone would have accused him of wanting to reign by force instead of by the consent of the people. He used to make his decisions sitting under a tree or on his own doorstep, after listening to the opinions of the elders who gathered round him in a ring. He mounted a dais or perhaps wore some special garment only when he had to offer a sacrifice or perform some other religious ceremony.

The Romans went to war with nothing resembling a proper military organization. The praetor who commanded the *centuria* or *decuria* had no badge of rank. The arms were mainly clubs, stones, and crude swords. It took quite some time for them to acquire helmets, shields, and armor, inventions which must have had the same effect in those days as the machine-gun and tank had in ours. Thus the great campaigns on which Rome embarked under its first warlike kings must have looked more like punitive expeditions than anything else and boiled down to man-to-man bashing contests, without a trace of tactics or strategy. The Romans won not only because they were the strongest but because they were the most convinced that their country had been founded by the gods to fulfil a great destiny and that to die for it was of no special merit—merely the settlement of a debt contracted at birth.

The enemy, once he had been defeated, ceased to be a "subject" and became an "object." The Roman who had taken him prisoner regarded him as his own private property. If that Roman was in a bad temper, he butchered the prisoner. If in a good humor, he took him home as a slave and could do what he liked with him: kill him, sell him, or make him work. The land was requisitioned by the state, which leased it to its subjects, and cities were often destroyed and populations deported.

By these methods Rome grew at the expense of the Latins in the south, of the Sabines and Aequi to the east, and of the Etruscans to the north. Romans did not dare venture on the sea, which was only a few miles away, because they had no fleet as yet and the peasant population had an instinctive distrust of the water.

The advent of a certain Etruscan dynasty, however, was to make radical changes in both domestic and foreign policy.

IV

The Merchant Kings

THE EXACT DATE OF THE DEATH OF ANCUS MARTIUS IS NOT known. It must have been about 150 years after the day that legend says Rome was founded, that is about 600 B.C. It seems that at the time there was one Lucius Tarquin in town (L. Tarquinius Priscus, we mentioned him before), and that he was a very different kind of man from those the Romans usually chose as their kings and magistrates.

He was not a local man but came from Tarquinia, the son of a Greek named Demaratus who had immigrated from Corinth and married an Etruscan woman. This mixed marriage had produced a lively, brilliant, broad-minded, and highly ambitious young man whom the Romans, when he settled in their midst, must have regarded with a mixture of admiration, envy, and mistrust. He was rich and extravagant among the poor and miserly, elegant in a community of rustics. He was the only one in a world of miserable illiterates to have studied philosophy, geography, and mathematics. As for politics, his Greek plus his Etruscan blood must have made him a highly resourceful diplomat. Titus Livy says of him: "He was the first to intrigue to get himself elected king and delivered a speech to assure himself of the support of the plebs."

We very much doubt that he was the first, but intrigue he certainly did. Probably the rich Etruscan families who formed a special minority saw that he was their man. Weary of being governed by Latin or Sabine shepherds and peasants who turned a deaf ear to their commercial and expansionist demands, they decided to put Tarquin on the throne.

One does not know exactly how it happened, but Livy's reference to the plebs gives us a very good idea. The plebs were a new element in Rome, or at least they had had no importance under the first four kings. Those kings had no need to address the plebs to get themselves elected since in their time there were no actual plebs. There were no social differences within the *comitiae curiatae,* which dealt with the investiture of the sovereign. All were citizens, all were landowners large or small, and therefore all of them had the same rights on paper even if in actual practice certain professional politicians of necessity imposed their point of view.

It was a perfect homespun democracy where everything was above board. Discussion took place among equal citizens and the only thing that counted in the distribution of appointments was prestige, the esteem in which one was held. This was all very well when Rome was a small town, confined to its own narrow circle of hovels where everybody knew everybody else and who was whose son and all about their past lives and how they treated their wives, how much they spent on food and how many sacrifices they offered to the gods.

By the time of the death of Ancus Martius the situation had completely changed. The necessities of the wars had stimulated industry and had of course favored the Etruscan element which supplied carpenters, blacksmiths, armorers, and merchants. Others had arrived from Tarquinia, Arezzo, and Veii and the shops were filled with assistants and apprentices who, as soon as they learned the tricks of the trade, set up shops on their own. The increase in wages had attracted peasant labor to the city; soldiers back from the wars did not want to return to the fields and preferred to stay in Rome where the prospects of getting women and wine were better. First and foremost, the victories had started a flow of slaves into the city and it was this mass of aliens which made up the *plenum* from which the word "plebs" is derived.

Lucius Tarquin and his Etruscan friends must have been quick to see the advantage that could be drawn from his mass of people who were mostly excluded from the *comitiae curiatae*, once they were persuaded that only a king who was a foreigner like themselves could assure them of their rights. That was the reason for his harangue and who knows what promises he made them. They might even have been promises that he later carried out! He was backed by sponsors who had money to spare for electoral propaganda and who were quite prepared to spend it provided they got a government more disposed than its predecessors to adopt the expansionist policy they wanted.

They succeeded. Lucius Tarquin was not only elected under the name of Tarquin Priscus but he remained on the throne for thirty-eight years. To get rid of him the "patricians," or big landowners, had to have him murdered. This turned out to be futile, however, because in the first place the crown passed to his son and then to his grandson, and in the second place because the rise of the Tarquin dynasty was the effect, rather than the initial cause, of a certain trend which the history of Rome had taken. It would have been impossible for her ever to return to her primitive and archaic social order.

This king of the merchants and the proletariat was authoritative, bellicose, systematic, and demagogic. He wanted a court, so he had one built for himself in the Etruscan style which was a much more refined style than that of Rome. He installed a throne where he sat in great pomp with a scepter in his hand and a plumed helmet on his head. He must have done this partly out of vanity and partly because he realized that the plebs, who elected him and whose favor he wanted to keep, loved pageantry and wanted to see their king in full dress, surrounded by a regiment of the household brigade. Unlike his predecessors who had spent most of their time making sacrifices or casting horoscopes, he concentrated on the profane, in other words politics and war. First he subjugated all Latium and then had another go at the Sabines, gnawing off a bit more of their land. For this he needed arms, which heavy industry supplied him—at a handsome profit—and miscellaneous provisions which the merchants produced for him, naturally making a nice little piece of change on the side. Republican anti-Etruscan historians claim that his reign was nothing but graft, an enormous racket, the triumph of the greased palm and the pork barrel, and that he did not use the loot from the vanquished for Rome but to embellish Etruscan cities, particularly his home town, Tarquinia.

We doubt the truth of this because it was precisely during his reign that Rome took a great step forward, especially in the matters of town planning and monuments. First of all he built the *cloaca maxima,* the sewer system, finally freeing the citizenry of their sewage, with which up until that period they had coexisted. At last the city really began to look like one, with well-laid-out streets, well-defined districts, houses that were no longer huts but proper buildings with sloping roofs, windows, and an *atrium.* And a *forum* or central square where all the citizens used to gather.

Unfortunately, in order to carry out this authentic revolution that transformed not only the external aspect of the city but also its way of life, Tarquin incurred the hostility of the senate. This body was the repository of the ancient traditions and in no way inclined to give over its control of the king. In other times they would have deposed him or forced him to resign. But now they had to reckon with the plebs, a multitude which so far had no adequate representation but who hoped Tarquin would remedy this and were ready to support him, even at the barricades. It was easiest to kill him, and the senators did just that; but they also made one colossal blunder. They did not kill either his wife or his child, convinced that she, because of her sex, and he, because of his tender years, were not in a position to hold on to the sovereignty.

They might have been right if Tanaquilla had been a Roman woman, accustomed to obedience. But she was an educated Etruscan and had shared not only her husband's bed but also his work, taking an interest in problems of state, administration, foreign policy, and reforms. She was much better informed about everything than the senators themselves, many of whom were illiterate.

When the king was murdered, she took his place on the throne and kept it warm for her son Servius who grew up to be the first and last king of Rome to inherit the crown without being elected.

The historians who came after Servius, all of them rabid republicans, tried to say derogatory things about him too, but without much success. Much against their will they had to admit that his rule was enlightened and that many important works were completed during his reign. First of all he built a wall around the city, thus providing employment for the masons, artisans, and specialists, who regarded him as their protector. Then he set his hand to that great political and social reform which was to become the basis of every subsequent Roman governing order.

The old division into thirty *curiae* was all very well for a city of thirty or forty thousand inhabitants all more or less of the same class, with the same merits and the same incomes. Now it had expanded enormously. Some people put the population of the city in Servius' time at 700-800,000. Most probably these figures refer not to the actual population of Rome but include the conquered territories. Nevertheless, the city must have had over a hundred thousand, and the great public works programs undertaken by Tarquin and Servius must have been partly motivated by an acute housing shortage.

Of all this mass of people only those already included in the *comitiae curiatae* had any say in matters and could vote. The others were still excluded, and among them were the big industrialists, merchants, and bankers, those in fact who provided the state with money for its wars and public works. Now was the time for them to get their reward.

First, Servius granted citizenship to the *libertini*, the sons of the freed slaves. There must have been thousands of them, and from that moment on they became his staunchest supporters. Then he abolished the thirty *curiae* which divided the electorate according to the quarter they lived in, and replaced them by five "classes," differentiated not on the basis of their place of residence but according to their wealth. To the first class belonged those who had at least 100,000 *asses;* those who had under 12,500 belonged to the last class. It is hard to say how much an *as* would amount to in today's money. Maybe ten lire or about a cent-and-a-half, perhaps more. The importance of these financial brackets is that they determined the political ones. Whereas in the *curiae* all were equal, at least formally, and all votes equally valid, the classes voted by *centuriae* but did not have an equal number of them. The first class had ninety-eight and the last class only one. In all there were 193 votes, and so in practice, the 98 votes of the first class were enough to get a majority. Even if the others formed a coalition, they could not win.

It was a sheer capitalist or plutocratic regime, giving the monopoly of legislative power to industry and taking it away from agriculture, i.e. the senate, whose members were not nearly so well off. What could they do about it? Servius did not even owe his election to them. He had inherited the crown from his father and had on his side all the money of the wealthy classes which owed to him their newly-acquired power, as well as the support of the lower classes to whom he had given employment and citizenship. With this backing, he surrounded himself with an armed guard to protect himself against his enemies, circled his head with a gold diadem and had an ivory throne made where he sat majestically with a scepter surmounted by an eagle in his hand. Whoever wished to approach him, patrician or commoner, senator or beggar, had to have himself announced and patiently await his turn in the anteroom.

It was difficult to get rid of a man like this and his enemies had to rely for the job on a nephew who had free access to the court.

Before risking the coup, this second Tarquin tried to get his uncle deposed for abuse of power, but Servius simply went to the *centuriae* who confirmed him king with great popular acclamation. (That great republican, Titus Livy, tells us this, so it must be true.)

And so there was nothing left but the dagger, and without much hesitation Tarquin the Second used it. But the senators' sigh of relief stuck in their throats when the murderer promptly seated himself on the throne without even pretending to ask their approval, as had been the custom in the good old days they hoped to restore.

The new sovereign immediately showed that he was even more tyrannical than the one he had sent to a better world, so much more so that they named him "the Proud" to distinguish him from the founder of the dynasty. They must have had a good reason for giving him this nickname, even if the story they later told about his fall is not true. It appears that one of his amusements was killing people in the Forum. And he certainly was an aggressive character, since he spent most of his reign in a series of wars. They were fortunate wars since the army under his command, which was by now several tens of thousands strong, not only conquered Sabina but also Etruria and its southern colonies as far as Gaeta. It was not always an active war; often it was only a cold one, as they say today. The fact remains that Tarquin, partly by force of arms and partly by diplomacy, was the ruler of something like a small empire. It did not extend to the Adriatic but it already dominated the Tyrrhenian.

Perhaps one of the reasons why Tarquin the Proud was so pugnacious was to make people forget that he had ascended the throne over the dead body of a generous and popular king. Successes abroad often serve to camouflage the internal weakness of a regime. In any case, it would appear that Tarquin's mania for conquest brought about his fall.

The story goes that one day he was encamped with his soldiers, his son Sextus Tarquin, and his nephew Lucius Tarquin Collatinus. The latter two began arguing in their tent about the virtue of their respective wives, each of them like a good husband upholding that of his own. Probably they both said: "Mine is an honest woman. Yours cuckolds you." So, the seed of doubt having been sown, they decided to go home that very night and surprise their wives. Immediately they jumped on their horses and started off.

In Rome they found the wife of Sextus consoling herself for her temporary widowhood by banqueting with some male friends and obviously not discouraging their advances. The wife of Collatinus, Lucretia, was passing the time weaving a garment for her husband. Collatinus triumphantly pocketed the wager and went back to camp. Sextus, humiliated and thirsting for revenge, set about courting Lucretia and finally, partly by violence and partly by guile, succeeded in overcoming her resistance.

After this infidelity, the poor woman sent for her husband and her father, a senator, told them what had happened, and then plunged a dagger into her heart. Lucius Junius Brutus, another nephew of the king (in fact it was his own father who had been murdered by Tarquin the Proud), summoned the senate, told them this infamous story, and proposed the removal of the Proud One from the throne and the expulsion of the whole family from the city (himself excepted, of course). Tarquin, when informed of this, rushed to Rome while Brutus was at the same time galloping to the camp. They probably crossed on the way. While the king was trying to reestablish order in Rome, Brutus was sowing seeds of disorder among the legions. They decided to rebel and march on Rome.

Tarquin fled north, taking refuge in the same Etruria from which his ancestors had come and whose pride he had humbled by reducing her to the status of vassal of Rome. It must have been a very bitter pill for him to beg hospitality from Porsena, the *lucumo* or chief magistrate of Chiusi, at that time called Clusium. But Porsena, a perfect gentleman, granted it to him.

In Rome they proclaimed a republic. As later, with the Plantagenets in England and the Bourbons in France, the monarchy of Rome lasted for seven reigns. It was now the year 509 B.C. and 245 years had elapsed *ab urbe condita*.

V

Lars Porsena of Clusium

AS PEOPLE ALWAYS DO WHEN THEY CHANGE REGIMES, THE ROMANS hailed the new one with enthusiasm and pinned on it all their hopes, including those of liberty and social justice. A great *comitia centuriata* was summoned, in which all the soldier citizens took part. It declared the monarchy well and truly dead, blamed it for all the errors and iniquities committed by the public administration during the entire two-and-a-half centuries of its life, and in the place of the king appointed two consuls, selecting the two chief protagonists of the revolution: the unhappy widower Collatinus, and the unfortunate orphan, Lucius Junius Brutus. As the former declined the job, his place was taken by Publius Valerius, who went down in history with the nickname of "Publicola," which means the people's friend.

Publicola gave proof of his friendship by proposing and getting the *comitia* to approve certain laws which remained fundamental for as long as the republic lasted. These decreed the death penalty for anyone who tried to take over a public appointment without the approval of the people and allowed any citizen condemned to death to appeal to the assembly, or *comitia centuriata*. Moreover they gave any citizen the right to kill without even a trial whoever tried to get himself proclaimed king. The latter law, however, forgot to define clearly the elements necessary for proving that somebody harbored this ambition. During the following years this came in very handy to the senate for getting rid of a number of inconvenient enemies whom they accused, naturally, of being would-be kings. In fact the system is still practiced in many countries: the would-be kings are now called "deviationists," "enemies of the fatherland," and "agents of foreign imperialism." Progress doesn't seem to change the crimes, only the tags attached to them.

In his democratic zeal Publicola also introduced the custom by which the consul, when he entered the enclosure of the *comitia centuriata*, had the lictors who preceded him lower the symbols of office, those famous *fasces* that Mussolini was later to bring back into fashion. This was to show that the authority came from the people, who, having delegated it to the consul, remained its arbiter.

These things were all very fine and for the moment had great effect. But once the ardor had cooled off, people began to wonder about the actual practical advantages of the new system. It was quite true that all citizens had the vote, but the *comitiae* still continued to function according to the rights of the classes, just as Servius had rigged things. So the wealthy of the first class, having ninety-eight *centuriae*, which meant ninety-eight votes, were still able to impose their will on all the others. In fact one of the first steps they took was to revoke the Tarquins' distribution of land in conquered territories to the poor. Thus a great many small landholders suddenly found their houses and land confiscated without notice. Not knowing what else to do they came back to Rome to look for work.

But there was no work in Rome, since the consuls, elected for only one year, could not carry out any long-range public works programs. These had been the specialty of the kings, the first five of which had been elected for life, while the last two were in fact hereditary. Furthermore, the republic was dominated by the senate, its creator, and was composed of landowners of Latin and Sabine origins. Compared with the spendthrift monarchy which had been dominated by industrialists of Etruscan and Greek origin, this was a stingy, tight-fisted bunch. They wanted to balance the budget, as we would say today, and follow a cautious financial policy, particularly as it was against their interests to increase the number of *nouveau riches*, their natural enemies.

In short, there was a depression, and the poor oafs who came in from the country to escape unemployment and starvation only found more starvation and unemployment. The daring contractors, who had been the mainstay of the Tarquins and had given work to thousands of specialists and tens of thousands of workmen, were either banished or had reason to fear that they would be. Places of public entertainment closed one after the other for lack of customers, who were thinned out for want of ready cash and by the puritanical atmosphere which all republics emanate or try to emanate. The propagandists of the new regime were forever haranguing the crowd not to forget the crimes that the kings had committed. It probably occurred to their listeners as they looked around them that these "crimes" also included the Forum where they stood at the moment, and which had been built by the execrated kings.

Another misdeed these propagandists were always harping on was that the late dynasty had tried to make Rome an Etruscan colony. This had some truth in it, but it was also thanks to this that Rome now had her Circus Maximus, her sewer system, her engineers, her artisans, her *histriones* (who were the actors of that time), her pugilists and gladiators (the protagonists of those spectacles the Romans loved so much), her walls, her drainage, her fortune-tellers, and her liturgy for worshipping her gods. All these were imports from Etruria.

Naturally not everybody realized this because not everybody had been to Etruria. The young intellectuals, however, were fully aware of it. They had studied at the Etruscan universities of Tarquinia, Arezzo, and Chiusi, where they had been sent by their fathers and which they remembered very well indeed. As a rule they did not belong to the patrician families, who educated their sons at home and were very careful to see that they did not become cultured men but simply men of character. They came from middle-class families and their lives were bound up with commerce, industry, and the liberal professions, the very things most drastically hit by the new trend of events.

For all these reasons discontent soon made itself felt. Unfortunately, it coincided with a declaration of war on the part of Porsena, who had been egged on by Tarquin.

We cannot tell with absolute certainty how they closed this deal, but, given the circumstances, we have no difficulty in guessing the arguments which the deposed monarch must have used to get the *lucumo* to come in on his side. The latter must certainly have pointed out that, although the Tarquins were of Etruscan blood, they had not been very good sons of Etruria insofar as they had continually harassed her with wars and punitive expeditions to the extent of becoming practically her overlord. The Proud One probably replied that while he and his two predecessors had been Romanizing Etruria, they had also been Etruscanizing Rome, conquering it from within, one might say, at the expense of the Latin and Sabine elements which had formerly predominated. The struggle had not been between foreign powers but between rival cities, daughters of the same civilization. Although Rome was the newcomer, she had not

tried to destroy the others, but to unite them under a single command so as to win the hegemony of Italy. Perhaps the Proud
One had made mistakes, perhaps he had been a little heavy-
handed now and then and had not shown enough consideration
for the independence of the Etruscan cities. But the Tarquins
had never treated any of them as they had treated Alba Longa,
for example, and so many other settlements and villages of
Latium and Sabina which had been razed to the ground. No
Etruscan city had ever been pillaged. And the merchants, artisans, actors, and pugilists of Tarquinia, Chiusi, Volterra, and
Arezzo, when they emigrated to Rome, had not been turned into
slaves. On the contrary, they had gone up in the world, and all
the economy, culture, industry, and commerce was virtually in
their hands.

That was to say, it *had* been in their hands, as long as Tarquins were on the throne to protect them. But what was going
to happen now, with this republic? The republic meant the return of the Latins and Sabines, those boorish, greedy, mistrust-
ful reactionaries, with their instinctive racial intolerance, who
had always harbored a smoldering hatred for the liberal, progressive, Etruscan bourgeoisie. It was no good deluding oneself
as to how they would be treated now. And their liquidation
would mean the consolidation at the mouth of the Tiber of a
hostile foreign power instead of a friendly (if at times slightly
obstreperous) people of the same race. Tomorrow this power
might join forces with other enemies of Etruria and contribute
to her downfall. Was Porsena prepared to stand idle and watch
such an alteration in the balance of power?

Instead, wasn't it a golden opportunity to prevent this
catastrophe by attacking Rome now, while chaos was rife within
and without? Particularly in Latium and Sabina where people's
bones were still aching from the blows they had received from
the Roman soldiery. One signal from the powerful *lucumo* of
Chiusi and all these cities would rise against their scant garrisons, and Rome would find herself divided and alone, at the
mercy of her enemies.

We know practically nothing about Porsena. Judging from
his acts, we must draw the conclusion that he combined the
qualities of a good general and a wise politician. He realized
that there was a certain amount of truth in Tarquin's arguments,
but before committing himself he wanted to be quite sure of

two things: that Latium and Sabina were really prepared to join him, and that in Rome itself there was a monarchist fifth column ready to facilitate things with an insurrection.

The insurrection actually took place, and forgetting what the Proud One had done to their grandfather, the two sons of the consul Lucius Junius Brutus took part in it. After the revolt had been ruthlessly suppressed, they were arrested and condemned to death, and it is said that their father insisted on being present at their decapitation.

The war, however, went badly for Rome. The various Latin and Sabine cities duly massacred their Roman garrisons and joined forces with Porsena who had come down from the north at the head of a confederate army made up of contingents from all Etruria. According to historians, Rome performed miracles of courage against this invasion. Mucius Scaevola, secretly finding his way into Porsena's encampment, mistook his victim, and then punished himself by putting his own hand on a red-hot brazier. Horatius Cocles alone withstood the entire Etruscan army at a bridge over the Tiber while his companions destroyed it behind him. But the war was lost. These legends prove it. Their tone of exaltation is one of the earliest examples of war propaganda. When a country suffers defeat, she invents or exaggerates "glorious" episodes to attract the attention of both contemporaries and posterity, and thus distract them from the final outcome. That is why heroes nearly always belong to the beaten armies. The winners do not need them. Caesar, for example, does not mention a single hero in his *Commentaries*.

The surrender of the city was, in today's terms, unconditional. She had to give back all her Etruscan territories to Porsena. The Latins also took advantage of this moment to attack Rome. She managed to save the situation at the battle of Lake Regillus, where the Heavenly Twins, Castor and Pollux, the sons of Jove, came to her rescue. Nevertheless, when the fighting was over, what had been a small empire under the kings found itself with a boundary which today would not quite reach Fregene in the north and fall short of Anzio in the south. It was an enormous catastrophe from which it took Rome a century to recover.

This war also claimed another powerful victim: Tarquin. He had already packed his bags to return to Rome, resume control, and wreak his vengeance, when Porsena stopped him and told him that he had no intention of putting him back on the throne. Did Porsena realize that the restoration of the monarchy was quite impossible, or did he mistrust the old master of intrigue who might forget, once he was back at the head of an army, the favors received, and start harassing Etruria all over again?

We are inclined toward the second theory. Etruria was an anarchical country in which every city wanted to be independent and could not bear to have its autonomy limited. Tarquin would have made Rome a definitely Etruscan city, but Etruria a definitely Roman province. Etruria wanted no part of this. But it cost her dear. Before the confederate army could even reestablish communications with the Etruscan colonies in the south where already the Greeks were beginning to filter in, the league which Porsena had formed with such difficulty had melted away. The *lucumo* retired to Chiusi and shut himself up there, while the Greeks advanced from the south and another terrible menace loomed large in the north: the Gauls, who were coming down from the Alps and submerging the Etruscan colonies of the Po Valley. Even in the face of this danger, Etruria did not find her unity, that unity Tarquin wished to give her in the name of Rome. The old king continued to intrigue, but in vain. The victorious cities of Latium, with Veii at their head, collaborated to prevent his return. They preferred to deal with a republican Rome whose internal difficulties they knew, and who was not in a position to take revenge. That revenge was in fact to be delayed for another century.

"Liberation" is always an expensive business. Rome paid for her liberation from her king with the loss of an empire. She had spent two and a half centuries gaining supremacy over central Italy and had achieved it under seven kings. The republic, in order to remain a republic, had to relinquish all of this colossal patrimony.

What then had failed to work under the monarchy and induced the Romans to make such a sacrifice to get rid of it?

The melting pot had not worked, that is, the fusion of the races and classes which made up the city. The first four kings had humiliated the Etruscan element which represented the middle classes: riches, progress, technique, industry, and commerce. The last three kings had humiliated the Latin and Sabine elements representing aristocracy, agriculture, tradition, and the army, whose political expression was the senate. Now the senate was getting its revenge—and by means of the republic, which was exclusively its creature.

From now on everything in Rome was to be republican, above all, its history, which began to be written in such a way as to discredit the monarchy and the spectacular successes Rome had achieved under it. This should not be forgotten when reading books on Roman history which, with one accord, date the beginning of the city's greatness from the time of the expulsion of the last Tarquin.

This is palpably unfair. Rome had already been a powerful capital under the kings, and it was largely due to their work that she became one again. The austere magistrates who came after them and wielded power "in the name of the people" found ready-made the materials for future triumphs: a well-laid-out city from the architectural and administrative point of view, a resourceful and cosmopolitan population, an elite of first-class technicians, a well-trained army, an already codified religion and language, and a diplomatic corps which had served its apprenticeship making and unmaking alliances with most of the people in the area.

These diplomatic talents were efficacious even at the moment of catastrophe. Rome hastened to sign two treaties, one with Carthage to assure herself of peace from the seaward side, and one with the Latin League to assure it on land. Both involved radical concessions. On the sea, Rome gave up every claim in Corsica, Sardinia, and Sicily, beyond which she was not to go with her ships and where she could only take on stores without landing. This concession actually cost Rome little, since she did not yet own a fleet worthy of the name.

The concessions she had to make on land were more painful. At the end of the war with Veii and her allies, Rome remained mistress of only 500 square miles and had to accept being an equal among equals in the Latin League. The *foedus*, the treaty of 493 B.C., begins with these emphatic words: "Let there be peace between the Roman and the Latin cities so long as the position of the sky and earth remains unchanged . . ." The position of the sky and earth had not changed in the slightest when less than a century later the Roman republic went on the

warpath again, on exactly the same one along which their ancient kings had stopped halfway, and proceeded to administer
an unforgettable lesson to the Latin cities.

VI

S.P.Q.R.

AFTER 509 B.C., THE YEAR IN WHICH THE REPUBLIC WAS FOUNDED,
all the monuments which the Romans erected all over the place
bore the initials *S.P.Q.R.*, which means *Senatus Populus-Que
Romanus:* "The Senate and the Roman People."

We have already described what the senate was, but not
the *populus*, a word which had little or nothing in common with
what we mean by the people. In those far-off days it did not include all the citizens, as it does today, but only two "orders," or
social classes: the patricians and the *equites*, or knights.

The patricians were those descended from the *patres* or
founders of the city. According to Livy, Romulus chose about a
hundred heads of families to help him build Rome. It was only
natural for them to help themselves to the best land and consider themselves a cut above the later arrivals. Thus the very
first kings had no social problems to cope with since all their
subjects were equal, and he himself was only one of them appointed to carry out certain functions of a mainly religious
nature.

Under Tarquin Priscus a great many other people began to
stream into Rome, especially from Etruria. The descendents of
the *patres* were very careful to keep their distance from these
newcomers and took refuge in the fortress of the senate, accessible only to members of their families. Each patrician bore the
name of his founder forbear: Manlius, Julius, Aemilius, Cornelius, Claudius, Horatius, Fabius.

As soon as these two groups, the descendents of the pioneers and the more recent arrivals, began to live together within
the city walls, two classes emerged in Rome: the patricians and
the plebs.

Very soon the patricians were heavily outnumbered. In order to defend their prerogatives, they did what all social classes do when they are crafty and find themselves in the minority—they called in some of the plebs to share their privileges and thus committed them to their side.

By the time of Servius Tullius there were already more than two classes. An important middle class had sprung up among the plebs, quite strong in number and very strong financially. When the king organized the new *comitiae centuriatae*, dividing the voters into five classes according to financial status, and giving the first, or millionaire's class, enough votes to beat the other four, the patricians were far from happy. They saw themselves literally outclassed as a political power by people with no family trees but much more money. So when Tarquin the Proud was expelled and the republic proclaimed, they realized that they could not stand alone against all the others. They resorted to an alliance with the moneyed bourgeoisie who like their counterparts in all ages asked nothing better than to be allowed to enter the aristocracy, that is, the senate. If the French nobility of the eighteenth century had behaved likewise, they would have avoided the guillotine.

These men of substance, as we have said, were called *equites*, or knights. They all came from commerce or industry and their great dream was to enter the senate. In order to make it come true, they not only always voted with the patricians but also they did not mind dipping into their pockets to get an appointment or office. The patricians made them pay by the nose. When a patrician married the daughter of a knight, he insisted on a queen's dowry, and even when the knight finally succeeded in becoming a senator, he was not admitted as a *pater*, or patrician, but as a conscript, for the assembly was composed of *patres et conscripti*.

"The people" then were made up of patricians and knights; the rest were plebs and did not count. This meant that all sorts of persons, artisans, small shopkeepers, clerks, freedmen and the like, were not at all satisfied with their lot. In fact the whole of the first century of the new Rome was taken up by a social struggle between those who wished to enlarge the concept of the people and those who wished to restrict it to the two aristocracies of birth and of money. This struggle began in 494 B.C., fourteen years after the proclamation of the republic when

Rome was assailed on every side, had lost all that she had won under the kings, and was reduced more or less to the status of a small town on an equal footing with other towns of the Latin League.

At the end of this ruinous war the plebs, who had supplied the soldiers for it, found themselves in a desperate state. Many had lost their farms because they were in territory now occupied by the enemy. In order to maintain their families when they were fighting, all of them had run heavily into debt, which in those times was not the normal state of affairs as it is today. The man who didn't pay up automatically became the slave of his creditor, who could lock him up in the cellar, sell him, or kill him. If there were several creditors, they were even authorized to divide up the corpse of the poor devil after they had finished him off. Although it appears that they never went quite as far as this, nonetheless the position of the debtor was far from comfortable.

What could these plebeians do to get a little justice? They had no voice in the *comitiae centuriatae* because they belonged to the lowest classes, had too few *centuriae* and therefore too few votes to impose their will. So they began to agitate in the streets and squares. Choosing orators from among the more intelligent of their fellows, they demanded the cancellation of debts, a new distribution of land to replace their lost smallholdings, and the right to elect their own magistrates.

The "orders" and the senate turned a deaf ear to these demands. Whereupon the plebs, or large masses of them, went on strike. They retired to Monte Sacro (or Mount Holy) some three miles from the city and said that from that moment on they would not supply a laborer for the land, a workman for industry, or a soldier for the army.

The last threat was the most serious, because at that very moment a new menace had arisen in the form of the Volsci and the Aequi. Just when a peace had been more or less patched up with their Latin and Sabine neighbors, these barbarous tribes came rolling down from the heights of the Apennines to the plains in search of more fertile land. They were already overrunning the cities of the league.

The senate, its back against the wall, sent delegation after delegation to the plebs to get them to come back to the city and collaborate in the common defense. Menenius Agrippa, to convince them, told them the famous story of the man whose limbs, to spite his stomach, refused to feed it, and ended up dying of starvation. But the plebs held out and replied that the choice was clear: either the senate would cancel their debts, free all those enslaved for debt, and allow the plebs to elect their own magistrates to defend them, or they would remain on Monte Sacro. Let all the Aequi and Volsci in the world come and destroy Rome.

In the end the senate gave in. It canceled the debts, freed the slaves, and put the plebs under the protection of two tribunes and three aediles elected annually by them.

This last provision was the first great victory of the Roman proletariat and gave them a legal instrument for winning others in their struggle for social justice. The year 494 B.C. is very important in the history of the city, and of democracy.

When the plebs returned, it was possible to put an army in the field to counter the menace of the Volsci and the Aequi. Rome was not alone in this war, which lasted about sixty years and involved her very survival. The common danger kept her Latin and Sabine allies faithful to her, as well as another neighboring people, the Hernici.

The story goes that a young patrician greatly distinguished himself in the close-fought battles of this war. He was called Coriolanus after a city which he had taken by assault. Being a die-hard conservative, he did not want the government to donate a free issue of grain to the starving population. The tribunes of the plebs, who meanwhile had been elected, asked for and obtained his exile. Coriolanus promptly joined the enemy's army, took command, and led it from victory to victory right up to the gates of Rome.

The senate sent him, as they had the plebs, delegation after delegation with appeals to desist but he refused to listen. Only when he saw his imploring wife and mother coming out to him did he give the order "to the rear, march." The Volsci reacted by killing him, but, left without a leader, they were defeated and forced to retreat.

In their wake came the Aequi who had already turned Frascati upside down. They managed to interrupt communications between the Romans and their allies, and the situation was so dismal that the senate granted the title and powers of dictator to L. Quintius Cincinnatus. With a fresh army he re-

lieved the surrounded legions and led them to final victory in
431 B.C. He then relinquished his command, having held it for
only sixteen days, and went back to his farm to get on with the
plowing.

Even before this happy ending, a new war had broken out
to the north against the Etruscan city of Veii. That city did not
intend to miss the chance of putting Rome down once and for
all. Veii had already committed a number of hostile acts while
Rome was busy defending herself against the Volsci and the
Aequi, acts which Rome had submitted to in the manner of the
English, that is, taking careful note of them. Then as soon as her
hands were free, she settled accounts. It was a bitter war which
also at one point required the appointment of a dictator—
Marcus Furius Camillus, a great soldier, but above all an honest
man. He brought a great innovation to the army: the *sti-*
pendium. Up until now soldiers had had to serve for nothing,
and if they were married, their families at home starved. The
satisfied troops redoubled their efforts, took Veii by assault,
destroyed it methodically and deported all the inhabitants as
slaves.

This great victory and the punishment which sealed it
filled the Romans with pride, quadrupled their territory until
it was well over 1,500 square miles, and gave rise to jealousy
and mistrust of Camillus. While he was conquering city after
city in Etruria, they began to accuse him in Rome of being
ambitious and pocketing the loot instead of handing it over to
the state. This so embittered him that he relinquished his command and, instead of returning home to clear his name, he went
into voluntary exile at Ardea.

Perhaps he would have died there, leaving a name be-
smirched by calumny, if the ungrateful Romans had not needed
him again to save them from the Gauls, the last and greatest
danger they had to face before starting on their career of conquest in earnest. The Gauls were a barbaric people of Celtic
stock who had come from France and overrun the valley of the
Po. They had divided that fertile territory among their tribes:
the Insubres, the Boii, the Cenomani, and the Senones. But one
enterprising tribe under the command of Brennus conquered
Chiusi, overthrew the Roman legions on the River Allia, and
marched on Rome.

Historians have wrapped this chapter, which must have

been a singularly unpleasant one for the city, in numerous legends. One of these is that when the Gauls were about to assault the Capitol, the geese sacred to Juno began to screech so loudly that they woke up Manlius Capitolinus. Thereupon, at the head of the defenders, he beat off the attack. If he did, the Gauls somehow got into the Capitol just the same, as well as into the rest of the city, from which the population had fled in a body to take refuge in the surrounding mountains. We are also told that the complete senate remained, sitting like statues on the rough benches of the Senate House, and that one of them named Papirius when he felt his beard pulled in derision by a Gaul (who may have wanted to find out whether it were made of stone) struck him in the face with his ivory scepter. Finally it is said that Brennus, having set fire to the whole of Rome, demanded I don't know how many pounds of gold to go away and insisted on rigged scales to weigh it on. When the senators protested, Brennus threw his sword on the plate for good measure and pronounced the famous phrase: *"Vae victis"*— "Woe to the vanquished!" At this point Camillus, popping up by a miracle from somewhere, is said to have replied: *"Non auro, sed ferro, recuperanda est patria"*—"Not with gold but with iron the country must be restored." Thereupon he placed himself at the head of an army—it remains a mystery where this had been hidden up to now—and put the enemy to flight.

The truth of the matter is that the Gauls took Rome by force of arms, sacked it and left, not pursued by legions but laden with booty. They were hearty and clumsy plunderers, and their conquests had nothing political or strategic about them. They assaulted, sacked, and retired, taking no thought for the morrow. If they had been able to imagine the vengeance Rome was to wreak for this humiliation, they would not have left a stone standing. Devastate it they did, but they did not destroy it. They then retraced their steps towards Aemilia and Lombardy. Camillus, urgently recalled from Ardea, got down to repairing the damage. He probably never even had a skirmish with the Gauls since they had already gone by the time he arrived. At any rate, laying aside his rancor, he reassumed the title of dictator and got busy reconstructing both city and army. The same people who had called him an ambitious robber now called him "The Second Founder of Rome."

While all this was happening on the surface, internally

Rome had attained a major objective with the law of the Twelve Tables.

This was a coup for the plebs, who had been demanding ever since they returned from Monte Sacro that the laws should no longer be left as the monopoly of the church which was in turn the monopoly of the patricians. They wanted laws to be published so that everyone would know his obligations and the penalties to which he might be liable. Up to now the standards by which the magistrates judged had been secret, contained in texts jealously guarded by the priests and mixed up with religious rites in which they claimed to divine the will of the gods. If the gods were in a good humor, a murderer could get away with it; if not, a miserable chicken thief might end up on the gallows. Since those who interpreted the divine will were patricians, the plebs felt defenseless.

Under pressure of external dangers from the Volsci, the Aequi, the Veientians and the Gauls, along with the threat of a second retirement to Monte Sacro, the senate gave in. It sent three of its members to Greece to study what Solon had done in this particular line. When these envoys returned, a commission of ten legislators was set up, called the Decemvirate. Under the presidency of Appius Claudius they drew up the Code of the Twelve Tables, which became the public and written foundation of Roman law.

This great achievement dates back to 451 B.C. a date that almost corresponds to the three-hundredth anniversary of the founding of the city.

Things did not run smoothly because the *decemviri* so much liked the plenary powers the senate had conferred on them to complete the job that at the end of the year they refused to part with them. This is said to be the fault of Appius Claudius who wished to continue in office to be in a position to overcome the resistance of a lovely and delectable plebeian, Virginia, of whom he was enamored. Her father, Lucius Virginius, went to him to protest. When Appius took a lofty tone, he stuck a knife in him and then, like Collatinus after the Lucretia business, hurried off to the barracks to tell his story to the soldiers and exhort them to revolt against the despot. The plebs in indignation once more retired to Monte Sacro and the army threatened to follow their example. So the senate, in emergency session, expressed regret to the *decemviri* that they could no longer keep them in office. They were therefore dismissed, Appius Claudius was banished, and executive power returned to the consuls.

It was not yet the triumph of democracy. This came a century later, with the proposals of Licinius and Sextius. But it was a great step forward. The *P* in *S.P.Q.R.* began to be *populus* as we understand it today.

VII

Pyrrhus

ROME EMERGED FROM THE HUMILIATION SHE HAD SUFFERED AT the hands of the Gauls and from her internal struggle between patricians and plebs with two trump cards in hand: first, supremacy in the league over her Latin and Sabine rivals who had suffered more serious devastation than she had without finding a Camillus to repair the damage; and second, a more balanced social structure, assuring peace among the classes. So when the smoke from the fires that Brennus left on his trail north cleared away, the city, brand-new and better organized, began to take a good look around in search of loot.

Campania had the richest and most fertile land in the neighborhood. It was inhabited by the Samnites, some of whom had remained in the mountains of the Abruzzi. Cold and hungry, these mountaineers regularly used to swoop down to plunder the herds and crops of their brethren in the plain. Under the threat of one of these incursions, the Samnites of Capua applied for Rome's protection. Rome was only too delighted to oblige, as it was the best way of splitting this people permanently in two and interfering in their private affairs. Thus began the first of the three Samnite wars, due to last about fifty years in all.

The first war against the people of the Abruzzi was a short one, from 343 B.C. to 341 B.C. Some people say it was never fought because the Abruzzans failed to turn up and the Romans did not feel like going into the mountains to flush them out. Be that as it may, the affair had one consequence: the "protection" by Rome of Capua, who began to feel so well protected that she invited the Latins to form a united front against their common "protector." The Latins agreed and Rome suddenly found that she had enemies instead of allies. It was an awkward moment, requiring the usual heroic episodes to overcome its difficulties. For the sake of discipline, the consul Titus Manlius Torquatus condemned his own son to death because, in spite of the order to stand firm, this son had left the ranks to reply to the insult of a Latin officer. And a colleague, Publius Decius Mus, when told by the augurs that the country could only be saved by the sacrifice of his life, advanced single-handed against the foe, quite happy to be slaughtered.

Whether or not these episodes are true, Rome at any rate won and abolished the Latin League which had betrayed her. This did away with the federal policy, in force up until then, and the "unitarian" policy of a single bloc was devised. Rome conceded different types of autonomy to the various cities which had made up the league so as to keep them from having interests in common. The good old system of divide and rule was beginning to creep in. There were to be no political relations between the subject cities themselves, only between each one of them and Rome. Colonizers were given free land in the Campania and became the outposts of Roman sovereignty in the south. The empire was being born.

The second Samnite war began without a pretext some fourteen years later in 327 B.C. The Romans had reached the outskirts of Naples during the previous war and had looked hard and long at this capital of the Greek colonies. They were fascinated by its long Hellenic walls, its gymnasiums, its theaters, commerce, and general liveliness, and one fine day they occupied it.

The Samnites, both of mountain and plain, realized that if the Romans were given a free hand they would devour the whole of Italy. So they made peace with each other and jointly attacked the legions in the rear. At first their army, composed of guerrillas rather than soldiers, was beaten; later, knowing the terrain better than the Romans, they lured them into the gorges of Caudium, near Benevento, and bottled them up there. After many vain attempts to break out of the trap, the two consuls were forced to capitulate and submit to the humiliation of

passing under the yoke of the Samnite spears. These were the
famous "Caudine forks."

Rome bided her time as usual and did not sue for peace.
Profiting by the experience, she reorganized the legions, making
them more mobile and maneuverable. In 316 B.C. she resumed
the struggle and once more found herself in trouble. The Etruscans to the north and the Hernici to the southeast tried to catch
her unawares. She defeated them separately and then turned all
her forces on the isolated Samnites. In 304 B.C. she conquered
Bovianum, their capital, and for the first time her legions crossed
the Apennines and reached the Adriatic coast of Apulia.

These successes worried the other peoples of the peninsula
so much that fear drove them into coalition and gave them the
courage to challenge Rome. This time, in addition to the Etruscans, the Lucanians, the Umbrians, and the Sabines, came in
too, determined even at the cost of their independence to defend their anarchy. They put together an army which met the
Romans at Sentinum in the Umbrian Apennines. They were
superior in numbers but instead of operating in concert, all the
generals commanding the different contingents shifted for themselves and were naturally beaten. Decius Mus, son of the consul
who had voluntarily died for his country, repeated his father's
gesture and thus guaranteed the family name its niche in history. The coalition broke up. The Etruscans, Lucanians, and
Umbrians sued for peace separately. The Samnites and Sabines
fought on for another five years and in 290 B.C. they surrendered.

Modern historians say that Rome undertook these wars
with a precise strategic objective in view, the Adriatic. We
believe that her legions arrived on the shores of that sea without knowing how or why, but simply in pursuit of the fleeing
enemy. Since the Romans of that time had no maps, they had
no idea that Italy comprised what today would be called a
natural geopolitical unit, that it was the shape of a boot, and
that to keep a firm hold on it one must be master of its seas.
Without knowing or propounding the theory, they quite simply
put into practice the principle of *lebensraum,* or vital space,
according to which a territory has to annex its neighbors in
order to live and breathe. Thus to guarantee the safety of
Capua, they took Naples. To guarantee the safety of Naples,
they conquered Benevento. At Tarentum, because there was
nothing but sea beyond it, they stopped.

At that time Tarentum was a Greek metropolis. It had made great progress, especially in the fields of industry, commerce, and art, under the guidance of Archytas who was half-philosopher, half-engineer, and one of the greatest statesmen of antiquity. It was not a warlike city. In 303 B.C. it had asked and received from Rome a promise that her ships should never round Cape Colonne, which meant that Rome would leave her in peace from the sea. Tarentum had been certain that Rome would never reach her over land, but now this was the very direction from which the legions were rolling down.

The pretext for war was supplied as usual by an appeal for protection, this time from the Thurii who were threatened by the Lucanians. As always on these occasions, Rome readily complied and supplied a garrison. This was sent by sea, no doubt with the deliberate intention of looking for trouble, as the ships had to round Cape Colonne to reach the Thurii. The Tarentines closed their eyes to this infraction of the pact, but when the ten Roman triremes demanded anchorage in their port, they considered it provocation, attacked them, and sank four ships.

They then realized that this act meant war, and that they would come off very badly unless they managed to get some powerful outside help. Where could they find it? Italy had not a single state left capable of opposing Rome. And so they had to send abroad for help, thus setting a precedent for a custom which long prevailed in the peninsula. They found that help just across the sea, in Pyrrhus king of Epirus, a country around what is now northwest Greece and southern Albania.

Pyrrhus was a curious character who might have lived to a ripe and comfortable old age if he had been content with his little mountain kingdom. But in the *Iliad* he had read of the deeds of Achilles and in his veins ran Macedonian blood, the blood of Alexander the Great. Everything conspired to make him rather like one of the *condottieri* of the fifteenth century, in short, the sort who looks for trouble. The proposal of the Tarentines was just what he had been waiting for. He embarked his army and met the Romans at Heraclea.

For the first time the Romans found themselves face to face with an enemy of whose existence they had never dreamed: elephants. At first they thought they were oxen, and in fact called them "Lucanian oxen." When they saw these monsters charge, they were panic-stricken, yet although they lost the battle they inflicted such heavy losses on the enemy that his victory was empty. The expression "Pyrrhic victory" has been used ever since to describe the conquest that carries too high a price.

The following year (279 B.C.) the Epirot repeated his performance at Asculum. Here again his losses were so heavy that when he looked at the battlefield he must have felt the same dismay that Napoleon III did a couple of thousand years later when he contemplated the field of Solferino. Pyrrhus then sent his secretary Cineas to Rome with peace proposals and with him two thousand Roman prisoners who were under oath to return if peace were not concluded. We are told that the senate was at the point of accepting the proposals when the censor Appius Claudius the Blind took the floor to remind the assembly that it was undignified to negotiate with a foreigner while his invading army was still encamped on Italian soil.

We tend to doubt the accuracy of this. For Rome, at that time, Italy meant only Rome itself. Yet there is no doubt that the senate rejected the proposals and that Cineas together with the two thousand prisoners, not one of whom broke his parole, returned and gave Pyrrhus such a vivid description of what he had seen at Rome that the Epirot decided to accept an appeal from the Syracusans for help against the Carthaginians, who were beginning to take an uncomfortable interest in Sicily. There, too, he did not have much success. The Greek cities he had come to defend could not agree among themselves and never gave him the contingents they had promised. Discouraged, he recrossed the straits to relieve Tarentum to which the Romans were now laying siege. By this time they were accustomed to elephants and faced them boldly. Pyrrhus was defeated in 275 B.C. at Malevento which, for the occasion, the Romans rechristened Benevento. Italy having proved unprofitable, Pyrrhus went back to try his luck in Greece where he presently met his death.

Exactly seventy years had elapsed (343–273 B.C.) since Rome had recovered as well as she could from the internal upheaval caused by the fall of the monarchy, had survived her struggle for existence, and embarked on her authentic campaigns of conquest. By now she was arbiter of the whole peninsula, from the Tuscan-Aemilian Apennines to the Straits of Messina. One by one the stars of all the little kingdoms which had once twinkled there were extinguished, including those of Magna Graecia, left without a protector once Pyrrhus had departed. Tarentum surrendered in 272 B.C., Reggio in 270 B.C.

After her experience with the Latin League, Rome realized that one could not put one's trust in protectorates and forced allies. Partly for this reason and partly because of the city's overpopulation, the Romans began really to Romanize Italy by the system of colonies, a process they had inaugurated after the first Samnite war. Enemy territory was confiscated and distributed to landless Roman citizens, especially to those with military merits. In fact most of it was assigned to veterans, men who could be relied on to rally promptly to their own defense —and Rome's. The natives naturally received them coldly, as robbers and oppressors, and from the name of one of them, a certain Caphus, a corporal in Caesar's army, the word *cafone* was later coined, a term of contempt meaning a coarse and vulgar person. This hostility also gave rise at this time to the mocking derisive sound—popularly known today as the "Bronx cheer"—with which the defeated peoples greeted the Romans when they entered their cities and which, it would seem, was at first mistaken for a manifestation of welcome.

Of course one cannot hope to enlarge one's territory from 300 to 15,000 square miles, as the Romans did during this period, without stepping on somebody's toes. On the other hand, all central and southern Italy began to speak the same language and to think in terms of nation and state instead of village and tribe.

During the course of these long and bloody years and as a direct result of the pressure of the wars, the plebs attained their objectives, one after the other, including the last and fundamental one that was guaranteed by the Hortensian law, named after the dictator who decreed it: that the result of a plebiscite automatically became law, with no need for ratification by the senate. Since the veto on marriages between patricians and plebs had been abolished, at least on paper by the Canuleian law of 445 B.C., the latter were no longer excluded from any right or magisterial office. And since the praetorship was open to them and the right of admission to the senate was given to those who had practiced at the bar, even this last citadel of the aristocracy was accessible to the plebs, albeit hedged with a thousand precautions and limitations.

All this had been achieved in the face of endless antagonisms which at times had endangered the survival of the city. But the fact that somehow or other it had been achieved goes to show that though the upper classes in Rome were hard-bitten conservatives, they had brains and could use them. They were not in the least ashamed of defending openly the interests of their caste and never pretended to flirt with the left wing as so many princes and industrialists do today. They paid their taxes, did ten years' hard military service, died at the head of their men, and whenever it was a question of choosing between their own privileges and the good of the country, they did not hesitate. That is why, even after they had accepted complete parity of rights with the plebs, they remained in power, as the English nobility still manages to do even in this socialist world.

During the period of rest the city allowed herself after the victory over Pyrrhus, a period she also used for digesting her prey, Rome put the finishing touches to the internal equilibrium and order of that large portion of the peninsula that was now hers. The Appian Way, which Appius Claudius had built to link Capua to Rome, was prolonged to Brindisi and Tarentum. This was the highway used not only by the soldiers but by the colonizers on their way to Romanize Benevento, Aesernia, Brindisi, Firmum, Hadria, and many other cities. Rome granted very little independence to the conquered, and respected it even less. Thus she bears prime responsibility for the lack in Italy of those communal and regional liberties that developed so vigorously in the Germanic world. Yet she brought the concept of the state, of which she was practically the inventor, to its highest expression, and placed it on those five pillars that still uphold it: the prefect, the judge, the policeman, the law, and the tax collector.

These were the instruments with which she set out to conquer the world. Let us now take a closer look at the reasons why she succeeded.

VIII

Education

IN THE WELL-NAMED "STOIC" ROME OF THOSE DAYS, EVERYBODY
lived dangerously. The danger began on the day of one's birth.
If one happened to be born a girl or with some physical defect,
one's father had the right to throw one out the door and leave
one to die. What's more, he often did. The healthy male child,
of course, was generally welcome, not only because he would
be useful to his parents later on by helping with the work, but
also they believed that unless someone was left to look after
their tombs and to celebrate the necessary sacrifices on them,
their souls would not go to heaven.

If all went well, that is if the baby had hit on the right
sex and physical endowments, he was officially received by the
gens eight days after his birth. The *gens* was a group of families
descended from a common ancestor who had given them his
name. The infant was usually given three names: the individual
or first name, such as Marius or Antonius, that of the *gens* or
real name, and that of his family, or surname. Women only had
the middle, the *gens* name, and were merely Tullia, Julia, Cornelia, whereas their brothers would be, let us say, Marcus
Tullius Aemilius, Publius Julius Antonius, and Caius Cornelius
Gracchus.

This strange habit caused no end of confusion since the
founder forbears numbered only about a hundred. There were
only so many *gens* names to go around, and so they were continually repeated, making necessary an added fourth or fifth
surname! For example, Publius Cornelius Scipio, who destroyed Carthage, added the names Aemilianus Africanus Minor
to his calling card. This distinguished him from the Publius
Cornelius Scipio who had beaten Hannibal and had added
Africanus Major to his name.

As can be seen, these were long, weighty, high-sounding
names that in themselves loaded a number of duties on their
infant owners. A Marcus Tullius Cornelius could not live in the
lap of luxury and give way to the caprices that are permitted

to little Dickie or Johnnie. These boys grew up anything but spoiled and from the tenderest age were taught that the family to which they belonged was strictly a military unit with one commander in chief, the *paterfamilias*. Only he could buy and sell because he was the sole owner of everything, including his wife's dowry. If she were unfaithful to him, or stole wine from the wine barrel, he could kill her without a trial. He had the same rights over his children whom he could even sell as slaves. Everything that they bought automatically became his property. The females could only escape from this paternal authority when he gave them in marriage to someone *cum manu*, that is by explicitly renouncing his every right over them. In this case the rights passed to the husband. Thus a woman always finished up as the appurtenance of some man, either her father, her husband, or, when she was left a widow, of her eldest son or a guardian.

This stern discipline which was gradually mitigated with the passing of the centuries was only tempered by *pietas*, or affection between husband and wife, parents and children. But almost nothing could affect the granite-like unity of the Roman family, which included grandchildren, great-grandchildren, and slaves, the latter being regarded simply as objects. The mother was called *domina* or lady, and was not confined to a *gynaeceum*, the women's quarters where Greek women had to live. She had her meals with her husband but sitting on the *triclinium* (a sort of rustic divan) instead of reclining as he did. As a rule she did not do much work with her hands, there being no servant shortage in those days; what with all the slaves they kept on capturing on the field of battle, every family had more than one. These were directed and supervised by the *domina*. For relaxation she wove the wool for the clothes of her husband and sons. No books, playing cards, theaters, or circuses—all were forbidden. Visits were rare and strictly formal, and a scrupulous ceremonial rendered them complicated and difficult. The *domus*, the house, was a sort of combined fortress and barracks in which the boys were drilled into unquestioning obedience.

They were taught that the fire in the hearth must never be allowed to go out because it represented Vesta, the goddess of life. It had to be kept going with fresh wood; bread crumbs had to be thrown on it during meals. On the mud or brick walls little ikons were hung; they were the *lares* and *penates,* the household gods who watched over the prosperity of the house and fields. On the door was Janus who with his two faces, one looking in and the other looking out, kept an eye on everyone. And standing guard all around were the *manes* or spirits of the ancestors who stayed in the vicinity even after death. Thus nobody could make a move without bumping into some supernatural guardian who belonged to the family. The family group was thus composed not only of the living but of predecessors and successors as well; it formed an economic, moral and religious microcosm of which the *pater* was the infallible pope. It was he who offered the sacrifices on the household altar, gave the orders, and meted out punishment in the name of the gods.

The religious atmosphere in which the Roman boy grew up did not aim to make a better, but a more disciplined man of him. Rather than inspiring him toward the noble ideals of goodness and generosity, it molded him into acceptance of those liturgical duties which turned his whole life into a rite. He was not expected to be altruistic, for example, but it was required, even insisted on that he should observe certain habits and participate in certain ceremonies. His prayers were always directed to immediate and practical ends. He addressed himself to Abeona to teach him how to take his first steps, to Fabulinus so that he could utter his first words, to Pomona so that the pears in the garden should grow sweet, to Saturn to help him sow, to Ceres to grant him a good harvest, and to Sterculus so that the cattle in the cowshed should provide enough manure.

None of these gods and spirits had any regard for morality, but they were incredibly fussy about formalities. Evidently they cherished no illusions about the human soul. Feeling that it had no real vocation for uplift, they left it to its own devices. What really interested them were not the sentiments but the deeds of the faithful. And they intended to keep these strictly regimented within the framework of those two great institutions of which they were the cement: the family and the state.

This was why they insisted on obedience to the father, fidelity to the husband, procreation, acceptance of the law, respect for authority, courage in war to the point of sacrifice, steadfastness in the face of death—all of which were decked out in sacerdotal authority.

Around the age of six or seven this careful and punctilious

formation of the character was followed by that of the mind, by
normal education. This was not organized by the state, as it is
today in public schools. It remained a family affair. Even in well-
to-do homes the father rarely relegated the job to a slave or a
freedman. This custom came much later when Rome was greater
and stronger but no longer stoic. Right up to the end of the
Punic Wars, fathers were their own sons' schoolmasters and
taught them what today is called culture and in those times was
called discipline.

The subjects were few and simple: reading, writing, grammar, history, and arithmetic. The Romans had a kind of ink con-
cocted from berry juice in which they dipped a small metal
implement and traced words on little boards of planed wood
(later they developed paper out of linen and parchment). Their
language had a very rigid syntax but a limited vocabulary with
no shades of meaning, much more adapted to drawing up legal
codes than to love stories and poetry. The Romans had no time
for such nonsense and anyone who wished to read it had to learn
Greek, a much richer, more flexible language. The first Roman
history textbook was in fact written in Greek, by Quintus Fabius
Pictor, but this was much later, in 202 B.C.

Up to this time history was just handed down verbally from
father to son by means of fanciful tales which appealed to the
children's imagination—stories like that of Aeneas, Amulius and
Numitor, the Horatii and the Curatii, Lucretia and Collatinus,
etc. These fictitious but self-improving historical legends were
reinforced by poetry, all of it sacred and commemorative in
tone. It was condensed in volumes entitled *Consular Archives,
The Books of the Magistrates, The Annals,* and so on, which
extolled great national events such as elections, victories, feasts,
and miracles.

The first to break away from these prescribed subjects was
a Greek slave, Livy Andronicus, who had been taken prisoner
during the sack of Tarentum and brought to Rome. Here he
began reciting the *Odyssey* to his owner's friends, who were
enthusiastic, and being highly placed personages, commissioned
him to make an entertainment from it for the great *ludi* or
games of 240 B.C. Livy Andronicus translated the Greek into
Latin verse, crude and irregular, and turned out a tragedy in
which he himself declaimed and sang all the parts as long as
his voice lasted. The Romans, who had never seen or heard any-

thing like this, were so delighted that the government gave
poets recognition from then on as a category of citizen and
allowed them to form their own corporation, with premises in
the temple of Minerva on the Aventine Hill.

But this also happened much later. For the moment, Roman
boys had no literature to read. Once they were able to spell and
had learned all the legends by heart, they went on to mathematics and geometry. The first consisted of simple sums counted off
on their fingers. Their written numerals were imitations of hand
signs: I is the graphic representation of a raised finger, V of an
open hand, X of two open and crossed hands. The Romans
counted with these symbols and with their prefixes (IV) and
suffixes (VI, XII). Later a decimal system evolved from this manual arithmetic, with fractions and multiples of ten, that is, of the
ten fingers. As for geometry, it remained archaic until the Greeks
came along to teach it; it was reduced to a bare minimum, just
enough for the rudimentary construction of the time.

There were no gymnastics. The wrestling ring and the gymnasium came much later, and were also of Greek import. Roman
fathers preferred to develop their sons' muscles by putting them
to work on the farm with spade and plow and then send them off
to the army which, when it did not kill them, sent them back
completely casehardened many years later. By the same token
there was no practice of medicine. The Romans were of the opinion that diseases were not caused by microbes but by the gods.
So there were two alternatives: either sickness was a sign that
the gods wished a man to depart from this life, and then there
was nothing to be done; or they just wanted to give him a temporary punishment and all one could do was wait. For every ill-
ness there was a prayer to a particular divinity. The "Madonna
of the Fevers" invoked by the Roman masses today is just the
modern version of the goddesses Febra and Mephitis who were
invoked back in those times.

As for recreation, even in their spare time the boys were not
allowed to do what they liked. After many hours of digging and
an hour or so of grammar, the senatorial father used to take his
offspring by the hand and drag him off to the hall opposite the
Forum where the senate held its sessions. There, sitting silent on
the benches, Roman boys, from seven or eight up, listened to debates on the great problems of the state—administration, alli-

ances, and wars—and learned early that mien of grave solemnity
which was to become their salient characteristic.

It was the army that gave the finishing touch. The richer
the citizen, the heavier the taxes he had to pay and the greater
number of years he had to serve. Ten years was the minimum
for anyone who wanted to embark on a public career. In practice only the rich were able to serve so long, as they were the
only ones who could afford to spend so much time away from
farm or shop. Even if somebody wanted to exercise his political
rights, that is, to vote, he had to be through with his military
service, for it was in his capacity as a member of the *centuria*
that he took part in the *comitia centuriata*, the highest legislative body of the state, divided, as we have said, into its five
classes.

The first class had ninety-eight *centuriae*, eighteen of which
were cavalry and the rest heavy infantry. All the recruits joined
up armed, at their own expense, with two spears, a dagger, a
saber, a bronze helmet, a breastplate, and a shield, which the
second class did not have, though in other respects their *accou-
trements* were identical. The third and fourth classes were without helmet, breastplate or shield. The fifth class was simply
armed with staves and stones. The basic unit of this army was
the legion, composed of 4,200 infantry, 300 cavalry, and various
supporting arms. Every legion had its own standard and it was
a point of honor for every soldier to keep it from falling into
enemy hands. In fact, when things looked unpromising, the
officers used to grab it and advance. In order to defend it the
troops had to follow and in this way the tables were turned at
the last moment in many a battle that was going badly.

In its earliest period the legion was divided into phalanxes,
six solid ranks of 500 men each; later, to make it more maneuverable, into maniples of two *centuriae*, companies of 200. Yet
the strength of this army did not lie in its order of battle but in
its discipline. Cowards were flogged to death and the general
could behead anyone, officer or soldier, for the slightest disobedience. Deserters and thieves had their right hands cut off.
The rations were bread and vegetables, and the men were so
accustomed to this diet that Caesar's veterans, during a year
when the wheat crop failed, complained at having to eat meat.

Boys were called up at the age of sixteen, and had already
begun to think about the regiment they were to join and in which

they would grow up. Discipline was so strict and fatigues so exhausting that everyone preferred battle service to drill. After the hard barracks life, death was no great sacrifice for these boys. Which was why they faced it with such indifference.

IX

The Career

THE YOUNG MAN WHO HAD SURVIVED TEN YEARS' MILITARY SERVICE could embark on a political career when he got home. But his election and his promotion by grades were subject to every kind of precaution and control.

It was the job of the assembly of the *centuriae* to sift the candidates for the various appointments which were on the plurality system, or held by more than one person. The first step was quaestor, an assistant to the higher magistrates in charge of finance and justice. He assisted in the control of state expenditure and collaborated in the investigation of crimes. He could not stay in office for more than a year, but if he had performed his duties well, he could present himself to the assembly for promotion.

If he had not satisfied the electors, he was rejected, and could not apply for any other appointment for ten years. But if they approved of him, he was made an aedile (there were four of them) and in this capacity, for one year only, he superintended buildings, theaters, aqueducts, and streets, and in fact all public buildings and buildings of public interest, including brothels.

If he produced satisfactory results in these duties, which were practically those of a city councilman, he could run for election to any of the four posts of praetor, a high civil and military appointment lasting for a further period of a year. Originally the praetors had been army generals but by now they had become more like high court judges and interpreters of the law. On the outbreak of war they resumed command of important units under the orders of the consuls.

When a man had reached the top in this career which was called *cursus honorum,* he could aspire to one of the two posi-

tions of censor, a five-year appointment. The length was due to
the fact that the census was only carried out every five years.
At that time everyone had to give an account of himself. The
principal duty of the censor was to ascertain, on the basis of his
investigations, the amount of tax every citizen should pay during the five-year period and also the number of years he had to
serve with the army.

These were not the only duties of the censor. He had even
more delicate tasks, tasks that made his post, especially when
held by a citizen of the caliber of Cato or Appius Claudius the
Blind, a great grandson of the famous *decemvir,* rival even that
of the consulship. For the censor had to make secret inquiries
into the past of any candidate for a public appointment. He had
to investigate the virtue of his women, the education of his
children and his treatment of slaves. This gave the censor the
right to poke his nose into anybody's private affairs, to lower
or raise a person in rank, and even to expel from the senate
those members whom he deemed unworthy. Finally it was the
censors who drew up the budget and authorized state expenditure. As is obvious, their powers were enormous and required
great shrewdness and probity on the part of those entrusted
with them. During the republican period, those nominated were,
generally speaking, up to their task.

At the summit were the two consuls, the two heads of
executive power. In theory at least, one of them had to be a
plebeian. In practice the plebs themselves almost always preferred a patrician. Only a highly educated and experienced man
could offer some guarantee of being able to guide the state
through increasingly complex and difficult problems. And then
there were the elections, which were run by a procedure which
allowed the aristocracy to commit practically any kind of sharp
practice. On election day the magistrate in office would scan the
stars to find out which candidates were *personae gratae* to the
gods. And since he claimed that he alone knew the language
of the stars, he could give out any interpretation he liked. The
awed assembly, accepting his verdict, would proceed to make
its choice only from among those competitors who were thus
approved.

Candidates appeared in a plain white toga without ornaments. This demonstrated the simplicity of their lives and the
austerity of their morals. Frequently they lifted their togas to

show the electors the wounds they had received in battle. If elected, they remained in power for one year, with equal authority. They took office on March 15, and when they relinquished it the senate generally admitted them as life members. Since in spite of everything the title of senator was the most sought after by everyone, it was only natural that the consul should do his best never to displease those who might confer it on him. In a certain sense, he represented the secular arm of that august body that did not count for anything from a strictly constitutional point of view, but in actual practice, by means of the stars and other devices, decided everything.

Like the first kings, the consuls were, above all, the heads of religious authority and directed the more important rites. In time of peace they presided over the meetings of both senate and assembly, and having listened to their deliberations, put them into effect by issuing the necessary decrees.

In time of war they became generals. They led the army, which they divided into two equal commands. If one consul were killed or taken prisoner, the other took over supreme command. If both were killed or taken prisoner, the senate declared an *interregnum* for five days, appointed an *interrex* to carry on, and then held new elections. All of which shows that the consul exercised for one year the same powers wielded by the ancient, non-absolute kings who preceded the Tarquins.

The office of consul, though naturally greatly desired, was also the most difficult. Apart from great energy, it required a good deal of diplomacy and tact to keep on good terms with both the senate and the popular assemblies who had elected the consuls and to whom they were answerable.

There were now three assemblies: the *comitiae curiatae,* the *comitiae centuriatae,* and the *comitiae tributae.*

The *comitiae curiatae* was the most ancient dating back to Romulus and the time when Rome was composed only of patricians. It had very important functions in the early days of the republic, such as the appointing of consuls. Later it gradually surrendered almost all its powers to the assembly of the *centuriae* which, in republican Rome, was the equivalent of the House of Representatives. Little by little the ancient and original assembly became a sort of College of Heralds that merely settled geneological questions, such as whether a citizen belonged to this or that *gens.*

The assembly of the *centuriae* was virtually the people under arms. All citizens who had done their military service belonged to it. Only foreigners, slaves, and those exempted from military service for reasons of poverty were excluded. Rome was grudging in granting citizenship, which carried such privileges as immunity from torture and the right of appeal to the assembly against the decisions of any public official.

The *comitiae centuriatae* was not a permanent assembly. It was summoned by a consul or a tribune and could not originate laws and decrees on its own. It could only vote yes or no, by a majority, to the proposals a magistrate laid before it. Its conservative character was guaranteed, as we know, by its division into five classes and the fact that the first class, composed of 98 patricians, cavalry officers, and millionaires, was enough to maintain a majority in a total of 193 *centuriae*. Since this class voted first and the count was announced immediately, all the rest could do was bow their heads.

There was some justice in this procedure. The Romans considered that rights should go hand in hand with duties and vice versa. Thus the richer one was, the heavier the tax one had to pay, and the longer one had to serve in the army. In return, one counted for more politically.

By the same token, the poor man counted for nothing. All he had was the advantage of paying small taxes and spending only a few months in the barracks. Politically he was powerless.

Eventually these outcasts began to organize into the so-called councils of the plebs which as time passed developed into the *comitiae tributae*, and were the weapon of the Roman proletariat in its uphill battle for greater social justice. These councils were started immediately after the withdrawal of the plebs to Monte Sacro, when they had been allowed to elect their own magistrates, those famous tribunes who had the right of veto on any law or ordinance which they considered contrary to the interests of the proletariat. These assemblies had the privilege of electing the tribunes. And gradually, they asked for and obtained the right to elect other defenders: the quaestors, the aediles of the plebs, and finally the military tribunes with consular powers.

The assembly of the plebs, like that of the *centuriae*, had no power other than to vote yes or no to the proposals of the magistrate who had summoned it. However, they voted indi-

vidually, and one man's vote was as good as another's, regardless of financial standing. The gradual growth of the power of
the Roman proletariat was marked by the increase in power of
this assembly as opposed to that of the other classes until finally,
after innumerable struggles, its decisions (called "plebiscites")
ceased to concern only the plebs, and were as binding as laws
on all citizens.

Since these two assemblies, the *centuriae* and the *tributae*,
were by their very nature bound to be antagonistic, the first
operating in the name of conservatism, and the second, in the
name of social progress, out to obstruct the maneuvers of the
former, one can well imagine how delicate the job of consul
must have been.

Nominally both consuls had the *imperium* or power of
command, which they displayed by having themselves preceded
wherever they went by twelve lictors, each of whom carried a
bunch of rods with an axe in the middle. They gave their combined names to their year of office, and this was registered on
the list in the consular archives. These status symbols, of course,
appealed to the ambitious. But the actual wielding of power was
a tricky business.

First, to be able to wield it at all, the two consuls had to be
in full agreement, since each had the right to veto the other's
decisions. What's more, they had to get the consent of the two
assemblies.

This near-paralysis in the executive power was precisely
what enabled the senate to come into its own. It was composed
of three hundred members, and the censors filled vacancies
caused by death by appointing an ex-consul or an ex-censor who
had particularly distinguished himself to take the dead man's
place. Also, the censors, or the senate itself, could expel members
who proved unworthy of the high honor.

The venerable body met in the Senate House opposite the
Forum and was convoked by the presiding consul. Its decisions
by majority vote, had no legal force theoretically, being merely
advice to the magistrate. But in practice the magistrate would
never have dared to lay a proposal before the assemblies without it having been previously approved by the senate. So in
effect the senate made the real decisions in all great matters of
state: war or peace, the government of the colonies and provinces. When a genuine crisis arose, the senate had recourse to a

special emergency decree, the *senatusconsultum ultimum*, which decided matters irrevocably.

Its true power lay more in its prestige than in its constitutional rights. A tribune, voted in by the plebs, could hardly be expected to be in sympathy with the senate, but when he sat there as a silent observer, as was his right, he usually came out with more conciliatory ideas than when he went in. The proof of this is that, as time passed, many tribunes became senators, thanks to the friendly attitude they had assumed during their periods of office toward what should have been the enemy's camp. Finally, the senate had a super-weapon in reserve for great occasions. When they could not get the magistrates to agree among themselves and with the people, they could nominate for six months or a year a dictator with, except for the disposition of state funds, otherwise plenary powers. The proposal was made by one of the consuls and could not be vetoed by the other. The nominee was chosen from among the ex-consuls who, by virtue of having held that office, were already senators. All the dictators of republican Rome save one were patricians. All save two respected the time limit laid down for them. And one of these, Cincinnatus, went back of his own free will to his plowing after holding supreme command for only sixteen days, and so passed into history with all the glowing colors of legend.

The senate did not exercise this prerogative very often, for though it did not always live up to its great name, it did not abuse it. Occasionally it would succumb to greed, especially in the exploitation of conquered territories; and occasionally, as it defended the privileges of its own caste, it would be deaf to the need for greater justice. Its members were not supermen—they made mistakes sometimes, or wavered, or contradicted themselves. But on the whole, in the history of all times and of all peoples, their assembly stands as a supreme example of political wisdom. They all came from families of statesmen, and each one of them had had long experience in the army, the law courts, and in administrative posts. They were at their worst in victory, when their pride and greed were unbridled, and at their best in defeat, when the situation called for courage and tenacity. Cineas, the ambassador sent by Pyrrhus to negotiate with the senators, said in admiration to his sovereign: "No wonder there is no king of Rome. Each of those three hundred senators is a king."

X

The Gods

THIS ORGANIZATION OF STATE AND MAGISTRATURE WAS MADE
possible only by the law, that is by the publication of the
"Twelve Tables of the Decemvirs," which were simultaneously
its cause, consequence, and instrument.

Up to that time Rome had lived under what was practically
a theocracy, in which the king was also the pope. As such, only
he had the right to settle disputes between man and man. He did
not do this according to a written legal code, but by consulting
the wishes of the gods, who kept him duly informed during religious ceremonies. At first the pope-king did everything himself.
But as the population increased and problems became more numerous and complicated, he had the clergy to give him a hand.
In fact the first Roman lawyers were priests.

A poor man who had or thought he had been wronged,
would hurry off to one of these priests to get an opinion. The
priest would give him one, after consulting secret texts to which
only he and his colleagues had access. For this reason no man
knew what his rights and obligations were. And only the priest
could tell him. Cases were heard according to a liturgy known
only to the priests. Since the clergy were all of aristocratic origin
or henchmen of the patricians, one can well imagine the verdicts
in cases of litigation between plebs and upper class citizens.

The first effect of the Twelve Tables was the separation of
civil from divine law, liberating disputing citizens from the
capricious will of the gods, or rather of those who claimed to
represent them. From this moment, Rome ceased to be a theocracy, and the ecclesiastical monopoly of the law gradually
crumbled. Appius Claudius the Blind published a calendar of
the *dies fasti,* indicating the days on which lawsuits could be
heard and the procedure to be adopted, facts which had hitherto been kept mysterious and known only to the priests. Later,
Coruncanius founded a regular law school whose graduates
became leading lights at the bar. The Twelve Tables, which
laid down the basic principles of all the legislation subsequently

adopted by Rome and the world, were made a compulsory subject for schoolboys. They had to learn them by heart. Thus these
codes also contributed to the formation of the Roman character
—orderly, severe, legalistic, and litigious.

From now on the priests, compelled to deal only with religious matters, tried without much success to put their own
house in order. They organized themselves into colleges, each
of which had a father superior elected by the assembly of the
centuriae. No particular training was needed to become one.
The priests did not form a caste apart and had no political
power. They were employees of the state, no more, and as it
paid their salaries, they tended to cooperate with it.

The most important of these colleges was that of the nine
augurs. Its job was to investigate the reactions of the gods to
the grave decisions about to be taken by the government.
Arrayed in sacerdotal finery and preceded by fifteen *flamines*,
the high priest in earlier times used to study the auspices by
observing the flight of birds, just as Romulus did when founding
Rome. Later the high priest did it by examining the entrails of
sacrificed animals. (Both these methods were learned from the
Etruscans.)

In the event of more serious crimes, a delegation was sent
to Cumae to interrogate the Sybil, high priestess of Apollo. As a
last resort they sent to consult the Delphic oracle, whose fame
had spread as far as Italy. Since the priests had no responsibilities except to the state, it was only natural that they should be
particularly receptive to suggestions made by the state, especially when these were accompanied by promotion or a raise in
salary.

The ritual consisted of a gift or sacrifice to the gods in order
to obtain their protection or placate their wrath. The procedure
was meticulous, and the slightest mistake was enough to force
them to repeat it as many as thirty times. In Latin, the word religion has a completely external and procedural connotation.
Sacrifice means, literally, to make something sacred. The offering
to the divinity which was thus made sacred naturally varied according to the income of the offerer and the importance of the
benefits to be gained. The poor father of a family, who acted as
spiritual director in his own home, sacrificed a piece of bread
and cheese or a glass of wine to obtain a good harvest. If the
drought continued, he might go as far as a rooster; if he were in

danger of being flooded out, he might even cut the throat of his pig or one of his sheep. But when it was the state offering a sacrifice to enlist divine favor for some great national undertaking, the Forum, where the ceremony usually took place, was turned into a shambles. Entire flocks were slaughtered while the priests intoned the formulas proper to the occasion. The entrails and particularly the livers were reserved for the gods, who had delicate palates. All the rest was eaten by the people, sitting around in a large circle. These ceremonies developed into gigantic banquets interspersed with prayers. A law of 97 B.C. forbade the sacrifice of human victims, which goes to show what had been the fate of a certain number of unfortunate slaves and prisoners of war. There were citizens who voluntarily offered their own lives to save the nation, such as Marcus Curtius who, in order to placate the gods of the lower regions during an earthquake, plunged into a chasm which immediately closed over him.

The so-called ceremonies of purification—of a farm, for instance, or a flock, or an army off to war, or even a whole city —were much more genteel. The priests would walk around the place or the group to be purified in a procession, singing *carmina* or hymns full of magic spells. This was quite similar to the ritual for *vota*, offerings to obtain some favor from the gods.

What gods?

The Roman state, which acted as religious impressario or producer, never succeeded in settling this matter satisfactorily. Perhaps it never wanted to. Jove was considered the most important of the tenants of Olympus but he was not their king, as Zeus was in Greece. Jove always remained a somewhat vague figure, a sort of impersonal force connected with the sky, with the sun, or the moon, or thunder and lightning, according to one's taste. Perhaps in early times he was the same person as Janus and only later became differentiated. During droughts, the rich Roman matrons used to go barefoot in processions to the temple, on the Capitol, of Jupiter the Thunderer to beg for rain. In time of war the doors of the temple of Janus were opened to allow him to reach the army and lead it in battle.

Equal in rank to those two were Mars, who had the month of March named after him and who, since he was the natural father of Romulus, had family connections with Rome, and Saturn, god of sowing who was, legend says, a prehistoric king and a professor of agriculture with communist tendencies.

After these came the goddesses. Juno was the goddess of fertility, of fields and trees, of animals and men, and her name was given to the month of June, considered to be the most propitious for weddings. Minerva, imported from Greece on the shoulders of Aeneas, protected wisdom and knowledge. Diana, goddess of the moon, superintended hunting and the woods, and in one of them, near Nemi, stood her majestic temple where she is said to have married Virbius, the first king of the forest.

Then followed a whole band of minor gods. Bacchus, god of wine and merriment, was quite prepared to dice for a harlot with the churchwarden of his temple. Mercury was supposed to have a weakness for merchants, orators, and thieves, evidently considered by the Romans as birds of a feather. Bellona specialized in wars . . . but it's impossible to name them all.

As the city grew and its dominion spread, the gods multiplied out of all proportion. Whenever the Romans conquered a state or a province, their first act was to steal the local gods and take them home, since they were convinced that the vanquished would not attempt revenge without their gods' help. And then, apart from these deities who were, in spite of privileged treatment, essentially prisoners of war, there were the *novensiles*, the gods that foreigners brought with them when they moved to Rome, so as to feel less like exiles and more at home. They set them up in temples paid for out of their own pockets. The Roman authorities never contested anybody's right to do this, in fact they went out of their way to be hospitable to one and all. Perhaps the state and its priests considered these imported gods, in a certain sense, as unsalaried policemen who would keep their followers in order. They even gave many of them a place in the official Olympus. In 496 B.C., Demeter and Dionysus, in a business merger, were taken in as partners and colleagues to Ceres and Liberus. A few years later Castor and Pollux, who had only recently been consecrated, showed their gratitude by coming down from Heaven to give the Romans a hand at the battle of Lake Regillus. And around 300 B.C., Aesculapius was arbitrarily transferred from Epidaurus to teach medicine in Rome. Gradually all these newcomers became permanent residents, especially the Greek gods who were more affable and cordial, less cold, punctilious, and remote than the Roman

deities. It was owing to Greek influence that a hierarchy gradually came into being, with Jove, carrying the same attributes
that Zeus had had at Athens, at the head. This was the first step
toward monotheistic religion which, starting with Stoicism and
Judaism, triumphed finally with Christianity.

This development came much later, however. The Romans
of the republic cohabited with a veritable mob of gods who,
Petronius said, were more numerous in some cities than the inhabitants. Varro estimated them at about 30,000. Their personal
activities and eternal meddling made life difficult for their wor-
shipers, who were never quite sure what line to take towards
their various discords and rivalries. Everywhere one turned, one
bumped into some object sacred to some god or other. When offended, they appeared in the guise of witches who flew by night,
ate serpents, killed babies, and stole corpses. They are referred
to continually in Horace, Tibullus, Virgil, and Lucan. They were
all the more dangerous because the Roman religion, unlike most
others, did not confine its deities to heaven. Although they lived
there too, they preferred to stay on earth most of the time, a prey
to the earthly urges of hunger, lechery, cupidity, ambition, envy,
and greed.

To save poor mortals from the immortals' malevolence, religious orders multiplied. Among them was a feminine one, the
vestals. Girls were recruited between the ages of six and ten and
did thirty years' service in complete chastity. They were the forerunners of our nuns. Clothed and veiled in white, their principal
duty was to water the earth with water drawn from a spring
sacred to the nymph Egeria. If caught breaking their vow of
chastity, they were bastinadoed and buried alive. Roman historians mention twelve cases of this treatment. At the end of thirty
years' service, they were received back into society with many
honors and privileges. They could even marry, though at that
age it was not too easy to find a husband.

The Romans did not have Sundays and weekends, but their
religion provided them feast days and days of rest. During the
year there were some one hundred, just about the same number
that there are today in Italy, though then they celebrated them
more seriously. Even the feasts of the Romans were austere and
commemorative, like the *lemuria* in May (the equivalent of All
Souls') which every head of a family celebrated at home by
filling his mouth with white beans and spitting them out all

around him, crying: "With these beans I redeem myself and my family. Depart, O souls of our ancestors!" In February there were the *parentalia* or *feralia*, and the *lupercalia*, when they used to throw wooden dolls into the Tiber to deceive the god, who demanded real men. Then there were the *floralia*, the *liberalia*, the *ambarvalia*, the *saturnalia*. . . .

Such anarchy reigned in this department that the main reason why the Romans drew up a calendar was to make a list of these festivals. In very early times the priests dealt with this matter, announcing month by month when they should be celebrated. Tradition gives Numa Pompilius the credit for settling the question by creating a fixed calender which remained in force until the time of Caesar. It divided the year into twelve lunar months, giving the priests the privilege of lengthening or shortening them provided that by the end of the twelfth a total of 366 days had elapsed. The priests so abused this prerogative, in order to favor or damage the interests of this or that magistrate, that by the end of the republic the Pompilian calendar had become quite useless, and was merely a source of controversy.

The daytime hours were measured by eye, according to the position of the sun in the sky. The first sundial, of Greek manufacture, was brought to Rome from Catania in 263 B.C. and set up in the Forum. Since Catania is four degrees south of Rome, the hour did not correspond, the Romans got angry, and there was confusion for a whole century because nobody knew how to put the contraption right. The days of the month were divided into the calends (the first), the nones (the fifth or seventh), and the ides (the thirteenth or fifteenth). The year which was called *annus* or circle began with March. Then came April, May, June, Quintile, Sextile, September, October, November, December, January, and February. A substitute for Sunday was the *nundina* which fell every nine days and corresponds to market day in modern country towns of Italy. The peasants left their fields to sell their eggs and fruit in town, but it was not a real holiday.

To have a really good time, the Romans had to wait for the *liberalia* and the *saturnalia*, when as one of the characters in Plautus says, "everybody could eat what he wanted, go where he liked, and make love to whomever he wanted, provided he left wives, widows, little boys, and little girls in peace."

XI

The City

IT IS NOT KNOWN EXACTLY HOW MANY INHABITANTS ROME HAD just before the Punic Wars. The figures given by historians on the basis of unreliable censuses are contradictory. Perhaps they do not take into account the fact that most of the people covered by the census did not live within the so-called *pomerium* or city wall, but in scattered country villages outside it. In the city itself there could not have been more than 100,000 souls, a modest population these days, but for those times it was enormous. Its ethnical composition must have made it already an international center, though not to the extent that it had been under the Tarquin kings. They, because of their Etruscan love of trading and the sea, had attracted too many foreigners, many of whom had been hard to assimilate. With the republic, the native Latin and Sabine elements grew stronger and took their revenge. Perhaps the city regulated immigration more strictly. This now came in from the neighboring provinces and was made up of more malleable types.

The city had not made much progress from the town planning point of view under the republican magistrates, who were miserly, rustic, and without ambition. Two main roads intersected inside the city, dividing it into four quarters. Each quarter had its own tutelary gods, the *lares compitales*, to whom statues were erected at every street corner. The streets were narrow, of beaten earth, and only later paved with stones taken from the river bed. The *cloaca maxima*, or sewer system, appears to have existed since the time of the Tarquins, and since it conveyed all the sewage of Rome into the Tiber, it infected the drinking water. In 312 B.C. Appius Claudius the Blind tackled and solved the problem by building the first aqueduct to provide Rome with clean fresh water drawn directly from wells. Thus for the first time the Romans, at least those with a certain standing, had enough water to wash themselves. The first *thermae*, or public baths, were built only after the defeat of Hannibal.

Houses had remained more or less as the Etruscan architects had built them. But their fronts had been smartened up with stucco and decorated with graffiti.

The dangers to which they had been continually exposed had induced the Roman builders to concentrate on temples, in the hope of earning the goodwill of the gods. On the Capitol three imposing temples, to Jove, Juno, and Minerva, had been built of wood faced with stone.

The city still lived by agriculture based on small private properties. A good proportion of the population, even in the middle of the town, after sleeping huddled together on straw, would get up at dawn, and loading spades and mattocks on the ox-drawn carts, go off to plow their own fields, which averaged about five acres per family. They were tenacious but not very enlightened peasants, who knew of no manure except the dung of their own animals and of no rotation of crops other than from grain to vegetables and back again. Many aristocratic families took their names from their own products. The Lentuli specialized in lentils, the Caeparii in onions, the Fabii in beans. Other products were figs, grapes, and oil. Every family had its chickens, its pigs, and very important, its sheep, which gave them wool for clothes.

On the eve of the Punic War, this idyllic picture of rustic life had undergone a complete change. The expeditions against neighboring peoples had depopulated the countryside. Abandoned homesteads had fallen into ruin. Undergrowth and weeds had spread over the fields of ex-soldiers, who returned to the city to earn a living. The new territories acquired from the beaten enemy were declared "public land" by the state, and sold to profiteers, grown fat on war contracts. In this way, large estates were created. The owners exploited these with slave labor (which was plentiful and cost next to nothing), while in the city a proletariat was formed of landless ex-peasants in search of employment.

But it was hard to find a job because industry had not progressed, but had actually receded since the Tarquin regimes. The subsoil, poor in minerals, was the property of the state and had been leased to unscrupulous and incompetent exploiters. Metallurgy had made little progress. Bronze continued to be more widely used than steel. Wood was the only fuel known, and the fine forests of Latium were hewn down to provide it. Only the weaving industry was relatively prosperous, and real factories had begun mass production.

There were four obstacles to industrial and commercial development. The first, of a psychological nature, was the mistrust of the Roman ruling classes (all of them landowners) of any activity that might strengthen the bourgeois middle class. The second was the lack of roads for the transport of raw materials and finished products. One of the two existing roads, the *via Latina*, which was built in 370 B.C., almost 150 years after the declaration of the republic, merely linked the city with the Alban Hills. Only Appius Claudius, who built the aqueduct some fifty years later, felt the need to construct one. In fact it bore his name and reached Capua. The senators reluctantly approved his grandiose project only because the generals also insisted on a road network. The third handicap to industry was the lack of a fleet, a deficiency that had existed ever since the Etruscan supremacy in Rome had ended. Small private shipowners had continued to build a few ships, but crews were timid and inexperienced. From November to March it was impossible to get them to leave the port of Ostia, where their boats remained stuck fast in Tiber mud, which once swallowed up two hundred of them in a single mouthful. They never ventured on anything more than minor coastal traffic because what with all the Greek and Carthaginian pirates who infested the waters to the east and the west, they were afraid to venture far from the coast. This makes all the more admirable the miracle which Rome accomplished only a few years later when her improvised fleets faced up to those of Hanno and Hannibal.

A fourth impediment to trade in early times was the lack of a monetary system. During the first century of the republic, the means of exchange was livestock. Chickens, pigs, sheep, donkeys, and cows were articles of barter. In fact the first coins bear the images of these animals and were called *pecunia* from *pecus*, meaning livestock. The first monetary unit coined was the *as*, a piece of copper weighing one pound. It had not been introduced for long when the state devalued it by five-sixths to to meet the expenses of the first Punic War. Which only proves that the inflation swindle has always existed and the technique has not changed over the centuries. On this occasion, the state floated a loan among its citizens who brought in all their *asses* to enable the state to fit out an army. Whereupon the state divided each one of them into six, and for every one received paid back one-sixth to the creditor.

For a long time this devalued *as* remained the only Roman currency. Its purchasing power was, it seems the equivalent of about eight cents. Then a more complicated system developed. The silver *sestertius* came in, which was worth two-and-a-half *asses*. Then came the *denarius*, equal to four *sestertii* and finally the gold talent, which must have been quite an ingot, since it was worth something like $4,000 and was probably never seen at all by ninety percent of the Romans.

Unlike ourselves, who regard our banks as churches, the ancient Romans treated their churches like banks, and deposited state funds in them because they thought they would be safer there from thieves. There were no government institutes of credit. Loans were made by the *argentarii*, whose little counting houses lay in an alley off the Forum. One of the laws of the Twelve Tables forbade extortion and fixed a maximum rate of interest at eight percent. All the same, usury flourished on the poor man's misery and needs. This was because what I have called industry was actually a seething mass of little artisan workshops in competition with one another, trying to lower the cost of their products by skimping on wages. Low-cost labor had no trade unions to protect it. Slaves did not go on strike against their masters because they were disorganized and lacked leaders. Every now and then they would work up really proper wars which were called *servili*, or slave wars, and would actually endanger the state.

On the other hand, they did have craft guilds known as "colleges," which appear to date back to the days of Numa. There were the guilds of the potters, the blacksmiths, the shoemakers, the carpenters, the flute-players, the tanners, the cooks, the bricklayers, the leather workers, the bronze workers, the weavers, and the actors, who called themselves "the artists of Dionysus." From this we can deduce the number of trades exercised by Roman townspeople. They were controlled by state officials, who did not allow questions of salary and wages to be discussed. When the officials felt that discontent was running dangerously high, they would authorize a free distribution of wheat. Members used to meet to talk shop, play dice, take a drop of wine, and help each other out, because they were all poor men

—even those who were free and had political rights. It is true that in peacetime they did little military service and paid no taxes, but in time of war they died like anybody else.

The Roman writers who flourished much later, those whose works have come down to us, have painted glowing pictures of stoic Rome. They did this for polemical reasons, to contrast the vices of their own epoch with the ancient virtues. But the republic was far from perfect, and even though the law was formed under its auspices, one can hardly say that justice triumphed.

It is true, however, that its citizens lived a more uncomfortable and ascetic life than those of the empire, and things were more orderly, and sounder. Morality even then was none too strict, but debauchery was kept in its place and did not contaminate family life, which was based on the chastity of the girls and the fidelity of the wife. After sowing their wild oats with the prostitutes, men married early, at about twenty. From then on, they were kept too busy trying to support wives and children to go on a serious binge.

Marriage was preceded by an engagement and was usually arranged by the two fathers, often without even consulting the interested parties. It was a definite contract, dealing mainly with hereditary and dowry matters. It was sealed by the young man putting a ring on the fourth finger of the girl's left hand through which, it was thought, a nerve passed that went straight to the heart.

Marriages were of two kinds: *cum manu* or *sine manu.* With the first, the commonest and most complete, the father gave up all his rights over his daughter to the son-in-law, who practically became her owner. With the second, which dispensed with a religious ceremony, he kept those rights. The *cum manu* kind came into force by *usus,* that is, after the couple had lived together for a year, by *coemptio,* (that is, by mock purchase), or by *confarreatio,* (when they had eaten bread together). The latter was reserved for patricians and required a solemn religious ceremony with hymns and processions. The two families met their friends, servants, and clients at the bride's home, and thence formed a procession to the house of the bridegroom, to the accompaniment of flutes, love songs, and coarse comments. When the procession reached its destination, the bridegroom asked "Who are you?" from behind the door, and the bride answered, "If you are so-and-so, I am so-and-so."

Thereupon the bridegroom lifted her up, gave her the front door key, and the two of them, with bowed heads, passed under a yoke to show that they submitted to a common bond.

In theory, divorce existed. The first one we hear about took place two-and-a-half centuries after the foundation of the republic, in spite of the fact that honor made it obligatory to divorce when a wife had committed adultery. (The husband was entitled to take such measures as he saw fit.) In those days women were rather plain and awkward, with short legs and heavy ankles and wrists. Blondes, who were extremely rare, were more highly prized than brunettes. At home, the women wore the *stola,* a sort of Abyssinian nightshirt of white wool which reached to their feet and was closed at the breast by a pin. When they went out, they wore over it the *palla* or cloak.

The men were more robust than handsome, with deeply tanned faces and straight noses. As boys they wore the *toga praetexta,* bordered with purple. When they had done their military service, they changed it for the *toga virile,* which was completely white and covered the whole body. It had a wide gathering which passed over the left shoulder, then under the right arm (which was thus left free) and returned to the left shoulder. The folds served as pockets. Until 300 B.C., the men wore beards and mustaches; later they adopted the habit of shaving, which to many appeared too daring and lacking in that gravity the Romans made such a fetish of, as today Italians make a point of nonchalance.

Spartan sobriety was the rule, even in the houses of the great. The senate itself sat on rough wooden benches in the Senate House, which in winter remained unheated. The Carthaginian ambassadors, who came to sue for peace after the first Punic War, greatly amused their spendthrift and sybaritic compatriots by telling them how, at the dinners offered them by the Roman senators, they always saw the same silver dish passed around. Evidently they lent it to one another.

We see the first evidence of luxury at the time of the second Punic War, since, when it broke out, a law was immediately passed prohibiting jewels, fancy clothing, and costly meals. The government wished above all to preserve a healthy frugal diet, based on breakfast of bread, honey, olives, and cheese, a lunch of vegetables, bread, and fruit, and an evening meal at which only the rich had meat or fish. Wine was drunk, but it was almost always watered.

The young respected the old. Possibly, in family circles and among friends, expressions of affection or tenderness may have been used. But generally speaking, relations between men were brusque. It was easy to die, and not only in war. The treatment of slaves was merciless. The state, tough enough with its own citizens, was downright savage with its enemies, though it did make some gestures of authentic moral grandeur. When, for instance, a hired assassin came with an offer to poison Pyrrhus, whose armies were threatening Rome, the senators not only refused to have anything to do with the deal, but warned the enemy king of the plot against him. Again, when Hannibal, having routed the Roman army at Cannae, sent ten prisoners of war to Rome to negotiate the ransom of another eight thousand, with the ten under oath to return to Hannibal if things fell through, and one of them broke his parole by staying at home, the senate put him in irons and returned him handcuffed to the Carthaginian general. Polybius says that this Roman gesture rather clouded Hannibal's victory, for it showed him the type of men he was up against.

By and large the Roman of this period was not unlike the figure idealized by historians like Tacitus and Plutarch. He had many shortcomings: no sense of individual liberty, no taste for art or science, no conversational gifts, complete indifference to philosophic speculation (which he mistrusted) and, above all, no sense of humor. On the other hand he was endowed with loyalty, frugality, tenacity, obedience, and practical sense. He was not cut out for understanding and enjoyment, but for conquering and governing the world.

Apart from religious festivals, he had few pastimes. Until 221 B.C. when the Flaminius was built, Rome had only one circus, the Maximus, attributed to Tarquin Priscus, where he could go to watch duels between slaves. These normally ended up with the death of the loser. At first the state put up the money. Later it was provided, with an eye to useful electoral propaganda, by the aediles. Some of them actually rose to the rank of consul by putting on good shows.

In addition to these, shall we say, "normal" amusements, there were also "triumphs" to enliven the austere and dreary lives of the Romans. These were accorded to a general returning from a victory in which at least 5,000 enemy soldiers had been slain. If the total had been only 4,999 he rated instead an "ovation," so called because it consisted of the sacrifice of an *ovis*, a sheep, in his honor.

For the triumph, an imposing procession formed outside the city gates, where the general and his troops had to lay down their arms and pass under a triumphal arch of wood and branches. This was the early model of arches later built of marble. A column of trumpeters headed the procession; after them came wagons laden with the spoils of war; then entire flocks and herds destined for slaughter; then the enemy chiefs in chains. Finally, preceded by lictors and flute players, came the victorious general himself, standing in a gaily-painted four-in-hand chariot, with a purple toga on his shoulders, a gold crown on his head, and holding aloft an ivory scepter and a laurel branch. He was surrounded by his children and followed by his relations, secretaries, advisers, and friends, all on horseback. He drove up to the temples of Jove, Juno, and Minerva on the Capitol, laid the booty down at their feet, had the doomed animals rounded up for slaughter and, as an additional offering, gave orders for the decapitation of the enemy commanders. The people shouted for joy. The climax came when the victorious soldiery were allowed to fling taunts, sarcasm, and jibes at their own general. To preserve him from a swelled head and delusions of infallibility, they heckled him, exposing his special faults and foibles. "Hey! Baldie!" they would shout at Caesar himself, "Lay off the married women, and stick to the prostitutes!"

XII

Carthage

CARTHAGE, LIKE ALL OTHER CITIES OF THE TIME, ATTRIBUTED ITS origin to a miracle of which it gave a romantic account. Dido, daughter of the king of Tyre, was said to have been its founder and was later venerated by her fellow citizens as a goddess. Made a widow, thanks to her brother who had killed her husband, she put herself at the head of a group of followers, took

ship and set sail from the extreme eastern end of the Mediterranean toward the west in search of adventure. Coasting along
North Africa past Egypt, Cyrenaica and Libya, she finally
reached a point about ten miles west of where Tunis now
stands. Here she landed and said to her companions: "Well, this
is where we build the New City." And that was what they called
it: New City, like Naples and New York. In their language it
was *Kart Hadasht,* which the Greeks later translated as *Karche-
don* and the Romans as *Carthago.*

Naturally things did not really go like this, but it is difficult
to get to the bottom of the matter because the Romans did to
Carthage, which unluckily stood on their path, exactly what they
had done to Etruria. They reduced it to such pulp that today it is
nearly impossible to find material for any exact reconstruction of
its history and civilization.

Certainly it was founded by the Phoenicians, a people of
Semitic race and language like the Hebrews. Great traders and
navigators, they sailed back and forth buying and selling a little
of everything. Fearing neither man nor the devil, they were the
first sailors in the world to go beyond the Pillars of Hercules, the
Straights of Gibraltar, and to sail down the Atlantic coast of
Africa and up the Spanish and Portuguese coasts. By the time
Rome had come into being, the Phoenicians had already founded
quite a number of towns along these routes. At first these must
have consisted simply of a shipyard, and a bazaar or market.
Leptis Magna, Utica, Bizerte, and Bône certainly originated in
this manner, and Carthage was one, perhaps even the most humble, of these sister cities, until circumstances made her the most
prominent.

These circumstances were mainly the military and commercial decline of Tyre and Sidon. These cities were unfortunate
enough to stand in the way of Alexander of Macedonia, who,
when Rome was still a village, threatened to become emperor of
the world and nearly succeeded. Menaced by his armies, the
plutocrats of these two cities, who, like all plutocrats, had more
cause to be frightened than other people, took steps to put themselves and their nest eggs in safety. In those days it was the fashion to take refuge in Carthage (nowadays the place to go to is
Tangier).

These new inhabitants, full of ready cash and initiative,
made the city grow, and drove the native population of poor

Negroes farther and farther back into the interior, keeping many
of them as servants and slaves. No longer content with trading
and the sea, they turned to the land. This is interesting, for it had
been thought up to that time that Jews were constitutionally un-
fitted for farming. The Semites of Carthage proved the opinion
wrong. They were expert in many types of cultivation, especially
of vines, olives, and fruits, and even the Romans had much to
learn from them. The greatest master of agriculture of ancient
times, Mago, was a Carthaginian.

Carthage had a perfectly balanced economy. Its excellent
and flourishing hardware industry turned out the best implements for cultivating, irrigating, and transforming the land into
market gardens and orchards. Most of the produce was loaded
into their ships, which were the biggest in the world, and sent off
to Spain or Greece. Shipowners financed explorers to discover
new markets. One of these, Hanno, sailed down the Atlantic
coast of Africa for over 1,200 miles in a solitary galley.

Other commercial travelers struck out overland on mules,
camels, and elephants, found gold and ivory, and brought their
treasures home. They used to cross the Sahara with the same
nonchalance with which Florentines now cross the Arno. On the
basis of their reports the government would send out a few ships
or a handful of soldiers to hold the strategic points, just as Venice
did later on.

For those days their economic and financial system was the
most advanced. Rome had hardly begun to coin crude metal
money when the Carthaginians already had banknotes, that is,
strips of leather differently stamped according to their value.
These circulated throughout the whole Mediterranean basin as
freely as the pound and the dollar did later. Their nominal value
was guaranteed by the gold which overflowed the state's coffers.
Whenever Carthage made a new conquest, the first thing she did
was to impose a tribute, and no light one, on the losers. Leptis,
for example, paid 365 talents, about $168 million, a year for the
privilege of being a vassal of Carthage.

The exploitation of her colonial empire was probably one of
the reasons for the defeat of Carthage when she came into conflict with Rome, though until this threat materialized, the Phoenician city enjoyed a prosperity unheard of up to that time.
Carthage had 200-300,000 inhabitants, none of whom lived in
huts like the Romans. Poor Carthaginians lived in tall buildings

with as many as twelve stories, rich ones in palaces with gardens and swimming pools. There were temples and public baths galore. As in London, the center of the metropolis contained the law courts and the treasury, surrounded by a triple bastion of walls and towers, a kind of Maginot line, which could hold up to 20,000 fully-equipped soldiers, 4,000 horses, and 300 elephants.

As for the people and their customs, we can only rely on the testimony of Roman historians. They, naturally cannot be expected to have been impartial. The language of Carthage must have been very similar to Hebrew, in fact, their magistrates were called *shofetes*, which certainly comes from the Hebrew *shofetim*. Their features betray a Semitic origin. They had olive complexions and generally wore long beards without mustaches and even in those days they used the turban. The poorer ones, who probably had interbred with the native population and consequently had darker skins, wore what in Egypt today is called "galábia," a long, loose gown falling to their sandaled feet. The upper classes dressed in the Greek style, clad in elegant costumes bordered with purple, and wore rings in their noses. The condition of women was inferior to that of the Athenians, but better than that of the Romans. They were usually veiled and kept indoors, but an ecclesiastical career was open to them and they could reach high rank. Otherwise they could always take up prostitution which, as in Japan today, was a flourishing and esteemed profession, or at least not despised.

Polybius and Plutarch agree in asserting that Carthaginian moral standards were low, which is most astonishing when one considers that they were Semites, people whose customs are usually puritanically strict. Both historians depict them as gluttons and drunkards, incorrigible profligates who were always ready for a brawl in the nightclubs and taverns. The *fides punica* or Carthaginian word of honor became a byword in Latin for treachery, but let's not forget that the history of Carthaginian treachery was written by Roman historians. Plutarch describes these ancient and implacable enemies of Rome as "servile toward inferiors and alternating between cowardice in defeat and cruelty in victory." Polybius adds that they looked at everything with an eye to the main chance. But it is well known that Polybius was an intimate friend of Scipio, the man who burned Carthage to the ground.

Naturally the Carthaginians had their gods too. They had

brought them along from their motherland, Phoenicia, but with changed names. Instead of Baal-Moloch and Astarte, as they were called at Tyre and Sidon, they called them Baal-Haman and Tanit. Under them were Melkart, which means "key to the city," Eshmun, the lord of riches and good health, and lastly, Dido, who held the same position in Carthage as Quirinus did in Rome.

Sacrifices were offered to all these gods, especially in time of need. For the minor gods it was merely a question of cows or goats, but when it was a matter of placating or ingratiating themselves with Baal-Haman, they used babies, putting them in the arms of his great bronze statue and letting them fall into the fire blazing below. They were known to burn as many as three hundred a day while the blast of trumpets and the thunder of drums drowned out their screams. Their poor mothers were expected to look on without a tear or a lament. It appears that it was the custom among the rich families, when they were asked to supply a baby, to buy one from the poor. But when Agathocles of Syracuse laid siege to the city, he made friendly relations between the classes as necessary as the help of the gods and this custom was forbidden.

On the whole the political system was not very different from that of Rome. Aristotle praised it highly, perhaps largely from hearsay and perhaps because there was no serious danger of dictatorship, a thing which he abhorred. As in Rome, the supreme legislative body was the senate, also composed of three hundred members. At first the majority of them came from the landed aristocracy. Gradually these were replaced by the wealthy and it became a plutocracy. The senate took the important decisions and transmitted them to the *shofetes,* who were roughly the counterparts of the Roman consuls. Only when they could not reach a decision did they ask the opinion of a sort of chamber of deputies, who had the right to vote yes or no, but not to make proposals of their own.

In theory also this senate was elective. In practice, however, as all the key posts were in the senators' hands, they could, either by corruption or fraud, successfully impose their own candidates. Above them there was only a sort of constitutional court composed of 104 judges, who kept a general eye not only on the constitutionality of the laws but also on the administrative expenditures. During the wars with Rome this court gradually became the real government.

Carthage did not attach much importance to her army because her African neighbors did not give her any trouble. The Carthaginians had no taste for barracks, and what barracks there were were full of mercenaries recruited from among the natives, mainly Libyans. Therefore the great achievements of Carthage during the century-long struggle with Rome should be attributed exclusively to the genius of her professional military men such as Hannibal, Hamilcar, and Hasdrubal, among the most brilliant generals of antiquity.

At sea, however, she was powerful, the strongest naval power of the time. In peacetime, her home fleet numbered 500 quinquiremes, which were more or less the equivalent of battleships, but light, speedy, and gaily painted in red, green, and yellow. Their admirals were highly competent seamen who, even without a compass, knew the Mediterranean like the ponds at the bottom of their gardens. They had repair shops, supply depots, and informers in all the inlets of the French and Spanish coasts, and their cartographic institute was up-to-date and modern. At the time Rome was busily establishing her hegemony over the peninsula and had not yet launched a fleet, the Carthaginians allowed no intrusion by sea between Gilbraltar and Sardinia. If any foreign vessel fell into their hands, they either commandeered or sank it, and drowned the crew without even asking where they came from or what flag they flew.

This, roughly, was Carthage at the time the Romans, having eliminated one after another of their rivals, had united the peninsula under their leadership and were now beginning to think of naval matters.

It should be noted that all the foregoing account has been reconstructed from very fragile materials. When Scipio put the city to fire and sword and razed it to the ground, he found among other things several libraries, but instead of bringing them to Rome he divided them among his African allies, who had little or no time for books and allowed them to molder into ruin. This is surprising in Scipio, who was a man of culture. That is why we do not possess a single one of its histories and have to make do with what Sallust and Juba succeeded in reconstructing. Some fragments of Mago and the testimony of St. Augustine confirm that Carthage had a culture of a high order.

The Greeks, despite the fact that they had the example of
Athens before them, declared that Carthage was one of the most
beautiful capitals in the world. But what remains of it is too scant
to confirm this. Its most important relics are those which archaeologists have excavated in the Balearic Islands. Here the Carthaginians founded a colony to which some of them perhaps escaped
at the moment of the massacre, taking with them some works of
art. All the rest is in the Tunis museum, where archaeologists
continue to bring all they manage to dig up on the site of the
city some ten miles to the west. In the museum one can admire
some fragments of sculpture taken from sarcophagi; the style is
graeco-phoenician. Then there is the usual pottery, mass-pro-
duced utility stuff of little value. Nothing remains of what seems
to have been the pride of Carthage—its craftsmanship. It is said
that the goldsmiths were masters of their art. Unfortunately, in
all times and in all wars, jewelry has been the most sought-after
kind of loot.

XIII

Regulus

THE PACT WHICH THE ROMANS HAD SIGNED WITH CARTHAGE IN 508
B.C. when they were trapped between an internal revolution and
wars with the Etruscans, Latins, and Sabines, bound them
under no circumstances to sail their ships beyond the Sicilian
Channel, and never to land in Sardinia or Corsica except in the
case of desperate straits, that is, to take on supplies or effect
repairs in some shipyard.

These were serious limitations, but Rome had not suffered
unduly from them with only an embryo fleet, which was in any
case entirely in the hands of Etruscan shipowners who had lost
their money and political influence with the proclamation of the
republic. Rome at that time counted for nothing on the sea. The
Latin-Sabine senators were all landlubbers and couldn't have
cared less. Rome had merely given up what she did not even
possess, and perhaps was in complete ignorance of the great

changes in the so-called balance of naval power which had been taking place during these years in the Mediterranean. Let's take a general look at the situation.

A war between the Phoenician and Greek fleets had been going on for centuries in the eastern basin, just east of the Sicilian Channel, and now the Greeks were winning. First the Aegean and then the Ionian Sea had fallen into their hands. Italy became aware of this when increasing numbers of the victors began landing on the southern and Sicilian coasts, founding colonies which became virtually an empire: Magna Graecia. Places like Catania, Syracuse, Heraclia, Croton, Messina, Sybaris, Reggio, and Naxos were flourishing cities for those times. Unfortunately, along with their gods, philosophy, sculpture, and theaters, these empire builders had also brought with them their besetting sin of quarrelsomeness. This vice was to be their downfall in the struggle against Rome. But for the moment they were the undisputed masters of the area.

In the western basin, however, the Phoenicians had gained control, thanks to their young colony Carthage, which in turn had founded numerous other colonies not only along the north African coast but also in Portugal, Spain, France, Corsica, and Sardinia. The western Mediterranean had in effect become a Carthaginian lake.

When Rome, under the kings, had been mistress of Etruria and consequently of her fleet, she had come up against Carthage several times. Probably these contacts had not always been distinguished by courtesy. In those times acts of piracy were fashionable and only involved the captains and crews who committed them. One ship used to attack another, even one of the same nationality, rifle it, throw the sailors overboard, and no more would be heard of the matter.

Then Rome had disappeared as a Mediterranean power. Only the Greeks of Magna Graecia and the Phoenicians of Carthage were left facing one another, the former to the east and the latter to the west of Sicily. In fact, the east coasts of Sicily were Greek, and those to the west were Carthaginian. They glowered at each other and lived in a state of "cold war," with moments of "shooting war," followed by armistices and détentes. Both sides were convinced that sometime there would have to be a fight to the finish, but neither imagined for a moment that a third party was going to be the winner.

Nobody can say for certain whether Rome knew what she was doing, and had weighed the pros and cons, when she decided to accept the offer of the Mamertines.

These were a band of mercenaries recruited by Agathocles of Syracuse from all over Italy to fight against the Carthaginians. When the time came for them to be demobilized, around 289 B.C., instead of going home where there was most likely a warrant out for their arrest, they banded together, assaulted, sacked, and exterminated the population of Messina, settling there as its masters. Thereupon they gave themselves the quaint and presumptuous name of Mamertines, which means Sons of Mars.

For the past twenty years, these warriors had been getting into every kind of mischief. They were in the habit of crossing the Straits of Messina and burning and destroying the villages on the Calabrian side. They had given trouble to both Pyrrhus and the Romans. Now, toward the end of 270 B.C., they found themselves besieged by Hiero of Syracuse, who was determined to get rid of them once and for all.

To avoid what would certainly have been an exemplary punishment, the Mamertines asked for help from the Carthaginians, who sent an army and occupied the city. Seeing that the system of dog-eat-dog had worked once, the Mamertines decided to try it again, and appealed to Rome to liberate them from their Carthaginian protectors. This was in 264 B.C. Two-and-a-half centuries had passed since the solemn pact of alliance had been signed between Carthage and Rome. On the whole it had always functioned properly and had been reconfirmed twenty years earlier, when Carthage had brought help to Rome in her struggle with Pyrrhus.

Sicily, to the Romans, was an Eldorado. And here was the chance to get a foot in there. Everyone who had visited the island told wonderful stories of its riches and beauty. The invitation of the Mamertines was hard to resist.

Even so, it might have been refused if the senators had been free to decide on their own. They knew what this intervention would lead to. But by this time certain decisions had to be left to the *comitiae centuriatae,* in which the industrial and mercantile middle classes, who always made a good piece of change out of wars and so were the biggest warmongers, had the real say. Those who had money hoped to mutiply it. Furthermore, it is difficult to raise objections to those who claim to speak in the name of the fatherland and manifest destiny.

The assembly decided to accept the offer and entrusted operations to the consul Appius Claudius. In the spring of 264 B.C., after several fruitless attempts, a small Roman fleet under the command of the tribune Caius Claudius succeeded in crossing the Straits and entering Messina, with the aid of the Mamertines. They took the Carthaginian general Hanno prisoner and offered him the choice of imprisonment or the withdrawal of his men from the city.

Hanno must have been a conciliatory sort of man. Only a few months previously he had sent back to Appius Claudius certain Roman triremes which had been wrecked by a storm on the Sicilian coast. Now, in the face of these grim alternatives, he did not hesitate, and at the head of his little army went back home, where as a reward they crucified him. Evidently Carthage was not prepared to swallow this insult, for they immediately put another army in the field, led by another Hanno.

When the new general landed in Sicily, the first thing he did was to come to terms with the Greeks. He immediately made an agreement with those at Agrigentum, and then at Selinus received the envoys of Hiero of Syracuse, who accepted an alliance with him. Clearly the Greeks preferred the devil they knew.

Appius Claudius, who had ben relying on the century-old discord between Greeks and Phoenicians, was taken by surprise, with the bulk of his army still in Calabria, so he resorted to deception. He spread the rumor that the new situation demanded his presence in Rome to receive new instructions. He even sent a few ships sailing north. The Carthaginians, reassured, relaxed their vigilance on the Straits, and Appius took advantage of this to land his troops, 20,000 strong, just to the south of Messina in view of the Syracusan camp, which he promptly attacked.

Hiero handled the situation well, but the unexpected appearance of the Roman army led him to suspect treachery on the part of Hanno. So he left him in the lurch and returned hastily to Syracuse. Having thus isolated the Carthaginians, Appius immediately threw himself on them, but this time without success. So he left a detachment to guard Messina and went off in pursuit of the other enemy whom he considered weaker. Hiero, a good soldier, inflicted a heavy defeat on the Romans, and Appius by a miracle saved his skin. He had to admit that the undertaking was not as easy as had been thought in Rome. So leaving part of his forces to keep an eye on Hanno, he returned to Rome to report and ask for reinforcements.

This matter was largely taken care of by the diplomats, who reestablished good relations with Hiero and brought him back to the Roman side. This was a good move. But it was necessary, at the same time, to have Agrigentum as well as Syracuse, and here diplomacy was powerless because there was a Carthaginian garrison at Agrigentum. So the Romans laid seige to it, and after seven months starved its defenders into a desperate sortie and battered them.

The Carthaginians immediately put a second army into the field under the command of Hamilcar, not Hannibal's father, another one. He figured that there was nothing to be done against the Romans on land, so proceeded to attack all their naval bases with his fleet, winning victory after victory.

Now the stuff of which Rome was made became clear. She had neither ships nor sailors, yet within a few months and by the combined efforts of all her citizens, she succeeded in fitting out 120 vessels. Hamilcar, who had 130, sailed against them without even taking the usual precautionary measures, and found himself up against the *corvi*, or gangways fitted with beaks or grappling irons mounted on the bows of the Roman ships. These prevented the enemy from maneuvering and enabled the Romans to fight a land battle at sea. Hamilcar lost a third of his forces and fled.

When the news broke, Carthage was dumbfounded, having been convinced that at sea they could teach anybody a lesson. Rome swaggered with pride and decided to cross the Mediterranean and carry the war to the heart of the enemy's country. A second fleet was added to the first, 330 vessels in all, with 150,000 men under the command of the consul Atilius Regulus. Carthage faced them with an equal force under Hamilcar. The encounter took place off Marsala. Rome's uncertain victory cost her twenty-four ships. The Carthaginians paid for their certain defeat with the loss of thirty, but Regulus was able to land in Africa at Cap Bon.

Now it was Carthage's turn to show what she was made of, and she did. She wavered slightly at the initial successes of the Romans who, with the help of the Numidians, had come to within about eighteen miles of the city, and sent envoys to sue for peace. Regulus on his own initiative imposed unacceptable conditions, whereupon the Carthaginians prepared for the death struggle. Having lost faith in their own generals, they turned over the command to a Greek from Sparta, Xanthippus, which today would be like giving it to a German from Prussia. He licked the army into shape by rough-and-ready methods, including summary executions, and introduced the new technique involving cavalry and elephants which Hannibal was later to exploit so brilliantly.

The decisive battle was fought near Tunis. Only 2,000 men of the Roman army, by bottling themselves up on Cap Bon, lived to tell the tale. Regulus was taken prisoner. It was the year 255 B.C.

It took Rome five years, morally and materially, to recover from this disaster, which had brought the war back to Sicily. During these five years, fortunes alternated, but they were generally more favorable to the Carthaginians. Then one day Hasdrubal, a new Carthaginian general, was beaten in an attempt to retake Palermo and left 20,000 dead on the battlefield. Carthage, war-weary and thinking that their adversary should be in the same state, took Regulus out of prison and sent him to Rome, accompanied by ambassadors to speak in favor of peace proposals. He had given his word of honor to return, should these proposals be rejected. The senate invited him to give his opinion, in the presence of the enemy plenipotentiaries, and Regulus maintained that it was necessary to continue the war. His view was accepted, and in spite of the entreaties of his wife he was returned to Carthage. Here they tortured him to death by preventing him from sleeping. His sons in Rome then took two high-ranking Carthaginian prisoners and kept them awake until they died.

The war continued. But now a new character appeared on the Carthaginian side: Hamilcar Barca, father of Hannibal and supreme commander of the army and navy. He was the inventor of commando raids, and he began launching them with devastating effectiveness on the coasts of the peninsula, giving the Romans the impression that he intended to land.

The senate, terrified, was unwilling to risk a new fleet against him. Military reserves were almost exhausted, and so were the resources of the treasury. In this moment of crisis, the wealthier citizens fitted out a fleet of 200 ships at their own expense and put them at the disposal of the consul Lutatius Catulus, who blockaded the ports of Drepanum and Lilybaeum. On their side, the Carthaginians sent 400 ships, laden with reinforcements, arms, and supplies. If they managed to land, it meant the doom of the Romans in Sicily. Against orders from the senate forbidding him to take the initiative at sea, and though seriously wounded, Catulus ordered his squadron to attack. The heavily-laden Carthaginian vessels were unable to maneuver. Some 120 of them were sunk and the rest limped back to Carthage. Hamilcar was cut off from home, and in spite of all his successes, had to ask for terms. Lutatius Catulus, having no desire to follow in Regulus' footsteps, immediately accepted Hamilcar's proposals and granted him the honor of arms and withdrawal of his men. He left the other conditions to the discretion of the senate.

In Rome, some people blamed Catulus for his indulgence and proposed renewing hostilities until the unconditional surrender of the enemy. Unconditional surrender is almost always a stupid objective and the senate quite rightly voted the idea down. They demanded from the Carthaginians withdrawal from Sicily, the return of all prisoners of war without ransom, and the payment within ten years of 4,400 talents. These were reasonable terms and Carthage hastened to accept them.

So ended the first Punic War. It had lasted almost a quarter of a century, 265–241 B.C. But both in Rome and in Carthage, everyone knew that this peace was only a truce.

XIV

Hannibal

BOTH SIDES WERE PRETTY BADLY BATTERED AT THE END OF THIS twenty-five-year struggle, but Carthage was worse off than Rome. Not only did she have to give up all Sicily, pay heavy reparations and accept the commercial competition of Rome in the whole Mediterranean, but thanks to internal conflict, she plunged into anarchy.

The government had refused to meet the arrears of pay

owed the mercenaries who had served under Hamilcar. Led by
Mathos, a truculent corporal who knew what he was about, they
revolted. Immediately they gained the support of the subject
peoples, particularly the Libyans. These also rebelled and
raised an army under the command of Spendius, a Neapolitan
slave, who laid siege to the city.

The rich merchants of Carthage were panic-stricken and
begged Hamilcar to free them from this menace. At first Hamilcar hesitated, as he did not like the idea of fighting against his
own ex-soldiers. But when they cut off the hands and broke both
the legs of his colleague Gesco, and buried 700 Carthaginians
alive, he decided to act. He called to arms all the young men he
could find in the beleaguered city, gave them some hard basic
military training, and with 10,000 men attacked an enemy of
40,000 strong. He broke through the blockading forces, drove
them into a narrow defile, blocked both ends, and waited for
them to die of starvation.

First they ate the horses, then the prisoners, then the slaves.
Finally, in despair, they sent Spendius to beg for peace. Hamilcar's only reply was to crucify him. The mercenaries attempted
a sortie and were massacred. Mathos, taken prisoner, was slowly
flogged to death. "It was," Polybius says, "the bloodiest and most
inhuman war in history." It lasted over three years and at the
end of it Carthage woke up to find that Rome had been busy
occupying Sardinia. She protested, but Rome, well aware of the
plight of her adversary, merely replied with a declaration of
war. To avoid this, Carthage accepted the loss of Sardinia,
added Corsica to it, and resigned herself to paying another
1,200 talents. In other words, to avoid war she accepted defeat,
and this time did not protest.

Rome, too, had been licking her wounds during this period.
The army was short of men and the currency had been devalued
by 83 percent. The policy of unification followed in the peninsula had, on the whole, produced good results, insofar as none of
the city's subject peoples had taken advantage of her reverses to
rebel. But the northern frontier was not yet secure. The Ligurians, who were incapable of founding their own state, were
nevertheless quite capable of sailing down the Tyrrhenian Sea
with their ships to harry commerce and raid the coasts, particularly those of Tuscany. In the northern Adriatic the Illyrians,
lurking among the rocky islands of Dalmatia, did likewise. And,

from Bologna to the Alps, in the whole of the Po Valley, the
Gauls were growing in strength, owing to the arrival of their
kinsmen from France, who not knowing the Romans, were not
afraid of them. If they were allowed to increase, there was always the risk of seeing them roll down again like an avalanche
as they had done under Brennus.

Having mopped up the remaining Carthaginians in Sicily
and occupied it (except for the Kingdom of Syracuse, which
was left to the faithful Hiero) with garrisons and colonies, Rome
proclaimed it a "province." It was the first of many which were
later to make up the empire. The second was Sardinia and Corsica together. Having thus established a certain administrative
order, the city decided to extend it beyond the Tuscan Apennines, which formed its northern frontier.

She began with the Ligurians, who were the most isolated
and the least dangerous, and perhaps it was not really a war
but a series of amphibious operations. It lasted five years, 238–
233 B.C., and required none of the usual heroic episodes. When
it came to an end, the Ligurians had become vassals and no
longer had a single ship that could disturb communications
with Sardinia and Corsica.

Then came the turn of the Gauls who in fact had already
taken the initiative by organizing, with the assistance of their
French relatives, an army of 50,000 infantry and 20,000 cavalry.
The Romans had always taken a disdainful view of these
doughty warriors, whom Polybius describes as "tall and handsome, and always spoiling for a fight, which they undertook
naked, except for a necklace or an amulet or two." But the senate was so perturbed at this new attack that, reviving a custom
which had fallen into disuse, they decided to propitiate the gods
with a human sacrifice, and buried alive a couple of victims,
who, of course, were chosen from among the Gauls. It can be
deduced that the gods were satisfied, because at Telamon the
legions succeeded in surrounding the enemy and practically
wiped them out once and for all. Some 40,000 Gauls fell on the
battlefield; another 10,000 were taken prisoner. All Italy up to
the Alps was now at the mercy of Rome and she called the rich
new province, her third, Cisalpine Gaul. She occupied the capital, Mediolanum, now Milan, and founded two powerful colonies, Cremona and Placentia (Piacenza).

She then turned east. In the course of a few years and by

means of expeditions similar to the ones she had mounted against the Ligurians, she reduced the Illyria of Queen Teuta to a tributary nation. Thus for the first time she set foot on the opposite shore of the Adriatic and made it a springboard for her successive conquests in the east.

While Rome was completing her conquest of the peninsula and securing herself from the east and north, Hamilcar in Carthage wasted no time. He was preparing for the coming struggle. As soon as he had subdued the revolt, he begged the government to give him an army to restore the shaken Phoenician prestige in Spain and to build up a base there for operations against Italy. On his side were the middle classes, who wished to regain their commercial monopoly in the Mediterranean, on which their prosperity depended. But he had against him the landed aristocracy, who did not want to risk losing their privileges in dangerous adventures.

Eventually a compromise was reached. Instead of an army corps, Hamilcar was granted only a division, but this was enough for him. A first-rate general, they had not given him the nickname "Barca" for nothing. In Phoenician it meant "thunderbolt." Before leaving at the head of his scanty command, he visited the church with his "lion cubs" as he used to call his son-in-law, Hasdrubal, and his three sons, Hannibal, Hasdrubal and Mago. Here, in front of the altar to Baal-Haman, he made them swear a solemn oath that one day they would avenge Carthage, and then embarked them with his troops.

A few months were enough for him to bring to heel the Spanish cities that had rebelled. He then began to recruit the natives to raise a proper army. Carthage did not lift a finger to help him. Hamilcar did everything on his own. He dug mines, extracted iron, and had it wrought into weapons. He monopolized trade to finance himself. Unfortunately death surprised him, still a young man, during a skirmish against a rebel tribe. As he lay dying, he nominated his son-in-law, Hasdrubel, as his successor. The latter held command for another eight years without giving anyone cause to regret his father-in-law. In the mining district he built a completely new city, which today is called Cartagena. On his death from an assassin's knife the soldiers acclaimed Hannibal, the eldest of Hamilcar's three sons, as their commander in chief. At this time he had spent seventeen of his twenty-six years under canvas with the troops. Furthermore, he still clearly remembered the oath which his father had made him swear.

Hannibal, if not the greatest in an absolute sense, was certainly the most brilliant of the military leaders of antiquity. Many put him on the same plane as Napoleon. Before his father took him to Spain he had received what was for those times a perfect education. He knew his history, languages (Latin and Greek), and, from the stories which Hamilcar had told him, he had a pretty shrewd idea of Rome, her strength and weaknesses. He was convinced, for example, that a defeat in Italy would separate Rome from her allies; that was what had happened in his father's time. He had not the slightest idea that Rome's policy was no longer federalistic. He was tough, frugal, and of boundless courage and cunning. Titus Livy tells us that he was always the first to go into battle and the last to come out. It may be that he had undue confidence in his own powers of improvisation. All Roman historians, including Livy, have emphasised his greed, cruelty, and unscrupulousness. It is true that the traps he set for the Romans were endless and diabolical, but this was the reason that his soldiers adored and had such blind faith in him. He had no need of badges of rank to maintain his prestige; indeed, he dressed like the troops and shared their hardships. Apart from being a master of strategy, he was also an excellent diplomat and unsurpassed at espionage.

As he was unknown to his compatriots, who had not laid eyes on him since he was nine, he could hardly expect them to agree to the opening of hostilities. So, instead of declaring war, he had to arrange for war to be declared on him. This was why, in 219 B.C., he attacked Saguntum.

Saguntum was a city allied to Rome, but ever since Hasdrubal's days, Rome had been pledged to regard everywhere south of the Ebro as a Carthaginian sphere of influence. Thus, since the city lay in that area, Hannibal had no difficulty in rejecting the by no means uncertain protest that he received from Rome. She was convinced that Carthage was still the frightened, unsettled city it had been during the mercenary revolts. Thus, with great cunning on one side and gross carelessness on the other, the second campaign began.

Hannibal spent another eight months under the walls of the city before taking it by assault as he was not prepared to risk leaving the excellent port of Saguntum open behind him to the

Roman fleet. Then, leaving his brother Hasdrubal to guard it and to train the reinforcements, he crossed the Ebro with 30 elephants, 50,000 infantry, and 9,000 cavalry. They were almost all Spaniards or Libyans and there was not a mercenary among them.

His difficulties began as soon as he reached the other side of the Pyrenees. The Gaulish tribes allied to Marseilles, which was in turn allied to Rome, offered resistance, regardless of the way Rome had treated their brethren of the Po Valley. Furthermore, when they knew that he intended to cross the Alps, 3,000 of his men refused to follow Hannibal. He did not force them; on the contrary, he freed from their obligations another 7,000 who appeared to be hesitant, and sent them home. Thus, rid of timid and irresolute troops, he marched north to Vienne and began the ascent.

It is not known exactly where he crossed. Some say it was by the Little St. Bernard, others by Mont Genèvre; most historians opt for the latter. In any case, at the beginning of September of 218 B.C. he reached the summit (still covered with snow) and gave his men two days' rest. He had already lost a thousand or so owing to the cold, exhaustion, precipices, and Celtic warriors. After this halt he began the descent, which was even more difficult, especially for the elephants. There were moments of crisis and despair in the hearts of these bold men but Hannibal kept up their morale by pointing out in the distance the beautiful Po Valley, which he promised them as a reward. About 26,000 men reached the bottom of the mountains, less than half the number that had started out. But the Boii and the other Gauls received them in a friendly manner, gave them supplies, and joined with them, so that together they massacred or put to flight the Romans of Cremona and Placentia.

Astounded by such audacity, the senate realized that this second war threatened to be even more dangerous than the first. They called up 300,000 men and 14,000 horses, part of which they entrusted to the first of the many Scipios who were to make the family name famous. This Scipio met Hannibal on the river Ticinus, allowed his front to be broken by the Numidian cavalry and lost the battle. Seriously wounded as he was, he would have lost his life as well, if his sixteen-year-old son had not saved him. (Sixteen years later this lad was to avenge his father at Zama.) This battle took place in October of 218 B.C.

Two months passed, and another army was sent to meet Hannibal on the Trebia. A second battle followed, and a second defeat. Eight months later Caius Flaminius, at the head of 30,000 men, marched against Hannibal, now master of all Cisalpine Gaul. Flaminius was so certain of victory that he took chains with him to put on the feet of the prisoners. Hannibal appeared to be trying to avoid a pitched battle. Actually, by cunning maneuvering of his patrols and by skirmishing, he enticed his enemy onto a plain near the shores of Lake Trasimenus, which was surrounded by hills and woods where he had concealed his cavalry. From these positions he entangled his enemy inextricably, and hardly a Roman, not even Flaminius, survived.

Titus Livy tells us that the news threw Rome into a panic, but the senate faced the situation with virile fortitude. The praetor, Marcus Pomponius, did not try to play down the communique about the defeat when he read it from the rostrum. "We have been defeated in a great battle," he said, "The danger is very serious."

Things were not looking too rosy, either, for Hannibal. As he drew nearer to Rome, he realized that his hopes of dividing her from her allies were unfounded. In Tuscany and Umbria the cities closed their gates before his army, which was unable to obtain supplies. In vain he liberated and sent home non-Roman prisoners. From the Apennines to Samnium, all Italy stood solidly by the city. All Hannibal could do was to change direction towards the Adriatic in search of more hospitable lands. His allies, the Gauls, who could see no farther than the tips of their own noses, began to desert now that they were getting farther away from their own region. Hannibal sent messengers to Carthage to ask for reinforcements. They were refused him. He sent to Hasdrubal, but he was being kept busy in Spain by the Romans, who had landed there. Hannibal continued his march south and found himself up against a new and embarrassing strategist.

Quintus Fabius Maximus had been appointed dictator, and had begun that "masterly inactivity" for which he was to go down in history as "The Delayer". He skirmished and laid ambushes, but refused to be drawn into battle. He just waited for hardship, hunger, and weariness to complete their work on the enemy, who were in fact desperate. Unfortunately the Romans got tired first and wanted a quick victory. They listened with approval to the malicious Minucius Rufus, Fabius' master of the horse and detractor, and Fabius was relieved of his command. It was divided between two freshly appointed consuls, Terentius Varro and Aemilius Paulus. The latter was an aristocrat of sound judgment, who was well aware that the Romans had not yet worked out a strategy capable of dealing with Hannibal. Varro was a plebeian, a better patriot than a general, who wanted what his electors wanted: a rapid victory. Since he spoke in the name of pride and nationalism, he got his way. He led his 80,000 infantry and 6,000 cavalry against Hannibal, who breathed a sigh of relief, although he only had 20,000 veterans, 15,000 unreliable Gauls and 10,000 horses. The only one he feared was Fabius Maximus.

The battle, the most gigantic of ancient times, took place at Cannae on the Aufidus. The Carthaginian, as usual, lured his enemy onto level ground suitable for the employment of cavalry and drew up his line of battle with the Gauls in the center, convinced that they would cut and run, which in fact they did. Varro plunged into the gap and Hannibal's wings closed round him. Aemilius Paulus, who had opposed the battle, fought gallantly and was killed together with another 44,000 Romans, including 80 senators. Varro, in company with the same Scipio who had saved his skin on the Ticinus, managed to escape. He took refuge in Canusium and from there returned to Rome.

The mourning population awaited him at the gates of the city. When they saw him coming they went to meet him with the magistrates at their head, and thanked him for having never doubted the fatherland. This was Rome's reply to the catastrophe.

XV

Scipio

ACCORDING TO THE EXPERTS CANNAE REMAINS AN EXAMPLE OF strategy unsurpassed in all history. Hannibal, the only commander ever to beat Rome four times running, lost only 6,000 men, of whom 4,000 were Gauls. But he also lost his secret for

success, as his enemies had finally caught on to the superiority
of cavalry.

For the time being it looked as though the invader had won
the day; the Samnites, the Abruzzans and the Lucanians revolted. At Croton, Locri, Capua, and Metapontum, the population massacred the Roman garrisons. Philip V of Macedonia
made an alliance with the victor. Carthage, elated, announced
the dispatch of reinforcements and certain young Roman patricians, already corrupted by Hellenic culture, meditated flight
to Greece, their ideal country. But these were isolated cases,
and Scipio, veteran of the two defeats of the Ticinus and Cannae, denounced them with words of fire. The people accepted
fresh taxation and further mobilization, the noble matrons
brought their jewels to the treasury and went to sweep the floors
of the temples with their hair. The government ordered a new
human sacrifice, no longer of two but of four victims, whereupon two Greeks and two Gauls were buried alive. The soldiers
refused to take their pay. Volunteers of thirteen and fourteen
left home to swell the slender garrison which was preparing to
defend Rome in her last battle against Hannibal.

Hannibal failed to appear. One still asks today why he was
unwilling to take a chance. Like Hitler after Dunkirk, this great
soldier, who had courage and to spare in battle, could not manage to screw up enough to tackle the last obstacle, even though
he knew it was almost defenseless. Was he suffering from the
illusion that he would get substantial reinforcements in time for
the great enterprise? Did he hope that the enemy would sue for
peace? Or had he still a healthy respect for Rome, in spite of
having beaten her four times? Whatever may have been the
cause, instead of exploiting the enormous success of Cannae, he
decided to take a rest. He sent home the non-Roman prisoners
and offered to return the Roman ones in exchange for a small
indemnity. The senate haughtily refused. Hannibal sent a
certain number of them to Carthage as slaves and used up the
others in gladiatorial games for the entertainment of his troops.
Then he advanced to within a few miles of Rome and made it
tremble before by-passing it to the east and heading for Capua.

For the moment the Romans did not pursue him; they were
painfully organizing a new army of 200,000 men. When this was
ready, they gave part of it to the consul Claudius Marcellus to
reestablish order in Sicily, now in revolt, kept a part for the

defense of the city, and sent another to Spain under the leadership of the two elder Scipios to keep Hasdrubal tied up.

By the following year Claudius Marcellus had conquered Syracuse, which had betrayed the alliance after the death of the faithful Hiero, and tried to hold out with the aid of the devices of Archimedes, the greatest mathematician and technician of antiquity. Among other things he had thought up were the "iron hands" which, from the confused and bewildering descriptions left us by historians, must have been cranes that lifted up the Roman ships. He also invented "burning mirrors" which set fire to ships by concentrating the rays of the sun on them. Perhaps these were only brilliant ideas that merely remained on paper. The fact is that the city fell just the same, and in the slaughter that followed, Archimedes himself lost his life.

To add to this success, which revived Roman prestige in the south, the two Scipios gave Hasdrubal several drubbings in Spain, and retook Capua, which fell in 211 B.C., when Hannibal had turned his back for a moment and was hoping to deceive the Romans by a pretended march on the city. The punishment of the unfaithful Capua was cautionary: all its chiefs were killed and the population was deported *en masse*. Terror spread over Italy and faith in Hannibal, "the liberator," was shaken.

Just at this moment arose a great leader who was destined to avenge all of Rome's humiliations. The two Scipios, who had been battling victoriously with Hasdrubal, were both killed in action, and Publius Cornelius, son of one and nephew of the other, and a twenty-four-year-old veteran of the Ticinus and Cannae, was sent to take their place.

He was too young to hold such a high command but in the face of such a serious emergency, the senate and the assembly decided to waive the law. Publius Cornelius Scipio had been a brave soldier and an excellent phalanx and cohort commander. On his return with Varro to Rome in the darkest hour after the defeat of Cannae, he had been the soul of the resistance. He was handsome, eloquent, and bore a great name. He was reputed to be a god-fearing, courteous, and just man, who did nothing, either in his public or private life, without first consulting the gods in prayer at the temple. He had, furthermore, managed to get himself a reputation among his fellow citizens for being lucky, in other words of being a favorite of the gods.

As soon as he arrived in Spain, where he found the army

besieging Cartagena, he gave a demonstration of the particular favors assisting him. To capture the city one had to cross a lagoon connected with the sea. The depth of the water made swimming necessary, an impossible feat for a man weighed down by breastplate, helmet, and arms. One morning Publius Cornelius assembled his men and informed them that Neptune had appeared to him in a dream. The god had promised to help him by lowering the level of the lagoon. The soldiery neither believed nor disbelieved this, but when all of a sudden they saw their general jump in and run across it, they acclaimed it as a miracle. They charged in after him, and more for the god's sake than Scipio's, stormed and took their objective.

Actually there was nothing miraculous about it. Publius Cornelius had merely discovered, while talking with some fishermen of Tarragona, the difference between high and low tide, a subject about which his veterans who were all peasants knew absolutely nothing. All the same, the energy and enthusiasm of troops are doubled once they are convinced that their general has divinity on his side. It began to be rumored that the father of Publius Cornelius was not Scipio at all, but a monstrous great snake, into which Jove in person had transformed himself. In fact, Scipio himself most likely started the talk. In those times the Romans were not above ruining their own mothers' reputations as long as they profited from it.

With this coup almost all Spain fell into the hands of Rome. Hasdrubal, who no longer had any reason for staying there, managed to escape, and together with his army, sped off to join his brother via France and the Alps. Somehow or other he succeeded in crossing them, but a message of his to Hannibal, announcing his imminent arrival and the route he was going to take, was intercepted by the Romans, who were thus fully in the know. Two new armies were hastily fitted out. One, commanded by Claudius Nero, saw to it that Hannibal was safely pinned down in Apulia. In any case the latter made no move because he had no idea of what was afoot. The other army, under the command of Livy Salinator, lay in wait for Hasdrubal in the most favorable position on the Metaurus, near Sena Gallica, and wiped out the Carthaginian forces. We are told that the head of the general, who was killed in the battle, was severed from his shoulders, taken to Hannibal's encampment, and thrown over the ramparts. Hannibal had already lost one eye from trachoma, but the remaining one enabled him to recognize the miserable remains of the brother he had loved like a son.

By now the Carthaginian felt that he had failed. Philip of Macedonia, after a platonic declaration of war, had allowed himself to be won over by Roman diplomacy and had made peace. The Italian rebels, intimidated by the example of Capua, sympathized with Hannibal but lent him no help. Eighty of the hundred ships which Carthage had sent him laden with reinforcements had been wrecked and sunk on the coast of Sardinia. Further, "the leisures of Capua," which became proverbial from that time on, had sapped the morale and physique of the valorous army of Cannae. One of his commanders had said to Hannibal when he refused to march on Rome: "The gods do not lavish all their gifts on one man. You know how to win victories, but you do not know how to use them." Perhaps there was more than a little truth in this judgment.

In 204 B.C. Scipio, having returned from his triumphs in Spain, was given command of a new and more powerful army, with which he embarked for Africa. The war now became a defensive one for Carthage. Alarmed, she hastily sent for Hannibal to come home and defend her. The man who came back after thirty-six year's absence, half-blind and worn out by fatigue and disillusionment, was still a great leader but no longer the prodigy who had set out from Cartagena. Half his troops refused to follow him and Roman historians say that he had 20,000 men executed for mutiny. He landed with the rest in 202 B.C. and hardly recognized the city he had left when he was nine. Then he took up a position with his remaining veterans on the plain of Zama, about fifty miles to the south of Carthage.

The two armies were about equal in strength and they stood and watched each other for many months, improving their positions. Then the Romans received unhoped for aid. Masinissa, king of Numidia, was deposed by his rival, Syphax, a friend and protégé of the Carthaginians. Masinissa therefore, complete with all his cavalry, joined Scipio.

Hannibal had always put his greatest trust in cavalry. Perhaps this is why, before giving battle, he wanted to play his last card: a try at a friendly agreement. He asked for a meeting with his opponent, and this was granted. At last the two great generals met face to face. The interview was short and evidently extremely polite. The participants came to the conclusion that there was no question of coming to an agreement, but judging by subsequent events, one is inclined to say that they got along very well together. (They could hardly fail to esteem each other highly.) They parted without rancor and immediately joined battle.

Hannibal, instead of taking the intiative, had for the first time in his life to submit to that of his adversary, who adopted his own pincer movements to beat him. In the ensuing disaster he displayed the same energy which he had shown twenty-five years before. He assailed and wounded Scipio in single combat. He attacked Masinissa. He formed and reformed his battered phalanxes five, six, ten times to hurl them into counterattacks, but to no avail. Some 20,000 of his men lay dead on the field. All he could do was to mount a horse and gallop off to Carthage. He arrived, covered with blood, summoned the senate and announced that he had lost not a battle but the war, and advised them to send envoys to sue for peace. They did so.

Scipio was generous. He demanded the surrender of the whole Carthaginian fleet, less ten triremes, the abandonment of any conquest in Europe, the recognition of Masinissa in an independent Numidia, and reparations of 10,000 talents. He left Carthage her Tunisian and Algerian possessions, though she was not to add others to them, and did not insist on the handing over of Hannibal, though the Roman people would have dearly loved to see him yoked behind the victor's chariot on the day of triumph.

Hannibal's compatriots showed none of the chivalry that his ex-enemy had done. The peace treaty had not yet been ratified when certain Carthaginians secretly informed Rome that Hannibal was already meditating vengeance and was doing his utmost to achieve it. Actually he was only trying to reestablish order in his country, and at the head of the popular party, was doing his best to destroy the privileges of the corrupt senatorial and mercantile oligarchy which had been really responsible for the defeat.

Scipio used all his influence to dissuade his countrymen from asking for the head of his great enemy, but without success. To avoid arrest and surrender, Hannibal had to flee on horse by night, galloping more than 125 miles to Thapsus, from which he sailed for Antioch. At that time King Antiochus was hesitating between war and peace with Rome. Hannibal counseled war and became one of his military experts. But in spite of all his skill, Antiochus was defeated at Magnesia and among other conditions the Romans insisted on the Carthaginian being handed over. So again Hannibal had to take flight, first to Crete and then to Bithynia. The Romans gave him no respite and finally surrounded him in his hide-out. The old general preferred death to capture, and Livy tells how, raising the poison to his lips, he ironically remarked: "Let us set the Roman's minds at rest, seeing they haven't the patience to wait for the end of an old man like me." He was sixty-seven and a few months later his victor and admirer, Cornelius, followed him to the grave.

It was this second Punic War which decided for many centuries the fate of the Mediterranean and Western Europe. The third was merely a superfluous postscript. It was the second that gave Rome Spain, North Africa, the dominion of the sea, and riches.

These acquisitions also brought about a transformation in the life of Rome, which was to prove not at all beneficial to the future of the city. In all, 300,000 men, the elite of agriculture and the army, had fallen in battle. Some 400 cities had been destroyed and half the farms had been pillaged, especially in southern Italy, which has never really recovered to this day.

The Romans 200 years earlier would have repaired this damage in the course of fifty years or so; their successors were not made of the same stuff. What now atttracted them was not work on the land but international trade. Instead of getting rich by patience, tenacity, and by living a frugal life and saving, it was easier, for example, to go to Spain where all one had to do was to scratch the earth to find iron and gold. Loot from the conquered peoples glutted the treasury, and the tribute paid by subject states, year after year, to the tune of billions, made every Roman citizen a *rentier* and gave him a distaste for work.

This economic boom unsettled society and made the framework on which it had rested up till now inadequate. A new bourgeoisie of middlemen and contractors sprang up and traditions were softened and relaxed. What today is called a "social life" began to develop, with intellectual, progressive salons. Faith in the gods weakened, as well as faith in that democracy which in moments of danger had had to rely on dictators with plenary power to save the country.

The crisis did not come all at once, but in those years after the downfall of Carthage its seeds were sown.

XVI

"Graecia Capta . . ."

ONE OF THE FIRST LOADS OF BOOTY WHICH ROME BROUGHT BACK from Greece was a group of some 1,000 intellectuals noted for their hostility to the city. Among them was a certain Polybius. He had a passion for history and taught the Romans how it should be written. "By what political system," he asked himself on arrival, "has this city been able to conquer the world in less than fifty-three years; a thing which no one else has succeeded in doing up till now?"

As a matter of fact Rome had taken much more than fifty-three years, but for the Greek Polybius, the "world" meant simply Greece, the conquest of which actually had not taken more than half-a-century. It had not however been the diabolical cunning of the senate and the Roman generals which had made that task so easy, but the fact that Greece, before being conquered, had already destroyed herself. Her disintegration had been internal, and all Rome had had to do was pluck the fruit.

The first dealings of the city with Greece dated back to the times of Pyrrhus. Even then Greece as a nation had already ceased to exist, or rather had given up all hope of ever becoming one. The various cities of which she was composed spent all their time fighting among themselves and not one of them was capable of keeping the others united in defense of their common interests.

The last attempt to create a Greek nation had come from outside, that is, from Macedonia, which the Greeks of Athens, Corinth, and Thebes regarded as a barbarous foreign country. It is true that it was little like Greece. The chains of mountains which enclosed it from the south had cut it off from the culture, customs, and civilization of the coastal cities. Anyway that civili-

zation was too urban and mercantile to have flourished in such a
harsh, rugged country of hidden valleys, sparse flocks, and lonely,
archaic villages. To make up for all this, the population had remained healthy, tough, and strong. They knew nothing about
grammar and philosophy but believed in their gods and obeyed
their masters—an aristocracy of big landowners whose only occupation was attending to their land and whose only pleasures
were tournaments and hunting. They went rarely and unwillingly to Pallas, the capital, not because the journey was arduous
but because the king happened to live in that dull country town
and they wished to have as little as possible to do with him. Only
Philip and his son Alexander had succeeded in overcoming their
reserve and uniting them in the great adventure of conquest.
Each brought his own contingent to Alexander's army. All together, first under the sole command of the father and then of
the son, they had occupied Greece, organized it, and tried to
coordinate its forces with those of Macedonia. Their object? To
conquer the world.

It was a wonderful adventure which only lasted as long as
its two protagonists. In 323 B.C. Alexander died in Babylonia at
the tender age of thirty-three. Although he had led his army
from victory to victory, to Egypt and India through Asia Minor,
Mesopotamia and Persia, his ephemeral empire faded away as
quickly as it had risen. To his generals, gathered around his bedside to ask him whom he designated as his successor, he replied:
"The strongest," but neglected to indicate who this might be;
perhaps he did not know. This is why his possessions were divided into five parts: Antipater took Macedonia and Greece,
Lysimachus Thrace, Antigonus Asia Minor, Seleucus Babylonia,
and Ptolemy Egypt. Naturally, they started fighting among themselves immediately.

Let us leave these "diadochs," as the five successors were
called, to their quarrels (which were of great advantage to Rome
later on), and concentrate on those that broke out immediately in
the kingdom of Antipater. He should have united Macedonia
with Greece, and had the union been really effective, Rome
would have found it a very tough nut to crack. But the Greeks
did not want this and did all they could to prevent it. When
Alexander died, Plutarch relates, the Athenians, who had received nothing but benefits from him, formed processions in the
streets and sang hymns of victory "as though they themselves

had overthrown the tyrant." Demosthenes, who had been the champion of the "resistance"—a resistance of words only—had his brief hour of glory and incited his fellow citizens to raise an army to resist Antipater. The army was raised and, naturally, defeated by the new king of Macedonia, an ignorant type with none of Alexander's weakness for the high civilization of Athens. He treated her just as he was accustomed to treating his own mutinous soldiers.

When Antipater died, leaving the throne to his son Cassander, Athens rebelled again. Again she was defeated and punished. And so it went on for years and years; rebellions followed by repressions. Finally Demetrius Poliorcetes (which means "conqueror of cities"), the son of Antigonus, arrived from Asia Minor and drove out the Macedonians. In Athens he was received as a conquering hero. They decorated a special apartment for him in the Parthenon, and he filled it with prostitutes and effeminate boys. Tiring of these pleasures, he proclaimed himself king of Macedonia and as such abolished the independence of Athens, which he himself had restored. He then turned the city over to another Macedonian garrison.

From this regime of anarchy, which lasted a century and which was made worse by a terrifying invasion of the Gauls, Greece emerged politically finished. In the wake of her merchant fleet and on the swords of Philip, Alexander, and their diadochs, her civilization had penetrated everywhere, from the Epirus to Asia Minor, to Palestine, to Persia, to Egypt, and even to India. Everywhere the ruling classes and the intellectuals were Greek or under Greek influence. Her philosophy, sculpture, literature, and science, transplanted to conquered countries, created new cultures. But politically, Greece was dead, and was to remain so for 2,000 years.

When Rome, by now free of Carthage, turned her eyes in that direction she saw a constellation of tiny states perpetually squabbling with one another. Polybius had no reason to wonder how she managed to conquer them in so short a time. As a matter of fact she could have done so in far less.

It all began because of Philip V, king of Macedonia. This state, bled white by Alexander, was no longer what it had been, but it was still the most stable in Greece. The Greek cities at this time were divided into two leagues, the Achaean and the

Aetolian, and only patched up their private quarrels to unite against Macedonia.

In 216 B.C. Philip, hearing that Hannibal had annihilated the Romans at Cannae, signed a pact of alliance with him and invited the Greeks to help him destroy Rome, a power which might become a menace to all of them. A conference was held at Naupactus, where the Aetolian delegate, Agelaus, speaking in the name of all present, urged Philip to put himself at the head of all the Greeks in this crusade. This seemed all very fine, but almost immediately in Athens and the other cities rumors started to the effect that Hannibal had given the Macedonian a free hand with the Greeks in return for his assistance. Suspicion, which had been momentarily allayed, at once flared up again and the Aetolian League sent envoys to Rome asking for help against Philip, who, now that he had to cope with Greece, was compelled to give up the idea of attacking Italy. Furthermore he had to sign a treaty with Rome, thus putting an end to the first Macedonian War before it had even begun.

After the battle of Zama, Pergamon, Egypt, and Rhodes, all of which had been molested by Philip, asked Rome for help against him. The city, which had a long memory and well re-called the maneuver of the Macedonian king after Cannae, sent an army under Titus Quintius Flamininus which trounced Philip in 197 B.C., in a battle on a ridge of hills called Cynoscephalae. Once Philip had been beaten, the road to Greece was open.

But Flamininus was a strange individual. Of a patrician fam-ily, he had studied at Tarentum, where he had learned Greek, and was an admirer of Hellenic civilization. Furthermore, he had "progressive" ideas. Instead of killing Philip, he put him back on his throne, in spite of the protests of his Greek allies, who claimed that they had won the battle of the Cynoscephalae. On the occasion of the great Isthmian Games held at Corinth and attended by delegations from all over Greece, he proclaimed that all her cities and peoples were independent, no longer sub-ject to garrisons or tribute, and free to govern themselves ac-cording to their own laws. His listeners, who had expected the Macedonian yoke to be replaced by the Roman one, were flab-bergasted; Plutarch says that they raised such a yell of enthu-siasm that a flight of crows, circling overhead, dropped down stone dead.

The Athenian skeptics did not have time to doubt the honest intentions of Flamininus. He put them into force at once by withdrawing his army from Greece. Having previously acclaimed him as their savior and liberator, they now criticized him for taking away a considerable number of souvenirs in the shape of works of art from certain cities of the Aetolian League. So they appealed to Antiochus, the latest heir to Seleucus, the king of Babylonia, to re-liberate them. It is not quite clear from what they were to be re-liberated, since Flamininus had left them as free as air.

Pergamon and Lampsacus, who were closer neighbors of Antiochus, knew him better and consequently what to expect from him. So they asked for help from Rome. The senate, which had never really believed in Flamininus' liberal, progressive experiment, sent another army under the command of Scipio, the hero of Zama. With a small force Scipio attacked Antiochus at Magnesia and routed him, despite the wise strategic counsels given him by his guest, Hannibal. Then Scipio wheeled north, defeated the Gauls, who were still encamped in the neighborhood, and returned to Italy without laying a finger on the Greek cities.

For several years Rome persisted in this policy of tolerance and respect, quite similar to that followed by the United States in Europe after World War II. She intervened in Greek internal affairs only when invited to do so, and then tried to support constituted authority. As a result she was unpopular with all the malcontents, who accused her of being reactionary. Perseus of Macedonia, who had succeeded Philip in 179 B.C., tried to profit from this state of affairs by calling on the masses for a holy war against the city. He had married the daughter of Seleucus, the successor of Antiochus, now his ally, and he also dragged in Illyria and the Epirus, practically the only other states to lend him help. A third Roman army under Aemilius Paulus, the son of the consul killed at Cannae, now arrived on the scene, and routed Perseus at Pydna in 171 B.C. Perseus was transported in chains to Rome to adorn the chariot of the victorious general.

Among other things, the secret files of the beaten enemy fell into the hands of Aemilius. They contained all the documents relating to the plot, with complete proof of the guilt of the various parties concerned. As a punishment seventy Macedonian towns were razed to the ground and Illyria and the Epirus devastated. Rhodes, which had conspired without taking an active part in the war, was deprived of her possessions in Asia Minor, and a thousand Greek sympathizers of Perseus, including Polybius, were taken to Rome as hostages.

This indicates that by this time Rome had abandoned the illusions of Flamininus and the other Greek-lovers, including the Scipios themselves, and had overcome her sense of inferiority towards Greece. She was now returning to her good old-fashioned methods of dealing with the conquered. Even now the turbulent Greeks did not realize what they were up against. Within a few years new proletarian classes who did not differentiate between socialism and nationalism came to power. The Achaean League was resuscitated and, when it learned that Rome was engaged in a third war with Carthage, it raised the banner of freedom all over Greece.

By now Rome was quite capable of fighting a war on two fronts, and while Scipio Aemilianus was embarking for Africa, the consul Mummius swooped down on Corinth, one of the more troublesome cities. He besieged and took it, killed all its menfolk, enslaved all its women, and having taken on board all the movable property he could lay hands on, burned it to the ground. Greece and Macedonia were then, with the exception of Athens and Sparta, united into a single province under a Roman governor. Athens and Sparta were granted a limited degree of autonomy.

Greece had at last found peace—the peace of a cemetery.

The third and last Punic War, so desired by Cato the Censor, was set in motion by Masinissa. Neither of them was destined to see the end of it.

Masinissa was one of the strangest personages of antiquity. He lived to be ninety, had his last son at eighty-six, and at eighty-eight still galloped at the head of his troops. After Zama he had got back the throne of Numidia, and since Carthage had given Rome a pledge not to go to war again, he never tired of tormenting her with his inroads and pillaging. Carthage protested to Rome, who paid no attention. But when she had paid up the last of her fifty annual indemnities for reparations, she decided to stand no more from Masinissa and attacked him.

At this time Cato's party had the upper hand in Rome, and he always finished speeches, no matter what they were about, with the refrain: "As for the rest, I think that Carthage ought to be destroyed."

Following his suggestion, the senate found a golden opportunity in the Masinissa incident. Not only did they forbid the Carthaginians to take any initiative, but demanded three hundred babies of noble birth as hostages. The babies were handed over amid the wails of their mothers, some of whom swam out to sea after the departing ships and were drowned. Seeing that the provocation had not worked, the Romans demanded the surrender of all arms, the entire fleet, and a large part of the harvest. When these demands were also complied with, the senate insisted that the whole population should withdraw ten miles from the city, which was to be razed to the ground. The Carthaginian ambassadors vainly objected that never in all history had such an atrocity been perpetrated, and threw themselves on the ground, tearing their hair and offering their own lives in exchange.

But Rome wanted war and war she was determined to have at all costs.

When this news reached Carthage, the infuriated mob lynched those responsible for handing over the babies, as well as the ambassadors, the ministers and all of the Italians they could lay hands on. Then, mad with rage and hatred, they called everybody to arms, including the slaves, and turned every house into a fortress. In two months of feverish activity they mustered 8,000 shields, 18,000 swords, 30,000 spears, and 120 ships.

The siege, by land and sea, lasted three years. Scipio Aemilianus, the adopted son of the son of the victor of Zama, won doubtful glory by finally taking the city. For another six days fighting continued, street by street and house by house. Sniped at by sharpshooters from the roofs and windows, Scipio destroyed all the buildings.

Those who in the end surrendered were only 55,000 out of the 500,000 inhabitants of Carthage. All the rest were dead. Their general, just for a change another Hasdrubal, implored and was granted mercy by Scipio. His wife, out of shame, hurled herself and her children into the flames of a burning building.

Scipio asked the senate's permission to put an end to this slaughter; their only answer was that not only Carthage but all its dependencies must be destroyed. The city burned for seventeen days. Its few survivors were sold as slaves and from then on its territory became a province under the generic name of Africa. There was no peace treaty for the simple reason that there was nobody left to sign one. The Carthaginian ambassadors were right: never had history seen such an atrocity.

Fortunately for Cato and Masinissa, they were spared remorse. They were already dead and buried.

XVII

Cato

IN 195 B.C., JUST AFTER THE SECOND PUNIC WAR, THE WOMEN OF Rome formed a procession and marched on the Forum to ask parliament to repeal the Oppian law, which had been passed during the austerity period of Hannibal's imminent threat to Rome, and which prohibited to the fair sex gold ornaments, colored garments, and the use of carriages.

For the first time in the history of the city, women took the lead in something. For the first time they took a political initiative or, in other words, stood up for their own rights. For five-and-a-half centuries, from the day of its foundation, the history of Rome had been a history of men, with women, an anonymous mass, acting merely as chorus. Those few whose names we know, Tarpeia, Lucretia, Virginia, probably never existed. They do not represent credible characters, but monuments to treachery or virtue. Roman public life was exclusively male. Women only counted in private life, in the home and family circle, where their influence was strictly confined to their functions as mothers, wives, daughters, or sisters of their menfolk.

In the senate, Marcus Porcius Cato, in his capacity as censor, entrusted with the surveillance of customs, opposed this female demand, and his speech, handed down to us by Livy, illuminates the changes that had taken place in the family and social life of the city.

"Gentlemen, if every one of us had maintained his authority and rights as a husband in his own home, we should never have reached this point. Now look at us. Female arrogance, having robbed us of our freedom of action in our families, is now destroying it in the Forum as well. Remember what a hard time we

had of it to keep our women in order and to restrain their licen-
tiousness, even when the laws permitted us to do so. Just imagine
what will happen from now on, if these laws are repealed and
women are legally put on an equal footing with ourselves. You
know what women are: make them your equals and in no time
you will find them lording it over you. In the end it will come to
this: the men of the whole world, who all over the world make
their women obey, will be ruled by the only men in the world
who are ruled by their women: the Romans."

Demonstrators drowned the orator in gales of derisive
laughter, but like all those who speak the truth, he was accustomed to that. The Oppian law was repealed and Cato uselessly
tried to get his own back by increasing tenfold the taxes on
luxury goods. When the wind begins to blow from a certain
direction, no censor has an earthly chance of stopping it. The
suffragettes, once they had taken the initiative, had no intention
of letting it slip from their grasp. Gradually they obtained the
right to administer their own dowries, which made them financially free and independent, or, to use today's expression, to
lead their own lives. Then followed the right of divorcing their
husbands, and if this proved impossible, they poisoned them.
Birth control became a more and more common practice.

Contrary to general belief, the man who was trying to put
a stop to these new fashions, all of Greek origin, was not in
the least an intolerable moralist with an acid tongue and liver
trouble. Quite the contrary. Marcus Porcius Cato was a plebeian
peasant from near Rieti, bursting with health and good humor,
who lived to the age of eighty-five (an almost legendary age
for those days). He died after achieving all his ambitions, including one particularly dear to his heart: that of making many
enemies.

Pure chance made him an outstanding political figure and
perhaps the most interesting personality of his period. He was
living in stoic simplicity on his tiny farm which he cultivated
with his own hands, when an old retired senator, Valerius
Flaccus, disgusted with the corruption of Rome, came to live
nearby. Valerius was an old-fashioned patrician of the type that
hated sophistication, and he took an instant liking to this horny-
handed young man, with his rough clothing, red hair, and miss-
ing teeth, who used to read the classics in secret as if they were
some unmentionable vice, but who had learned from them to

write and speak in a clear-cut and unadorned style. Owing to their common tastes and ideas they became friends, and Valerius encouraged Marcus (who was called Porcius because his family had always bred pigs and Cato because all his ancestors had been cunning) to become a lawyer. This was the profession leading into public life and perhaps the senator launched him on it with this very object in view, hoping to leave a successor to combat the modernistic trend, which old age prevented him from doing in person.

Cato tried his hand and won a dozen cases, one after the other, before the local courts. Then, with an assured clientele, he set up a law office in Rome, stood as a candidate in the elections, and set off on the so-called "course of honors" with the alacrity of a Hannibal. Aedile at thirty in 199 B.C., praetor in 198, three years later he was consul. Then he began again. Tribune in 191, censor in 184, he held one office after another until a ripe old age, particularly in wartime, when he changed his civil for military rank. He was more at home in camp than in the Forum because in camp he could invoke discipline (which he considered the foremost virtue) with more propriety. As a general he appears to have been a stickler, but his soldiers forgave him because he always marched on foot with them, fought with cool courage and allowed everyone a pound of silver out of the booty, which he then turned over to the senate intact, not keeping an ounce for himself.

This was a rule which the Roman generals had nearly always observed up until the Punic Wars, yet later on it had become an exception. When the takings were abundant, the government used to wink at the part the victor pocketed. Quintus Minucius had brought back 35,000 pounds of silver and 35,000 *denarii* from Spain; Manlius Vulso 4,500 pounds of gold from Asia; 400,000 *sestertii*, something well in excess of $280 million, had been extorted from Antiochus and Perseus. It was only natural that the honesty of the Roman generals and magistrates who had always been poor, thrifty, and miserly should succumb to this downpour of gold, and Cato's battle to prevent it was doomed to failure. Nonetheless he fought it.

In 187 B.C., when he was tribune, he asked Scipio Africanus and his brother Lucius, who had returned victorious from Asia, to account for the sums paid out by Antiochus in war reparations. It was a perfectly legitimate request but it came as a surprise to Rome since it raised doubts as to the impeccability of the hero of Zama, who was really above suspicion. It is not clear what led Cato to take this step. He must have been well aware of the African's integrity and immense popularity. Perhaps he simply wished to reestablish the principle, which was falling into disuse, that Roman generals, whatever their names or merits, should render their accounts; or was there perhaps at the bottom of it a violent dislike for the Scipio clan, who were aesthetes, Hellenists, and moderns?

Perhaps it was for both reasons. In any case, the request set the oligarchy of ruling families, who practically held the monopoly of power in the aristocratic circles of the senate, against Cato. Until Sulla's times the history of Rome is practically that of a few dynasties; the same names are continually cropping up. Of the last 200 consuls of the republic, half had come from only ten families and the other from sixteen. Of all these the Scipios were the most distinguished, from the one who had fallen on the Trebia to the one who had triumphed at Zama and whose adopted son was later to destroy Carthage.

The African, in spite of his injured pride, was prepared to respond, but was prevented from doing so by his brother Lucius. He took from his briefcase the documents showing his receipts and expenditure and tore them up in front of the senate. For this gesture he was brought before the assembly and sentenced for fraud, but he escaped punishment owing to the veto of one of the tribunes, a certain Tiberius Sempronius Gracchus, of whom we shall hear more presently. In confirmation of what we have said above about government by dynasties, this tribune happened to be a relation of the accused, having married his daughter Cornelia. The hero of Zama, summoned before the assembly for judgment, interrupted the debate by inviting its members to the temple of Jove to celebrate the anniversary of his great victory, which chanced to fall on that same day. The members accepted, but when they returned to parliament and summoned the general again he refused to appear, and embittered by their insistence, retired to his villa at Liternus where he remained until his death. His persecutors finally left him in peace, but Cato justly deplored the fact that for the first time in the history of Rome the military merits of a defendant had frustrated justice, and denounced in this episode the first symptoms of that individualism and hero worship which would shortly corrupt society and destroy democracy.

It may be asked how, with such powerful adversaries as women and the "mafia" of aristocratic families, this implacable troublemaker still managed to remain in power and to get himself elected every time he stood for office. Few people liked him, but his honesty in those corrupt times and his asceticism in that effete age had the same effect on everybody as remorse. He was what all of them should have been, would have liked to have been, but unfortunately were not. That was why they respected and voted for him even though they detested him. Furthermore, he was a great orator. This is odd, since he had started his literary career by publishing a treatise against orators, anticipating Verlaine's famous phrase: "When you meet oratory, wring its neck." Nevertheless, by dint of telling others how not to speak, he had learned to speak well himself. What little remains of his speeches is enough for us to recognize him as being greater than Cicero, who was certainly more rounded, dignified, and high-sounding, but less direct, effective, and sincere. All of which proves that there is no eloquence, literature, music, painting, or anything else without moral strength and firm conviction to sustain it.

Cato salted even his most severe tirades with humor. When for example, as censor, he had Manilius expelled from the senate for kissing his wife in public and was asked whether he himself had never done the same thing, he replied: "Yes, but only when it is thundering. That is why bad weather always puts me in a good temper." Even when they brought him to trial (and it appears that they tried to do that forty-four times under one pretext or another), he never lost his good humor and laughed just as often as he snapped back. It could not have been much fun to have to face him in cross-examination, with his ready sarcasm, his bitter gibes, his battle-scarred face, red hair, and uneven teeth. Nobody would ever have overthrown him if, at a certain moment, he himself had not wearied of the useless struggle and retired of his own free will to write books, an occupation which he secretly despised. He did so because he wanted to pit Latin texts against those which all the other literary men were composing in Greek, a language which threatened to gain the monopoly of Roman culture.

De Agricultura is in fact his only surviving text, and is the first book in real Latin prose to have been published in Rome. It is a curious practical manual in which advice on methods of curing rheumatism and diarrhea is mixed up with vaguely philosophic theories. As for his views on various methods of farming, here they are: "The best," he says, "is profitable cattle raising. And then? Moderately profitable cattle raising. And then? And then plowing and sowing." Cato did not wish to return to agriculture but to grazing.

No one had a stronger presentiment of the decadence of Rome than he, or diagnosed more accurately the root of the infection: Greece. He had studied the language and, educated and alert as he was under his coarse clothing, he realized that Hellenic culture was so superior to Roman culture and so much more refined that it was bound to corrupt it. He called Socrates "a gossipy old maid" and approved of the judges who had sentenced him to death as a corrupter of the laws and traditions of Athens. "Mark my words," he wrote to his son, "if those people manage to contaminate us with their culture, we are lost. In any case, they have already started with their doctors who, with the excuse of healing us, have come here to destroy the 'barbarians.' I forbid you to have anything to do with them." He would rather have seen him dead than cured by Greek medicines.

It is most probable that this phobia led to his insistence on *delenda est Carthago* for which he has remained famous. More than preventing the revival of the Phoenician city, he was aiming at distracting Rome from the temptation of conquering Greece. He wanted his country to look westward, not to the east, from which only vice and disaster could come. Perhaps he was very disappointed at the rapidity with which Scipio concluded the task. He would have preferred a defensive war against ten Hannibals to an offensive one against Hellas. When he saw the consuls Marcellus, Fulvius, and Aemilius Paulus come back from Greece with their wagons laden with statues, paintings, metal cups, priceless furniture, and embroidered materials, and the people rushing to see these marvels eagerly and discussing fashions, styles, hats, sandals, silverware, and cosmetics, he must have torn his hair.

He died in 149 B.C. when the senate had already decided to send the last Scipio *ad delendam Carthaginem*. Perhaps this decision gave him a last ray of hope, or at least we like to think so. Had he lived a little longer, he would have seen that the destruction of Carthage was completely useless. In fact, once that city had disappeared from the face of Africa and the Mediterranean, the Romans had no eyes, ears, and thoughts but for Phidias, Praxiteles, Aristotle, Plato, refined cookery, makeup, and the intellectual ladies of Athens.

XVIII

". . . ferum victorem cepit"

HORACE, MUCH LATER, CONFIRMED THOSE FEARS WHICH CATO HAD expressed, with a verse: *Graecia capta ferum victorem cepit*— "Captive Greece her captor captive made." To accomplish this she used several weapons: religion and the theater for the plebs, philosophy and art for the upper classes, who were not yet educated, but unfortunately would become so later.

To Polybius, when he was taken to Rome as a prisoner, religion still seemed to be deep-rooted. "The characteristic," he wrote, "for which, in my opinion, the Roman Empire is superior to all others lies in its religion. What in other nations would be considered deplorable superstition here in Rome is the very cornerstone of the state. Everything connected with it is adorned with pomp, and it so conditions public and private life that nothing can compete with it. I think the government must have created it especially for the masses. It would not be necessary if the people were made up exclusively of enlightened persons, but for the multitude, always stupid and prone to blind passions, it is just as well that there should be fear to keep them in check."

It is understandable that to such a man, fresh from Greece, where skepticism was boundless, the Romans who still retained a glimmer of faith must have seemed like so many monks. But it was only a glimmer, though certain liturgical forms ("pomp," Polybius calls them) were still respected from force of habit. Even Cato, though he endeavored to preserve all the old customs and beliefs, wondered in a public speech how the augurs, who all knew each others' little tricks, managed to keep a straight face when they met in the street. On the stage, Plautus was able with impunity to ridicule Jove in the role of the seducer of Alcmena and to present Mercury as a clown.

Yet the public, who applauded these irreverent comedies, had years before, at the news of the disaster of Cannae, rushed to the Forum crying: "To which god must we pray for Rome to be saved?" Evidently the Romans only remembered in moments of danger that they had gods, yet of the many with which their paradise swarmed did not know the right one for the job. The government's answer was also odd. They decided to entrust the safety of the city not to a Roman god, as had always been the case up till then, but to a Greek goddess, Cybele. Her statue was to be brought to Rome from its home in Pessinus, Asia Minor. Attalus, king of Pergamon, agreed to the removal. Thus Magna Mater, as the goddess was re-christened, arrived one fine day at Ostia where Scipio Africanus was waiting to receive her at the head of a party of noble matrons. The rumor went around Rome that the ship, which had run aground at the mouth of the Tiber, had been refloated and steered upstream into the heart of the city by the vestal Virginia Claudia's sheer force of chastity. Whether or not they believed this, everybody burned incense as the goddess passed on her way to the temple of Victory escorted by the procession of matrons. The senate was rather shocked and perplexed when it found out that the Great Mother had to be ministered to by self-castrated priests. None were available in the religious colleges of Rome. Eventually some were rounded up from among the prisoners of war and ordained for the purpose.

From this moment, Greek ceremonial spread, and was applied not only to overseas gods but also to the Roman ones. As a result, the ceremonial, instead of being austere and gloomy, as it had been up to now, became lighthearted and orgiastic. In 186 B.C. the senate was astonished and alarmed to discover that the masses were particularly devoted to Dionysus, and had made him their favorite deity, flocking to his temple and enthusiastically offering sacrifices to him. The reason is understandable. These sacrifices consisted of gigantic banquets, copious libations, and considerable laxity in the relations between men and women. They were, in fact, anything but sacrifices. The police raided these junketings, rounded up and arrested 7,000 participants, condemned a few hundred to death, the rest to prison, and suppressed the cult. But when the police have to be called in to protect the morals of the people it means that they are already beyond protection.

Indeed, one could see this quite well in the theater, which was fast becoming the real temple of Rome.

The first theatrical experiment had been that of Livy Andronicus, the Tarentine-Greek prisoner of war. In 240 B.C. he had written, acted, and sung the *Odyssey* in crude verse. As we have said, the public and government were so delighted by this show that they had allowed the actors to form a corporation, and to organize the so-called *ludi scenici* on the occasion of the great annual feasts.

Five years after that historic occasion, another prisoner of war, a Neapolitan this time, Cnaeus Naevius, produced another play. It ridiculed the abuses and hypocrisy of Roman society with the briskness of an Aristophanes. The people were highly amused but the influential families took offense and protested. They were too crude and obtuse to appreciate satire, which is at home only among really civilized peoples. Poor Naevius was arrested and had to retract. He wrote another comedy, certainly with the intention of never again offending anybody, but as he was a very witty man, this was beyond him. Again his pen let slip a few more barbs, for which he paid by being deported. In this way Rome lost a playwright who might have founded an original theater, not a banal imitation of foreign models, and a humorist who might have taught these dreary, pedantic people the art of recognizing, laughing at and even remedying their own defects. Naevius, continuing to write in exile, left a very poor dramatic poem on Roman history which is patriotic to the point of being silly.

From then on the Roman theater merely aped the Greek until a third foreigner came along to give it a touch of originality. Quintus Ennius was an Apulian with an Italian father and a Greek mother. He had studied at Tarentum, where he had seen and fervently admired the dramas of Euripides. Then he had gone to do his military service. His courage in Sardinia had attracted the attention of Cato, who was there as quaestor and who brought him back to Rome. His *Annals*, an epic story of Rome from Aeneas to Pyrrhus, was, until Virgil appeared, the national poem of the city. But his first love was the theater, for which he wrote about thirty tragedies in which his principal butt was the zealotry of bigots. Here in the words of one of his leading characters are his religious convictions: "I assure you, my friends, that the gods do exist, but they don't care in the least what we mortals do. How, otherwise, can one explain that good is not always rewarded by good and evil by evil?" Cicero, who reports this speech that already showed the influence of the theories of Epicurus, assures us that the applause was loud and long. Ennius advised his followers to put a little but not too much philosophy into their plays. Unfortunately, he was the first to ignore this wise maxim. He insisted on writing such highbrow drama that the public turned their backs on him and flocked to the farces of Plautus, the first real Roman playwright.

He arrived from Umbria in 254 B.C. and even his name made people laugh; Titus Maccius Plautus meant Titus the flat-footed clown. He began his theatrical career as an extra, saved a little money, invested it in an unlucky speculation, and lost the lot. Then, in order to eat, he started to write. At first he adapted Greek comedies, putting in topical gags about current Roman events. When he saw that the public laughed at these more than at anything else, he abandoned his foreign models and began to write originals, using as plots day to day happenings of the city and inaugurating a truly contemporary theater of manners. Plautus soon became the idol of the public, who loved his cheerful good humor and loud Rabelaisian laughter. His *Miles Gloriosus* had his audiences rolling in the aisles. Everybody liked him and they even stood for his *Amphitryon*, which contained an irreverent satire on Jove, presented as a vulgar Don Juan who, in order to seduce Alcmena, passes himself off as her husband, invoking and offering sacrifices to himself.

In 184 B.C., the year Plautus died, Terence, a Carthaginian slave, arrived in Rome. Terence had the luck to hit on the house of P. Terentius Lucanus, an educated and affable senator, who discovered the talent of his servant, and freed him. Terence, originally called Publius Afer, adopted his name out of gratitude. When he had written his first play, *Andria,* he read it to Caecilius Statius, a well-established and highly successful author of the day whose works have all perished. Suetonius says that Statius was so impressed that he invited his visitor to lunch, although he was dressed like a tramp. Despite the fact that he frequented society salons and became fashionable among the upper classes, Terence never achieved the general popularity of Plautus. His second play, *Hecyra*, failed. The audience walked out in a body when they heard that a duel between a gladiator and a bear was about to begin at the Circus. However, Terence had a success with *The Eunuch*, which earned him 8,000 sesterces, about $6,400, for two performances on the same day. In Rome it was murmured that the real author of these works was Laelius, the brother of Scipio, and a great friend and patron of Terence. The latter, with great tact, never either confirmed or denied this gossip, and perhaps to get away from it, decided to go to Greece. He never returned. On his way back he died of an illness in Arcady.

The intellectual and sophisticated circles of the time had the same devotion for Terence that their French counterparts of today had for Gide. Cicero defines him as "the most exquisite poet of the republic." Caesar, who knew his literature, and was more forthright, considered him a perfect stylist but a *Menander dimidiatus*, a half-baked Menander, on the stage. True, his plays never lapse into the vulgarities of Plautus. Their characters are more complex, more subtle, their dialogue more meditated and richer in double meanings. Unfortunately they were all written in a language which was no longer "of the people," and so the people sensed its artificiality. And they booed.

More and more people now attended the theater, particularly since admission was free. The premises were rudimentary, erected only for feasts and dismantled afterward. They consisted of a wooden structure, which supported the stage, in front of which there was a circular "orchestra" for the ballets which accompanied the show. Some of the spectators stood, others lay on the ground, and others sat on benches which they had brought from home. Only in 145 B.C. was a permanent theater built. This was also of wood, without a roof, but with fixed seats arranged in a circle which in the Greek style completely surrounded the stage. Anybody could go there, even slaves who, however, were not allowed to sit, and women, who were relegated to the back rows.

The prologue, recited by an actor before the curtain went up, included recommendations to mothers to blow their children's noses before the show began, or to take home those who sniveled. They must have been noisy undisciplined audiences, frequently interrupting the performance with ribald comment and salacious remarks. Often they did not notice when the show was over, which in fact always ended with a *nunc plaudite omnes*—an invitation to applaud.

The actors were generally Greek slaves, except for the star, who could be a Roman citizen. But the latter lost his political rights on taking up this career, just as in France until the seventeenth century. Men also played the women's parts. As long as the public was limited in number, they made do with a sketchy makeup, but when in the last century before Christ houses were filled to capacity, they introduced the use of masks to distinguish the characters. These were called *personae* from the Etruscan *phersu*. Thus *dramatis personae* literally means "masks of the drama." The players in a tragedy wore *cothurni*, which were short boots, and in a comedy the *soccus* or shoe without heels.

As today, there was unceasing conflict between what the public wanted and a censorship which kept productions under rigid surveillance. It was for violation of one of the laws of the Twelve Tables, which banned political satire and even authorized the death penalty for it, that poor Naevius had been banished. To avoid the same fate, his successors borrowed everything from Greece: scenes, characters, situations, costumes, and even the names of coins. The reasons for this censorship were, as usual, bureaucratic and stupid. They did not mind a certain amount of obscenity, provided there was no hint of criticism of the government or of prominent citizens.

Fortunately the aediles, who staged these shows for the entertainment of the public and who were also after their votes, were always on the side of the authors. Plautus must have had some very powerful bigwigs to let him get away with what he did. It is thanks to him that the Roman theater ever existed except as a translation from the Greek. Without it we should have been deprived of that mirror of society which for better or worse has been bequeathed to us.

This general relaxation was made possible because of the now-prevailing atmosphere of free thinking. It had been imported by the "Greeklings," as the Romans called them, with a scorn that did not prevent those same Romans from taking them on as teachers. Prisoners of war, brought over as hostages and slaves, were the first grammarians, orators, and philosophers to open schools in Rome. In 172 B.C. the senate discovered among them two disciples of Epicurus. These were banished. A few years later Crates of Mallos, director of the State Library of Pergamon and chief exponent of the Stoic school, came to Rome as an ambassador and broke his leg. While waiting for it to heal he gave lectures.

In 155 B.C. Athens sent three philosophers (all she had left by now) on a diplomatic mission: Carneades, a disciple of Plato, Critolaus the Aristotelian, and Diogenes the Stoic. These three also gave lectures. When Cato heard Carneades assert that the gods did not exist and that justice and injustice were merely a matter of convention, he rushed to the senate and demanded that the three Athenians be repatriated.

He had his way. It was little use though, since Greek culture was being fostered by many of the Romans themselves, and the most influential of them were already steeped in it. Flamininus had at his home a gallery of sculpture by Polycletes, Phidias, Scopas, and Praxiteles. Aemilius Paulus had helped himself to the library of Perseus, and had brought his children up on it. When he died, the youngest of these children was adopted by Cornelius Scipio, the son of the African. The boy took over the name and, as Publius Cornelius Scipio Aemilianus, emulated his grandfather by destroying Carthage, and became head of this powerful clan which he converted to Hellenism. With his good looks, wealth, pleasant manner, keen intelligence, and incorruptible honesty (he only left thirty-three pounds of silver and two of gold when he died), he had everything necessary to make him a favorite in the aristocratic salons now springing up everywhere. Polybius lived for years as a guest in his house. A daily caller was Panaetius, another aristocratic Greek from Rhodes, and of the Stoic school. His book *On Duty*, which Scipio probably suggested and inspired, was a bible for the gilded youth of Rome. Unlike the ancient stoics, the modern ones did not preach absolute virtue, nor did they insist on complete indifference to fortune or misfortune. They were only propounding a substitute, full of decent compromise, for a faith which could no longer sustain the Roman way of life. Indulgence was taking the place of the severe puritanism of earlier days.

Scipio's drawing room exerted an enormous influence. Apart from Flamininus, Caius Lucilius and Caius Laelius were outstanding. Their friendship with the master of the house inspired Cicero's book, *De amicitia*. Lofty ideas were exchanged.

Beauty was acclaimed. Refined manners, original and precious ideas and, above all, pure, polished, accentless speech were *de rigueur:* this speech, thanks to Catullus, a habitué of these circles, became that of literary and cultured Rome. But when uttered by Terence's characters it was jeered at by the public as artificial and too remote from its own.

XIX

The Gracchi

IT WAS IN ONE OF THESE SALONS THAT THE SEEDS OF REVOLUTION were sown. Contrary to general belief, revolutions never originate among the proletariat that provides the manpower for them, but among the aristocratic or bourgeois classes, which are then consumed by them. Revolutions are always more or less a form of suicide, since a class is only eliminated when it has already eliminated itself.

Cornelia, daughter of Scipio Africanus, had married Tiberius Sempronius Gracchus, the tribune who had vetoed the sentence on Lucius, the brother of the hero of Zama. Since his intervention had saved his wife's uncle it was an example of nepotism in reverse. However, notwithstanding this pardonable lapse, he continued to enjoy a well-deserved reputation for integrity. Elected censor and then twice as a consul, he had governed Spain in a liberal and enlightened manner. Cornelia had given him twelve children of whom nine died young. On his death, Cornelia was left with only two boys, Tiberius and Caius, and a girl, Cornelia, who was either born deformed or became so through infantile paralysis.

Cornelia the mother was an exemplary widow and a great educator. She must also have been good-looking since, according to Plutarch, an Egyptian king asked her to marry him. She replied haughtily that she preferred to remain the daughter of one Scipio, the mother-in-law of another, and the mother of the Gracchi. At that time the second Cornelia had already married the destroyer of Carthage. It was not, it appears, a love-match but a marriage of convenience, as was usual in that society composed of families and dynasties, constantly reinforcing their alliances.

Cornelia was also something that up to then had never been seen in Rome, a great intellectual and a charming hostess. Her drawing room, where the greatest names in politics, art, and philosophy used to foregather, anticipated those of certain French ladies of the eighteenth century; indeed its functions were more or less the same. The leading lights, partly for family reasons, were the so-called Scipio set, with Laelius, Flamininus, Polybius, Caius Lucilius, Mucius Scaevola, and Metellus Macedonicus. As regards birth, intelligence, and experience, it was the best Rome could offer. But what a difference there was between these new leaders and their fathers and grandfathers! To begin with, these moderns accepted the inspiration of a woman. Further, they had a bath every day, were fastidious in dress, and not in the least convinced that Rome should give lessons to the world. On the contrary, they believed that Rome should take lessons from Greece.

Conversation in this salon was not revolutionary but "progressive." It must have been similar to that of today's left-wing liberals or radicals. Since they were all highly placed personages, they knew what they were talking about, and what they said was re-echoed in senate and government circles.

The situation of Rome, far from being bright, called forth wide criticism and the darkest forebodings. The city was having trouble in digesting the immense empire which she had so rapidly devoured. The grain of Sicily, Sardinia, Spain, and Africa, because of free slave labor, was glutting the market at a very low price and bringing economic ruin on the rural Italy of the small landowners. Those small and medium landowners, who had been the most effective bulwark against Hannibal and had made the best soldiers in the war against him, were unable to face the competition. They were selling their modest farms, which were being absorbed by the big estates. A law of 220 B.C., which forbade the senators to engage in commerce, obliged them to invest the capital they had accumulated from the spoils of war in agriculture. Further, much of the land requisitioned from the enemy had been ceded to speculators in return for the money they had lent the state. Neither these speculators nor the senators were any longer country gentlemen. Accustomed to living in town, with its comforts and ease, politics and business, they had no intention of abandoning it and returning to the simple frugal life of their stoic ancestors. Thus they did what certain barons of southern Italy do today. They acquired an estate, turned it over to an agent, who drove the laborers and over-exploited the resources of the soil with no thought for the future, in order to make it yield as much as possible for the owner and himself.

Another social and moral crisis arose from the economic one: this society, which had been founded on its small, free farmers, now relied more and more on loot from abroad and slavery at home. A torrent of slaves kept pouring into Rome. In 177 B.C. 40,000 Sardinians were imported in a single batch, ten years later 150,000 Epirots. "Wholesalers" in this human commodity used to follow the legions who captured them, so as to lay in their supplies. With the downfall of the Greek and Macedonian empires, these dealers had by now reached Asia, the Danube, and the frontiers of Russia. Slaves were so plentiful that transactions in 10,000 at a time were normal on the intercontinental market of Delos. The price fell to eighty cents a head.

In the towns it was the slaves who provided the labor for the artisans' shops, the offices, banks, and factories, thus throwing those citizens who had previously done the work into unemployment and indigence. Their relations with the contractors varied with the temperament of the latter. Although they were not bound to show any special regard for slaves, some tried to treat them humanely. A limit was put to these humanitarian considerations by the economic law of competitive prices. The trend was to demand more of them and make fewer concessions.

In the country the plight of slaves was even more in contrast to the time when they had been a rarity, had been taken into the family, and often finished up by becoming part of it, rather like poor relations. The modest size of the property and the shortage of hands had made relations with the owner direct and human. Now, on the big estates, where slaves were employed in droves, the owner never appeared and in his place was an overseer chosen from the dregs of the population, who made drastic economies on the food and clothing, which was the only salary due these poor wretches. If they disobeyed or complained, they were put in chains and thrown into underground cells.

In 196 B.C. slaves revolted in Etruria. The legions killed them all; many were crucified. Ten years later another revolt broke out in Apulia: the few who survived the repression were imprisoned in a mine. In 135 B.C. a full-scale servile war broke out in Sicily under the leadership of Eunus, who massacred the population of Enna, occupied Agrigentum and in a short time, with an army of 70,000 mutinous slaves, made himself master of almost the whole island, defeating a Roman army in the process. It took six years to put an end to it. Punishment was of course on a proportionate scale.

In the year 133 B.C. Tiberius Gracchus, the son of Sempronius and Cornelia, was elected tribune. He had grown up in his mother's salon with radical ideas drummed into his head by his tutor Blossius, a philosopher from Cumae. From adolescence he had thought about nothing but politics. He was what is usually called an idealist, but how far his ideas, which were excellent, served his ambition, which was enormous, and vice versa, not even he himself knew. This after all is the quandary of all idealists. He knew a great deal about the predicament of the country, partly because it was continually and knowledgeably discussed in the salon, and partly from what his brother had told him after going to study it at first hand in Etruria and returning horrified by what he had seen. Tiberius realized that Italy would be ruined if its agriculture fell irretrievably into the hands of speculators and slaves, and that no sound democracy could flourish in Rome if the people were corrupted by continual unemployment and relief handouts.

The only remedy for slavery, city life, and military decadence seemed to him to lie in a bold agrarian reform. So as soon as he was elected, he put his reform proposal before the assembly. It consisted of three proposals: 1) no citizen could possess more than 250 acres, which could be increased to 500 if he had two or more sons; 2) all lands distributed or leased by the state should be returned to it at the same price, with an indemnity for any improvements carried out; 3) these lands should be divided up and redistributed to poor citizens in lots of about twelve or fifteen acres each, with the obligation not to sell them and to pay a modest tax on them.

These were reasonable proposals and fully consistent with the Licinian laws, which had been passed more than two centuries previously. Tiberius, however, made the mistake of presenting them in a demagogic and rabble-rousing speech quite out of keeping with his social position. "Our generals," he said speaking from the rostrum, "encourage you to fight for the temples and the tombs of your ancestors. It is a vain and false appeal. You have no paternal altars. You have no ancestral tombs. You fight and die just to provide luxury and riches for those over you."

It was well delivered because Tiberius was an excellent speaker, but it contained unfortunately subversive elements. The senate declared the proposals illegal, accused their author of aiming at a dictatorship, and persuaded Octavius, the other tribune, to veto the proposals. Tiberius replied with a motion whereby a tribune, when he acted against the will of the assembly, should immediately be deposed. The assembly approved this motion, and Tiberius' lictors forcibly ejected Octavius from his bench. The law was then passed and the assembly, fearing for the life of Tiberius, escorted him to his house.

He was probably not welcomed home that day with the unanimous enthusiasm he may have expected. Perhaps only Cornelia continued to regard him as one of her "jewels," as she had once called him and Caius. The others must have been somewhat shaken, not so much by the laws which he had imposed and which were in complete harmony with the political and social outlook of the salon, but by the unconstitutional methods he had used against Octavius. Scandalized, they withdrew their support when he stood again for the tribuneship in spite of a precise ruling which definitely forbade it.

He was obliged to do this because the senate threatened to put him on trial as soon as his term of office expired. Abandoned by his own family and friends, Tiberius, to curry favor with the plebs, swung even further to the left. He promised if reelected to shorten military service, to abolish the monopoly of the senators in court juries, and, since at that moment Attalus III of Pergamon had just died and left his kingdom to Rome, he proposed selling all its mobile property and using the proceeds to help the peasants to equip their farms. Here he slipped into pure demagogy and presented his opponents with valid arguments against him.

On the day of the elections Tiberius appeared in the Forum with an armed bodyguard and wearing mourning to make it quite clear that if he were not elected he would be condemned to death. While voting was in progress, a group of senators headed by Scipio Nasica burst in with clubs in their hands. The prestige which the senate still held, and which Gracchus had foolishly overlooked, is shown by the fact that the friends of Tiberius respectfully fell back before these patricians and left him standing alone. He was killed by a blow on the nape of the neck, and his body, together with those of some hundreds of his followers, was thrown into the Tiber.

His brother, Caius, was refused permission to recover and bury it.

This took place in 131 B.C. Seven years later, December 10, 124, the second of Cornelia's "jewels" took his brother's place as tribune. We understand him better and rate him higher than his brother, since he seems to have been more of a realist, and more sincere. He also was a magnificent orator: Cicero considered him the greatest (after himself, of course). He had fought bravely under his brother-in-law, Scipio Aemilianus, at Numantia and he had great self-control. In fact he proceeded by degrees, never trying to browbeat or accomplish everything in a hurry.

During these seven years the agrarian laws of Tiberius, which the senate, having killed their author, had not dared to repeal, had produced good results despite the fact that their application had involved many difficulties of a practical nature. The census had registered 80,000 new citizens, who had become, as such, owners of a piece of land, but many protests had been made by the old proprietors. They were adamantly against the dismemberment or confiscation of their lands, and entrusted their cause to Scipio Africanus. It is not very clear why he accepted the defense of interests which were contrary to his own ideas. Perhaps he was induced to support them by those very family reasons which should have led him to abstain. He was on increasingly worse terms with his wife, Cornelia, and one morning in 129 B.C. he was found murdered in his bed. It has never been discovered who killed him. Naturally the gossips of the aristocratic households, where they were detested, put the blame on his wife and mother-in-law.

Having grown up amid so many misfortunes and in a house by now deserted even by its most intimate friends, Caius went ahead cautiously with the application of the laws of Tiberius. He set up new agricultural colonies in southern Italy, he won over the soldiers by decreeing that from now on they would be equipped at state expense, and he fixed the price of grain at a "political price" which was half the market price. By this last

measure, which later became the strongest weapon in the hands
of Marius and Caesar, he won all the masses of the city to his
side.

The following year, on the strength of these successes, he
was again able to stand for the tribuneship without incurring his
brother's fate, and was elected. He now thought he could play
his trump cards, but here he made a mistake. He proposed add-
ing to the 300 senators-by-right another 300 elected by the assembly, and extending citizenship to all the non-slaves of Latium
and to a good proportion of those of the rest of the peninsula.
But he failed to reckon with the boundless indifference of the
Romans to their brethren of Latium or the peninsula. The senate
promptly took steps to exploit its adversary's tactical error. It
egged on Livy Drusus, the other tribune, to make even more
radical proposals: that the tax imposed by the Tiberian law on
new proprietors should be abolished, and that 42,000 landless
Roman citizens should be given new allotments in twelve new
colonies. The assembly immediately approved these projects
and, when Caius went back there, he found that Drusus had
stolen his thunder.

He stood for election a third time but was rejected. His supporters claimed that there had been trickery, but he calmed them
down and retired to private life.

The senate, recognizing that he could be a menace so long
as he lived at all, indicated its readiness to reward anyone who
would kill him. The assembly realized that this would be the first
step towards nullifying the legislation of the Gracchi, and so
their sympathizers attended the next session armed. One of them
hacked a conservative to bits because he had used threats against
Caius. The next day the senators appeared in full battle array,
each of them attended by two slaves. Partisans of the Gracchi
entrenched themselves on the Aventine, and Caius tried to act
as mediator. When he met with no success, he dived into the
Tiber to escape his enemies' assassins. Just as his pursuers were
catching up with him on the opposite bank, he ordered one of his
slaves to kill him. The slave obeyed, and then drawing the blood-
stained dagger from his master's heart, plunged it into his own.
One of the Caius's followers severed his head from his trunk,
filled it with lead and took it to the senate which had offered to
pay for it with its weight in gold. He not only pocketed the reward but was restored to political favor. The mob which had

applauded their hero Caius so loudly did not blink an eye at his
assassination. They were too busy looting their hero's house.
Cornelia, mother of two murdered sons and a widow suspected
of homicide, put on mourning. The senate ordered her to remove it.

XX

Marius

SOME 250 OF HIS FOLLOWERS WERE KILLED WITH CAIUS. ANOTHER
3,000 were arrested. For the moment it looked as if the conservatives had won and a drastic repression was expected. It did not
materialize. The senate set aside the agricultural reforms, but it
did not touch the subsidy on grain or try to renew the monopoly
of the aristocracy in the juries of the law courts. Evidently it
realized, in spite of its temporary victory, that the situation did
not justify radical restorations.

For some years there remained in force a hand-to-mouth
regime which did not try to alter what the Gracchi had started
so prematurely and with so many tactical errors. With the excuse of giving further aid to the small landowners created by
the agrarian laws, they allowed them to sell the lands they had
been assigned. Deprived of government backing, they did so,
and the big estates came back into being on the usual basis of
slave labor. Appianus, a very moderate democrat, admitted that
during those years in all Rome there were not even about 2,000
landowners. All the others were landless and their situation
grew worse from day to day.

The last straw was the so-called African scandal in 110 B.C.
Micipsa, who had succeeded Masinissa on the throne of Numidia, had died six years previously and had left his bastard son
Jugurtha as regent and guardian to his two legitimate heirs, still
minors. Jugurtha killed one and declared war on the other. This
survivor appealed to Rome, as protector of his kingdom, for
help. The city sent out an investigating committee which
Jugurtha bought off with a handsome bribe and which, on its

return to Rome, corrupted the senators who were to examine its findings. It was not until Quintus Metellus, a comparatively honest man, was elected consul, that a general was found disposed to make war on the usurper instead of accepting his bribes.

Though without newspapers in those days, the people knew quite well what was going on both in public and behind the scenes. The hatred they had been nursing for the aristocracy since the murders of the Gracchi flared up violently when they learned that Metellus, one of the better aristocrats, was opposing the election of one of his commanders, Caius Marius, to the consulate just because he was not a patrician. Although he was comparatively unknown, the assembly voted solidly for Marius and gave him command of the legions. The reason was that at the time (as in all times when a democracy is at its last gasp) people were saying: "What we need is a Man. . . ."

And, purely by chance, they found one. Marius was an old-fashioned character of the kind that by now was only to be found in the provinces. Like Cicero, he was born at Arpinum, the son of a poor farmhand. The army, which he had joined very young, had been his university. He had earned promotion, medals, and the scars which seamed his body at the siege of Numantia. On his return he had made a good marriage. He had married Julia, the sister of a certain Caius Julius Caesar, whose family was nothing exceptional, being only small landed gentry. Julia already had a son by a previous marriage, another Caius Julius Caesar, who was to get himself talked about for thousands of years. Thanks to his military prowess, Marius had been elected tribune. He had taken advantage of this not to go in for politics and show his incapacity, but to return to his soldiers with a higher rank, still under the command of Metellus. The latter, bogged down in the war with Jugurtha, was scandalized when he had discovered that his subordinate wanted to go to Rome to stand for the consulate. It was out of place and presumptuous on the part of a poor peasant, even though the consulate was in theory open to the plebs.

Marius, a touchy, vindictive man, was offended, and once elected, claimed the command from Metellus, who was forced to give it up to him. The war immediately began to move at a different pace. In a few months Jugurtha was forced to surrender and adorned the victor's chariot when Marius was given a

superb triumph by the people of Rome, who saw in him their
champion. They did not know that it was not Marius who had
struck the decisive blow against the usurper of Numidia, but a
quaestor of his named Sulla, who had much the same relation
to Marius that Marius had to Metellus.

For the moment, however, Marius was the hero of the city.
Ignoring the provisions of a constitution, by now on its last legs,
Rome confirmed him as consul for six years running. Danger
from outside had not, indeed, ended with Jugurtha. It was
actually more serious than ever because of certain Gauls. They
had returned to the attack. More numerous and aggressive than
before, the Cimbri and the Teutons had reappeared, rolling
down like an avalanche from Germany into France. A Roman
army which had met them in Carinthia had been destroyed.
They had then destroyed a second army on the Rhine, and then
a third, and a fourth. The senate sent a fifth, under the command of two patricians, Servilius Caepio and Mallius Maximus.
Out of jealousy, they did nothing but quarrel between themselves and annul each other's actions. At Arausio (Orange),
80,000 legionaries, the pride of the aristocracy which had produced these inept generals, and 40,000 auxiliaries died on the
field of battle. Rome waited tensely, expecting to be assailed by
these hordes. Fortunately they crossed the Pyrenees instead of
the Alps and began pillaging Spain. When they came back
again, Marius, who had now been consul for four years, was
ready.

He had raised a new type of army, his really great innovation, which was later to give his relative Caesar his military
might. He had realized that it was no longer possible to rely on
citizens declared "fit for military service" just because they belonged to one of the five classes and were, in duty bound, however unwillingly, to serve. Instead, he resorted to the indigent
and unemployed, offering them good pay, plenty of loot, and a
generous portion of land after victory. He was replacing the
national army by a mercenary one; a risky operation, and in the
long run a disastrous one, but made necessary by the decadence
of Roman society.

He led his proletarian recruits with a cadre of veteran non-
coms beyond the Alps, toughened them with forced marches,
gave them battle training in operations against minor objectives,
and finally had them build an entrenched camp near Aix-en-

Provence in a locality through which the Teutons were bound
to pass.

The Teutons were so numerous that they streamed past it
for six days, derisively asking the Roman sentries on the ramparts whether they had any messages for their wives at home.
These Teutons were just the same as they had been three centuries earlier: tall, fair-headed, very strong, extremely courageous, and with absolutely no notion of strategy. Otherwise
they would never have left such a powerful enemy in their rear.
They paid for it dearly. In fact a few hours later, Marius fell on
them from behind and exterminated 100,000 of them. Plutarch
says that the people of Marseilles erected palisades with their
skeletons and that the land that year, fertilized by so many
corpses, yielded an unprecedented harvest.

After this victory, Marius returned to Italy and lay in wait
for the Cimbri near Vercellae, where Hannibal had won his
first victory. Like their Teuton brothers, the Cimbri showed
more courage than brains. Naked in the snow, they advanced
boldly against the Romans, using their shields as sledges to
slide down the icy slopes and howling joyfully as if it were
a sporting event. Here, as at Aix, it was more of a shambles than
a battle.

In Rome, Marius was acclaimed as a "second Camillus" and,
as a token of gratitude, they gave him all the booty captured
from the foe. He thus became enormously rich, the owner of
lands "as vast as a kingdom" and for the sixth time running was
elected consul.

In the game of politics, which he now had to learn to play,
our hero, as is often the case with heroes, showed himself much
less expert than in handling legions. He had made promises to
his men which he now had to keep. And to keep them he was
forced to ally himself with the leaders of the popular party:
Saturninus, the tribune of the plebs, and Glaucia, the praetor.
This pair of scoundrels was adept at every kind of parliamen-
tary skullduggery, and their one aim was to feather their own
nests using the highly popular Marius as a front. The land was
actually distributed in accordance with the laws of the Gracchi,
but, to gain votes for the party, the poiltical price of wheat, already low, was reduced by another nine-tenths. This absurd
measure jeopardized the financial balance of the state. Even the
more moderate of the popular party hesitated. The senate per-

suaded a tribune to veto it but Saturninus, contrary to the constitution, presented the law. Riots began. The candidates for the consulate of 99 B.C. to be elected as the colleagues of Marius were Glaucia, for the popular party, and Caius Memmius, one of the patricians still commanding some respect, for the Conservatives. The latter was murdered by Saturninus' assassins, and the senate, resorting to the emergency measure of the *senatusconsultum ultimum* for the defense of the state, ordered Marius to see that justice was done and order reestablished. Marius hesitated. In fact he had done little else since entering politics. He had aged, grown fat, drank heavily, and now he had to choose between open rebellion and the liquidation of his friends. He took the second course. He ordered Saturninus, Glaucia, and their followers to be stoned to death by the conservatives, whom on that occasion he himself led. Then, realizing that he was unpopular with the patricians because he was an uncertain ally, and with the people because he was a certain traitor, he retired full of rancor and left on a journey to the Orient.

Less than two years had elapsed since the Romans had hailed him in triumph as a "second Camillus." Had he accepted their subsequent ingratitude a little more philosophically, he would have gone down in history with an untarnished name. But being of a primitive nature, governed by his passions, consumed by unfulfilled ambition, and more than ever convinced that he was "the man of the hour," he returned without hesitation when events called him back and played a rather shady role.

In 91 B.C. Marcus Livy Drusus was elected tribune. He was a patrician, son of the man who had opposed Tiberius Gracchus, and father of the girl who was later to marry a certain Octavian, the future Caesar Augustus. He put up three fundamental reforms to the assembly: the distribution of other new lands to the poor, the restoration of the monopoly in the juries to the senate, after the addition of 300 new members to it, and the granting of Roman citizenship to all free Italians. The assembly approved the first two proposals. The third was never discussed, for its author was killed by an unknown assassin.

Immediately the whole peninsula was up in arms. After two centuries of union with Rome, it was still treated as a conquered province. Squeezed dry by taxes and by military levies, it was subject to laws passed by a parliament in which it had no representation. The main task of the Roman prefects in the various capitals of the provinces had been to stir up strife between rich and poor so as to keep them perpetually disunited. Only a few millionaires, by wire-pulling and bribery, had obtained Roman citizenship. Furthermore, in 126 B.C. the assembly had made it illegal for the Italians of the provinces to immigrate to the city, and in 95 B.C. had expelled those who were already there.

Rebellion spread like wildfire, except in Etruria and Umbria, which remained faithful. The others recruited an army, which was stronger in despair than in lances and shields, especially in the case of the slaves who had quickly made common cause with the rebels. The latter proclaimed a federal republic with its capital at Corfinium, and so turned it into a "servile" war as well as a "social" one. In the panic which spread in Rome, where nobody had any illusions as to the vengeance that these outcasts were saving up for their secular oppressors, the myth of Marius, man of the hour, was revived. He improvised an army by his usual method and led it from victory to victory, with no scruples as to the cost in human lives. He devastated and massacred up and down the whole peninsula. When 300,000 men had fallen on both sides, the senate decided to grant citizenship to the Etruscans and the Umbrians as a reward for their fidelity and also to all others who were prepared to lay down their arms and take an oath of loyalty.

The peace which followed was that of a graveyard. It reflects little credit on the man who imposed it. Furthermore, Rome kept her word by incorporating her new citizens into ten new "tribes," who voted *after* the thirty-five Roman ones that composed the *comitiae tributae*. In other words the new citizens had no chance at all to modify a decision. To obtain full democratic rights they had to wait for Caesar, welcoming him with such enthusiasm that they did not realize that he really meant to end all democracy.

A year later the war, no longer servile or social, but civil, broke out again. This time Marius did not confine himself to taking advantage of it; he personally provoked it. But like the popular party earlier, the conservatives now discovered their own man of the hour. He was Marius' former subaltern and quaestor in Numidia—Sulla.

XXI

Sulla

SULLA WAS ELECTED CONSUL IN THE YEAR 88 B.C., IMMEDIATELY after the end of the servile and social revolution which Marius had so bloodily repressed. Sulla's nomination, supported by the conservatives, was unusual and somewhat unconstitutional, as he was a man who had never followed a regular *cursus honorum*.

Lucius Cornelius Sulla came from a family of impoverished minor aristocrats. He had always shown a marked distaste for those two great passions of his contemporaries, a military uniform and a magistrate's toga. In the course of a misspent youth he had been kept by a Greek prostitute older than himself, whom he had abused and mistreated. He had never been interested in politics or serious matters and most likely had never had a regular education. But he was well read, knew Greek and its literature well, and had a refined artistic taste.

His underlying talents, which were enormous, might never have been revealed if he had not been elected quaestor somehow or other, given a captain's rank in the army of Marius in Numidia and directly involved in the undoing of Jugurtha. It was he who persuaded Bocchus, king of Mauretania, to hand over the usurper. This brilliant stroke crowned a series of successes won by the sword. Sulla had shown himself a magnificent commander, cold, cunning, and extremely brave, and his men would follow him anywhere. War interested and amused him because it involved hazard and risk, two things he always liked. He therefore continued to follow Marius in his campaigns against the Teutons and the Cimbri and made a valuable contribution to his victories.

When he returned to Rome in 99 B.C., Sulla could easily have stood for higher office. But for the moment he had had enough, and plunged back for four years into his former life among prostitutes, circus gladiators, starving poets, and penniless actors. One day he suddenly presented himself for election as praetor and was defeated. This so injured his pride, which in him took the place of ambition, that he put himself up for aedile, was elected, and delighted the Romans by offering them the first fights against lions in the amphitheater. Naturally the next year he was praetor and, as such, took command of a division in Cappadocia to reduce its rebelling king to obedience. He returned to Rome victorious with a rich enough booty, but not so rich, evidently, as that which he himself had pocketed. Tired of being in debt, he wished to finance his own electoral campaigns rather than depend on a party. He did not, in fact, belong to any. Being a patrician by birth, but poor, he regarded the aristocracy, who looked down their noses at him, with the same indifference and contempt as he did the plebs, who did not accept him as one of them. He had always lived his own life among outsiders, and his quarrel with Marius was not at all on political grounds but just that he had had Bocchus give him a bas-relief in gold which depicted the king of the Moors handing over Jugurtha to himself instead of Marius.

Sulla stood for the consulate of 88 B.C., not for political reasons but to obtain command of the army. This was being mobilized against Mithridates of Asia Minor, where he had fought against Ariobarzanes of Cappadocia, which was in turmoil as usual. A woman was the deciding factor in Sulla's election. He had, in fact, divorced his third wife, Claelia, after showering gifts on her, in order to marry a fourth: Caecilia Metella, widow of Scaurus and daughter of Metellus the Dalmatian, pontiff and prince, which is to say, president of the senate. It was owing to this connection with one of its most powerful families that the aristocracy began to see Sulla as their champion. They backed his election and gave him the coveted command.

The tribune, Sulpicius Rufus, tried to invalidate his appointment. He proposed to the assembly that it be transferred to Marius, who, although almost seventy, was still out for position, office, and honors. Sulla, not the type to forego anything, rushed off to Nola where the army was fitting out. Instead of embarking it for Asia Minor, he marched back with it to Rome. Here Marius had improvised another army to resist him. Sulla won with ease and rapidity, Marius fled to Africa, and Sulpicius was killed by one of his slaves. Sulla, on the rostrum, held up the severed head and rewarded the murderer for services rendered by granting him his freedom; he then had him killed for his treachery. After this there were very few reprisals. With his

35,000 men encamped in the Forum, Sulla proclaimed that no proposal of law could be put up to the assembly without the prior consent of the senate, and that the future voting in the *comitiae* was to be carried out by *centuriae*, according to the old constitution of Servius. Then, after getting himself confirmed in his military command with the title of proconsul, he allowed two consuls, the patrician Cnaeus Octavius and the plebian Lucius Cornelius Cinna, to be elected to look after home affairs and he himself left on his eastern expedition.

Before he was in sight of the Greek coast, back in Rome Octavius and Cinna had already begun to brawl. Fighting began on the streets, with the conservatives, or *optimates*, on one side and democrats, or *populares*, on the other. The servile and social war of two years before flared up into civil war. Octavius won and Cinna fled. Nevertheless in a single day more than 10,000 corpses were piled up on the paving stones of the city.

Marius hastened back from Africa to join Cinna, who was melodramatically touring the provinces to stir up revolt, his toga in rags, his sandals worn out, his beard long, and his battle-scars carefully displayed. In no time he raised an army of 6,000 men, mainly slaves. With this he marched on the now defenseless capital. It was downright slaughter. Octavius awaited his death sitting calmly on the consul's bench. The heads of the senators, hoisted on pikes, were paraded through the streets. A revolutionary tribunal condemned thousands of patricians to death. Sulla was relieved of his command, his property was confiscated, and all his friends were killed. Caecilia alone was saved because she managed to escape and reach her husband in Greece. Under the new consulship of Marius and Cinna, terror reigned for a year. Vultures and dogs devoured the bodies denied burial and left in the streets. Freed slaves continued to sack, burn, and pillage until Cinna, with a detachment of Gaulish soldiers, surrounded and killed the lot. For the first time in the history of Rome foreign troops were used to reestablish order in the city.

Marius died in the midst of the bloodshed, worn out by alcohol, spite, and unsatisfied ambition. Cinna remained alone, virtually dictator. Valerius Flaccus, who had been elected in the place of Marius, was sent east with 12,000 men to depose Sulla.

Cut off from the homeland, the latter was busy besieging Athens, which had allied itself with Mithridates, who in turn was on his way from Asia with an army five times larger than Sulla's.

The situation was desperate and might have become hopeless if Sulla had allowed himself to be surprised beneath the walls of the city by both Flaccus and Mithridates. Those who knew him well used to say that a fox and a lion slumbered in Sulla, and the fox was much more dangerous than the lion. Thanks to a number of timely miracles, which he managed to arrange for, his soldiers were convinced that he was a god and therefore infallible. He was, in fact, a formidable general who understood his men perfectly and knew with cold precision how to exploit their strength and weaknesses. As he had run out of money, he paid his troops by allowing them to sack Olympia, Epidaurus, and Delphi. But he always restored discipline immediately afterwards. Impregnable Athens was stormed in a surprise attack and Sulla's soldiers were rewarded by being given a free hand. "Nobody knows how many people they killed," says Plutarch, "but in the streets blood flowed in rivers and flooded the suburbs."

After days and days of massacre, Sulla, who, in spite of his love for Greece and her culture and art, had looked on with complete detachment, said that the survivors must be forgiven in the name of the dead. Having reorganized his phalanxes, he led them against the army of Mithridates, who was advancing on Chaeroneia and Orchomenus. Sulla defeated him in a masterly battle and pursued the remnants across the Hellespont into the heart of Asia. He was just preparing to deliver the final blow to the last of the enemy forces when Flaccus arrived with orders to relieve him of his command.

The two generals met. At the end of their conversation Flaccus had not only given up all idea of carrying out his orders but of his own free will had put himself under Sulla's. When Flaccus' second in command, Fimbria, tried to rebel, Sulla offered an advantageous peace to Mithridates. He undertook to respect his kingdom within its old frontiers, and insisted only on reparations consisting of eighty ships and 2,000 talents to pay his men and take them home. He then marched against Fimbria in Lydia, but did not need to beat him, since Sulla had such prestige that as soon as they saw him, Fimbria's troops came over to him. The abandoned Fimbria committed suicide.

Sulla retraced his footsteps without passing up the opportunity of helping himself to treasures and squeezing cash out of all the provinces *en route*. He crossed Greece, embarked his army at Patras, and landed at Brindisi in 83 B.C.; Cinna, who was rushing to halt him, was killed by his own soldiers and a revolution broke out in Rome.

Sulla had brought back magnificent booty for the government, 15,000 pounds of gold and 100,000 of silver. But the government, still in the hands of the popular party, headed by Marius's son, Marius the Younger, proclaimed him a public enemy and sent an army against him. Many patricians escaped from Rome to join him. Of these Cnaeus Pompey, one of the most brilliant of the gilded youth, brought a small personal army composed of friends, clients, and servants of his family.

Marius the Younger was soundly beaten in battle, but before fleeing to Praeneste he sent orders to his followers in Rome to kill all the patricians still left in the city. The praetor summoned the senate, as was his right, and all senators on the black list were butchered on their benches. The murderers then evacuated the city to join Marius and the other popular forces now preparing to play their last card against Sulla. The battle of the Collina Gate was one of the bloodiest of antiquity. Of the 100,000 and more of Marius' men, over half were killed and another 8,000 prisoners were slaughtered out of hand. The heads of their generals, stuck on pikes, were carried in procession around the walls of Praeneste, the last bastion of the popular party, which soon surrendered. Marius killed himself, and his head, too, was cut off, sent to Rome and hoisted in the Forum.

The capital accorded Sulla a colossal triumph on January 27 and 28 of 81 B.C. The general was followed by an enthusiastic procession of people Marius had exiled, all with wreaths of flowers on their heads, who acclaimed him as father and savior of the country. This time not even the soldiers hurled rude remarks at their leader; they cheered him with the rest. Sulla performed the ritual sacrifices on the Capitol and then harangued the crowd. With becoming modesty he attributed the incredible series of successes which had brought him there to good luck. This being the case, he requested—or rather, insisted—that he be given the title of *felix*, which literally means "happy" but which, on this occasion meant kissed by destiny, annointed of the Lord or, in short, "the man of providence." The people bowed to his will and decided to erect in his honor the first equestrian statue in gilded bronze ever seen in Rome.

This was not the only innovation that Sulla brought in to emphasize his absolute authority. He was the real inventor of the cult of personality. He coined new money with his profile on it, and put "The Feasts of the Victories of Sulla" into the official calendar. Under his dictatorship he treated Rome like any other conquered city, garrisoned by his soldiery and subjected to ferocious repression. Forty senators and 2,600 knights who had sided with Marius were condemned to death and executed. Rewards up to $8,000 were given to those who handed over, dead or alive, any fugitive proscript. Even many of those who had tried to avoid compromising themselves by not siding with anybody were suppressed or exiled, especially if they were rich. Sulla needed their money for his soldiers. Forum and streets were gaily decorated with heads, as they are decorated nowadays with colored balloons. One of the accused was a young man called Caius Julius Caesar, who, being a nephew of Marius on his mother's side of the family, had refused to abjure his uncle. Mutual friends intervened and the young man was let off with banishment. As he signed the sentence Sulla said, "I am being stupid. There are a lot of Mariuses in that lad."

For two years Sulla governed autocratically. To fill the gaps in the population caused by the civil war, he granted citizenship to foreigners, mainly to Spaniards and Gauls. He distributed land to over 100,000 veterans, especially in the Cumae region, where he himself had a farm. To discourage city-dwelling he abolished the free distributions of grain. He reduced the importance of the post of tribune and reestablished the rule of a ten years' interval for anyone standing for the consulship a second time. The senate, decimated by massacres, was repopulated with 300 new members from the faithful upper middle classes, and all those rights and privileges which it had had before the Gracchi were restored to it. It was definitely an "aristocratic restoration." He made a thorough job of it and then disbanded the army, decreeing that in the future no armed forces could camp in Italy. Considering his mission completed, to the astonishment of all he returned his powers to the senate and restored government by the consuls. Then, just like any other private citizen, he retired to his villa at Cumae.

By this time Caecilia Metella was dead. She had fallen ill just after her husband's triumph, and since it was an infectious disease, he had had her taken to another house, where he left her to die like a mangy cur.

Shortly before his abdication, Sulla, by now almost sixty,

had met Valeria, a beautiful girl of twenty-five, whom chance had placed by his side at the Circus. Seeing a hair on the dictator's toga, she removed it with two fingers. Sulla turned to look at her, amazed first at such barefaced audacity and then at such luscious beauty. "Don't mind me, Dictator," she said, "I only want a hair's share of your good fortune." This appears to have been Sulla's only disinterested love. Soon afterward he married her, and it may be that the desire to enjoy his beautiful young wife to the full influenced his decision to abdicate.

The day on which he relinquished power and lay down the insignia of office he went home through the dismayed and awestricken silence of the crowd. Someone began to follow him and call him names. Sulla did not even turn around. He merely remarked to the few friends who accompanied him: "What an imbecile! After this, no dictator in the world will ever be disposed to give up his power."

He spent the last two years of his life with Valeria, hunting, talking philosophy with his friends, and writing his memoirs, of which very few fragments have reached us. It appears that "The Happy One" was really happy at the close of his life, a life that had been a full one without disappointments or regrets (he was incapable of remorse), as he had always wished it to be. He remained vigorous and active until his dying day, living among his veterans at Cumae and settling their disputes in his imperious and abrupt manner. When a certain Granius disobeyed him over some trifle, he had him brought into his room and strangled by his servants just as in the good old days when he had been dictator. His pride and arrogance did not diminish even when he found himself face to face with death, which was knocking at his door in the form of a malignant ulcer which may have been cancer. With his cold blue eyes under his golden mane and his pale face, described by Plutarch as looking like "a mulberry sprinkled with flour," he continued to conceal his sufferings with a cheerful smile and bantering words. Before he died, he dictated his own epitaph: "No friend has ever done me a service and no enemy has ever done me an injury which I have not repaid in full." It was true.

XXII

A Dinner in Rome

THE RESTORATION OF SULLA HAD ONE FUNDAMENTAL DEFECT: IT
denied the exigencies which had led to the revolution. For the
creation of a dynamic and lasting work its author had lacked
one essential quality: faith in mankind. Not that mankind de-
serves it, but it expects it in those who propose to govern it.
Sulla did not believe in anything, least of all in the possibility of
reforming his fellowmen. His love for himself was so great that
there was none left for others. He despised them and was convinced that the only thing to do was to keep them in order. This
was why he had set up a formidable police organization which
he left in the hands of the aristocracy—not because he had any
particular regard for them, but because he was convinced that
the *populares* were even more contemptible, and that any reform of theirs would have been a step in the wrong direction.
The consequences were that ten years after his death, his political structure had fallen to pieces.

The patricians, finding themselves with all this power in
their hands, exploited it to steal, corrupt, and kill instead of
using it to reorganize the government and society. By now
everything was just a question of money. It was standard practice to buy election to an office. There was even a vote-getting
organization with its specialized technicians: the *interpreti* (ex-
plainers), the *divisori* (bribe-givers), and the *sequestri* (the go-
betweens). Pompey, to get his friend Afranius elected, invited
the chiefs of the tribes to his palace and bargained for their votes
as if they had been so many sacks of apples. The law courts were
even worse. Lentulus Sura, when acquitted by a jury with a
margin of two votes, clapped his hand to his forehead and exclaimed: "Damn it! I bought one too many. And with prices
what they are today!"

Since everything was a question of money, money had become everyone's chief preoccupation. Capable and honest officials in the administration did still exist, but the majority were
incompetent plunderers. To obtain a post in the government of
a province, they would not only forego a salary, but would actu-

ally pay to get the post, they were so sure of being able to make a handsome profit on it within a year. And profit they did, out of taxes, robbery, and the sale of the inhabitants as slaves. When Caesar was assigned to Spain he owed his creditors something like $840,000; in one year he repaid every penny. Cicero earned himself the reputation of being an honest man because in his year as governor of Cilicia he put aside only $96,000. This he trumpeted abroad in his letters as a good example.

The soldiers behaved no better. Lucullus returned home a millionaire from his campaigns in the orient. From the same part of the world Pompey brought back booty of ten or eleven million dollars for the state treasury together with another twenty-four million for his private one. It was so easy to multiply one's capital, if one had enough to buy an appointment, that bankers would lend money to anybody who did not have it at 50 percent interest. The senate forbade its members to practice this ignoble usury but the ban was skirted by using somebody else's name. Even men of the dignity of Brutus were associated with moneylenders, who controlled their capital by lending them money on these exorbitant terms. In the hands of such a corrupt ruling class, Rome had become a pump which sucked money out of its empire to enable one class of satraps to maintain an increasingly magnificent tenor of life in ever more insolent luxury.

One evening Cicero began to pull Lucullus leg about the name he had earned himself as a gourmet. Cicero, a young lawyer from Arpinum, was the son of a well-to-do farmer who had given him a good education. When he was twenty-seven and almost unknown, he had taken on a famous but decidedly risky case, that of defending Roscius against Chrysogenes, who was a great favorite of Sulla, then dictator. Cicero won the case with a masterly harangue. Then possibly fearing reprisals from Sulla, he left for Greece. He stayed there for three years, studying the language, the oratory of Demosthenes and the philosophy of Posidonius who was a mediocre exponent of Socrates and the Stoic school. Three years later, with Sulla safely dead, he returned, married Terentia (and her considerable dowry), and in his capacity as a lawyer, went in for politics. He immediately had on his hands another *cause célèbre*. This time it was against Verres, a senator who, as governor of Sicily, had thieved and swindled but was supported by the entire aristocracy. Cicero found himself up against Hortensius, the prince of the Forum and trusted advocate of the aristocracy and senate. It was a little like the Dreyfus affair of its time, with the patricians ranged on one side and the people, particularly the wealthy *equites* of the middle classes, on the other. Again Cicero won, and thus replaced Hortensius as leader of the bar and became the idol of the social class from which, it so happens, he had sprung.

Lucullus, an ex-general of Sulla's, had served for eight years in the orient against Mithridates. He came from a poor aristo-cratic family with a scandalous reputation. His father was said to have extorted money from the rebellious slaves in Sicily, his grandfather to have stolen statues, and his mother to have had more lovers than hairs on her head. All this may have been slander. In any case, Lucullus as a young man showed no signs of these vices. His only fault was an enormous ambition. But he also had all the qualities that make for success: brains, elo-quence, education, and courage. As long as Sulla, who had a weakness for him, was alive, his career had been easy. On the death of his protector, he had not hesitated to continue it through the favors of a woman, Precia, who, owing to the impor-tance of her lovers, had great influence. Through Precia he ob-tained the proconsulship of Cilicia. This enabled him to go on commanding, waging, and winning wars, and enriching himself with the spoils. To become a leader of the caliber of Marius, Sulla, and Caesar, he lacked but one quality—an understanding of men. Although he led his soldiers from victory to victory, he so exhausted them that they finally mutinied. Having ob-tained his command by intrigue, by intrigue he lost it again. Recalled to Rome, he retired from public life and proceeded to enjoy his wealth. This was enormous, and he splashed it lavishly around. His villa at Misenum had cost over $1,600,000, the estate at Tusculum extended to more than 50,000 acres, and the palace he had built on the Pincius was famous for its sculpture gallery, for the precious manuscripts he had looted in the east, and the gardens, in which he cultivated plants like the cherry (till then unknown in Rome) with the diligence of a fanatical botanist. Above all his palace was famous for its kitchens, where the most exquisite delicacies were prepared.

As we were saying, Cicero, one evening, with a group of friends, began pulling Lucullus' leg about his *gourmandise*

being just a pose, and offered to bet that if one were to visit his
house without warning the cooks, one would sit down to the
simple supper of a peasant or a soldier. Lucullus accepted the
challenge. He invited everybody to come and see for themselves
and merely asked permission to send orders for the table to be
laid for all of them in the Hall of Apollo. This was enough to
let his servants know what was afoot. A dinner in the Hall of
Apollo could not cost less than 200,000 sesterces. As hors
d'oeuvres, shellfish, fledglings with asparagus, oyster patties,
and shrimps were obligatory. Then came the actual dinner,
breasts of suckling pig, fish, duck, hare, turkey, peacocks from
Samos, partridges from Phrygia, lampreys from Gades, sturgeons
from Rhodes. And cheeses, and cakes, and wines.

Plutarch, who tells the anecdote, does not name the guests
who came to this banquet, but they must have been the cream
of Roman society. Certainly there must have been Marcus Licinius Crassus, the aristocratic son of one of Sulla's most famous
commanders, who had killed himself rather than surrender to
Marius. Sulla had compensated the orphan by letting him buy
at bargain prices the properties of the proscribed followers of
Marius, and allowing him to organize the first fire brigade ever
seen in Rome. When a fire broke out, Crassus used to rush to
the scene, but, instead of extinguishing the flames, he would
make a bid right on the spot for the burning building to the
proprietor, who was usually only too glad to get rid of it. When
it was his, Crassus got the pumps in action. Otherwise he let it
burn.

Another guest who certainly must have been present at this
feast of Lucullus was Titus Pomponius Atticus. Although of
bourgeois descent, he was a more refined type of aristocrat.
Being of an immensely wealthy family, he had no need to soil
his hands with unsavory practices, and had confined himself to
finishing his education in Athens. There he had met Sulla, who
had taken such a liking to him that he had wished to have him
as a collaborator. But Atticus declined. He preferred to continue his studies. He then invested his capital, which amounted
to over a million-and-a-half dollars, in a cattle-ranch in the
Epirus, apartments in Rome, a school for gladiators, and a
publishing firm for books of cultural value. Cicero, Hortensius,
Cato, and many others made use of him, not only as their financial adviser, but also as their bank. Such was his reputation and

prestige that although he lived simply as a true epicurean, there was no salon in Roman society where he did not have a standing invitation, and no party that he did not attend.

There must also have been Pompey, the favorite and son-in-law of Sulla who somewhat ironically used to call him "the Great." Of equestrian birth, he was also the "prince charming" of Rome's gilded youth. Before he was twenty-one he had won his first battle and a triumph, and was so seductively handsome that the courtesan Flora used to say that she could never leave him without giving him a kiss. He was considered an upright young man, which for those times he was, endeavoring to do his best for everybody as though he were doing it for himself. He was said to have many ambitions; actually he had only one: to be superior in everything to everybody, but this was probably more vanity than ambition.

None of the personages at this dinner would have been found in the stoic Rome of three centuries before. This was not only because of the fashionable cut of their clothing, the food that they ate, and the fine, flowing, clear Latin they spoke, sprinkled with literary allusions, but because the gathering would include women, who had emerged from their state of subjection. Clodia, the wife of Quintus Caecilius Metellus, and, at that time, the "first lady" of the city, set the mode for the others. She was a feminist, went out alone at night, and when she met a friend, instead of modestly lowering her eyes, as had always been the custom, she used to put her arms around him and kiss him. She invited her male friends to dinner when her husband was away, and asserting that women should have the right of polyandry, she practiced it unreservedly. Taking lovers by the dozen, she jilted them with much charm and no remorse. The poet Catullus, obsessed by her and madly jealous, celebrated her in immortal verses under the name of Lesbia. Celius, another discarded lover, tried to get his own back by accusing her in court of having tried to poison him and publicly called her *quadrantaria*, "a quarter-of-a-cent," the price of a cheap prostitute. Clodia was fined, not because she was guilty, but because she was sister to Publius Clodius, one of the leaders of the radical party, detested by the now all-powerful aristocrats and sworn enemy of Cicero. Celius's cause was supported by Cicero who explained that he was loath to accuse a lady, especially a lady who had been such a very good friend to so many men.

With such examples before their eyes, it was difficult for girls to become good wives and mothers. Marriages, arranged entirely for political and financial considerations, were contracted and dissolved with the utmost ease. Pompey, to help his career, divorced his first wife to marry Aemilia, Sulla's stepdaughter. When she died he married Julia, the daughter of Caesar, who in turn changed wives five times and was regularly unfaithful to all of them. "This city," Cato used to say, "is nothing but an agency for political marriages qualified by horns." Marriage *cum manu*, the kind which did not admit of divorce, had practically disappeared in order to allow couples to annul at will. A simple letter sufficed. Children were unwanted because they would have been a bother and had by now become a luxury afforded only by the poor. Freed from the chores of pregnancy and breast feeding, wives looked around for distractions and found them in love affairs and culture, which had now begun to be fashionable.

The literary tastes of this rich and frivolous society did not center on the major writer and poet of the time, Lucretius. The author of *De rerum natura* was probably an aristocrat, but owing to ill health lived a very retiring life. He was subject, it seems, to a recurring form of depressive mania, and his inspiration was too lofty, tragic, and profound to win popular favor. Catullus, an easy, sentimental poet, was all the rage. This rich, miserly bourgeois from Verona was always complaining of how hard up he was, but he had a house in Rome, a villa at Tivoli, and another on Lake Garda. The ladies adored him because he only spoke of love and had rendered soft and debonair a language which seemed to have been devised solely for legal codes and proclamations of victory. Apart from him, the other best-known writers were Marcus Coelius, a penniless aristocrat with radical sympathies, Licinius Calvus, an amateur poet and orator not without talent, and Helvius Cinna, who, after the death of Caesar, was mistaken for one of his murderers and killed by the mob. These literati, all left-wing intellectuals, were against dictatorship but did nothing to defend democracy. Perhaps their influence was greater than they deserved because, as well as social circles and the ladies to make their works known, by now they had the advantages of a proper publishing business.

Atticus had introduced parchment, out of which he made "volumes," which means "rolls," with pages composed of two or three columns of manuscript. Special slaves whose only pay was their keep were employed to copy them by hand. Authors too were unpaid, except for an occasional gift. Practically speaking, only the rich could afford to take up literature. An edition usually ran to about 1,000 copies, which were distributed to the booksellers, to whom book lovers would go to buy them. It was one of these booksellers, Asinius Pollio, who started Rome's first public library.

This technical progress stimulated output. Terence Varro published his essays on Latin and rustic life. Sallust, between one political battle and another, published his *Storiae*, magnificently written but highly partisan, and Cicero, who had now become undisputed master of the art of oratory, put out his speeches in book form, of which only fifty-seven have come down to us.

In short, culture was no longer the domain of a few lone specialists. It had begun to spread throughout society, a society which, by now, had definitely turned its back on the primitive customs and healthy ignorance of the first republican era. What is usually called the "Golden Age" of Rome was approaching, and like all golden ages, it was the prelude to the death agony of its civilization.

XXIII

Cicero

POMPEY AND CRASSUS, WHOM WE MET IN THE PREVIOUS CHAPTER, were not just frivolous business men, but politicians as well. They intended to play important parts, and succeeded, even though they both paid for it later with their lives.

As favorites of Sulla, their careers at first had been easy. On the retirement of the dictator the senate put them in command of two armies to quell the rebellions in Spain and Italy.

Spain had already rebelled several times against the malpractices of the Roman governors. Now useless cruelties had been added to these malpractices. In 98 B.C. the general Didius, imitating his predecessor Sulpicius Galba, lured an entire tribe of natives into his camp with the promise of a distribution of land. He then exterminated them. One of his officers, Quintus Sertorius, indignant at such barbarity, deserted, called the other tribes to arms, and organized them into an army. With it, he beat the Romans steadily, for eight years. During that time he also governed the province wisely. As Metellus, the general the senate had sent to conquer Sertorius, could not pull it off, he promised something like $320,000 and 25,000 acres of land to anyone who succeeded in killing him. Perperna, another Roman refugee in Sertorius' camp, managed to knife him, but instead of going and picking up his reward, he preferred to take over from the dead man and continue the war on his own account. The senate sent out Pompey, who easily defeated, captured, and killed the renegade. In this way Spain was restored to the malpractices of it governors.

Meanwhile a far more serious rebellion was soaking Italy in blood. Lentulus Battiades ran a school for gladiators at Capua, which was attended by slaves being prepared for what was almost certain death in the circus for the amusement of the spectators. One day two hundred of them tried to escape and seventy-eight succeeded. They pillaged the district and elected as their chief a Thracian whose name was Spartacus. He must have been a man of good family and notable qualities. This Spartacus tried to rally the millions of slaves in Italy, organized an army of 70,000 of them thirsting for freedom and revenge, and taught them how to make arms for themselves. He then beat the generals the senate sent against him. He was not intoxicated by these victories. A shrewd politician, he knew too well that in the long run it was a hopeless struggle. He therefore led his horde toward the Alps intending to cross them, disband his men, and send them home. This at least is what Plutarch says. But his followers wanted to turn back to continue pillaging town and countryside. Although Spartacus, who must have had a conscience, tried to stop this brigandage, he did not like to leave them in the lurch. He was beaten in one battle, whipped Cassius in another, and finally found himself face to face with the city, confronting her with the fearful prospect that all the slaves of

Italy and those in Rome itself might join the insurgents and overwhelm her.

Command was then given to Crassus and the flower of the aristocracy enrolled as volunteers under his banner. Spartacus, realizing now that he was up against the empire, withdrew to the south. His intention was to ferry his men to Sicily and then to Africa. Crassus gave chase, caught up with the rear guard, destroyed it, and continued the pursuit. In the meantime Pompey and his legions were on their way from Spain by forced marches. Recognizing that the game was up, Spartacus attacked, plunging into the thickest of the fray and killed two centurions with his own hand before falling, so hacked up that afterward it was impossible to identify his body.

The majority of his men died with him. About 6,000 were rounded up in the woods and crucified along the sides of the Appian Way.

This was in 71 B.C. On their return to Rome, the two victorious generals did not send their armies home, according to the law and the wishes of the senate. There was no love lost between them, for both had been born too rich, too fortunate, and too ambitious. However when the senate refused Pompey a triumph and the distribution of land he had promised his veterans, Pompey and Crassus united, and encamped threateningly around the city.

Immediately the *populares,* who since the death of Sulla had been waiting for the chance to get even with the aristocracy for their high-handedness, took their side. Proclaiming them as their champions, they elected them as consuls for the year 70 B.C. Pompey and Crassus were anything but *populares.* By birth they belonged to the upper middle class, but the blind egotism of the aristocracy had been steadily driving that class into the arms of the proletariat. In fact, the first steps taken by the two consuls were to restore to the tribunes the powers taken from them by Sulla and to remove from the patricians monopoly of the court juries, readmitting the *equites.* After this they came to an agreement over the division of personal gains. Pompey was to take over from Lucullus the supreme command in the orient and given the rank of admiral to suppress the Mediterranean pirates, who were making the trade routes to Asia Minor unsafe for shipping. In return he undertook to reopen the oriental markets for the investments of the banker friends of Crassus, who thus became their supreme patron.

In the senate a single voice was raised in favor of the measure, that of a still almost unknown young man who was not exactly popular among his aristocratic fellows: Julius Caesar. The assembly unanimously approved it at the urging of another young man: Cicero. The victory of the assembly and Pompey marked the end of patrician supremacy, and was to have a decisive effect on subsequent events. Immediately after Pompey's departure at the head of 125,000 men, 500 ships, and with 150 million sesterces, trade with the east revived. As a result the price of grain, mainstay of the landed aristocracy, fell.

Only one thing happened to mar this peaceful and progressive return to democracy and stiffen the forces of reaction. We only know Lucius Sergius Catiline from the descriptions of his enemies and, in particular, of Sallust and Cicero. Cicero describes him as "a turbulent individual, on permanently bad terms with god and man, who could never find rest either asleep or awake: hence his ashen complexion, his bloodshot eyes and his epileptic gait: in short, his madman's appearance." The trouble is that Cicero, through his wife, was stepbrother-in-law to a vestal virgin, whom Catiline had been accused of deflowering. At the trial he had been acquitted, but in society people said that it was true and that one should not be surprised, since to please his mistress he had already murdered his own son.

Perhaps the hostility that he met everywhere was another reason why Catiline, though of aristocratic descent, became one of the most rabid of the *populares*. His program was radical. He demanded the cancellation of all the debts of all the citizens. It was also whispered that he had organized a band of 400 desperadoes to assassinate the consuls and take over the government.

Actually no one ever saw this famous band. Catiline merely presented his candidature for the consulship, evidently hoping, as had been the case with Pompey and Crassus, that his name would rally all the anti-senatorial currents. But the upper middle classes, being the creditors to whom the debts were owed, were naturally indisposed to support him. They were with the plebs when it was a question of limiting the monopolies of the aristocracy, but they were with the aristocracy, and consequently the senate, when it came to finance and the state.

This can be seen from Cicero's attitude. He put himself up as rival candidate to Catiline and got himself elected as representative of "concord between the orders," so becoming for that year, spokesman for the alliance between the aristocracy and the upper classes.

Having lost the election, Catiline began hatching the famous plot. He secretly assembled a few thousand followers at Fiesole and set up a conspiracy within Rome itself. All sorts of people took part in it, slaves, senators, and two praetors, Cethegus and Lentulus. Backed by these elements, he ran again in the elections the following year and to make sure of the result arranged for the assassination of his rival and of Cicero. At least that was the version Cicero gave when he appeared on the Field of Mars, attended by an armed bodyguard, for the counting of the votes. Catiline failed again.

On the seventh of November, 63 B.C., Cicero said that during the night the conspirators had come to his house to kill him but had been driven off by his guards. The next day, meeting Catiline in the Senate House, he pronounced the famous oration against him (*Quousque tandem abutere, Catalina, patientia nostra . . .?* "How long, Catiline, will you continue to abuse our patience . . . ?") which is still the torment and delight of schoolboys. One day was not enough for this arraignment. He needed three. It was his masterpiece and he poured into it in equal measure all the treasures of his rounded, sonorous eloquence and his vanity. A magnificent piece of theater.

On the third of December Cicero managed to get a warrant issued for the arrest of Lentulus, Cethegus, and five other conspirators of high rank. He did not dare do the same to Catiline, who departed in silence to join his troops in Tuscany. On the fifth Cicero demanded that the prisoners be condemned to death and was supported by Silanus and Cato the Younger. Again only one fresh, young voice spoke up in defense of the accused, that of Julius Caesar, faithful advocate of the *populares*. He asked for simple detention. His oratory, in contrast with Cicero's, was sober and bare, and when he had finished speaking some young aristocrats tried to kill him. Caesar managed to escape, and while Cicero went to the prison to enforce the sentence, Mark Antony, the other consul (father of a young man who was destined to become more famous than himself) left at the head of the army to destroy Catiline.

The battle took place near Pistoia. Not one of the insurgents surrendered. Closing round their banner—the eagles of Marius —and Catiline, who shared their fate, they fought to the last man.

The first to be surprised and delighted at the energy he had shown was Cicero. He had not suspected that he had it in him. In a speech to the senate he modestly declared that the task he had undertaken had been so great as to surpass all human limits. Having thus laid his claim to deification, he went on to say that he would have likened himself to Romulus if the salvation of Rome had not been a much more glorious achievement than its foundation.

The senators may have smiled at this outburst but willingly decreed him the title of "Father of His Country," and when he relinquished his appointment, at the end of 63 B.C., they escorted him home as a mark of their esteem. Cicero had villas at Arpinum, Puteoli and Pompeii, an estate worth 50,000 sesterces at Formiae, another worth 500,000 at Tusculum, and a palace worth 3,500,000 on the Palatine. These were all properties bought with "loans" from his clients, because the law forbade lawyers to accept fees. These loans were, naturally, never paid back. Moreover Cicero had thought up another way of getting rich: by wills in which he had himself made heir. In the course of thirty years he inherited 20 million sesterces from his clientele, nearly $1,600,000.

It was logical that a man of this kind should preach "concord among the orders." He wanted a balance which was neither the savage reaction of an aristocratic caste to which he did not belong, nor yet a form of progressiveness which would have led to general equality.

Rich, prince of the Forum and "Father of His Country," he appeared to have everything. He lacked, however, the most important thing of all: peace at home. Terentia was a virtuous and intolerable wife, who poisoned his life with her nerves and rheumatic twinges. Furthermore, she was no less eloquent than her husband. Two orators in one house are one too many and at home the prince of the Forum yielded the gavel to his wife. She used it to complain interminably about something or other. When she finally decided to leave him a widower, Cicero replaced her with Publilia, whose dowry was no whit inferior to that of her predecessor. But then he got rid of her because she did not get along with his daughter Tullia, who received his only true and disinterested affection.

After the Catiline affair, Cicero's political star began to wane, though it flickered again briefly under Caesar. Caesar was sometimes his enemy and sometimes his friend, as we shall see, but Cicero never forgave him for being just as good an orator as himself, though in a different style. He became increasingly absorbed in his literary pursuits. To these we owe some of the finest passages in Latin. Above all, we appreciate his letters for their freshness and wealth of autobiographical anecdotes. He wrote a great number of them and they reveal him to us just as he was: a glutton for work, a tender father, a shrewd administrator of public and private funds, a good friend to friends (who might be useful to him), and a peacock so unconscious of his vanity that he immortalizes it in impeccable prose. Such is his candor that it redeems his conceit and almost converts it into a virtue.

XXIV

Caesar

AT THE MOMENT WHEN CATILINE FELL DEAD, METELLUS NEPOS, one of Pompey's commanders, arrived in Rome as a sort of advance guard. He had landed at Brindisi after a brilliant series of victories in Asia Minor, and had come on ahead to run for praetor. Once elected, he was to do his best to promote Pompey's reelection as consul.

He carried out the first part of his program with the votes of the *populares*, but found himself associated with Marcus Cato, a representative of the most deadly conservatives, who after the victory over Catiline, were under the impression that they had again become masters of the situation. They saw no good reason for supporting the ambitions of Pompey, who would have asked nothing better than to become their exponent. If they had chosen him they might have saved themselves or at least delayed their own downfall, so great was Pompey's prestige. But most conservatives were jealous of him, his riches and his successes, and thought they could do quite well without him.

Once more only one voice in the senate struck a discordant note. It was that of Caesar, who was also a praetor supporting Pompey. There was a tumult in the assembly that day. Caesar, together with Nepos, was deposed. He was rescued by the crowds, who gathered to protect him, ready to revolt. He calmed them down and sent them home. For the first time the senate realized that he might have to be taken seriously. His deposition was rescinded.

Caius Julius Caesar was then twenty-seven years old and, like Sulla, came from a poor aristocratic family. Its origins had been traced back to Ancus Marcius and Venus, but after these dubious progenitors, it had not contributed any further outstanding individuals to the history of Rome. Its members had been praetors, quaestors, and even consuls, but they were all quite ordinary people. Their house stood in the Subura, a sort of East Harlem or Arab quarter of Rome. Here Caesar was born in either 100 or 102 B.C.

We know nothing of his youth except that he had a Gaulish tutor, Antonius Grifo, who, apart from teaching him Latin and Greek, may have given him useful information about his northern neighbors. During his adolescence he suffered from headaches and epileptic fits; his ambition at the time was to become a writer. He grew bald early. Being ashamed of this, he tried to hide it by combing his hair from the back over onto his forehead. He used to spend a lot of time every morning at this complicated operation.

Suetonius reports him as being tall, rather plump, fair-skinned, with black, vivacious eyes. Plutarch says he was thin and of medium height. Perhaps they were both right: one is describing him as a young man, the other in later life. His long tours of military service must have hardened him. Since boyhood he had been an excellent horseman who could gallop with his hands crossed behind his back. Often he used to march at the head of his troops and sleep in wagons. His diet was simple. He was always cool and level-headed. It cannot be said that he was handsome. Under his bald and over-massive skull protruded a square chin, a bitter, twisted mouth framed by two deep creases, and an out-thrust lower lip. In spite of this he was always lucky with women. He married four times and had in-

numerable mistresses. His soldiers called him *calvus moechus,*
the bald adulterer, and when they marched through the streets
of Rome on the occasion of a triumph they would shout: "Look
out, men! Lock up your wives. The bald seducer is back!" and
Caesar was the first to laugh.

In contrast to the legend which makes him out to have been
pompously solemn, Caesar was actually a man of the world,
courtly, elegant, broad-minded, and with a great sense of humor.
He could laugh off and reply to quips at his own expense with
mordant sarcasm. He was indulgent about the vices of others
because he wanted others to be indulgent toward his. Curio
called him "husband to all the wives and wife to all the husbands in Rome." One of the reasons that the aristocrats hated
him was that he was always seducing their wives, who, it seems,
lined up to be seduced. Among them was Servilia, the half-
sister of Cato, who became for this reason implacably hostile to
Caesar. But Servilia was so devoted to him that, on retiring from
the post of mistress, she offered him her daughter Tertia in her
place. Caesar rewarded the generous mother by allotting her
the belongings of certain proscribed senators at one-third of
their value. Cicero made a pun about this, saying that the
bargain was made *Tertia deducta.* Pompey himself, though he
was handsomer, richer, and at that time more famous than
Caesar, had to put up with the latter's seduction of his wife,
though he repudiated her. Caesar made amends by giving him
his own daughter in marriage.

This extraordinary personage, around whom from now on
the history of Rome and the world was to revolve, was from a
moral point of view a son of his time. In fact he started off in a
far from promising way. Having finished his studies at about
sixteen, he went off to Asia with Marcus Thermus on one of the
many campaigns there, but instead of making a good soldier, he
became a favorite of Nicomedes, king of Bithynia, who had a
weakness for good-looking boys. On his return to Rome at the
age of eighteen, he married Cossutia in deference to his father's
wishes. When his father died, Cossutia was discarded for Cornelia, the daughter of that Cinna who previously had succeeded
his uncle Marius. This strengthened ties already binding him to
the democratic party.

When Sulla set up his dictatorship, he ordered Caesar to
divorce her. Caesar, though he changed wives as easily as he

changed his toga, boldly refused. He was condemned to death, and Cornelia's dowry was confiscated. Then mutual friends intervened and Sulla let him off with exile. Caesar repaid this act of clemency by calling it stupidity, but he was wrong. Sulla fully understood the "stupidity" he was committing and confided to intimate friends: "That boy is worth many Mariuses." Perhaps he had a private liking for him.

When the dictator retired, Caesar returned to Rome. Finding it still in the hands of reactionaries, who detested him because he was the nephew of Marius and Cinna's son-in-law, he left again for Cilicia. At sea he was captured by a pirate crew, who asked twenty talents, something like $64,000, for his ransom. Caesar insolently replied that this was too little for a person of his worth and that he preferred to give them fifty. He sent his servants to raise the money and passed the time of waiting writing poetry and reading it to his unappreciative captors. Caesar called them "barbarians" and "cretins" and promised to hang them the first chance he got. He kept his word. As soon as he was liberated he hurried to Miletus to charter a flotilla. He pursued and captured the buccaneers, recovered his money (or, rather, that of his creditors which he did not even bother to repay), and as a gesture of clemency to the pirates cut their throats before hanging them.

He himself tells of this adventure in letters to friends, but we would not swear to its authenticity. Caesar was not yet the sober and dispassionate writer of *De bello gallico* who, having won many battles, had no need to romanticize them. It was a talkative, arrogant, dissipated young scamp who returned to Rome in 68 B.C. and presented himself as a candidate for the office of quaestor. He put himself heavily into debt with Crassus, whose wife, Tertulla, he seduced, and used the money to buy the necessary votes. He was given a governorship and a military command in Spain, fought against the rebels, and returned to Rome with the reputation of being a good soldier and a wise administrator.

In 65 B.C. he stood again and was elected aedile. He thanked his supporters by financing superspectaculars for them but he also did one other thing: he put Marius' trophies, which Sulla had removed, back in the Capitol. Three years later Caesar was appointed propraetor in Spain. His creditors held a meeting and asked the government not to let him leave before settling his debts. He himself admitted owing them 25 million sesterces. Crassus as usual lent him the money. Caesar returned to the Iberians, subdued them almost completely, and brought such booty back to Rome that the senate granted him a triumph. However, this may have been a dodge to prevent him from running for a consulship, since his candidature could not be presented during his absence and the law forbade the winner of a triumph to return to Rome before the ceremony. Caesar returned anyway, leaving his army outside the gates of the city. It was in the coming electoral campaign that he was to make his first great political moves.

The conservatives hated him because he had stood up for Catiline, brought back the trophies of Marius to the Capitol, and was now presenting himself as leader of the *populares*. They could easily have prevented his success by putting somebody against him with the prestige of a Pompey, whom, as we have said, they rejected because they were jealous of his victories and riches. Pompey was indeed so rich that he could afford to keep his own private army, the one with which he had landed at Brindisi from the orient and which could have elected him dictator by force. Generously, Pompey demobilized it and entered Rome to celebrate his triumph with only a small following of officers. Courageous in battle, Pompey was timid about political responsibilities and always avoided anything illegal or against the rules. The senate knew this. They took advantage of it to snub him, and to refuse to distribute to his soldiers the lands he had promised them. Caesar saw in this a golden opportunity of winning him over to the side of Crassus and himself.

This masterpiece of diplomacy was sealed by a tripartite agreement: the first triumvirate. Pompey and Crassus put their enormous influence and their immense wealth at Caesar's disposal to get him elected consul. When he came to power he was to distribute the land to Pompey's soldiers and assign to Crassus the contracts he was after.

Thus Cicero's famous "concord between the orders," that is, the alliance between the aristocracy and the upper classes, broke up. The upper classes, who saw in Crassus and Pompey their legitimate representatives, made common cause with the *populares* of Caesar, and in this way the aristocracy remained isolated, stupidly and arrogantly convinced that they had no need

for help or to share their privileges with anybody. They put up
an insignificant personage, Bibulus, as their candidate. He was
elected, but they could not prevent Caesar, a man of very different cut, from being elected as well.

Caesar fulfilled his obligations to his allies. He immediately
proposed the distribution of the land and the ratification of the
measures taken by Pompey in the east. The senate opposed
them. Caesar brought the proposals directly before the assembly. The Gracchi had done the same thing and it had cost them
their skins; but times had changed. Bibulus applied his veto,
saying that, on interrogation, the gods had been unfavorable.
The assembly laughed in his face. A proletarian emptied a
chamber pot over his head. The proposals were carried by a
heavy majority. Pompey became Caesar's son-in-law by marrying his daughter, Julia; the middle classes and the mob fell into
one another's arms and had the time of their lives for months at
the expense of the triumvirs, who organized magnificent dis-
plays at the Circus for them.

In this atmosphere of popular favor it was easy for Caesar
to put into effect his economic and social reforms, which were
essentially those of the Gracchi. The senate opposed them all,
and sent Bibulus to announce that the gods disapproved of
them. The assembly did not care a hoot about the gods. They
laughed at Bibulus, who finally shut himself up at home and did
not again emerge. Since it was the custom to name the year after
the two consuls, the Romans called 59 B.C. "that of Julius
and Caesar."

He concluded it by procuring the election of Gabinius and
Piso as his successors in 58 B.C. He had married Piso's daughter,
Calpurnia, after getting a regular divorce from his third wife,
Pompeia. The latter was about to stand trial for indecency and
sacrilege and was accused of admitting her lover, Clodius, dis-
guised as a woman, into the enclosure sacred to the goddess
Bona, of whom she was a priestess. This last at least was true.
Clodius, a handsome, ambitious, and unscrupulous young aristocrat, often used to visit Caesar, whose politics he admired as
well as his wife. It is not absolutely certain that she was his
accomplice when he was caught in his impious deed. Caesar,
called upon to give evidence, defended Pompeia's innocence.
When the judge asked him why in that case he had divorced

her, he replied: "Because Caesar's wife must be above suspicion." He also testified in favor of Clodius, saying that he did not consider him capable of such an act, although it would appear he had managed to accomplish much worse ones, for example seducing his own sister, the famous Clodia, the Lesbia of Catullus, and wife of Quintus Caecilius Metellus, whom Cicero had lashed with his malicious tongue. Resentful busybody that he was, the great lawyer also came to give evidence against her brother. But Caesar set Crassus to work; he bought the judges and Clodius was acquitted.

Why Caesar had been so keen on saving this rascal became clear immediately afterwards. Clodius ran for tribune of the plebs and, although he had dishonored Caesar's wife, Caesar supported him. Evidently, having installed his father-in-law and an intimate friend on the consular bench, he wanted somebody in his debt at the head of the proletariat. Toward his wife's honor he could not have been more indifferent. The Clodius affair had given him an excuse to get rid of a wife who was no longer of service to him and to acquire another whose family connections were extremely useful. His last act before leaving office was to nominate himself proconsul of Cisalpine Gaul and the Narbonne for a period of five years. Since the law forbade any troops to be stationed south of the Apennines, whoever commanded those north of them was practically master of the entire peninsula. Caesar by now was determined to be that master.

He knew the senate would do its utmost to thwart him, but he had demonstrated that one could govern perfectly well without it by submitting laws for the direct approval of the assembly. He had gone even further: he had decreed that all debates held by the senate should be taken down and published daily. In this way the first newspaper was born. It was called *acta diurna* and it was free because it was affixed to the walls so that every citizen could read it and keep an eye on what his rulers were saying and doing. This invention was of enormous importance; it sanctioned the most democratic of all rights. The senate, which in the past had owed much of its prestige to its secrecy, was now accountable to public opinion, a blow from which it never recovered.

With Gabinius and Piso as Consuls to guard his rear, with an adventurer susceptible to blackmail as leader of the plebs, with the friendship of Pompey, with the financial support of

Crassus, with the senate under restraint and compelled to make public its decisions, Caesar could now leave Rome in quest of what he still lacked: a faithful army and military glory.

XXV

The Conquest of Gaul

WHEN CAESAR WENT NORTH IN 58 B.C., GAUL WAS ONLY A NAME TO the Romans. They knew the southern provinces, which they had reduced to vassalage to assure their land communications with Spain; they had no idea of what lay beyond them to the north.

To the north there was nothing which today might be called a nation. The Celtic tribes scattered throughout the various regions spent their time fighting one another. Caesar, who among other things was a great journalist and a shrewd observer, noted that each of these tribes was divided into three classes: the nobles or knights, who had the monopoly of the army, the priests or Druids, who had the monopoly of religion and education, and the people, who had only the monopoly of hunger and fear. Caesar considered that to dominate these tribes and to keep them divided, it would be enough to set the nobles against the nobles. Each of them, to make war on the others, would draw a section of the population in his wake. There was only one danger: that the Druids might get together and form a spiritual center of national unity. Therefore it was necessary to have all of them on the side of Rome.

Caesar liked the Gauls for two reasons: first, because one of them had been his earliest tutor, and, secondly, because they were the blood brothers of the Celts of Piedmont and Lombardy, whom Rome had already subjugated and who supplied her crack infantry regiments. If he could extend this domination to the whole of France, he would have found an inexhaustible reservoir for his armies.

Caesar had insufficient forces for a regular conquest. For all that vast territory he had been given four legions, fewer than 30,000 men. Moreover, at the moment he assumed command,

400,000 Helvetii were pouring out of Switzerland and threatening to submerge the Narbonne, while 150,000 Germani were crossing the Rhine into Flanders to reinforce their kinsman, Ariovistus, who had settled there thirteen years previously. All Gaul, in alarm, appealed to Caesar for protection. Without even referring to the senate, he enlisted another four legions at his own expense, and sent word for Ariovistus to come and parley with him. Ariovistus refused and Caesar, to consolidate his prestige in the eyes of his new subjects, had no choice but to war against him and the Helvetii.

There followed two bold, lightning fast campaigns. Beaten in spite of their enormous numerical superiority, the Helvetii asked to be allowed to withdraw to their own country. Caesar agreed, provided they became vassals of Rome. The Germani were literally wiped out near Ostheim. Ariovistus escaped but died shortly afterward. Caesar, the impenitent and debt-ridden libertine, was proving himself a formidable general on the battlefield.

Taking advantage of this success which had left all Gaul stunned with amazement, Caesar invited it to unite under his command to avoid future invasions. The Gauls were prepared to do anything but agree among themselves. Many tribes rebelled and appealed for help to the Belgians. These came running. Caesar defeated them, defeated those who had called them in, and then announced to Rome somewhat prematurely that the whole of Gaul had been subdued. The people were beside themselves, the assembly applauded and the senate made a wry face. Caesar, suspecting that the conservatives were preparing treachery, went back to Italy and summoned Pompey and Crassus to Lucca to work out a common plan of defense: the second triumvirate.

Rome had, indeed, been in the throes of convulsions ever since Caesar had relinquished the consulship. The leader of the aristocrats up to that time had been Cato, a rather obtuse reactionary but an honest man. Perhaps he might have been a little bit more open-minded if he had not borne the name of his grandfather, the great censor, who had had the narrowest mind on record. This name was his ruin. It obliged him to play a part which may not really have convinced him. In order to maintain the austerity of the ancient customs he used to go about barefoot, without a tunic, continually grumbling against innovations.

The first Cato had done the same thing, but his grumble had
been seasoned by honest hearty laughter, pungent sarcasm, a
bellyfull of beans, and copious draughts of chianti. The grandson had a gloomy, disagreeable expression, and the sour tongue
of an old maid obsessed with remorse for her uncommitted sins.
Perhaps he got on everybody's nerves because he first got on his
own by having to behave like a professional moralist and wet
blanket. Even so, he was an odd kind of moralist since he saw
nothing wrong in his wife Marcia taking the lawyer Hortensius,
Cicero's handsome and eloquent rival, for a lover. In fact,
Plutarch reports, when Cato found out about it he asked the
adulterer: "Do you want her? I'll lend her to you." When Hortensius died shortly afterwards, Cato took Marcia back and
went on living with her as if nothing had happened.

Nevertheless this strange man had his good points. Above
all he was honest, and this explains how, in an epoch when
everything, particularly votes, could be bought, he never got
further than praetor. The senators, whose political privileges he
defended and who had no time for honesty, would have preferred him to have used more suitable weapons against the general corruption and the new enemy they were up against. This
enemy was Clodius who had become ruler of Rome after Caesar's departure. It was he who fixed it with the assembly for
Cato to be sent to Cyprus as proconsul. Cato obeyed, and the
conservatives were left without their leader.

Luckily for them, Clodius was a better demagogue than
he was a politician, and consequently had no sense of proportion. In his blind hatred of Cicero he began persecuting him and
forced him to escape to Greece. He then confiscated his patrimony and razed his palace on the Palatine to the ground.

Cicero, though not so important in Rome as he thought
himself, was still something of a national institution and Pompey
and Caesar were the first to disapprove of such measures. However Clodius would not come to heel and rebelled against his
two powerful masters. Having enlisted a gang of hooligans, he
began terrorizing the city. Quintus Tullius, Cicero's brother,
who had asked the assembly to recall the proscript, had an
attempt made on his life and escaped by the skin of his teeth.
Pompey, in order to get the request granted, had to engage
another gang of thugs to beat the rebellious fool at his own
game. Its leader was Annius Milo, an aristocrat with little

money and as few scruples as Clodius. In the ensuing struggle
Rome turned into something like Chicago of forty years ago.

Cicero, who was given a great welcome on his return, now
became legal adviser to the triumvirs, his saviors. He pleaded
their cause in the senate, arranged for Caesar to be granted
more funds for his troops in Gaul, and had Pompey made com-
missary, a sort of Secretary of Agriculture, for six years, with
full powers to solve the peninsula's food problems. Early in 56
B.C., however, Cato returned from Cyprus, where he had performed his duties brilliantly, and under his leadership, the
senate resumed its struggle with the triumvirs. Calvus and
Catullus flooded Rome with epigrams against them and, when
the patrician Domitius stood for the consulship of 56 B.C., he
based his electoral campaign on the repeal of Caesar's agrarian
laws. Cicero, sniffing the wind as usual, thought that it was
blowing hard enough from the right, and siding with Domitius,
denounced Caesar's father-in-law, Piso, for embezzlement.

It was to remedy all this that the triumvirs held their
meeting at Lucca, where it was decided that Pompey and
Crassus should stand for the consulship again and that, after
their victory, they should reconfirm Caesar for another five
years as governor of Gaul. On the expiration of their term of
office, Crassus was to have Syria and Pompey Spain. Then the
three of them would be masters of the whole army.

The plan worked because the riches of Crassus and Pompey, with the contributions of Caesar who now held the purse
strings of the whole of Gaul, were enough to buy a majority.
Thus the proconsul was able to return to his provinces where a
new German invasion was imminent. Caesar massacred the in-
vaders, driving them back across the Rhône. Then, with a small
detachment, he crossed the Channel and for the first time
Roman soldiers set foot on English soil. It is not quite clear
why he went. Most likely to see what was there. He stayed a
few days, defeated the few tribes that crossed his path, made
a few notes, and came back again. The next year with larger
forces he repeated the expedition. He whipped a native army
under Cassivellaunus and went as far as the Thames. He might
have gone even further had he not heard from Gaul that a
revolt had broken out behind his back.

For the moment Caesar took it as a matter of ordinary
administration. Landing on the continent, he routed the Eburo-

nes, who had started the revolt, and left the bulk of his army to garrison their northern provinces. Then he returned to Lombardy with a small escort. He had only just got there when he learned that the whole country was in ferment and united for the first time under an able leader, Vercingetorix. Caesar knew him: he was a warlord from the Auvergne, a land of tough mountain warriors, son of a certain Celtillus, who had been killed by his own men because he had decided that he wanted to be king of a united Gaul. Perhaps this young fellow had nursed the same ambitions as his father and had hoped to be crowned by Caesar, who had been friendly to him. Disappointed, he had rebelled but, wiser than the others, he had appealed to nationalist sentiment and assured himself of the support of the Druids, who had given him their blessing.

Vercingetorix now stood with powerful forces between Caesar in the south and his army in the north. The situation could not have been worse, but Caesar faced it with his usual audacity. Recrossing the Alps with his meager columns, he began to move north through France, by now completely hostile country. Day and night he led his men on foot through the snow of the Cevennes, heading for the enemy's capital. Vercingetorix hastened to defend it. Caesar left Decimus Brutus in charge and he himself, with a few horsemen as escort, slipped through the enemy lines towards his main body. He concentrated it, beat the Carnutes at Cenabum and the Bituriges at their capital Avaricum separately, and sacked both cities. He had to withdraw before Gergovia because he was harried by the Aedui, whom he had considered the most loyal of his allies and who had now abandoned him.

Alone in hostile territory and confronting ten-to-one odds, he thought the game was up. Staking all on a single throw, he marched on Alesia. Here Vercingetorix had massed his army, and Caesar laid siege to it. Immediately the Gauls came down from all directions to liberate their leader. Some 250,000 men concentrated against the four Roman legions. Caesar ordered his men to erect two ramparts: one facing the beleaguered city and the other the relieving forces. Between these two bastions he disposed his troops with their few remaining arms and rations. After a week of desperate resistance on two fronts the Romans were starving, but the Gauls, fallen into anarchy, had begun to withdraw in disorder. Caesar says that if they had stuck it out for another day they would have won.

Vercingetorix in person came out of the hard-pressed city to beg for mercy. Caesar granted it to the city, but the rebels became the property of the legionaries, who sold them as slaves. Their unfortunate leader was taken to Rome where, one year later, he followed his victor's chariot in chains and was "sacrificed to the gods," in the current phrase.

Caesar spent the rest of that year in Gaul, stamping out the embers of the revolt. He did so with a severity unusual in a man who had always been magnanimous toward a beaten adversary. Once he had meted out punishment by executing the leaders, he resumed his usual routine of clemency and pacification. By these means he converted the Gauls into a tractable people, faithful to Rome. This can be attested by the fact that during the civil war with Pompey, they did not make the slightest attempt to shake off their fragile bonds.

Rome did not realize the magnitude of her proconsul's gift. She only saw a new province twice the size of Italy with 5,000,-000 inhabitants to exploit. Little did she imagine that Caesar had founded a nation which was destined to perpetuate and spread her language and her civilization throughout Europe. In any event she was at the time too busy with her own internal strife to have time for any larger considerations.

After his consulship Crassus had left for Syria, as agreed at Lucca. In his craving for military glory he had declared war on the Parthians, had been beaten by them at Carrhae and, while he was negotiating with the victorious general, the latter had killed him and sent his severed head to be used as a stage prop in one of the plays of Euripides. Pompey, on the other hand, had given himself an army to govern Spain and had remained with it in Italy, adopting an attitude that presaged little good. His strongest link with Caesar had been broken by Julia's death. Caesar offered to replace her with his granddaughter, Octavia, and when the widower declined, he offered to take Pompey's daughter as a wife in place of Calpurnia, whom he would have divorced. In Rome one exchanged the status of father-in-law for that of son-in-law with the utmost nonchalance. Pompey refused this offer also. He was no longer interested in a family link with Caesar, because he had finally come to an agreement with the conservatives and now came into the open as their champion. Knowing that Caesar's pronconsulship was due to expire in 49 B.C., he had his own extended until 46 B.C. This way he would be the only one of the two to have an army.

Democracy, under the blows of Clodius and Milo, who had reduced it to a question of bludgeons, was on its deathbed. In the end Milo killed Clodius, who had recently burned his house down. The plebs treated the dead man as a martyr. Taking his corpse to the Senate House, they set fire to the building. Pompey called in his troops to quell the riots and thus became master of the city. Cicero hailed him as the "consul without a colleague" and the phrase went down well with the conservatives since it allowed them to give him the powers of a dictator without using the unpleasant name. Pompey quartered his entire army in Rome and under its domination the assembly held its sessions and the law courts their trials, including that of Milo who, although defended by Cicero, was condemned for the murder of Clodius. Cicero later published his speech for the defense; when Milo, who had fled to Marseilles, read it, he exclaimed: "Oh, Cicero, had you really spoken the words you have written, I should not be here now eating fish!" It *is* possible that the prince of the Forum's written speeches did not always correspond with his spoken versions.

Pompey again proposed the law that required the presence of the candidate in the city before he could run for consul. The assembly, occupied by his troops, approved it. This ruled out Caesar, who could not come back before the day fixed for his triumph. It was 49 B.C. and his term was due to expire on March 1, but Marcus Marcellus proposed that this date be anticipated. The tribunes of the plebs used their veto, but this veto implied a democratic legality which no longer existed. Cato added his proposal that Caesar should be brought to trial and banished. It was the least they could do to repay him for having conquered Gaul.

XXVI

The Rubicon

CAESAR'S HESITATION BEFORE UNLEASHING CIVIL WAR HAS BEEN THE delight of many writers. It also has made famous a little stream which otherwise no one would ever have heard of—the Rubicon, near Rimini, which marked the boundary between Cisalpine Gaul, where the proconsul could keep his troops, and Italy proper, where the law forbade him to take them. Historians have described Caesar on its banks, wrapped in meditation and gnawed by doubt. In actual fact he had already made his decision or rather his enemies had forced it on him before he got there.

In order to avoid a conflict between Romans, he had accepted the proposals put forward by Pompey and the senate, who by now were one and the same thing. These were that he should send one of his few legions to the east to avenge Crassus and give another back to Pompey, who had lent it to him for operations in Gaul. But when the senate definitely replied with a refusal to allow him to stand for consul and offered him the choice of disbanding his army or being declared a public enemy, Caesar realized that if he chose the first alternative he would be handing himself over helpless to a state which was out for his blood. He made a final proposal in a letter which his subordinates, Curio and Antony, took to read to the senate. Caesar offered to demobilize eight of his ten legions if they would extend his governorship of Gaul until 48 B.C. Pompey and Cicero pronounced themselves in favor. The consul Lentulus drove the two envoys from the hall. Cato and Marcellus then asked the senate, which reluctantly agreed, to grant Pompey the necessary powers to prevent the "state from being endangered." This was the formula for imposing martial law. It put Caesar with his back squarely to the wall.

He paraded his favorite legion, the thirteenth, and addressed his soldiers as *commilitones* and not as *milites*. He had the right; apart from being their general, he had been their real comrade. For ten years through every kind of difficulty, wisely alternating indulgence with strict discipline, he had led them to victory. These veterans were experienced regular soldiers, who knew their job and how to size up their officers. They felt respectful affection for Caesar, who rarely had to rely on rank to assert his authority. So when he told them how matters stood and asked them how they felt about taking on Rome, their own country, in a war, they were all for it and said so, although they knew that if they lost they would be treated as traitors. They were almost all Gauls from Piedmont and Lombardy, a people to whom Caesar had given citizenship, a fact which the senate obstinately refused to recognize. Their general was their country. When he warned them he had not even the money for their pay, their answer was to deposit their savings in the legion's funds. Only one deserted to go over to Pompey: Titus Labienus. Caesar, who considered him the most able and trustworthy of his commanders, sent his baggage and pay after him, as the fugitive had gone off without it.

In the grey dawn of a January morning in 49 B.C., he "cast the die," as he himself put it. That is to say, he crossed the Rubicon with one legion, 6,000 strong, against the 60,000 Pompey had assembled. At Picenum he was joined by the twelfth, at Corfinium by the eighth. He formed another three from local volunteers, who had not forgotten Marius and saw in his nephew his successor. "The towns open their gates to him and greet him like a god," wrote Cicero, who was beginning to doubt whether he had backed the right horse. Actually, Italy had gotten pretty tired of the conservatives and offered no resistance to the rebel, who rewarded her with long-sighted clemency: no looting, no killing, no imprisonment.

During this bloodless march on Rome, Caesar continued to try to find a compromise or at least to give that impression. He wrote to Lentulus pointing out to him the disasters that would befall Rome in a fratricidal struggle. He wrote to Cicero telling him to inform Pompey that he was prepared to retire to private life if they guaranteed his safety. Without waiting for a reply, he continued to advance against Pompey, who was retreating toward the south.

In spite of the fact that they had rejected Caesar's offers, the conservatives had abandoned Rome, declaring that they would consider as enemies any senator who remained there. Laden with money, pretensions, and insolence, each with his servants, wives, mistresses, small boys, luxurious tents, fine linen, uniforms, and plumes, these aristocrats were noisy camp followers of Pompey, muddling his brain with their idle chatter. Pompey had never had a very strong character even when young. Now aged and asthmatic, fearful of making a decision, he continued to withdraw as far as Brindisi, where he embarked his army, still twice the size of his enemy's, and ferried it over to Durrës in Albania, on the pretext that he wanted to train and discipline it before the final battle.

Caesar entered Rome on the sixteenth of March, leaving his army outside the city. He had rebelled against the state but he still respected its laws. His request for the title of dictator was refused by the senate. He then asked that an armistice commission should be sent to Pompey. This, too, the senate refused. He asked to be allowed to dispose of treasury funds and the tribune Lucius Metellus applied his veto. Caesar replied: "It is as difficult for me to utter threats as it is easy for me to carry them out." The treasury was immediately put at his disposal and Caesar, before emptying it, paid in all the booty accumulated during his recent campaigns. Even theft had to be legal.

The conservatives prepared their counterattack by mobilizing three armies: that of Pompey in Albania, that of Cato in Sicily, and another in Spain. They reckoned on forcing Caesar and Italy to surrender from hunger, without having to fight a battle which they feared. Caesar sent two legions to Sicily under the command of Curio. Curio followed Cato, who had sailed for Africa, attacked him without adequate preparation, was beaten, and died during the battle, asking Caesar's pardon for the trouble he had caused him. In order to make sure of the corn supply, Caesar went in person to Spain. He underestimated the strength of Pompey's following there and found himself in difficulty. But in moments of danger Caesar was always at his best. One day, while being besieged, he diverted the course of a river and became the besieger. The enemy surrendered, and Spain was again under the control of Rome. The people, freed from the specter of famine, gave Caesar a rousing welcome and the senate granted him the title of dictator, which Caesar now refused. They elected him consul and that was enough for him.

With his customary rapidity he set the internal affairs of the state in order without recourse to trials, banishments, or

confiscations. Then he mustered his army at Brindisi, embarked
20,000 men on the twelve ships he had available and landed
them in Albania on the trail of Pompey. The latter was
astounded, as he had been convinced that nobody would have
dared cross, in the winter, a stretch of water patrolled by his
powerful fleet. Why he did not at once attack his rash opponent,
who had come within reach in such small strength, will never
be known. He even had a storm on his side. It sank Caesar's
squadron and prevented him from ferrying the rest of his army
across from Italy. In the boat in which he was still trying to get
off the Albanian coast to go fetch them, Caesar shouted to his
terrified oarsmen: "Don't be afraid: you are carrying Caesar
and his star." The storm, however, cast him back on the rocks.
If Pompey had taken the initiative at that moment the star
would never have risen again.

The weather finally turned fair. One of Caesar's finest
generals, Mark Antony, arrived to reinforce the demoralized
troops with men and supplies. Before attacking, Caesar says he
sent fresh peace proposals to Pompey which had no effect.
Neither did Caesar's attack. Pompey held fast, took a few
prisoners and killed them. Caesar also took a few and enlisted
them. His veterans admitted that the battle had gone badly
because they had not fought hard enough, and asked to be
punished. Caesar refused, and they begged him to lead them
back into battle again. Instead he led them into the granary
that was Thessaly to rest and refresh them.

In Pompey's camp Afranius advised returning to Rome,
now undefended, and leaving Caesar to his fate. The majority
were for giving him the *coup de grâce* because they thought he
was already beaten. Pompey, having no ideas of his own, followed the majority opinion, went after Caesar, and caught up
with him on the plain of Pharsalus. He had 50,000 infantry and
7,000 cavalry; Caesar had 22,000 infantry and 1,000 cavalry. On
the eve of the battle there were great banquets in Pompey's
camp, speeches, and drinking of toasts to certain victory. Caesar,
in contrast, had a ration of corn meal and cabbage with his men
in the mud of the trenches. He issued firm orders to his officers,
while among his enemies there were a thousand armchair strate-
gists with a thousand different plans, and a commander in chief
who was waiting for them to suggest one to him.

Pharsalus was Caesar's masterpiece. While losing only 200

men, he killed 15,000 and took 20,000 prisoners. These he ordered to be spared. He then celebrated his victory by eating, in Pompey's sumptuous tent, the dinner which cooks had prepared in honor of Pompey's triumph. That hapless general was at the moment galloping towards Larissa, still followed by his entourage of worthless aristocrats, among whom there was a certain Brutus, whose corpse Caesar had looked for on the battlefield in terror of finding it. Brutus was the son of his former mistress, Servilia, Cato's half-sister, and perhaps Caesar himself was his father. Finally Caesar received a letter from him in Larissa, asking his pardon and begging it also for his brother-in-law Cassius, who had married his sister Tertia, Servilia's daughter, and had been taken prisoner with other followers of Pompey. Caesar immediately gave free pardon to both of them because Rome in those days was what the writer Ennio Flaiano says Italy is today: a country not only of poets, heroes, and navigators, but also of uncles, nephews, and cousins.

Pompey, having joined his wife at Mytilene, sailed with her for Africa. His intention was probably to take command of the last of the senatorial armies, the one which Cato and Labienus were organizing at Utica. His ship cast anchor in the waters of Egypt, a vassal state of Rome, administered through the young king Ptolemy XII, who was a degenerate completely under the thumb of his vizier or prime minister, a rascally eunuch called Pothinus. Pothinus had already heard about Pharsalus and thought that he would earn the gratitude of the victor by murdering the vanquished. Pompey was knifed in the back under the eyes of his wife as he stepped ashore from a launch. His head was sent as a present to Caesar, who turned his own aside when it was shown to him. Caesar did not care for blood, even that of his enemies, and there is no doubt that he would have pardoned Pompey, had he taken him alive.

As he was in the area, before returning to Rome Caesar decided to straighten out matters in Egypt, where for some time they had been going badly. Ptolemy, according to his father's will, should have shared the throne with his sister, Cleopatra, after he had married her. (Love affairs between brother and sister occurred frequently in Egypt up until Farouk: they were part of the "local color.") When Caesar arrived, Cleopatra was not there; Pothinus, the better to further his own interests, had had her locked up. Caesar secretly sent for her. In order to reach him, she had herself hidden under the covers of a bed which the slave Apollodorus was to take to the apartments of the illustrious guest in the royal palace. Caesar found her there when he turned in for the night, with momentous consequences.

The following day he settled matters between brother and sister, that is, he practically gave them complete sovereignty at the expense of Pothinus, whom he had killed on the grounds, possibly true, of treasonable conspiracy. Unfortunately the city rose against Caesar. The Roman garrison sided with the rebels. Caesar and his few men turned the royal palace into a fortress, sent a messenger to Asia Minor for reinforcements, burned his fleet so that it should not fall into enemy hands (unluckily the fire also spread to the great library, the glory and pride of Alexandria), and in a raid which he himself led swimming, captured the island of Pharos, and the lighthouse. Here he waited for his reinforcements to arrive by sea. Ptolemy thought he was lost, joined the rebels, and nothing was ever heard of him again. Cleopatra courageously stood by Caesar who, when his men arrived, routed the Egyptians and put her back on the throne.

He remained nine months with her, at the end of which she gave birth to a baby who was named Caesarion so that there should be no doubt as to who his father was. Caesar must have been very much in love to be so deaf to the appeals of Rome. The city had now fallen into the clutches of the Milo gangs, back again from Marseilles. Finally, hearing that Caesar intended to make a long cruise with Cleopatra up the Nile, his own soldiers mutinied. A rumor had spread among them that their general wanted to marry and stay in Egypt as king of the Mediterranean.

At this Caesar roused himself, and at the head of his men went off to Asia Minor, where, at Zela, he "came, saw, and conquered" Pharnaces, the rebel son of Mithridates. Then he sailed for Tarentum, where Cicero and other ex-conservatives came to meet him with ashes on their heads. With characteristic magnanimity Caesar cut short their contrite speeches by shaking hands with them. Then with Cleopatra, rigged out like a belly dancer, and with Caesarion, her bawling brat, he returned to a turbulent Rome with his "war prize" and to his wife Calpurnia, who didn't blink an eye because she was used to him by now.

Yet she was probably the first to notice that Cleopatra had a nose that was a little bit too long. And we can be sure that this made her quite happy.

XXVII

The Ides of March

THE SITUATION IN ROME WAS NONE TOO BRIGHT. GRAIN WAS NO longer arriving from Spain where Pompey's son had organized another army, nor from Africa, which Cato and Labienus controlled with an army as big as the one which had been defeated at Pharsalus. At home chaos reigned. Cicero's son-in-law, Dolabella, had joined up with Caelius, the successor of Clodius, leader of the extremists. Between them they had decreed the cancellation of all debts, which meant a financial crisis, and had called back from Marseilles Milo, the grand master of demagogy and the blackjack. Mark Antony, who as Caesar's representative had to keep order, and who as a soldier was rough and ready in his methods, had called in the troops. About a thousand Romans had been butchered in the Forum. Caelius and Milo fled to stir up revolt in the provinces, where various legions had mutinied.

Caesar, accustomed to battling with the right wing, that is, with the reactionaries, hated to have enemies on the left; he did not want to end up like Marius, who had been obliged to massacre his own supporters in order to save the situation. He began to unravel his political tangle with the soldiers, "because," he said, "they depend on money, which depends on force, which depends on them." He visited the mutinous legions alone and unarmed, and with his customary calm told them that he agreed that their claims were legitimate. He went on to say that he would satisfy them when he got back from Africa, where he was going to fight "with other soldiers." At these words, Suetonius says, the veterans were overcome by guilt and shame. They shouted that this could not be, that they were Caesar's soldiers and intended to remain so. Caesar pretended to hesitate and then gave way for the simple reason that he had no other soldiers. Not only was he a great general, he was also an extremely artful one. At the end of December 47 B.C. he embarked the troops, burning with the desire to redeem themselves, and by April 46 B.C. he had laid Thapsus under siege. Here he found 80,000 men waiting to go against him under the command of Cato, Metellus Scipio, his former henchman, Labienus, and Juba, king of Numidia.

Again he was facing three-to-one odds, again he lost the first round, again he won the decisive battle. It was appalling. This time his soldiers did not obey his orders to be merciful, and slaughtered all the prisoners. Juba committed suicide on the battlefield and Scipio, overtaken at sea, was killed. Cato shut himself up in Utica with a small detachment. He advised his son to submit to Caesar and distributed all his available funds to those who wished to try to escape. He then invited his most intimate friends to dinner, discussed Socrates and Plato with them, retired to his room, and split open his stomach with a dagger. His slaves found him and called a doctor, who did what he could to replace his intestines, which were bursting out of the wound. While the doctor was bandaging him up, Cato pretended to be unconscious, but when left alone he removed the bandages and reopened the wound with his own hands.

They found him dead with his head resting on the pages of Plato's *Phaedo*. Caesar, grieved, said that he could not forgive him for having deprived him of the opportunity of forgiving him. He gave him a solemn funeral and was merciful to his son. Perhaps he felt that this unpleasant and in many respects insufferable man was taking the virtues of republican Rome to the grave and so would willingly have exchanged his life for that of many of his friends: Cicero, for example.

After a short period in Rome, Caesar went to Spain to destroy the last of Pompey's armies. He routed it at Munda and could at last devote himself entirely to the task of reorganizing the state. He had the power to do so because the senate had given him the title of dictator, first for ten years and then for life. It was a gigantic undertaking which called for a ruling class. This Caesar did not have. He invited his aristocratic ex-adversaries, who were the most competent, to collaborate with him, but their only answer was sarcasm and conspiracies. They continued to harp on the old story of his projected marriage to

Cleopatra and the transfer of the capital to Alexandria. Caesar could only count on a small group of faithful friends who knew little about administration. With these he formed a sort of ministry: Balbus, Mark Antony, Dolabella, Oppius, etcetera. The assembly was on his side so he reduced the senate to a purely consultative body. He increased it in number from 600 to 900 by admitting new members, drawn partly from the middle classes of Rome and the provinces, and partly from his old Celtic officers, many of whom were sons of slaves.

This maneuver formed part of a much vaster plan. Caesar had shown a glimpse of this plan when he had granted citizenship to all Gaul south of the River Po. The senate had never ratified this measure but now had to accept its extension to all of Italy. Caesar had realized that no good could be expected from the Romans of Rome—soft, degenerate, and incapable of producing anything but parasites and deserters. He knew that the only good lay in the provinces, where the family had remained intact, customs sound, and education severe. He was planning to renew the framework of the administration and the army with these provincials of peasant or lower-middle-class origin.

This was his radical change. He tried to put it into effect by means of the great agrarian reform planned by the Gracchi. To insure its success, he called in the industrial and commercial middle classes to finance the operation. Great capitalists like Balbus and Atticus became his bankers and advisers. In this enterprise Caesar displayed the same energy he had displayed as a general in battle. He insisted on seeing, knowing, and deciding everything himself. He would not stand for waste or incompetence. The policy of full-time employment of labor fitted in perfectly with his passion for building. He was a born builder and was happiest when most busy.

Instead of annoying him, the gossip of his enemies amused him, and he used to have it told to him so that he could pass it on to Calpurnia, with whom he had gone back to live after the Cleopatra interlude. In his own way, he was a good husband. He compensated his wife for his countless infidelities with a thousand attentions, profound esteem, and affectionate companionship. He always had something to tell her when he came home. Here he treated his collaborators and subordinates with the well-bred aloofness natural to him. He dressed with care and only took advantage of one of the prerogatives which were

his due as dictator: that of wearing a laurel wreath to conceal
his baldness. He did everything with an air, even the forgiveness
of someone who had injured him. He went even farther. Whenever possible he preferred to know nothing about the injury.
This is why he burned without reading it the correspondence
that Pompey had left in his tent at Pharsalus and Scipio in his at
Thapsus. When he learned that Sextus was preparing to avenge
his father in Spain, he had his sons, who had remained in Rome,
sent to him; he made his two enemies, Brutus and Cassius, governors of provinces. Perhaps in this magnanimity there was a
measure of contempt for mankind, a trait which quite often
accompanies greatness. Perhaps his complete disregard for the
dangers which threatened him was also rooted in this contempt.
He could not have been blind to the fact that plots were going
on all around him and must have known that generosity is a
stimulant, not a cure for hatred. But he thought his enemies
lacked the courage to take action. He dreamed of new under-
takings: of taking vengeance for Crassus on the Parthians, of
including Germany and Scythia in the Empire.

In February of 44 B.C. he was already drawing up his plans
for these campaigns when Cassius became the ringleader of a
conspiracy to kill him. Cassius tried to draw Brutus into it, Brutus whom Caesar still loved as a son (perhaps because he knew
he was). Novelists and playwrights have tried to make this
young man a hero of republican liberty. It is doubtful whether
he really was. The conspiracy was cloaked in noble ideals; it
claimed that its object was the death of a tyrant who aimed at
a king's throne which he intended to share with Cleopatra, the
foreign harlot, then leave to his bastard Caesarion after trans-
ferring the capital to Egypt. Had he not had his statue erected
beside those of the ancient kings? Had he not had his own
image put on the new coins? Power had gone to his head, already deranged by a recurrence of his epileptic fits. Better both
for him and his memory that he should be killed before he got
a chance to destroy the liberty and supremacy of Rome.

These were probably the arguments which the "lean and
hungry" Cassius used to convince his brother-in-law. Nevertheless, perhaps those which tipped the scale were quite different,
of a more personal and secret nature. Brutus may have hated
Caesar not because he did not know that he was his father, but
because he did. Perhaps he had never forgiven his mother for

making a bastard of him. These are mere suppositions, for Brutus was taciturn and reserved. One very doubtful source reports that in a letter to a friend he wrote: "Our ancestors taught us never to tolerate a tyrant, even though he happens to be our father." It is only too easy to attribute such thoughts to a man after he has put them into practice.

Brutus was an educated man, who knew his Greek and philosophy. He had governed Cisalpine Gaul, which Caesar had entrusted to him, honestly and efficiently. He had married his cousin Portia, daughter of his uncle Cato. This certainly could not have made him favorably disposed toward the dictator. The most alarming thing about him was the fact that he wrote essays about virtue. Virtue is one of those respectable ladies who are best loved, if at all, in silence.

During the first few days of March, after indoctrinating him carefully, Cassius came to tell Brutus that on the coming Ides, that is to say on the fifteenth, Caesar was going to make his great *coup*. His right-hand man, Lucius Cotta, was going to propose to the assembly, already determined to approve, that the dictator be proclaimed king. The excuse was that the Sybil had predicted that the Parthians, against whom he was preparing an expedition, could only be defeated by a king. One could not rely much on the opposition of the senate. Its recent reform had given the majority to the followers of Caesar. The only remedy before it was too late was the dagger. This conversation took place in the presence of Portia, who supported Cassius's point of view. To show that she could keep the secret, even under torture, she drove a dagger into her thigh. Brutus gave in; he had to show he was worthy of such a wife.

That evening Caesar was dining at home with some friends and, according to the custom of Roman hosts, he proposed a topic of conversation. "What death would you prefer?" Everyone had his say. Caesar pronounced himself in favor of a rapid and violent end. The following morning Calpurnia told him that she had dreamed of him covered with blood. She begged him not to go to the senate, but a friend, who was privy to the plot, came to fetch him: Caesar went with him and just missed another friend, a loyal one, who came to warn him of the conspiracy. In the street a soothsayer shouted to him to beware of the Ides of March. "They are already here," said Caesar. "They aren't over yet," replied the other. Just as he was entering the

Senate House, somebody put a roll of parchment in his hand. Caesar thought it was just another of the usual petitions and did not unroll it. He still held it in his hand when he died: it was a detailed denunciation.

He was barely inside the Capitol when the conspirators were on him with their daggers. The only person who could have defended him, Mark Antony, had been detained in the entrance hall by Trebonius. Caesar at first tried to protect himself with his arm, but gave up when he saw Brutus among his assassins. It is very probable that he really did say to him: "You, too, my son?" as Suetonius says he did.

He fell, his body full of dagger holes, at the feet of the statue of Pompey. He himself had had it put there and he used to bow to it whenever he passed. The deed left its own authors dismayed and uncertain. Brutus gave a rousing cheer for Cicero, calling him "Father of His Country," and asked him to make a speech. Horrified at the idea of getting involved in this business and realizing that oratory would be out of place, the great speaker was speechless for the first time in his life. Mark Antony entered and saw the corpse stretched out on the floor. Everybody expected him to give way to an outburst of vindictive rage. Instead, "the faithful one" did not say a word and went out in silence. Outside, perturbed by the news, which was just beginning to spread, a crowd was gathering. Fearfully the conspirators appeared in the entrance. Some of them tried to explain what had happened, justifying it as a triumph of liberty. The word "liberty," however, no longer had any fascination for the Romans. They began to growl menaces. The conspirators hastily retired, barricaded themselves inside the Capitol and, putting their armed servants on guard, sent a message for Mark Antony to come and get them out of their predicament.

The "faithful one" came the next day, when Brutus and Cassius had in vain already made a second speech to calm a crowd that was becoming ever more threatening. By a clever speech in which he asked for the maintenance of order in exchange for the punishment of the guilty, he more or less succeeded in calming them. He then went to Calpurnia, who was prostrate with grief, and had her give him Caesar's will in a sealed envelope. This he delivered to the vestal virgins, as was the custom in Rome, without opening it. He was quite sure that he had been designated heir. Then he secretly sent for the troops encamped outside the city. Returning to the senate, he made a speech of Caesarean stature designed to restore order and reduce tension. He approved the proposal made by Cicero for a general amnesty on condition that the senate ratify all Caesar's outstanding projects. He also promised governorships to Brutus and Cassius, which would enable them to get out of Rome. And he had them to dinner with him the same evening.

On the eighteenth he pronounced the eulogy at Caesar's funeral. This was the most solemn one ever seen in Rome. The Jewish community, grateful to Caesar for the kind treatment they had received from him, followed his bier, mingling with his veterans and singing their ancient mournful hymns. The soldiers threw their arms, the gladiators and actors their costumes on the pyre, and the entire populace kept vigil around the coffin the whole night long.

The following day, Antony had the vestals hand him back the will. He opened it in the presence of the highest authorities of the state and read it aloud in public. Out of his private income, which amounted to about a 100 million sesterces, Caesar left a sum to every Roman citizen. His magnificent gardens he gave to the City of Rome as a public park. The rest was to be divided among his three great-nephews, one of whom, Caius Octavius, he had adopted as his son and designated heir.

The "faithful one" who forty-eight hours after his chief's assassination had invited his murderers to dinner, had been justly repaid for his strange fidelity.

XXVIII

Antony and Cleopatra

APART FROM A FEW INTIMATE FAMILY FRIENDS WHO HAD SEEN him as an adolescent, nobody in Rome knew this Caius Octavius, who was destined to change his name twice and, under the last one, Augustus, was to go down in history as the greatest Roman statesman. His grandmother had been Julia, Caesar's sister, who had married a rich, vulgar provincial from Velletri.

His father had had quite a successful career and had finished up as governor in Macedonia. As for the boy, he had grown up under almost Spartan discipline, had been diligent in his studies, and his great-uncle Caesar, who had no legitimate son in spite of all the wives he had married, had taken him into his home and had grown fond of him. He took him to Spain with him in the winter of 46-45 B.C., when he went to eliminate the last remnants of the Pompeians, and on that occasion had admired the will power with which he put up with hardships which his health could ill support. He suffered, in fact, from colitis, eczema, and bronchitis, ailments which became worse with time and compelled him to live, even in battle, like a chick in cotton wool, with bellybands, shawls, woollen caps, a whole drug store of pills, ointments, and syrups, and a doctor always at hand. He did not drink, ate like a sparrow, and had a terror of draughts. Still, he faced the enemy with the coolest courage and never took any action, even the most ordinary one, without first carefully weighing the pros and cons.

Caesar, the brilliant, daring improviser, so broad-minded and irrationally generous, so easy in his speech and vivacious in his gestures, must have taken a liking to him because of the contrast between them. He followed his studies, giving him guidance in strategy and administration, and, as soon as he was seventeen, gave him a small command in Illyria to obtain experience in military life and government. It was here that toward the end of March a messenger reached him with the news of his uncle's death and of his will. He hurried off to Rome, and contrary to the advice of his mother went to see Mark Antony who treated him disdainfully and called him "little boy."

He did not take offense and calmly asked whether the money Caesar had left to the Roman citizens and soldiers had actually been distributed. Antony replied that there were other more urgent matters to be attended to and so Caius Octavius, who now, owing to his adoption, had taken the name of Caius Julius Caesar Octavian, borrowed the money from rich friends of the dead man and distributed it according to his instructions. The veterans began to look with a favorable eye on this "little boy," who to them seemed to be a chip off the old block.

The irritated Antony announced some days later that an attempt had been made on his life and that he had found out from the would-be murderer that Octavian had organized the attempt.

Octavian asked for proof and since this was not forthcoming, hastened off to the two legions which he had recalled from Illyria, joined forces with the two consuls in office, Hirtius and Pansa, and the three of them marched against Antony.

Octavian was only eighteen at the time and for this reason the senate was on his side. The aristocrats were alarmed at Antony's arrogant attitude. Defrauded as he felt of Caesar's heritage, he was now trying to seize it by force. In his few days of power he had ransacked the treasury, appropriating millions for himself, had arbitrarily occupied Pompey's palace, and had nominated himself governor of Cisalpine Gaul. This was his excuse for keeping an army in Italy and thus becoming its master. The senate realized that if they let him get away with it they would have another, and worse Caesar on their hands. Consequently they decided to support Octavian, who seemed less likely to give them trouble. Cicero lent his oratory to the struggle against Antony in a series of "Philippics," mainly aimed against his private life. This gave him plenty of scope. Antony, who was now thirty-eight, had spent his years in feats of military prowess, acts of arrogance, generous gestures, and obscene conduct. Even Caesar, who was fond of him and far from being strait-laced, must have been shocked at the harem of both sexes which his general, even in wartime, used to cart around with him. Antony was an ignorant, profligate, vigorous, full-blooded, and violent aristocrat. Cicero, poking his nose into his past, found plenty of grounds there for all his accusations.

The battle between the two armies took place near Modena, and Octavian was so outrageously lucky that he was the only general to survive; Hirtius and Pansa were killed, and Antony, beaten for the first time in his life, fled. The victor returned to Rome at the head of all the troops quartered in Italy, and went straight to the senate to insist on his appointment as consul, the abolition of the amnesty for the Ides of March conspirators, and their sentence to death. The senate, which had counted on using him as a tool, was indignant and offered resistance. Whereupon Octavian summoned another of Caesar's lieutenants, Lepidus, sent him to make peace with Antony, and the three of them established the second triumvirate, thus demonstrating that the youngster had learned his uncle's lesson. The senate bowed its head and in the days that followed had leisure to reflect that a dictator's successor always makes one regret his predecessor.

Patrols of soldiers were stationed at all the gates of the city and the great purge began. Three hundred senators and 2,000 officials, indicted for the murder of Caesar, were tried and executed after the confiscation of all their possessions. Anyone who fled had a price of 25,000 *drachmae*, about $16,000, put on his head. Most of them preferred to kill themselves, a gesture reminiscent of the great Romans of ancient times. The tribune Salvius gave a banquet, drank poison, and left as his last wish the order that dinner should continue in the presence of his corpse. His wish was granted. Fulvia, the wife of Antony, had the innocent Rufus hanged at the door of his own house only because he had not wanted to sell it to her. Her husband was not in a position to stop her because at that moment he was in bed with the wife of Coponius, who by this arrangement saved her husband's life.

Antony's sweetest revenge was upon Cicero, not only because the "Philippics" had stuck in his throat, but because he wanted to avenge Clodius, whose widow he had married, and Lentulus, Antony's stepfather, whom Cicero had had killed in prison during Catiline's conspiracy. The "Father of His Country" had tried to escape by embarking at Antium. Unfortunately, he suffered from seasickness, which seemed worse than death to him and forced him to land at Formiae. Antony's battalions swooped down on him. Cicero forbade his servants to offer resistance and meekly extended his neck. His decapitated head and right hand were taken to the triumvirs. Antony was overjoyed, and Octavian was, or pretended to be, indignant. He had never cared much for Cicero, who had played a double game with his uncle, and had allied himself with Caesar's murderers after praising him so highly when he was alive. Octavian himself he had described as *"laudandum adolescentem, ornandum, tollendum."* It sounded like praise but *tollendum* not only meant "to be exalted," but also "to be killed." There was little doubt about the interpretation of a double meaning when it came from the mouth of Cicero. Thus died the greatest orator of Rome, victim of his own oratory.

All that remained to be done was to punish the principal guilty parties, Brutus and Cassius. They had departed as governors of Macedonia and Syria respectively and had joined forces, thus creating the last of the armies of republican Rome, which was not destined to leave a happy memory of itself in those provinces. Palestine, Cilicia, and Thrace were literally stripped bare. Whole populations, particularly the Jews, who had not the wherewithal to pay their tribute, were reduced to slavery. Virtue did not prevent Brutus from besieging, starving, and driving to mass suicide the inhabitants of Xanthus. When they arrived the armies of Antony and Octavian were welcomed as "liberators."

The battle took place at Philippi in September of 42 B.C. Brutus broke Octavian's line of battle. Antony broke through that of Cassius, who had himself killed by an attendant. Octavian was in bed in his tent with one of his usual attacks of influenza, so Antony waited for him to recover before setting out with him in pursuit of Brutus. The latter, when he saw his men waver, threw himself on a friend's sword. Antony looked for his body and, when he found it, in pity covered it with his purple tunic. He remembered that Brutus had set only one condition for joining the plot against Caesar: that Antony should be spared.

At Philippi the greatest names of the aristocracy fell with the republic. Those who were not killed in battle committed suicide, as did the son of Hortensius and the son of Cato. They were all that remained of the flower of the ancient Roman patrician class and at least they proved themselves brave soldiers to the very end. At home only the craven and corrupt remained. These people would do anything to avoid hardship and danger and were quite prepared to accept even the dividing up of the great empire by the victors. Octavian took the European slice, Lepidus was given Africa. Antony chose Egypt, Greece, and the Middle East. Each of the three knew that the arrangement was purely temporary and, except for Lepidus, who was satisfied with what he had gotten, hoped sooner or later to get rid of the other two. The most likely to succeed was Antony, who believed in military force only, and knew that as a general he was superior to his colleagues.

The first thing he did was to send a message to Cleopatra, ordering her to come to him at Tarsus to answer the accusation of having helped and financed Cassius. Cleopatra obeyed. On the day fixed for her appearance, Antony prepared to receive her on a majestic throne raised in the middle of the forum, and in the presence of the population, who were all agog at the thought of the forthcoming trial. Cleopatra arrived on a ship with red sails, a golden prow, and a silver-plated keel. The crew was composed of her maids, dressed as nymphs, who thronged around a lamé canopy under which she lay, provocatively attired as Venus, intent on the melodies played to her on pipes and flutes. When the news of this extraordinary apparition on the waters of the River Cydnus spread around town, everybody rushed to the port to see her, as they do today to see Sophia Loren. Antony was left alone in a towering rage. He sent for her and she replied that he was expected on board for dinner. Furious, Antony went, still considering himself the judge and her the accused. When he saw her, he was dumbfounded. He had met her as a little girl in Alexandria; seeing her again as a mature woman, it was only too obvious why Caesar had been enthralled by her. His generals were already at her feet. Dinner began with his haughty accusations and ended with his giving her Phoenicia, Cyprus, and large helpings of Arabia and Palestine. She rewarded him that very night, and when she left took him with her to Alexandria, where he seems to have forgotten all about the precarious nature of his position. Cleopatra, on the other hand, remembered it well. She entirely understood that the empire could not tolerate three masters. Though she probably did not love Antony, and perhaps had never loved anybody, she intended to use him as the instrument for the operation which with Caesar she had failed to carry through.

While all this was going on at Alexandria, Octavian was laying the foundations of the reunification. It was not easy. Sextus Pompey was busy again in Spain and blocking supplies. Unemployment was spreading, inflation threatened, and the senate was proving obstructive unless adequately bribed. On top of all this, Antony's wife, Fulvia, perhaps to get her husband out of Cleopatra's spell and back to Rome, organized a plot with his brother Lucius. They raised an army and stirred the Italians to revolt. Marcus Agrippa, Octavian's most trusted lieutenant, had to intervene to put down this uprising. Lucius surrendered at Perugia and Fulvia died of anger, disappointment, and jealousy.

In these events Antony, egged on by Cleopatra, saw his

opportunity. He assembled his army and sailed with it for Brindisi, where he besieged Octavian's garrison. However, the soldiers on both sides refused to fight and so their generals were obliged to make peace. This was sealed by Antony's wedding to Octavian's sister, Octavia.

History does not relate Cleopatra's reaction to this episode, which put an apparent end to her projects. Separated from her, Antony seemed to have recovered some of his reason. He took his wife to Athens, where she endeavored to interest him in the monuments of its culture and the lessons of its philosophers. This interlude ended with his sending her back to Rome and setting out with his legions for Persia. Here Labienus, son of Caesar's treacherous general, was organizing an army in the service of its rebel king. Cleopatra joined Antony at Antioch, and though she disapproved of the undertaking and refused to finance it, she accompanied her lover. He vainly pursued the enemy for three hundred miles, lost a good proportion of his 100,000 men, imposed a theoretical vassalage on Armenia, proclaimed himself victor, and treated himself to a solemn triumph at Alexandria, thus scandalizing Rome, who considered that she had the monopoly of such ceremonies. Antony then gave notice of divorce to Octavia, which broke the only link he had with Octavian, married Cleopatra, endowed the two sons he had had by her with all the Middle East, and named Caesarion heir to the crown of Egypt and Cyprus.

In this way he rendered inevitable the conflict with Octavian, who was preparing for it with his usual cautious tenacity. He, too, had had his sentimental complications. He had fallen in love—it is difficult to imagine—with Livia, the wife of Tiberius Claudius Nero, who was in her fifth month of pregnancy. Although Octavian was still under thirty, he had already been married twice before: first to Claudia and then to Scribonia, who had given him a daughter, Julia. Now he divorced Scribonia and amicably persuaded Tiberius Claudius Nero to do the same with Livia. He adopted her two sons, Tiberius, who was almost full-grown, and Drusus, who was about to be born, as if they had been his own.

These domestic affairs settled, he turned to the work of reconstruction. Sextus' blockade was broken with the destruction of his fleet, order was restored, and a newborn confidence put hoarded capital again into circulation. Marcus Agrippa, besides being a good general, was an incomparable minister of war. In fact he was the real reorganizer of the great army which was to restore unity to the Roman Empire.

XXIX

Augustus

IN THE SPRING OF THE YEAR 32 B.C. A MESSENGER FROM ANTONY arrived in Rome with a letter to the senate. In this the triumvir proposed that he and his two colleagues, having restored the republican institutions, should all three simultaneously resign their positions and commands and retire to private life. The proposal was so astute that it is easier to imagine it originating with Cleopatra than with Antony.

Octavian was embarrassed. To escape from his dilemma he published Antony's will which he said he had obtained from the vestals with whom it had been deposited. It designated as Antony's sole heirs the two sons he had had by Cleopatra and nominated her as regent. There are grave doubts as to the authenticity of this document. However, it served to confirm the suspicions which all Rome harbored with regard to "the Serpent of the Nile." It also enabled Octavian to embark on a war of "independence" that he declared, with much perspicacity, on Cleopatra and not on Antony.

It was a naval war. The two fleets met at Actium. Octavian's commanded by Agrippa, though inferior in numbers, defeated the enemy, who retired in disorder to Alexandria. Octavian did not go in pursuit. He knew that time was on his side and that the longer Antony stayed in Egypt the more he would be softened by orgies and idleness. Instead, he landed in Athens to settle the Greek situation and then returned to Italy to put down a revolt. After this, he again set out on a wide sweep through Asia Minor to isolate Antony by destroying the alliances he had made there. Finally he closed in on Alexandria. On the way he received three letters: one from Cleopatra, together with a scepter and crown, symbols of her submission, and two from Antony suing for peace. To Cleopatra he replied that he would leave her on the throne if she killed her lover. All things considered, it is surprising that she ignored the offer.

With the courage of despair Antony attacked and gained a partial victory. This however was not enough to prevent Octavian from enclosing the city in a trap. The next day Cleopatra's mercenaries surrendered and the news reached Antony that the queen was dead. He tried to kill himself with a dagger. When he learned that she was still alive, he had himself carried to the tower in which she was barricaded with her handmaidens and died in her arms.

Cleopatra asked permission to bury the body and sought an audience. Octavian agreed. She appeared before him as she had done before Antony—perfumed, bistered, and clad only in queenly veils. Under those veils, however, there was now a woman of forty, not twenty-nine, who revealed all too plainly the sad ravages of time. Augustus needed no great strength to resist her temptations and informed her that he was going to take her to Rome to adorn his triumph. She put an asp to her breast and let it poison her. Her handmaidens did likewise.

Octavian settled the question of the succession in characteristic manner. He allowed the two corpses to be buried side by side, killed young Caesarion, and sent back the two sons of the dead couple to Octavia, who brought them up as if they had been her own. So as not to humiliate Egypt by making her a Roman province, he proclaimed himself king, helped himself to her enormous treasure, put a prefect in charge and went home. Here he quietly did away with Antony's eldest son by Fulvia.

By now he was just thirty-one and absolute master of all Caesar's heritage. The senate no longer had the desire, or the strength, to dispute it with him. But out of caution he refrained from asking for the throne. Octavian was aware that the word "king" still held odious memories. There was no point in awakening certain ideas slumbering in torpid consciences. The Romans had ceased to believe in democratic institutions. They knew the corruption to which they were heir. They did, however, care about the form. They wanted order, peace, safety, a good administration, a sound currency, and their savings guaranteed. Octavian set about giving them these.

He paid off the army, which now numbered half a million, with the gold brought back from Egypt, keeping only 200,000 men under arms, calling himself their *imperator*, a purely military title. He settled the rest of the soldiers as peasants on lands specially acquired for the purpose. He cancelled the debts of private citizens to the state and initiated a great public works program. But these were just the first and easiest steps. Like Caesar, Octavian did not wish to confine himself to mere administration, but also wished to carry out gigantic reforms and reconstruct the whole of society on the lines laid down by his uncle. Octavian was the real inventor of bureaucracy. He gathered around him a sort of cabinet, composed of experts whom he had the knack of choosing well. There was a great organizer like Agrippa, a great financier like Maecenas, and various generals, including Octavian's stepson, Tiberius, soon to become prominent.

As almost all these belonged to the upper-middle class, the aristocrats complained that they had been excluded. Octavian, therefore, chose some twenty of them, all senators, to form a sort of privy council which gradually became the mouthpiece of the senate and ratified its decisions. The assembly still continued to meet but more and more infrequently, and it never made any attempt to oppose Octavian, who stood for the consulship thirteen times running, and naturally was elected every time. In 27 B.C. he suddenly placed all his powers in the hands of the senate, proclaimed the restoration of the republic, and announced his intention of retiring to private life. He was only thirty-five at this time and the sole title he had accepted was the new one of "prince." The senate responded by abdicating in its turn and handing all his powers back to him, begging him to accept them. They also conferred on him the name of "Augustus," meaning the "increaser," an adjective which later became used as a noun. Octavian accepted with an air of resignation. It was a comedy, perfectly acted on both sides, and it proved that the conservative and republican front was dead. Even the proudest senator preferred a master to chaos.

The master, however, continued to show discretion in the use of his powers. He lived in Hortensius' very splendid palace, but he did not transform it into a court, and kept a monastically furnished little room with a study on the ground floor as his personal apartment. Even when, many years later, the building was destroyed by fire and he built another one like it, he insisted that these two rooms should be identically rebuilt. He

was a sober creature of habit who kept to a strict timetable. As
he considered himself the first servant of the state, he worked
very hard and used to put everything in writing: not only the
speeches he was to make in public, but also those he made at
home to his wife and family. Not until Franz Josef of Austria,
to whom he was similar in many respects, can history produce a
sovereign so attached to duty, so respectable, prosaic, and un-
attractive. Or one so unhappy in his family affections.

These embraced Julia, his daughter by Scribonia, Livia, his
third wife, and his two stepsons, Drusus and Tiberius, whom
she had brought with her. Livia was an irreproachable wife, if a
little dull and too ostentatiously virtuous. She brought up her
children well, did a great deal for charity, and bore her husband's various infidelities with resignation. Everything leads one
to believe that she was far less interested in love than she was
in the power of Augustus and the careers of her sons. These, in
fact, made rapid headway. Generals at the age of twenty, they
were sent to subdue Illyria and Pannonia. Augustus, who had
brought about the *pax Romana,* soon gave up the idea of war
and new annexations, but he wanted to guarantee the boundaries of the empire, which were continually threatened. Drusus,
his favorite, extended them from the Rhône to the Elbe to make
them safer, beating the Germans brilliantly, but during the
battle he fell from his horse and was seriously injured. Tiberius,
who adored him, and who was in Gaul at the time, galloped four
hundred miles to get to him. He arrived just in time to close his
eyes. The death of this gay, impetuous, and expansive lad was a
great blow to Augustus since he had intended to make him
his successor. Now he hoped that Julia would give him another
heir.

This lively, sensual, and flighty girl was the apple of his
eye. At the age of fourteen he had married her to Marcellus,
son of his sister Octavia, the widow of Antony, but Marcellus
had died shortly afterward. Julia had then become the gayest
widow in all Rome. She enjoyed not only misbehaving but
also talking about it. Her father, who had begun to issue laws
for the promotion of public morality, decided that he might get
her back on the straight and narrow by finding her another
husband. He chose Marcus Agrippa, his minister of war who,
after the victory at Actium, had become his most trusted and
able collaborator. A great soldier, gentleman, and engineer, he

had pacified Spain and Gaul, reorganized trade, and built roads. He was the only important figure of whom it was never murmured that he made money on the side. Augustus, who was a planner by nature, and thought he had the right to interfere with the happiness of others, did not worry about the fact that Agrippa was forty-two and Julia was eighteen and that the former already had a wife with whom he was very happy. He insisted on his divorcing and remarrying.

The couple could not have been more ill-suited to one another, even though they did bring five children into the world. These, somewhat surprisingly, all resembled Agrippa. Julia, when brazenly asked for an explanation, would reply with equal brass: "I only embark new sailors on the ship when it is already laden." Eight years later Agrippa died. Julia again became the Merry Widow of Rome. To put a stop to all this, Augustus insisted on a third marriage, this time to Tiberius, whom he now saw, or whom Livia made him see, as a possible regent for the empire until such time as Julia's sons, Gaius and Lucius, came of age. Tiberius was already happily married to Agrippa's daughter, Vipsania. But this happiness did not coincide with that planned by Augustus. He destroyed it and replaced it with sheer misery. When, instead of being Agrippa's son-in-law, he took his place as Julia's husband, Tiberius had to put up with all that the most wretched husband has ever had to put up with from a wife. When he could not stand it any longer, he retired to private life in Rhodes, where he spent seven years studying. Julia's scandals, meanwhile, put even the memory of Clodia in the shade. Gaius and Lucius died, one of typhoid and the other in battle, and Augustus, now sixty, was shattered by these misfortunes. Consumed by eczema and rheumatism and increasingly under the thumb of Livia, he finally banished his daughter to the island Pandateria for immorality. He then recalled Tiberius, and though he never really like him much, adopted him as his son and heir.

Perhaps at that moment he thought he was going to die. His colitis and influenza gave him no respite and he never took a step without his private doctor, Antony Musa. He had become crotchety, suspicious, and cruel. For a mere indiscretion he had the legs of his secretary, Tallus, broken, and to protect himself from nonexistent plots he invented the police, that is to say, those praetorians or bodyguards, who later were to play such a nefarious role under his successors. Ever more skeptical, and embittered by his sufferings, he clearly saw the failure of his work of reconstruction. True, there was the *pax Augusta*. The sailors from the east used to come and thank him for the safety with which they now sailed the seas, but Varus, with three legions, had been massacred on the Elbe by the German, Arminius, and the frontier had had to be withdrawn to the Rhône. Augustus guessed that on the other side, in the depths of their forests, the Germanic tribes were in a ferment. Trade, revived by Agrippa, was flourishing and the currency, stabilized by Maecenas, was sound. The administration was functioning, the army was strong, but the great moral reform had failed. Divorce and birth control had destroyed the family and the Roman race was almost extinct. The last census had shown that three-quarters of the population were freedmen or sons of foreign freedmen. Hundreds of new temples had been built but the gods they housed were, in effect, not there, since the people no longer believed in them. Morals cannot be renewed without a religious basis. Augustus had tried to revive the ancient faith without believing in it himself. The result was that the people pretended to adore him as a god.

Julia, who died in exile, had left Augustus a granddaughter, called Julia like her mother. Unfortunately she showed every sign of taking after her in more than name. Her grandfather had to have her, also, exiled for immorality. Broken by this new grief, he thought of starving himself to death but his sense of duty and the certainty that he had not long to live prevailed. In fact, for those times, he lived to a very great age.

He was seventy-six and convalescing after an attack of bronchitis when death surprised him at Nola. That morning he had worked as usual from eight until midday, the perfect official, signing decrees and answering correspondence. Sending for Livia, with whom he was about to celebrate his golden wedding, he bade her an affectionate farewell. Then, like a great Roman, he turned to those present and said: "I have played my part well. So, my friends, let me leave the stage with your applause."

Before cremating the corpse, the senators bore the coffin all around Rome on their shoulders. They should have been glad to get rid of him, but unfortunately they knew that Tiberius was his successor-designate.

XXX

Virgil, Ovid, Horace, and Livy

MANY YEARS BEFORE, WHEN HE HAD RETURNED VICTORIOUS FROM
his campaign against Antony, Augustus had found Maecenas
waiting for him at Brindisi with a young poet from Mantua
named Virgil. Virgil was the son of a civil servant of Celtic
birth, whose little farm, in which he had invested all his savings,
had been confiscated by the army. The boy had then come to
Rome and published a book of poems, the *Eclogues*, which had
been well received. Maecenas had become his protector. He
planned to use him as a propagandist for Augustus, and this was
why he had come to introduce him.

Augustus had the author read him the unpublished manuscript of the *Georgics*. He took a liking to him for two reasons
which had little or nothing to do with art. First of all, Virgil was
sickly and broken-down like himself and so they could talk for
hours about their respective infirmities. And, secondly, these
poems extolled the pleasures of that same rustic, frugal life to
which Augustus wanted all the Romans to return. Actually, as
Seneca points out, Virgil described the country with all the
mannerisms, style, and artificiality of a city dweller, but Augustus did not have the sensitivity to notice this. The only thing that
really mattered to him was that Virgil's poetry had didactic virtues. He rewarded the author by having his confiscated farm
restored to his father. Virgil, however, did not return there. He
far preferred writing about the countryside while sitting in
Rome. But he was greatly obliged to Augustus, and with the aim
of celebrating his victories composed the *Aeneid* in his honor.
He wrote slowly, with great diligence and attention to style.
Since, with the income from the farm and the generosity of
Maecenas, he no longer had to earn his living and had no other
amusements, he spent most of his day working. He never married, because of his ill health. His friends in Naples, where every
now and then he used to winter, nicknamed him the "little
virgin." Augustus was anxious to see the finished work. Occasionally Virgil read him a passage but he never reached the end
of it. In 19 B.C. he interrupted his writing to visit the emperor in

Athens, and as he lay dying at Brindisi, where he had been taken, he begged his friends to destroy the manuscript of the poem. Perhaps he deemed the epic not to be his vocation and preferred to leave other, fragmentary elegiac compositions to posterity. Augustus prevented the dead man's wishes from being carried out. Thanks to his desire to preserve this uncompleted monument to his own glory, he saved for us an authentic masterpiece.

Augustus' interest in literature was not confined merely to Virgil. It also included many other writers, among them Horace and Propertius. Maecenas, who backed them, used to present them to him, and thus gave his name to all patrons of the arts. This excuses him for the extremely poor verses which he himself insisted on composing. After Atticus had first established his publishing firm, many others had sprung up and a flourishing business had come into being. Editions of 5,000 or 10,000 copies, at from $1.50 to $3.00 a copy, all handwritten by slaves, were sold out in a few months. Books were becoming a necessary adjunct for the interior decoration of any self-respecting household, even if they were never read. Orders came pouring in from the provinces.

This fashion had a great influence on society. Instead of remaining rude and warlike, it became increasingly intellectual and literary. This was the reason why Augustus saw the fad for reading as an instrument for his moral reforms. Until old age and sufferings made him susceptible and touchy, he was always tolerant of epigrams and satires, even those aimed directly at him. He had public libraries built, and advised Tiberius to go easy on punishments and censorship. He even went so far as to compose some verses himself to send to a certain Greek who used to wait for him every day when he came out of his palace so that he could read him his own. This Greek rewarded him with a gift of a few *denarii* and a very courteous letter in which he excused himself for not being able to pay better owing to his poverty. Augustus was highly amused at this sally and had him sent 100,000 sesterces.

These writers and poets, however, rather let the emperor down by devoting the worst of their efforts to state propaganda and the best to aiding and abetting the deplorable tendencies of an ever more libertine and cynical society. The public did not want the great themes of glory, religion, and nature but preferred those of love and dalliance. The minstrel for these new motifs was Ovid, a lawyer from the Abruzzi, who had embittered his father by refusing a political career, proclaiming that he had been personally chosen by Venus to sing of Eros. He married three women, loved numerous others, and wrote about all of them with the utmost frankness. He openly declared that he did not give a damn for all the various little Catos who criticized him. The success of his sugary, lascivious verse led him to believe that he was a great poet. The last modest words of his *Metamorphoses* are: "I shall live on in the centuries to come."

This ink was hardly dry when he received an order from Augustus sending him into exile at Tomis on the Black Sea. The exact reason for the emperor's punishment has never been known. Ovid is said to have been having an affair with Augustus' granddaughter Julia. In fact she was banished at roughly the same time. Like all men to whom success comes easily, Ovid had no fortitude in adversity. His laments from his place of exile, *Ex Ponto* and *Tristia,* are more to the credit of his elegiac vein than his character. In spite of the fact that he sent a thousand letters vainly imploring mercy from the emperor and help from his friends, he never returned to Rome alive.

Generally speaking, although it has been called the Golden Age, the Augustan period did not see a literary and artistic flowering comparable to that of Greece under Pericles or Italy during the Renaissance. Under this bourgeois emperor, a correspondingly bourgeois taste developed. The middle course often means mediocrity. The qualities which were most appreciated were moderation and a sense of proportion, seasoned with a certain good-humored and homespun skepticism. In fact the most representative writer of the time is Horace.

He was the son of an Apulian tax collector who wished to make a lawyer out of him. At great sacrifice he sent him to study first at Rome and then at Athens. Here Horace met Brutus, who was preparing for the battle of Philippi. Brutus took a liking to the young man and immediately put him in command of a legion, which may give us some idea as to why his army was beaten. In the middle of the battle Horace threw away his helmet, shield, and saber and fled to Athens to write a poem about how sweet and noble it was to die for the fatherland.

Repatriated, without a penny to his name, he got a job as assistant to a quaestor. Since he was not invited to society salons and did not know any respectable women, he began to write verse about the ladies of easy virtue with whom he consorted. One day Virgil, having read a book of his, spoke of it enthusiastically to Maecenas, who expressed a desire to meet the author. Maecenas immediately liked the rather vulgar, vainglorious, and timid little provincial and recommended him as a secretary to Augustus. Horace, however, refused what to anybody else would have seemed a gift from heaven. This was partly because he was neither ambitious nor greedy. Most of all, probably, it was because he had no intention of tying his destiny to that of a politician who one day might get killed and involve him in the same fate. Maecenas, to enable him to devote more leisure to literature, gave him a villa with fertile lands in the Sabine hills. It was excavated in 1932 and gives us some idea of the magnate's generosity. It had twenty-four rooms, a spacious portico, three baths, a beautiful garden, and five dependent farms.

Now that he was a well-to-do landowner, Horace could devote himself to his true calling, that of the moralist. His *Satires* are priceless vignettes of everyday Romans of his time. He took them from the street, not from history or high society, and presented each one with cynical detachment. Every now and then, to keep in well with the government, he used to write a poem in rhetorical and insincere praise of Augustus. The latter was highly flattered and commissioned him to complete his *Odes* with a secular *Carmen* in which his deeds and those of Drusus and Tiberius were to be extolled. Horace set about it. He had to seek inspiration in Glory, Fate, and Infallible Destinies, none of which attracted him in the least. Exhausted and bored, he finished this dreary poem after having interrupted it a thousand times to write the *Epistolae* to his friends, especially to Maecenas. These, together with his *Satires*, remain his masterpiece. He became ever more sedentary owing to ill health which compelled him to take great care of himself and to observe a rigid diet. In vain Maecenas encouraged him to travel; Horace preferred to stay in Rome or, better still, in his villa, where his diet was a forkful of homemade spaghetti, a minute portion of boiled meat, and a stewed apple. To make up for this, he wrote poems about convivial friendship, succulent banquets, deep potations, and making love to Glycera, Neaera, Pyrrha, Lydia, Lalage, and countless other females who either never existed or whom he hardly knew. For virtue he had the stoic's respect, for

pleasure the epicurean's appreciation, but he could not practice
one or the other owing to his heartburn, rheumatism, and liver
trouble.

He was fully aware of the decadence of society, and despite his own complete lack of belief, attributed it to the decay
of religion. The fear of death cast a gloom over his latter years,
during which he even refused to go to Rome. His letters are
pervaded with it. "You've loved, eaten, and drunk enough and
now it is time for you to pass on," he used to repeat to himself.
He died at the age of fifty-seven, leaving his property to the
emperor, and asked to be buried beside Maecenas, who had
died a few months previously. His wish was granted.

What the period of Augustus did not contribute to art and
philosophy was compensated for by the contribution to history
made by Titus Livy. He was born at Padua, and, like Virgil, was
a Celt. He, too, according to the wishes of his family, should
have become a lawyer, but being disgusted by the contemporary city, he preferred to make a study of ancient Rome. Unfortunately he has left us nothing in writing about his personal
affairs. He was too busy composing 142 books, starting *ab urbe
condita*, from the foundation of the city, and continuing with the
Horatii and the Scipios. Only about forty of these have been
handed down to us. It was an enormous work, carried out with
scrupulous care and attention to detail. No wonder that when
he got as far as the Punic Wars he had had enough and wanted
to stop. It was Augustus who encouraged him to go on.

This is rather surprising, considering that the works of Livy
are one long hymn of praise for the great republican, conservative aristocracy and, as such, opposed to Caesar and Caesarism.
But they are also a paean to the ancient, austere customs and to
the Roman "character." This was what the emperor liked. We
have some reservations as to the accuracy of Livy's accounts,
especially when he has his personages make lengthy speeches,
which sound more like himself than them. His is a story of
heroes, an enormous tapestry of episodes that carries the reader
away rather more than informing him. If one is to believe Livy,
Rome, like Italy in Mussolini's time, was inhabited only by
warriors and seafarers of absolute rectitude. They merely conquered the world to improve its morals and make it a better
place. According to him, men are divided into the good and the
bad. In Rome there were only the good and outside only the

bad. From his point of view, even a great general like Hannibal becomes a common rascal.

All this does not alter the fact that Livy's history, which took up an entire fifty years of its author's life, remains a great literary monument, perhaps the greatest achieved under the auspices of Augustus.

XXXI

Tiberius and Caligula

THE ONE THING THAT CAN CERTAINLY BE SAID ABOUT TIBERIUS IS that he was born under an unlucky star. When his mother brought him as a boy into the home of Augustus, the emperor only had eyes for his brother Drusus. Drusus was as attractive, lively, arrogant, and impulsive as Tiberius was timid, reserved, thoughtful, and sensitive. He might well have become jealous and resentful. Instead, he looked up to Drusus with affection and risked his life in an effort to save him when he was injured in Germany. He even escorted his brother's bier from the Elbe to Rome on horseback. It took him years to get over his grief.

He had studied a lot, and as soon as he was given an army, he won numerous victories over warlike and crafty enemies like the Illyrians and the Pannonians. When they gave him provinces to administer, he organized them with efficiency and honesty. At the age of twenty they already called him "the little old man" because of his gravity. He devoted his few leisure hours to polishing his excellent Greek and studying astrology. This gained him a reputation as a heretic. He never moved in society or went to the Circus. Possibly the first woman to engage his affection was his wife Vipsania, the daughter of Agrippa, a lady of great virtue and of domestic habits similar to his own.

Had he been allowed to stay married to her perhaps his character would have remained as it had been in his youth, that of a simple, serene Stoic, generous with his friends, and more exacting with himself than with others. The fact that his soldiers adored him proves this. In Rome he was hated for being the personification of a virtue which was a reproach to all. Augustus, however, made him divorce his wife in order to marry his own daughter, Julia, delightful but wayward, and eminently unsuitable as a companion to one of his nature. Why did Tiberius give way? It was true that the inheritance was at stake but he had never seemed to attach much importance to it. He had been an industrious subordinate of his stepfather but had never tried to curry favor with him, preferring to be esteemed rather than loved. Certainly Livia must have been instrumental in procuring his compliance. She may have been an exemplary wife to Augustus but she was a bad mother for Tiberius, out for his advancement even when it cost him his happiness.

Tiberius bore his matrimonial misfortunes with dignity. It was said that he refused to denounce Julia for adultery (as was his duty and legal right) to avoid annoying Augustus, but in fact he withdrew from public life and retired as a private citizen to Rhodes, where he most likely spent his most peaceful period. The emperor then banished Julia. Her two sons Gaius and Lucius being dead, he sent for Tiberius again, and we can once more discern the hand of Livia. When Tiberius finally succeeded Augustus he was already fifty-five. His first step was to appear before the senate and ask it to relieve him of his responsibilities and to restore the republic. The senate thought that he was simply striking a pose (perhaps he was) and although it detested him, begged him to remain. When it asked his permission to name a month after him, as it had done for Augustus, Tiberius replied: "What, pray, will you do from the thirteenth heir onwards?"

With this sardonic attitude toward every kind of adulation, the chaste and taciturn Tiberius set about the job of governing with much equity and shrewdness. On his death he left the state much richer and more prosperous than it had been when he had taken it over. Unluckily he became the victim of the pens of Tacitus and Suetonius, two republican historians, who made him the scapegoat for all the evils of the period.

The most serious charge against him is that of adopting his nephew Germanicus as his son and heir and then having him murdered. Germanicus was the son of Drusus and of Antonia, a niece of Augustus. He was a handsome, intelligent, vivacious, and courageous boy who was very popular in Rome. Tiberius sent him to the east as governor to gain experience. It was, however, insinuated that he had exiled him because he was jealous of him. As he died out there, people said that Piso, on the orders of Tiberius, had murdered him. Piso committed suicide to avoid trial. Agrippina, the widow of Germanicus, was among the most implacable of Tiberius's accusers but Antonia, the boy's mother, stood up for him. And between a wife and a mother, the truth is more likely to lie on the side of the mother.

Another accusation made against him was that of cruelty to Livia. He certainly owed the throne to her but she could not have been very easy to get on with. She claimed the right to countersign imperial decrees and would frequently remind Tiberius that but for her he would still have been an *émigré* in Rhodes. Moreover, she considered herself mistress of the household and when he went out refused to let him have the keys. Finally Tiberius went to live by himself in a modest and gloomy apartment where there was nobody to nag him. Even so, he still had to put up with Agrippina who had another claim on him: the life of Germanicus. This Agrippina, apart from being his niece (having married the son of his brother Drusus), was also his stepdaughter. She was the child of Julia's marriage to Agrippa and, when Julia married Tiberius, Agrippina came with her. She was a greedy and querulous woman with all the vices and not one of the good qualities of her mother, who had been charming, witty, and generous. She had had a son by Germanicus, a certain Nero, who now, according to her, should be designated heir in the place of his dead father. Tiberius endured her carping with patient resignation. "Do you really feel so wronged because you are not empress?" he used to ask. Tiberius also had a son, Drusus, by his beloved and virtuous Vipsania, but he was a vicious wastrel and Tiberius had disinherited him. He actually was looking for an heir, but was uncertain whether Nero was the right choice.

A series of plots were hatched against him, which were reported by Sejanus, the commander of the praetorian guard of the palace. It is uncertain how genuine they were, but gradually Sejanus became the only man Tiberius trusted. As a result he allowed him to bring the strength of the guard up to nine cohorts, little realizing what a terrible precedent he was setting. At which point he retired to Capri.

One can hardly say that he ceased to rule while he was there but he transmitted all his orders through Sejanus. The latter altered them to suit himself and so became the real master of the city. Finally he unearthed still another conspiracy involving Titius Sabinus, Agrippina, and Nero, and received authority to punish them. The first was executed, the second banished to Pandateria, and the third committed suicide. By now Drusus was dead, as was the "Mother of the Fatherland," the derisive name by which Livia was called.

One day his sister-in-law Antonia, the mother of Germanicus, at the risk of her life sent Tiberius a secret note warning him that Sejanus was now plotting to assassinate him and take his place. Tiberius, in spite of his age, rushed to Rome, arrested the traitor and handed him over to the senate for trial. As the senate had lived for years in terror of this satrap, not only Sejanus but all his friends and relations were executed. His adolescent daughter was duly deflowered before the trial because the execution of virgins was prohibited by law. His wife committed suicide, but not before she had written a letter to Tiberius denouncing Livilla, the daughter of Antonia, as one of Sejanus' accomplices. Tiberius had her arrested and she starved herself to death in prison. Agrippina also killed herself. The Tiberius who emerged from this orgy of bloodshed and familial treachery was naturally no longer the man he had been. He lived another six years, and it appears that his mind was deranged. In 37 A.D. he decided to leave Capri, and during his journey through Campania was taken ill, possibly with a heart attack. When his courtiers saw that he was recovering, they put a pillow over his head and suffocated him.

Tiberius had kept the peace, improved the administration, and enriched the treasury, but although the empire seemed intact, its capital had become increasingly corrupt. To arrest this decay, the strong hand of a great reformer was needed. Perhaps Tiberius thought he discerned the necessary qualities in the second son of Agrippina and Germanicus, Caius. The soldiers among whom he had grown up in Germany used to call him Caligula, or "Little Boot," because of the military footwear he always wore.

At first, he seemed to have been a good choice. Caligula was generous to the poor, restored a semblance of democracy by giving back its powers to the assembly, and was noted as a brave and conscientious soldier. The sudden change in him can only be explained by some mental disease: a typical case of schizophrenia or dissociation of the personality. He began having fits of terror at night, especially during thunderstorms when he used to wander around the palace crying for help. Tall, well-built, and athletic, he used to spend hours in front of the mirror making faces at himself. He was very good at this, as he had pop-eyes, while a bald patch on top of his head made him look like a friar. At one time he had a craze for everything Egyptian and insisted on introducing Egyptian customs into Rome. He made the senators kiss his feet and duel with gladiators in the Circus, where they regularly got killed. He also made them elect his horse, Incitatus, consul, and built a marble stable and an ivory manger for it. Still aping Egypt, he took his sisters as mistresses. One of them, in fact, Drusilla, he actually married and nominated heiress to the throne. He then repudiated her in order to marry Orestilla on the very day she was to marry Gaius Piso. He stopped at his fourth wife, the rather ugly Caesonia, who was already pregnant when he met her. To her he was devoted and faithful. Who knows why?

Because of their hatred of the monarchy, Dion Cassius and Suetonius may have exaggerated somewhat, but Caligula must certainly have been a criminal lunatic. One morning he woke up in a rage against bald men. He ordered all those he could find to be fed to the wild beasts of the Circus who, owing to a famine, were ravenous. Then came the turn of philosophers and he sentenced them all to death or deportation. Only his uncle Claudius, because he was considered mentally deficient, and the young Seneca, because he pretended to be seriously ill, were spared. Not knowing whom to persecute next he forced his grandmother, Antonia, to commit suicide because, looking at her one day, he found that she had a beautiful head but that it sat badly on her shoulders. Finally he picked on Jove. He said that Jove was an inflated balloon and that he had wrongfully usurped the position of king of the gods. He therefore had the heads removed from all his statues and replaced by his own.

All this was a pity because in his rare moments of lucidity he was friendly and witty with a turn for repartee. To a Gaulish cobbler who called him a mountebank to his face he replied: "True, but do you think my subjects are any better?" In fact, if they had been they would have found a way of getting rid of him. Instead they applauded him and the senators were the first to kiss his feet.

It took the praetorian commander Cassius Chaerea to rid
Rome of this pest. Caligula as a matter of routine took delight
in heaping obscene insults on everyone, but this Cassius was
touchy and one evening, as he was escorting the emperor along
the corridor of the theater, he knifed him. The city could hardly
believe its ears. They suspected that it was a trick of Caligula's
to expose and punish those who were pleased at his death. To
convince everybody that it was true, the praetorian guard also
killed his wife, Caesonia, and shattered his baby daughter's
skull against the wall.

This was a suitable end to the personages concerned and
the sinister atmosphere of terror and madness in which they had
lived. Such, by now, was Rome, the capital of an empire where
regicide was the only alternative to unbridled tyranny. Incapable of killing their own tyrants, the Romans had to resort to
mercenaries.

XXXII

Claudius and Seneca

THE PRAETORIANS, HAVING KILLED CALIGULA, WERE MASTERS OF
the situation and intended to remain so. They looked around for
a successor with whom they could do as they liked. The most
suitable choice seemed to be the dead man's uncle. This was
fifty-year-old Claudius, who had been crippled by infantile
paralysis, stammered, and wore a permanently dazed expression.
On the night of the murder he had been found hiding behind a
pillar, trembling with fear.

He was the son of Antonia and Drusus, son of Germanicus.
Protected by a well-earned reputation for being a half-wit, he
had escaped all the tragedies of the Claudian family. If he was
pretending, one must admit that he did it very well, for ever
since he was a child even his mother used to call him an
"abortion," and when she wanted to malign anyone, she used to
say he was "even more of a cretin than my poor Claudius."

It is hard to say how much he put it on to keep out of trouble. In any case he was the only surviving member of his family. He dragged his deformed legs and spat in everybody's face when he spoke to them. He was tall and obese and his nose was red from soaking up wine. He spent his life keeping out of everybody's way, studying and writing history. He also wrote an autobiography, spoke Greek, and was a student of geometry and medicine. When he appeared before the senate to be proclaimed emperor, he said: "I know that you consider me a poor imbecile, but I am not. I have pretended to be one. That is why I am here today." He then rather ruined the effect of these initial remarks by making a speech on methods of treating snake-bites.

Claudius started off by giving a handsome reward to the praetorians who had elected him, but in return insisted that Caligula's murderers be handed over to him. He had them executed. This, he said, was to lay down the principle that "emperors should not be murdered." Then, with a stroke of the pen, he cancelled all the decrees of his predecessor and set about reorganizing the administration. In this task he displayed a common sense and equilibrium that nobody had suspected in him. Convinced that none of the senators were any good, he formed a cabinet of technicians recruited from among the freedmen and, together with these, began studying and carrying out great public works. He used to enjoy making calculations and projects. His pet scheme was the draining of Lake Fucinus, where he employed 30,000 workers for eleven years digging a tunnel to drain off the water. When all was ready, as a final spectacle before the lake was dried up, he offered the Romans a naval battle between two fleets manned by 20,000 condemned criminals. These saluted him with the famous cry: "Hail, Caesar! Those who are about to die salute thee!" They then sank one another and drowned. The public, thronging the surrounding hillsides, roared with delight.

Everybody also laughed when, in A.D. 43, this hard-drinking emperor with the half-baked, amiable expression set out at the head of his army to conquer Britain. He had never done any soldiering (he would certainly never have passed a medical examination), and Rome was convinced that he would run away at the first brush with the enemy. When the word went around that he was dead, grief was genuine and general. The Romans were sincere in their liking for this emperor of theirs, who with all his extravagances, had proved to be the best or, at least the most human of them all since Augustus.

Actually Claudius was far from dead and had really conquered Britain. He now returned, bringing with him its king, Caratacus, who was the first of the kings conquered by Rome ever to be pardoned. Naturally, the credit for this victory should go to the generals rather than to Claudius. Nevertheless, it was Claudius who appointed the generals and he knew how to choose them. Vespasian was one who learned his trade under him.

Unfortunately this worthy emperor was an incorrigible wolf. He had already had (and been unfaithful to) three wives when at the age of almost fifty he married the fourth. This was the sixteen-year-old Messalina. Messalina has gone down in history as the most infamous of all queens. Perhaps this is not true. She may simply have been the most licentious. As she was not particularly good-looking, whenever a young man did not want her, she used to get Claudius to give him the necessary orders. Dalliance thus became a patriotic duty. Claudius' sole condition was that Messalina would allow him similar freedom. On the whole they were a well-matched couple, but a difficulty arose when Claudius decided to restore Roman morals to their primitive austerity. A wife like Messalina hardly set the best of examples. One day, during his absence, she even married Silius, who was her lover at the time. His ministers informed the emperor, telling him that Silius was aiming to replace him on the throne. Claudius returned, had Silius killed, and sent a couple of praetorian guards to arrest Messalina, who was hiding in her mother's house. Fearing her vengeance, these guards stabbed her to death in her mother's arms. Claudius ordered them to kill him, too, if he ever gave any indication of wanting to get married again.

He did so the following year. His fifth wife was virtuous and made him regret her shameless predecessor. Agrippina, daughter of Agrippina and Germanicus, was his niece. She had already been married twice and from her first husband she had had a son, Nero, whose career was her main interest in life. She was another Livia, only worse. At the age of thirty she had little difficulty in establishing her ascendancy over a failing husband. She kept him away from his advisers, put her friend Burrus in command of the praetorian guard and started a new reign of

terror. Death warrants bearing Claudius' signature turned out
after his death to have been forged. The poor man, though in
his dotage, at a certain moment seemed to realize what was going on. He resolved to do something about it, but Agrippina
intervened by serving him a dish of poisoned mushrooms. Nero,
who was not devoid of a low sense of humor, later said that
mushrooms must be a food of the gods, seeing that they had
managed to make a god out of a poor creature like Claudius.

Nero in Sabine dialect means "strong," and for the first five
years of his reign the son of Agrippina gave promise of a wise
and magnanimous strength. For this, however, thanks were due
less to him than to Seneca, who governed in his name.

Seneca was a Spaniard from Córdoba, a philosopher who
had inherited a large fortune. He had already achieved no-
toriety before Agrippina engaged him as her son's tutor. Caligula had sentenced him to death for "impertinence" but then
had pardoned him because he suffered badly from asthma.
Claudius had exiled him to Corsica because of an affair with his
aunt Julia, a daughter of Germanicus. Seneca remained there
for eight years, writing excellent essays and some pretty awful
tragedies. We do not know who suggested him to Agrippina as
the most suitable man to bring Nero up according to the principles of Stoicism, a philosophy of which Seneca was a distinguished exponent. In any event, in the course of a few days,
the exile became tutor to the future master of the empire.

He was a strange character. He took unscrupulous advantage of his position to increase his private fortune but did not
use it to improve his style of living. He ate sparingly, drank
only water, and slept on a bed of planks. He was faithful to his
wife from the day he married her. When accused of being too
fond of money and power, he used to reply: "I do not praise the
life I lead. I praise the life I ought to lead, the life of which I
so falteringly try to follow the pattern." At the height of his
career he was publicly accused by a pamphleteer of embezzling
300 million sesterces of state funds, of making a profit on them
by usury, and of getting rid of his rivals and enemies by denouncing them to justice. Seneca, who at the time could have
had anybody he wanted to destroyed, made no attempt to
eliminate his accuser. However, according to Dion Cassius, he
continued to practice usury.

When his pupil came to the throne, Seneca provided him

with a noble speech to read in the senate. In this the new emperor gave his word he would only exercise the powers of commander in chief of the army. Probably nobody believed him, but for five years the promise was kept. During this time all other powers were in the hands of Agrippina and Seneca. Things went quite smoothly as long as these two agreed. Nero, with their guidance, made some wise decisions. He rejected the proposal of the senate to erect gold statues to him. He refused to sign death warrants, and when as a rare exception he had to sign one, he waved the pen and exclaimed: "Would that I had never learned to write!" He really gave the impression of being a decent youth whose main interests were music and poetry. Nobody imagined that these harmless diversions might one day become dangerous.

In the end Agrippina went too far; that is, she wanted to manage things on her own. Seneca and Burrus were alarmed, and to neutralize Agrippina, urged Nero to use his authority. Agrippina, in a fury, threatened to undo all the good work by putting Britannicus, the son of Claudius, on the throne. Nero forestalled her by doing away with Britannicus and confining his mother to a villa. During her period of confinement she did a disservice to history by writing a book of memoirs about Tiberius, Claudius, and Nero. Suetonius and Tacitus helped themselves liberally to material from this book, and as it was dictated by vengeance, one can have serious doubts about its accuracy.

For as long as Nero accepted the precepts of Seneca, Rome and the empire remained peaceful, the frontiers secure. Trade flourished and industry progressed. Unfortunately the time came when the pupil, still barely twenty, began to listen to a new preceptor, one who offered greater encouragement to his artistic tendencies. This was Caius Petronius, the arbiter of Roman elegance and prototype of the dandy.

It is hard to recognize in this rich aristocrat, whom Tacitus describes as being of refined and delicately voluptuous tastes and of ironic and exquisite conversation, the Caius Petronius who was the author of the *Satyricon,* a book so vulgar that it verges on obscenity, with banal and trite situations. If they are one and the same Caius Petronius, it means that there is not a world but a whole universe of difference between the author's actual life and the way he wrote about it. Whatever the truth of the matter, Nero was fascinated by Petronius. He had met him in society and considered him the model of refinement and culture, irresistible to men and women, an unerring connoisseur of the arts. Nevertheless he was more influenced by the indifferent poet and his literary doctrines. Nero now chose the characters from the *Satyricon* as his companions and with them indulged in orgies in all the unsavory quarters of Rome.

For the moment the austere Seneca had no objections. In fact it is quite possible that he encouraged his pupil in these pursuits in order to keep his mind off problems of state which he preferred to solve alone or with Burrus. Thus for a number of years the empire continued to prosper under an increasingly debauched emperor. Trajan later described the first five years of Nero's reign as "Rome's greatest period." The young sovereign was, however, fated to get mixed up with Poppaea, an Agrippina in the full flower of her beauty. She was determined to become empress and, in order to do so, made Nero act as emperor. Nero was twenty-one when he met her, and already had a respectable wife, Octavia, who put up with her husband's infidelities with great dignity. He also had a mistress, Acte, who was another respectable woman and in love with him. Nero betrayed them both with the licentious, sensual, and calculating Poppaea. This moment marks the turning point in his life and the beginning of new tribulations for Rome.

XXXIII

Nero

FATE HAD ALWAYS BEEN UNKIND TO AGRIPPINA, BUT THE CLOSING episodes of her life are worthy of an ancient Roman matron. She had no hesitation in giving a downright refusal to her son, Nero, when he came to ask her consent to his divorce from Octavia. Tacitus claims that she even went so far as to offer herself to him.

Although he had confined her to a villa, Nero was still frightened of her. He was, however, just as frightened of Pop-

paea, who refused herself to him and scorned him for his fear
of his mother. In the end Poppaea was able to convince him
that Agrippina was plotting against him. Not daring to have her
executed, he twice tried to have her assassinated: first by poison
and then by having her thrown into the river. Agrippina was
prepared for this. Perhaps she was kept informed of what was
going on in the palace by some faithful servant. The first time
she saved her life by taking an emetic, the second time she
swam. Nero's guards had to do likewise and follow her to the
other bank. One cannot help wondering what were the feelings
and thoughts of this woman when she found herself pursued by
the hirelings of the son for whom she had sacrificed a lifetime.
When the killers reached her, she showed no emotion. She
simply said: "Strike here," and pointed to the womb that had
given birth to Nero. When the naked corpse of his mother was
brought to him, Nero merely remarked: "Funny, I never realized that I had such a good-looking mother." And perhaps his
only real regret was that he had not accepted her offer.

As in the case of Caligula, there is no other supposition
than madness to explain such behavior. Perhaps the blood of
the Claudian family was tainted by syphilis, a congenital disease
which affects the brain and appears to have been very prevalent
in Rome.

History assures us that Seneca was not involved in this
abominable crime. However, since he continued to collaborate
with the emperor, he must have condoned it. Perhaps he hoped
to keep Nero back from the brink of the precipice. If he did
cherish this hope, he was soon deluded. When he tried to per-
suade Nero that competing in the Circus and singing tenor in
the theater was conduct unbecoming in an emperor, Nero took
no notice. Further, to show how little consideration he now had
for his tutor, he ordered the senators to compete with him in
these athletic and musical contests. He said that they were in
the Greek tradition and that the Greek tradition was superior
to that of Rome. On the whole, the senators probably deserved
this treatment, but some of them still retained a spark of dignity. Thrasea Paetus and Helvidius Priscus criticized the emperor openly and his spies accused them of conspiracy. After
the murder of his mother, Nero had shown a certain amount of
clemency but now he indulged in an orgy of bloodshed. As the
treasury (left to him by Claudius in flourishing condition) had

been drained by his extravagance, Nero compelled his victims
to leave him their wealth. Seneca criticized these measures. But
the real reason he lost his place was because he also criticized
his master's poetry. Yet he most likely gave a sigh of relief when
he retired to his villa in Campania. Here as a writer he tried to
make up for his failure as a preceptor. Burrus had died some
months before and been succeeded by the villainous Tigellinus.

With nobody to keep him in check Nero ran completely
wild. Physically, he has been described at twenty-five as having
yellow hair worn in braids, bleary eyes, and a bulging paunch
over short, rickety legs. Poppaea, now his wife, could twist him
around her little finger. Not content with making him divorce
Octavia, she forced him to banish her. Since the Romans disapproved of this and adorned her statues with flowers, she persuaded him to have her murdered. Octavia did not die well.
She was terror-stricken and begged for mercy. She was barely
twenty and should have been the faithful consort of a good
husband, not the heroine of a tragedy.

Nero felt no remorse, because in the meanwhile he had
had himself deified. Luckily, gods are exempt from the twinges
of conscience. His pet project now was to build a brand-new,
golden palace to serve as a temple to himself. He designed it in
such colossal dimensions that he could not find a suitable building site for it in the crowded center of Rome. For some time he
had been grumbling that the city had been badly constructed
and that it ought to be entirely rebuilt according to a rational
plan. In A.D. 64 the famous fire broke out.

Had he really set fire to the city himself? Perhaps not. He
was at Antium at the time and, returning posthaste, displayed
unsuspected energy in the rescue work. The fact that public
opinion promptly accused him shows that even if he did not
start the fire, people considered him quite capable of such an
act. This time, strangely enough, he did not react to the accusations against him. He did not even prosecute the authors of the
pamphlets and lampoons holding him up to public execration.
Anticipating other heads of totalitarian states, he took the view
that, before repairing the damage, one should find somebody to
make responsible. Thus (Tacitus says) he picked a religious
sect which had recently established itself in Rome. This sect
took its name from a certain Christ, a Jew, who in the days of

Tiberius, had been sentenced to death in Palestine by Pontius
Pilate.

Nero knew nothing else about the Christians when he arrested all those he could lay hands on, and after a summary
trial put them to the torture. Some were thrown to the wild
beasts, others crucified, others smeared with resin to serve as
torches. The Romans had not taken very much notice of these
people before, but after this mass martyrdom they began to regard them with a certain curiosity. At last the emperor was able
to rebuild the capital exactly as he wanted it. In this task, which
took up all his time, Nero showed great ability, but while the
new Rome was rising, much finer than the old, Poppaea died of
an abortion. Malicious tongues immediately said that during a
quarrel her husband had kicked her in the stomach. This may
have been so. In any case, it was a blow to Nero, who simultaneously lost the wife he loved and the heir for whom he was
hoping. Wandering grief-stricken through the streets, he happened on a youth named Sporus whose features bore a striking
resemblance to those of the dead woman. Nero took him back
to the palace, had him castrated and married him. "A pity
Nero's father didn't do the same," commented the Romans.

While the emperor was superintending construction work
on his new palace, his spies discovered a plot to put G. Cal-
purnius Piso on the throne. There were the usual arrests, the
usual tortures, the usual confessions. One of these gave the
names of various intellectuals, including Seneca and Lucan.

Lucan, another Spaniard from Córdoba, was a distant
cousin of Seneca. He had come to Rome to study law but had
made the unforgivable mistake of winning a poetry prize in a
contest in which Nero was also a competitor. The emperor forbade him to write any more. Lucan disobeyed and wrote a
rhetorical and mediocre poem, definitely republican in sympathy, on the Battle of Pharsalus. He could not publish it, but
he read it aloud in aristocratic circles where it had great success
with those who no longer had the courage to stand up to
tyranny but hankered after freedom. Did he really take part in
the plot or was his name put down by police informers knowing
of Nero's dislike for this rival? Under interrogation he admitted
his guilt and gave the names of other accomplices including, it
appears, his mother and his cousin Seneca. Condemned to death,
Lucan invited his friends to a big party and ate and drank with

them. He then slit his veins and died reciting his own verses against despotism. He was only twenty-six.

Perhaps Seneca first learned that he had taken part in Piso's plot from the emperor's messenger when the latter arrived in the Campania to inform him of his conviction. He had just written a letter to his friend Lucilius which ended with the words: "As for myself, I have lived long enough and I consider that I have had my deserts. I now await my death." When, however, death actually appeared in the guise of this envoy, he objected, saying that there was no reason to inflict the penalty. For a long time now he had taken no part in politics. He was merely looking after his health, which was liable to break down at any moment. This was the same excuse he had used to Caligula. It had enabled him to live to the age of almost seventy. The envoy returned to Rome but Nero was inexorable. So Seneca calmly embraced his wife, Paulina, dictated a farewell letter to the Romans, drank the hemlock, opened his veins, and died much more stoically than he had ever lived. Paulina tried to do likewise, but the emperor had her veins sutured. Time has blurred the contradictory nature of Seneca, the man, but has preserved his works as a writer. They reached a high standard. He was a past master of the art of essay writing and of reconciling the preaching of self-denial with the practice of doing exactly as one pleases. Such a teacher will never lack pupils.

Having disposed of his enemies, Nero left for a tour of Greece. Here, he said, they understood art better than in Rome. He competed in a horse race at the Olympic Games, fell off and came in last. The Greeks proclaimed him victor just the same. Nero showed his appreciation by exempting them from tribute to Rome. The Greeks, quick to see how the land lay, let him win all the other contests and organized a vociferous claque in the theater whenever the emperor sang. It was strictly forbidden to leave during the performance and some women even had babies there. In return, the Greeks were granted full citizenship.

On his return to Rome, Nero decreed himself a triumph, and unable to display any enemy trophies, displayed those he had won as a charioteer and tenor. When he claimed the admiration of his subjects he was in good faith. He thought they really felt it for him. He was therefore more astonished than worried when he heard that Julius Vindex had called Gaul to arms against him. Mobilizing an army against the rebel, the first thing he did was to order a large number of specially-built wagons to carry stage scenery. Between battles he intended to act, play music, and sing so that he could be applauded by the troops. While these preparations were going ahead, the news arrived that Galba, the governor of Spain, had joined Vindex and that the two of them together were marching on Rome.

For a long time the senate had been waiting for such a chance. Having made certain of the benevolent neutrality of the praetorian guard, they proclaimed the rebel proconsul Galba emperor. Nero suddenly found himself alone. When he asked an officer of the guard to accompany him in flight, he received, in reply, a line from Virgil: "Is it, then, so hard to die?"

For him it was very hard. He procured some poison but shrank from swallowing it. He thought of plunging into the Tiber, but could not screw up enough courage. Finally he hid in the villa of a friend on the via Salaria, some six miles from the city. Here he heard that he had been condemned to death "in the ancient manner," namely by flogging. Appalled, he seized a dagger to stab himself but first he tried the point and found that "it hurt." When he heard the sound of hooves outside the door he decided to cut his throat. His hand shook so much that his secretary, Epaphroditus, had to guide it to the carotid artery. "Oh, what an artist dies with me!" he murmured with his last breath. Galba's guards respected his corpse, which was reverently buried by his old nurse and his first mistress, Acte. Strangely enough, for a long time afterward his grave was covered with freshly-gathered flowers. Many people in Rome did not believe that he was dead and thought that he would be coming back. Ideas like these, as a rule, originate from regret or hope.

Could it be that on the whole Nero was not so black as he has been painted?

XXXIV

Pompeii

POMPEII WAS DESTROYED BY AN ERUPTION AND EARTHQUAKE ON the twenty-fourth of August in A.D. 79. This calamity earned the city posthumous fame. It had just over 15,000 inhabitants, who lived mainly by agriculture, and no great event had ever been connected with its name. On the fatal day Vesuvius was hidden beneath a murky black cloud. From this a torrent of lava surged down, and in the course of a few hours Pompeii and Herculaneum were buried. Pliny the Elder, who commanded the fleet lying at anchor at Puteoli, was among other things a keen geologist. He sailed his ships there at full speed. Either he wanted to see what was going on, or else he intended to evacuate the inhabitants who were fleeing desperately toward the sea. Blinded by fumes and trampled on in the panic, Pliny was overtaken and buried by the lava. About 2,000 people lost their lives in this disaster, but under its shroud of lava the city was preserved intact. When some two centuries ago archaeologists began excavating it, what they gradually revealed gives us a very clear picture not only of the architecture but also of the way of living of a small provincial town in the Golden Age of the empire.

The center of the town was the forum. This originally must have been the market for cauliflowers, a vegetable for which the district was famous. Later it developed into an open-air theater, used both for dramatic performances and games. It was surrounded by public buildings. There were the temples of Jove, Apollo, and Venus, the town hall, and shops. The life of the town obviously centered in the forum. Behind this lay a maze of narrow alleys, the commercial quarter. It was full of little shops and artisan's workrooms and echoed to the sound of hammers and axes, saws, planes, and files. To this uproar were added the shrill shouts of women and children, cats, dogs, and streethawkers, still so characteristic of this beautiful but far from silent country, especially in the south. The most persistent traits of a people are its faults. Pompeii gives us some idea of the agelessness of the Italian habit of defacing walls and using them as propaganda vehicles for opinions, loves, and hates. Whereas today we use posters, chalk, or charcoal, our ancestors resorted to *graffiti*, or carving on the stone. The method, not the subject matter, is the only thing that varies. It is clear that the Italians have always thought, said, and yelled the same things. Titus promised to love Cornelia forever and a day, Caius invited Sempronius to go and jump in a lake, and Julius guaranteed peace and prosperity to everybody if they elected him quaestor. Numerous were the "vivas" in honor of Majus, an aedile who at his own expense had signed up the gladiator Paris to perform in the local amphitheater. This could seat 20,000 spectators, 5,000 more than the total population of the city. The extra seats were evidently for the use of people from the surrounding countryside.

Houses were comfortable, even luxurious. They had very few windows and were only rarely centrally heated. Ceilings were of cement, sometimes decorated with mosaics, and floors were of stone. Only the larger mansions had bathrooms but some even had swimming pools. But there were three public baths, each complete with its gymnasium. Kitchens were well equipped with every kind of utensil: frying pans, pots, and spits. In one private library 2,000 volumes in Latin and Greek were found. Little is known of the furniture because it was made almost entirely of wood and has crumbled away. However, bronze ink-pots, pens, lamps, and statues, all in the Greek style, have survived. These are of good quality and refined workmanship.

All this conveys the impression that life in the provincial cities during the prosperous centuries of the empire must have been comfortable and well organized. Of course none of them could compete with Rome in public amenities, variety, social gatherings, and entertainments. On the other hand, their citizens were safe from persecutions or at least suffered from them to a lesser degree. The vices of decadence took longer to reach them and even then were tempered by the greater solidity of the sound provincial traditions. It was with good reason that Caesar and later Vespasian tried to fill the gaps in the Roman aristocracy and senate by admitting the bourgeois provincial families. After the fall of Rome one of the reasons why Roman civilization survived and the barbarians were absorbed was that wherever they set foot in the peninsula they found cities with a superior organization.

Unlike today, the cities in the south were superior to those in the north. This was because, before experiencing Roman civilization, they had already experienced that of the Greeks. Naples was the most famous because of its temples, its sculpture, its blue sea and sky, the subtle craftiness of its citizens, and (as still today) their indolence. People came from Rome to winter there. The surroundings, Surrentum, Puteoli, and Cumae, were dotted with villas. Capri had long been discovered and Tiberius had made it fashionable by choosing it as his habitual residence. Puteoli, because of its sulfurous waters, was the most famous spa of antiquity.

Tuscany was another region abounding in cities with a past, cities that had been built by the Etruscans. The most important were Chiusi, Arezzo, Volterra, Tarquinia, and Perugia, then considered part of that region. Florentia had only just come into being. She was the least conspicuous of them all and had no idea what the future held for her.

Further north beyond the Apennines began the fortress-cities, built as military strongholds for the armies engaged in the struggle against the Gauls: Mantua, Cremona, Ferrara, and Piacenza. Still farther north was the big commercial city of Como, which considered Mediolanum (Milan) as a sort of poor relation. Turin had been founded by the Taurine Gauls, but only began to be a real city when Augustus made it into a Roman colony. Venice had not yet been founded, but the Venetians had already arrived from Illyria and had founded Verona. Herodotus tells us that the chiefs of their tribes used to pool the girls, sell the prettiest by auction and with the proceeds provide a dowry for the plain ones, thus finding husbands for all.

This is not a complete catalogue, only a few examples. Roughly speaking, one may say that Italy has been well provided with cities ever since those days. Almost all those existing today sprang up at about this time.

In the provinces, democratic liberties lasted longer than in Rome itself, in spite of the fact that the city government was apt to be very paternalistic. It consisted of the *curia*, a sort of miniature senate, which as in Rome exercised control over magistrates freely elected by the citizens. The choice of candidates was, however, strictly limited to the rich, as magistrates were not only unpaid but were also expected to make up deficits in the municipal budget out of their own pockets.

The election of a candidate was celebrated with a gigantic banquet to which everyone was invited. On the occasion of his birthday, or the marriage of his daughter, and so forth, he had to give another one. Furthermore, success in office, the possibility of standing for it again, or of aiming even higher depended on the public works and entertainments which the dignitary had paid for with his own money. Inscriptions on stones have been found in many localities testifying to the prodigality (and the vanity) of these administrators, who often ruined their families to gain the esteem and votes of their fellow citizens. At Tarquinia, Desumius Tullus, in order to defeat his rival, and ignoring the protests of his children, promised to build public baths and spent 5,000,000 sesterces on them. At Cassino a rich widow donated a temple and an amphitheater. At Ostia, Lucilius Gemala paved the streets. Whenever there was a shortage, all of them used to buy wheat and distribute it free to the poor, who were not always grateful. At Pompeii there are *graffiti* which accuse officials of only having given the people half of what they had salted away by graft when in office.

Until the time of Marcus Aurelius, interference by the central government in the municipal affairs of the provincial towns was rare and almost always such as to encourage rather than hinder their development. The emperors, almost all of whom were rapacious in the administration of foreign provinces, had a perhaps not-altogether-disinterested weakness for Italy. It was here that they recruited their soldiers and supporters. The republic had always treated the peninsula badly. It had had to conquer and subdue it, and had often been betrayed by it. Under the empire, however, it had become the outskirts of Rome. The emperors often used to visit its cities and every visit meant gifts, subsidies, and tax exemptions in return for the enthusiastic welcomes which they regularly received. Each sovereign tried to outdo his predecessor in munificence. The empire was manna from heaven for the Italian provinces. They enjoyed only its benefits—law and order, well-kept roads, brisk trade, a sound currency, and security from invasion. The palace plots, police persecutions, trials, and purges had nothing to do with them.

XXXV

Jesus

AMONG THE CHRISTIANS MASSACRED BY NERO IN A.D. 64 FOR COM-
plicity in the burning of Rome, was Peter, their leader. After
seeing his wife taken away to be tortured, Peter was condemned
to be crucified. At his request he was crucified upside down because he did not feel worthy of dying in the same position as his
Master, Jesus Christ. The sentence was carried out in the very
place where the great church bearing his name now stands.

Peter was a Jew from Judaea, one of the provinces most
harassed by imperial misrule. Two-and-a-half centuries previously, by miracles of courage and diplomacy, it had successfully
shaken off the Persian yoke and, for about seventy years, had
regained its independence under the guidance of its priest-kings,
from Simon Maccabaeus onward. Their court was the Temple
of Jerusalem and it was in this edifice that the Jews united to
beat off the invasion of Pompey, who intended to annex their
territory to Rome. They fought with the courage of despair, but
would not give up the Sabbath respite which their religion imposed. Pompey noticed this, chose precisely the Sabbath to attack, and 12,000 people were slaughtered. The Temple was not
sacked, but Judaea became a Roman province. A few years
later it rebelled, and paid for the attempt with the liberty of
30,000 of its citizens who were sold as slaves. Later it regained
a glimmering of independence under a foreign king, Herod,
who tried to introduce Greek civilization and pagan architecture. Herod was in his way a great king, intelligent, ruthless,
and picturesque. He was clever enough to remain a protégé of
Rome without becoming her slave. He presented his subjects
with an even more beautiful Temple, but it was decorated with
images which the austere Hebrew faith categorically rejects as
sinful and contrary to the Law.

Under his successor, Archelaus, the Jews rebelled again.
The Romans once more sacked Jerusalem, sold another 30,000
citizens as slaves, and Augustus, to settle matters once and for
all, made Judaea a second-class province under the governor-

ship of Syria. Shortly before this new arrangement came into force, a minor event took place in the country, which at the time attracted no attention but which was later to have a considerable effect on the destiny of all humanity. At Bethlehem, near Nazareth, Jesus Christ was born.

For a couple of centuries the authenticity of this event was put in doubt by a school of critics who tried to deny the existence of Jesus. Now all doubts have been removed or, rather, only one, of secondary importance, remains: of the exact date of that birth. Matthew and Luke, for example, say that it was during the reign of Herod who, according to our system of reckoning, died three years before Christ was born. Some say that it was April, others May. The twenty-fifth of December, 753 *ab urbe condita*, was arbitrarily established 354 years after the event and became official.

History is of little use in helping us to reconstruct the childhood of Jesus. It merely provides contradictory testimony, vague dates, doubtful episodes. It contains little to contradict the version given so poetically by the gospels: the annunciation to Mary, the virgin wife of Joseph the carpenter, the birth in the stable, the adoration of the shepherds and the three wise men, the slaughter of the innocents and the flight into Egypt. History only helps to give us some idea of the condition of the country at the time Jesus was born and of the inspiration he found there. These are the only elements on which one can rely.

Judaea, or Palestine, was a ferment of religious and patriotic feeling. Its inhabitants numbered about 2,500,000, of whom a 100,000 were concentrated in Jerusalem. There was no unity of race and creed. In some cities, in fact, the majority were Gentiles, or non-Jews, mostly Greeks and Syrians. The country districts, on the other hand, were solidly Hebrew. The poor peasants and humble artisans who inhabited them were thrifty and industrious, pious and austere. They spent their lives in work, prayer, and fasting, and were awaiting the coming of the emissary of Jehovah, their God. He, according to the sacred scriptures (which were also the Law), was to save his people and establish the Kingdom of Heaven. They traded very little. Indeed, it appears that they were entirely devoid of that genius for speculation for which they later became so famous (and feared).

The limited amount of home rule granted them by Rome

was administered by the Sanhedrin, or council of elders. This consisted of seventy-one members presided over by a high priest and was divided into two classes: the conservative and nationalist Sadducees who were more interested in earthly matters than heavenly ones, and the bigoted Pharisees, theologians who passed the time interpreting the sacred texts. There was also a third, extremist sect, that of the Essenes, who practised a form of communism. They pooled the profits from their labors, used implements made with their own hands, and ate in silence at a common table. They ate so little that they often lived for over a hundred years. On the Sabbath they did not even move their bowels, as they considered it contrary to the Law. The scribes, to whom Jesus so often refers, were not a sect but a professional class mainly composed of Pharisees. They roughly correspond to our notaries and clerks of the court. One of their duties was to consult the sacred scriptures, from which they drew the precepts according to which society was to be regulated.

Not only all politics, but all Hebrew literature and philosophy had a profoundly religious basis, as it still does today. The keynote was expectation of the Messiah, who would one day come to deliver his people from evil, of which Rome was considered the incarnation. Most of the Jews were convinced that the Messiah of this redemption would be a Son of Man and a descendant of the house of David, as Isaiah had prophesied. Had not David, the legendary king of the Jews, driven out Evil and replaced it by Good: love, peace, and prosperity?

This hope now began to be shared by other pagan peoples subject to Rome. These peoples had lost their faith in their destinies as nations and had sublimated their hopes onto a spiritual plane. But in no other country was the expectation so eager and breathless as in Palestine. Signs and portents indicated that the great appearance was imminent, and some people even passed their days in the open space in front of the Temple praying and fasting. Everybody felt that the Messiah could not delay his coming much longer.

Even so, Jesus had some difficulty in getting himself recognized as the awaited Son of Man. It appears that he himself only realized his divine nature after listening to the sermons of John the Baptist, a distant relation of his, John being the son of a cousin of Mary. As John was his forerunner, we usually

JESUS (221)

imagine him as being much older than Jesus. Actually, it seems that they were almost the same age. John lived on the banks of the Jordan, clad only in his own long hair, and ate nothing but herbs, locusts, and wild honey. Calling on the people to purify themselves by the rite of baptism, he promised them the advent of the Messiah as a reward for their sincere repentance.

Jesus came to visit John "in the fifteenth year of the reign of Tiberius," when he must have been about twenty-eight or nine. Jesus substantially accepted John's teachings and made them his own, but refrained from baptizing. He then began to spread these teachings among the people. Shortly afterward, John was arrested by the guards of Herod Antipas, the tetrarch of Jerusalem. Luke and Matthew tell us that John was arrested because he had criticized the marriage of Herod to Herodias, the wife of his brother Philip. Salome, the daughter of Philip, so pleased the tetrarch by her dancing that he offered to give her anything she asked for. At the suggestion of her mother, she asked for John's head and her wish was granted.

It was after this occurrence that the mission of Jesus entered its decisive stage. He began to preach in the synagogues, and judging by the consensus of testimony which remains to us, there must have been something supernatural about him which immediately attracted the multitudes. Every now and then he would accompany his preaching with miracles, but he performed them with reluctance. He forbade his followers to exploit them for purposes of publicity and refused to consider them "proofs" of his omnipotence.

Jesus had gathered a group of close collaborators around him, the twelve Apostles. The first was Andrew, a fisherman who had been a follower of John's. He brought with him Peter, another fisherman, impulsive, generous and, at times, timid to the point of cowardice. James and John, the sons of Zebedee, were also fishermen. Matthew, on the other hand, was a "publican" (today we would call him a civil servant), that is, a functionary of the hated Roman government. Judas Iscariot administered the common purse of the Apostles.

After the Apostles came seventy-two disciples, who preceded Jesus barefoot to the cities he intended to visit in order to prepare the people for his teachings. Then came a whole throng of his faithful followers, men and women who lived together in brotherly love according to the rule of the Essenes.

The Sanhedrin did not at first worry very much about Jesus for two reasons: first because his followers were still few in number, and secondly, because the ideas which he preached were not on the whole incompatible with the Law and its dogma. The advent of the Redeemer and of the Kingdom of Heaven was part of the Hebrew doctrine of the Messiah, as were the moral precepts which Jesus taught. "Love thy neighbor as thyself" and "Turn the other cheek . . ." and the like were already accepted in the religious code of the Jews. "I have not come to destroy the law of Moses, but to apply it," Jesus used to say.

The breach with authority came only when Jesus announced that he was the Son of Man, the Messiah for whom all had been waiting. The multitude in Jerusalem acclaimed him as such on his return from a preaching tour in the surrounding country. The Sanhedrin was alarmed mainly for political reasons. They feared that Jesus might take advantage of the belief that he was the Messiah to provoke a rising against Rome, a rising which would inevitably end in another massacre.

On the evening of the third of April, A.D. 30 he was informed that the Sanhedrin had decided to arrest him on information supplied by one of his Apostles. Nevertheless he dined with them at the house of a friend and during this last supper told them that one of them was about to betray him and that he had now but a short time to spend with them. The soldiers seized him that very night in the garden of Gethsemane. When asked, in front of the Sanhedrin, if he were the Son of Man, Jesus replied: "Yes, I am." He was therefore brought before the Roman governor Pontius Pilate, and charged with blasphemy.

Pontius Pilate was an official who later finished his career somewhat ingloriously. He was removed for embezzlement and cruelty. But from the bureaucratic point of view, he did not behave too badly in Jesus' case. He asked Jesus whether he still maintained his claim to be king of the Jews, but did so in a jocular tone of voice, perhaps hoping that the accused would say no. Jesus, however, answered yes, and explained to him the kind of kingdom he intended to establish. Peter says that he had decided to die in order to redeem the sins of all mankind.

Pilate reluctantly pronounced the sentence which this confession implied: death by crucifixion. Jesus was nailed to the cross, between two robbers, at nine in the morning. During his agony he wavered for one brief moment, when he murmured:

"My God, my God, why hast thou forsaken me?" At three in the afternoon, he died.

Two influential members of the Sanhedrin obtained permission from Pilate to bury the corpse. Two days later Mary Magdalene, one of the most ardent followers of Jesus, went to visit the tomb and found it empty. The news flew from mouth to mouth and was confirmed by the earthly appearances of Christ, in flesh and blood, to his disciples.

Forty days after his official death he ascended to Heaven, according to the Hebrew tradition and the prophesies of Moses, Elijah, and Isaiah. His followers then scattered throughout the world to announce the great news of his resurrection and imminent return.

XXXVI

The Apostles

AT FIRST THIS MISSIONARY WORK WAS ONLY CARRIED ON IN PALESTine and those neighboring lands where there were Jewish colonies. This was because the Apostles had tacitly agreed that Jesus was the redeemer of the Hebrew people only and not of all men. The question of the universality of Christianity only arose and was solved after Paul's mission to Antioch, and his success among the Gentiles of that city.

Paul was, for the dissemination of the new faith, what Peter was for its organization. He was a Jew from Tarsus, son of a well-to-do Pharisee (thus of middle-class origin) and he had inherited that most precious of privileges: Roman citizenship. He had studied Greek and had been a pupil of Gamaliel, the president of the Sanhedrin. He had keen intelligence, a typically Jewish capacity for splitting hairs, and a difficult character. He was imperious, impatient, and often unjust. Paul's first reaction to Christ (whom he had never met) and the Christians was one of violent antipathy. He considered them heretics. When Stephen, one of their number, was condemned for breaking the Law, he enthusiastically took part in stoning him. One day he learned that the Christians were gaining proselytes at Damascus and asked the Sanhedrin's permission to investigate their activities there. On the way he was struck by a blinding light and heard a voice say: "Paul, Paul, why persecutest thou me?" "Who art thou?" he asked in amazement. "I am Jesus," came the answer. Paul remained blind for three days. Then he went to be baptized and soon became the most able propagandist of the new faith.

For three years he preached in Arabia. Then he returned to Jerusalem to obtain Peter's pardon for his past record as a persecutor. From there he went with Barnabas to organize the work of conversion among the Greeks of Antioch. When the Apostles learned that the two missionaries did not insist on circumcision when accepting Gentile converts (as Moses had prescribed), they sent for them to know the reason why. With Peter's support, Paul won his case, but the dispute broke out again after his second visit to Greece. The majority of the Apostles were still faithful to the Law, attended the Temple, and did not want to break with their people and traditions. If they were to have their way, Paul felt, Christianity would never amount to more than a Hebrew heresy. He sustained his theories in public sermons and was in serious danger of being lynched by the crowd. They actually wanted to put him on trial for blasphemy, but he was saved by his Roman citizenship, which gave him the right of appeal to the emperor. Ultimately they sent him by ship to Rome, where he arrived after a highly adventurous voyage.

In the city they listened to him patiently without understanding a word he was talking about. Gathering that it had nothing to do with politics, they treated him well and awaited the arrival of his accusers. They allowed him to choose his own house and merely put a sentry at the door. Paul invited the leaders of the Jewish colony to his house, but was unable to convince them. Even the few of them who were already Christians repudiated with horror the idea that baptism was more important than circumcision. They far preferred Peter, who arrived shortly afterward and received a much warmer welcome.

Paul succeeded in converting a few Gentiles, but he remained isolated. Animated as he was by implacable missionary zeal, he gave vent to his feelings by writing the famous *Epistles* to all his old friends in Corinth, Salonika, and Ephesus. These still remain the basis of Christian theology. According to some historians he was acquitted and went on to preach in Asia and Spain, but was arrested again and brought back to Rome. It appears that this is not true. Paul was never released. In the bitterness of his solitary exile, he lost faith, little by little, in the imminent return of Christ to earth or rather he transferred his hopes to the next world, thus putting his seal on the true message of the new religion.

We do not know how, when, or why he was tried again. We only know that the charge was "Disobedience to the orders of the emperor and claiming that the real king was a certain Jesus." It is quite possible that apart from this there was nothing against him. The police, however, did not waste time on details and, hearing Paul call Jesus "king," when Nero was actually on the throne, they arrested and condemned him. A legend runs that he died in A.D. 64 on the same day that Peter was crucified and that the two, meeting on their way to execution, embraced one another as a sign of peace. This is hardly likely. Peter was killed with the other Christians who were slaughtered wholesale for the fire of Rome. But Paul was a citizen and as such had the right to a certain amount of regard. In fact he was only beheaded. Two centuries later the Church built a basilica over the place where he is believed to have been buried—St. Paul's Outside the Walls.

How many converts had Christianity made in Rome at the time of the death of the two great Apostles?

It is impossible to give exact figures, but we doubt that they were more than a few hundred—at the most a thousand or so. This is proved by the fact that the authorities paid little attention to them. The accusation of incendiarism was not part of a policy of persecution, but only an improvised ruse to divert suspicion from Nero. The ensuing massacre seemed to have wiped out the sect once and for all. Then, like so many massacres, it proved to have been a stimulant. This was due to the organization given to the sect by Peter.

The Christians met in *ecclesiae*—churches or congregations. These in early times were not at all secret or conspiratorial. Comparisons made today with the communist cellular organization are ridiculous and unfounded. In the *ecclesiae*, they preached love, not hatred. No political propaganda was carried on, and furthermore there was not the slightest secrecy. Whoever came in was received without suspicion or mistrust. An-

other of today's erroneous beliefs is that the Christians all came
from the lower classes, "the scum of the earth," as Celsus was
later to call them. Nothing could be more inexact. All classes
were represented. They were mainly industrious folk, who set
aside what money they had to assist the poorer Christian com-
munities. Lucian, the unbeliever, called them "imbeciles who
share everything they possess." Tertullian, the convert, cor-
rected him. He called them "people who share everything the
others keep for themselves and keep for themselves the only
thing the others share: their wives."

They had only one discrimination and this was forced on
them by circumstances. They differentiated between townspeople and country people. For obvious reasons the first converts came from the city. In town regular meetings were
possible, the discontent was more acute, and minds were more
critical. In the country, traditions and customs had deeper roots
and there was greater moral strength to support them. That is
why the Christians began to call disbelievers "pagans," that is,
villagers, from *pagus* meaning village.

The first aim of the pioneers was to set an example of clean
and decent living. One can imagine the prestige and fascination
that this was bound to exert in a capital which was steadily becoming more degenerate and shameless. The Hebrew origin of
the new faith and of its first converts is shown by the austerity
it imposed. The religious services, which were still limited to
prayers, were open to women, but they had to be veiled. St.
Jerome used to say that women's hair was enough to distract an
angel and wanted to have them all cropped. An orderly domestic
life was their fundamental rule. The feast of the Sabbath, also
of Hebrew origin, was celebrated with a communal supper,
which began and ended with prayers and reading from the
scriptures. The priest blessed the bread and wine, which symbolized the body and blood of Jesus, and the ceremony ended
with the kiss of love, exchanged by all. This must have given
rise to some theological difficulty, since shortly afterward it was
limited to an exchange between men and men and women and
women, with the recommendation to keep the lips closed, and
if it were found pleasurable not to repeat it.

Abortions and birth control were execrated by the Christians in the midst of a society which practiced both on an increasing scale and was gradually dying from them. It was in fact

obligatory for the faithful to take in foundlings and to adopt and educate them in the new religion. Homosexuality was banned, and divorce was only permitted at the request of the wife if she happened to be a pagan. The ban on going to the theater met with less success. But generally speaking, the rules remained strict, especially when they were observed almost exclusively by Jews. Gradually, with the increase in the numbers and importance of the Gentiles, they became less rigid. The austere feast of Saturday slowly developed into the more cheerful one of Sunday.

On the "Lord's Day" they gathered around the priest, who read a passage from the scriptures, led the prayers, and preached a sermon. This was the first rudimentary liturgy, which later developed into a more precise and complicated ritual. In early times the congregation also took a more active part, as they were allowed to "prophesy," that is, to expound concepts while in a state of religious ecstasy. These then had to be interpreted by the priest. This custom was abolished because it threatened to give rise to chaos in the very field where the Church was now making every effort to establish order: questions of theology.

Only two of the seven sacraments were administered at this time. As the first converts were adults, no distinction was made between baptism and confirmation. Then as Christian babies began to be born, the two sacraments were separated, the second becoming the confirmation of the first. Marriage was not a religious ceremony; the priest merely gave it his blessing. Much greater attention, however, was paid to funerals. From the moment a man was dead, he became the exclusive responsibility of the Church and everything had to be arranged for his resurrection. Each corpse had to have its own tomb and the priest officiated at its burial. Tombs were constructed after the manner of the Syrians and Etruscans, in crypts excavated in the walls of long subterranean tunnels called catacombs.

This custom lasted until the ninth century and then fell into disuse. The catacombs became the object of pilgrimages. Then the earth covered them and they were forgotten. In 1578 they were rediscovered by pure chance. Their ramifications were so complicated and tortuous that people thought that they had been built as hiding places for the "conspiracy" and many novels have been based on this hypothesis.

These were the foundations upon which the new religion arose. It was no longer limited to one people and one race, like Judaism, or to a social class, like the paganism of Greece or Rome, who both considered their religions as a monopoly of their "citizens." Its moral loftiness, the great hope it kindled in the hearts of men, and the missionary urge it inspired caused Tertullian to declare with pride: "We are only of yesterday, but already we fill the world."

XXXVII

The Flavii

IT WAS A RABIDLY ANTI-SEMITIC EMPEROR WHO INVOLUNTARILY rendered a great service to the Christians. He committed the colossal blunder of persecuting the Jews and, by dispersing them throughout the world, encouraged the diffusion of the new faith.

Vespasian came to the throne in A.D. 70 after the fearful interregnum which followed the death of Nero, the last of the Julio-Claudian dynasty. Nero had been succeeded by the rebel general Galba, an aristocrat no worse than many others. He was bald, fat, and arthritic and had a mania for economizing. As soon as he was proclaimed emperor, his first act was to order all those who had received gifts from Nero to return them to the state. This cost him the throne and his life, since among the beneficiaries were the praetorian guard. Three months after his proclamation, they met him in the Forum riding in his litter and cut off his head, arms, and lips. In his place they proclaimed the financier Otho, a fraudulent bankrupt who looked as though he would administer public money in the same carefree way he had handled his own.

Hearing this news, the armies stationed in Germany under Aulus Vitellius and in Egypt under Vespasian rebelled and marched on Rome. Vitellius arrived first, only to bury Otho who had committed suicide. He then abandoned himself to his one great passion—Lucullan banquets. He was so busy gorging that he neglected to march against the forces of Vespasian which had meanwhile landed. The bloody battle of Cremona decided this war of succession. Vitellius was beaten and the Romans were treated to an unexampled slaughter. Tacitus says that the people crowded to their windows to cheer on the contenders as though they were at a football match. In the intervals the combatants looted the shops and set fire to them. If certain of them, accosted by prostitutes, disappeared into doorways with these ladies, they were knifed in the back by clients from the other side. Vitellius was captured in his hide-out as he was preparing to attack his dinner. With a halter around his neck, they dragged him naked, a target for excrement, through the city. He was then tortured with painstaking care and thrown into the Tiber.

A city which gloated over fratricide, armies which rebelled, emperors who were pelted with human filth only a few days after being greeted with hosannas: this was what had become of the capital of the empire.

Titus Flavius Vespasian hadn't lived there very long. He had been born at Rieti in the provinces, had then gone into the army and seen quite a good deal of the world. He was not of noble birth, but descended from a middle-class country family, and had earned promotion on his own merits. Two qualities he admired above all: discipline and thrift. When he came to the throne he was sixty but did not look it. He had a completely bald head and his face, open, rugged, and honest, was framed by two enormous hairy ears. He detested aristocrats whom he considered wastrels, and never suffered from the temptation to pass himself off as one of them. When an expert in genealogy came and told him that he had traced his family tree back to Hercules, the walls shook with his laughter. When he received some dignitary he would feel the material of his tunic to see whether it was too fine and sniff it for the traces of scent: two refinements he hated.

His first task was to reorganize the army and the finances. The first he put into the hands of regular officers, almost all like himself from the provinces. For the second he took a short cut. He sold all the highest state appointments at fabulous prices. "What does it matter?" he used to say, "They are all robbers, however we promote them. It is much better for them to get their promotion by returning some of their ill-gotten gains to the state." He used the same method for taxation. Collection was entrusted to officials picked from among the most rapacious.

These he unleashed with full powers in all the provinces of the empire. Regardless of the effect on the wretched populations, revenue was collected with unprecedented punctuality. Then as soon as the extortions had been completed, Vespasian recalled all the officials, to Rome, heaped praises on them, and proceeded to confiscate their illicit personal profits. As the budget was now balanced, the money went to compensate the victims. His son Titus, full of puritanical scruples, came to protest against these methods. They were repugnant to his high-minded, somewhat priggish nature. "When in the temple I act the priest," replied his father, "With brigands I act the brigand." To increase revenue he invented those little edifices now so associated with French civilization. But the French remember their origin, and one of the more polite terms for a public urinal is *vespasienne*. The emperor set an entrance fee for those who used them and a fine for those who did not. There was no choice. Relieving oneself outside cost more than doing so inside. Titus again protested. His father held a coin under his nose and asked: "Does this smell of anything?"

This upright and worthy son, whom he loved tenderly, was the cynical emperor's greatest worry. Vespasian did not aim to reform humanity and abolish its vices, merely to keep it in its proper place. To give Titus experience of men he sent him to discipline Palestine, where the last and most terrible rebellion had broken out. The Jews defended Jerusalem with unprecedented heroism. According to one of their historians, 2,000,000 of them perished: according to Tacitus, 600,000. To stamp out resistance Titus set fire to the city and flames destroyed the Temple. Some of the survivors killed themselves, some were sold as slaves, others fled. Their dispersion, begun some six centuries before, now become the authentic *diaspora*. Like the soldiers of Napoleon who carted *The Rights of Man* around in their knapsacks, in their bundles many of these poor emigrants carried the Word of Christ.

Full of paternal pride, Vespasian granted Titus a triumph which was somewhat out of proportion to the military value of his undertaking and in his honor built in the Forum the famous arch which bears his name.

Soon afterward it was his turn to be emperor. One day, after a wise reign of ten years, the wisest Rome had enjoyed since Augustus, Vespasian went home to Rieti on holiday. He often went there to visit boyhood friends, hunt the hare, have a chat, eat a plate of crackling pork and beans, and play a hand or two of cards. Unfortunately this time he had the fatal idea of taking the waters of Fonte Cottorella for his kidneys. Either the cure was unsuitable or he micalculated the dose, for he was seized by violent gripes and at once realized that there was no remedy for them. "*Vae*," he remarked with characteristic humor, "*puto deus fio*." ("Alas, I think I am becoming a god.") This was because in Rome it was the custom to deify all emperors when they died. After three days and nights of dysentery, yellow as a lemon and with beads of sweat standing out on his brow, he still had the strength to get up. He met the astonished gaze of those present with a short laugh to show he realized that he was being theatrical and murmured: "Yes, I know, I know, but what can I do about it? An emperor has to die on his feet."

Titus, who succeeded him, was a very lucky sovereign because he did not have time to make mistakes. He would have been bound to make them, not because of his failings, but because of his good qualities: honesty, frankness, and generosity. He never signed a death warrant. Whenever he discovered a plot he used to send a warning message to the conspirators and another to reassure their mothers. During the two years of his reign Rome suffered a terrible fire, Pompeii was buried by Vesuvius, and all Italy was devastated by a pestilence. Titus emptied the treasury to make good the damage. While personally tending the sick he caught the plague and died at the age of forty-two. Everybody regretted him except the man who succeeded him on the throne, his brother Domitian.

It is difficult to know what to make of this last representative of the Flavian dynasty. Of contemporary writers, Tacitus and Pliny have given us the blackest, and Statius and Martial the rosiest picture of him. They do not even agree on his physical appearance. The first two describe him as bald and pot-bellied, with spindly legs, the second as being handsome as an archangel, timid, and gentle. One thing is certain: he must have suffered a great deal from the preference Vespasian had always shown for Titus. On the death of their father he laid claim to half his power. Titus agreed but then Domitian refused and began to conspire. Dion Cassius says that, when Titus fell ill, Domitian hastened his end by covering him with snow.

His reign was rather like that of Tiberius, and in some respects their characters appear to have been similar. Their reigns had identical starts: wise and careful, with a touch of puritanism. Domitian was a keen moralist and engineer. The job he liked most was that of censor, which gave him the chance to control morals. The ministers he gathered around him were technicians particularly well qualified to rebuild the fire-devastated city. He did not want war. When Agricola, governor of Britain, tried to push the frontiers of the empire as far as Scotland, he relieved him of his command. Perhaps this was his most serious mistake. Agricola was father-in-law to and adored by Tacitus, who took it upon himself to pass judgment on all the men of his time. So it's quite understandable that the great historian did such a thorough demolition job on Domitian.

Unfortunately it takes two to keep the peace and Domitian had to reckon with the Dacians. They crossed the Danube, beat the Roman generals, and compelled the emperor to take over command of the army. He was making progress when the governor of Germany, Antoninus Saturninus, rebelled with a number of legions. This forced the emperor to make a premature and unfavorable peace with the Dacians and perhaps gave rise to his obsessions. He began to see plots everywhere and established the most exaggerated of personality cults. Sitting on a real throne he insisted on being called "Our lord and god." Visitors had to kiss his feet. He, too, like Nero, banished all philosophers from Italy because they denied his absolute power. Christians he beheaded because they denied his divinity. The senators hated him, flattered him and countersigned his death sentences. These senators included Tacitus, his implacable future critic.

In a fit of persecution mania, Domitian suddenly remembered that his secretary, Epaphroditus, was the same man who, a quarter of a century before, had helped Nero to cut his throat. Fearing a repetition of that event, he sentenced him to death. This alarmed the other officials of the palace so that they organized a plot in which even the empress Domitia took part. One night they stabbed him, Domitian defending himself savagely to the bitter end. He was forty-five years old and for fifteen of them he had reigned, first as the wisest, and then as the most disastrous, of sovereigns.

Thus, in the obscurity from which it had risen, ended the second dynasty of the successors of Augustus. Of the ten emperors who had succeeded one another in the course of 126 years, (from 30 B.C. to A.D. 96) seven had died a violent death. There was something not working right with a system which turned even well-disposed men into bloody tyrants. This something was a much more decisive factor than the congenital disease which had perhaps tainted the blood of the Julio-Claudians. Its origin must be sought in the transformation Roman society had undergone during the previous three centuries.

XXXVIII

Epicurean Rome

THE ROME OF THIS PERIOD, WHICH IS GENERALLY CALLED "EPICU-rean," had a population which some estimate at 1,000,000, others at 1,500,000. It was divided into the usual orders and classes. The aristocracy was still numerous but, apart from the Cornelii, chroniclers of the time no longer mention the great names of the past: the Fabii, the Aemilii, the Valerii, and so forth. Decimated first by wars, to which they contributed a high proportion of casualties, then by persecutions, and finally by birth control, these illustrious families were virtually extinct. They had been replaced by others, with fewer ancestors and more money, who came from the industrial and commercial midddle classes of the provinces.

"In high society today," Juvenal used to say, "the best thing is to have a barren wife. Everybody will be agreeable to you, hoping to be remembered in your will. If your wife is capable of childbirth, who can tell whether she will not present you with a little Negro?"

Juvenal was exaggerating a little, but the evil he denounced was real enough. Marriage, which during the stoic period had been a sacrament and was to become so again with Christianity, was now a casual pastime. Having children, once considered a duty to the state and the gods (who only promised an afterlife to those who left somebody to look after their tombs), was now regarded as a wearisome nuisance to be avoided. Though infanticide was no longer permitted, abortion was a common practice. If it were unsuccessful, the newborn baby was simply left at the foot of a "dairy-column," so called because professional state-employed wet nurses went on duty there to feed the foundlings.

Under the influence of these customs, the biological and racial structure of Rome had changed. What citizen had not a few drops of foreign blood in his veins? The Greek, Syrian, and Israelite minorities put together made up a majority. Even in Caesar's time the Jews were so strong, thanks to their united front, that they constituted one of the principal props of his regime. Few of them were rich, but on the whole they formed a disciplined and industrious community of sound morals. One cannot say the same for the Egyptians, Syrians, and other Orientals, who controlled the murkiest commercial activities.

Unless she were really hard up, the Roman mother who had had a child immediately got rid of it by turning it over first to a wet nurse, then to a Greek governess (the equivalent of today's English or German nanny), and finally to a pedagogue, another Greek, to be educated. Failing this, she sent him to one of the schools which by now had sprung up almost everywhere. These were not state schools, but private, coeducational ones run by *magistri*. The pupils attended elementary classes until they were twelve or thirteen, when the sexes were separated. The girls completed their education in special colleges where the principal subjects taught were music and dancing. The boys went to a secondary school directed by grammarians who, being for the most part Greek, laid emphasis on the Greek language, literature, and philosophy. Thus Roman culture was almost entirely overlooked. The courses of the rhetoricians took the place of the university which had no fixed curriculum. There were no examinations, no theses, no degrees. There were only lectures followed by discussion. These courses cost up to 2,000 sesterces, somewhere between $320 and $400 a year. Petronius complains that they taught only abstractions of no practical value in everyday life. They did, however, develop the typically Roman predilection for controversy, sophistry, and quibbling, vices which have been inherited by the Italians.

The wealthier families sent their sons to finishing schools abroad: Athens for philosophy, Alexandria for medicine, and Rhodes for oratory. They spent so much money keeping them there that the thrifty Vespasian, to put a stop to the drainage of currency, preferred to engage the most illustrious professors in those cities and bring them to Rome. Here they taught in state institutes and were paid 100,000 sesterces a year.

The morals of young men, even in stoic times, had never been outstanding. After the age of sixteen it was taken for granted that the boy would go to brothels and nobody paid much attention if he also had an affair or two, with men or women. This was in primitive times, when the bawdy houses were fourth-rate and the boy's period of debauchery finished when he was called up for military service. He then got married and started on a life of austerity. But in later times, young men got themselves exempted from military service, and the brothels had become luxurious. The inmates were expected to entertain clients not only with their more obvious charms, but with conversation, music, and dancing, rather like the geishas in Japan. Clients continued to patronize them even after they were married.

Things were a little stricter for girls as long as they remained such, but they generally got married before they were twenty. Otherwise, they were considered old maids. Married, they enjoyed almost the same amount of liberty as their husbands. Seneca considered a husband lucky if his wife made do with only two lovers. One epitaph on a tomb runs as follows: "For forty-one years he was faithful to the same wife." Juvenal, Martial, and Statius speak of middle-class women competing in the Circus, driving their own gigs through the streets of Rome, and stopping under the porticos for a chat, "offering," as Ovid says, "the delicious sight of their naked shoulders to the passerby."

Intellectual ladies also flourished. Martial's friend, Theophila, was able to discourse fluently on the subject of Stoic philosophy. Sulpicia wrote poetry—about love, naturally. Women organized clubs where lectures were given on "Duties to Society," a very popular topic in all societies where such duties are lightly regarded.

People had put on weight. The statues of this period, compared with the bony, angular effigies of stoic Rome, show us a softer race, fattish from idleness and overindulgence at the table. Beards were no longer worn. Tonsorial parlors increased in number, and the first shave was an occasion marking a boy's entry into adult life. Most men wore their hair cropped close but certain dandies let theirs grow and wore it in braids. The purple toga having become the exclusive privilege of the emperor, all the others now wore a white tunic or shirt and sandals with the thong inserted between the toes.

Women's fashions had also become more elaborate. No self-respecting lady ever spent less than three hours in the moring over her coiffure, helped by half-a-dozen female slaves. Many pages of literature were devoted to this art. Bathrooms were littered with razors, scissors, hairbrushes, creams, powders, cosmetics, oils, and soaps. Poppaea had invented a facial, a mask soaked in milk to wear at night to improve the complexion, and this had been widely copied. The milk-bath was quite commonplace, and wealthy women used to travel followed by herds of cows so that they would always have a supply of fresh milk available for the purpose. Specialists prescribed diets, exercises, sun-treatment, and massage. Certain beauticians made their fortunes by creating original hairstyles, hair swept back or gathered in a chignon at the nape of the neck, kept in place by a net or pretty ribbons.

Underwear was of silk or linen and the brassière was just coming into fashion. Stockings were not worn. Shoes also were elaborate, made of soft, light leather, embroidered with gold filigree. They had high heels to remedy that unfortunate defect of Roman women, short legs and a low-slung behind.

In winter furs were worn, and these were usually presents from husbands or lovers stationed in the northern provinces of Gaul and Germany. In all seasons great display was made of jewelry, a ruling passion with these ladies. Lollia Paulina used to go about loaded with 40 million sesterces, scattered about her person in the shape of precious stones. Pliny gives us a list of over a hundred varieties. One senator was proscribed by Vespasian because he wore an opal ring reputed to be worth $250,000. The strait-laced Tiberius tried to restrain this exhibitionism but failed. If the luxury trades had been abolished, Rome would have risked an economic crisis.

Interior decoration was on a par with this magnificence and perhaps even surpassed it. A palace worthy of the name had to have a garden, a marble portico, and not fewer than forty rooms. It contained salons with onyx or alabaster pillars, walls inlaid with precious stones, floors and ceilings of mosaic, cedar-wood tables with ivory legs, oriental brocades (Nero had spent nearly

$500,000 on these), Corinthian vases and wrought-iron beds with mosquito netting. There were about a hundred servants: two behind the place of each guest to serve his meals, two to take his shoes off simultaneously when he went to bed, etcetera.

The great Roman aristocrat of this period rose at about seven in the morning. The first thing he did was receive his clients for a couple of hours, offering each of them his cheek to kiss. After a frugal breakfast he received and returned the visits of his friends. This was one of the most rigidly-observed obligations of Roman social life. To refuse to give assistance to a friend making his will, to attend his son's wedding, to read his poetry, to support his election, or to guarantee his promissory notes was regarded as very bad form. Only after the fulfillment of these duties was one free to think about one's own personal affairs.

This rule also held good for people of more modest standing. The middle classes worked until midday, ate a light lunch and then went back to work. However, all of them sooner or later, according to their working hours, used to meet at the public baths. There has never been a people as clean as the late Romans. Although every palace had its own swimming pool, there were over a thousand baths open to the general public, each one with an average capacity of a thousand clients at a time. They were open from dawn till one o'clock for women and from two till sunset for men; later mixed bathing came in. The entrance-fee, service included, was about a cent and-a-half. Having undressed in a cabin, one went to the gymnasium to practise boxing, throwing the javelin, basketball, jumping, or throwing the discus. Then one went for a massage. Finally the actual bath began, which followed a strict procedure—first the *tepidarium* of warm air, then the *caldarium* of hot air, then the *laconicum* of steam, where soap, a novelty from Gaul, was used. Finally, to obtain a healthy reaction, one plunged into the icy water of the swimming pool.

After all this one dried off, anointed oneself with oil, dressed, and went into the gaming room to play chess or dice. Otherwise one went into the lounge to talk to the friends one was certain to meet there. One could also have dinner in the restaurant and, even if it were on a modest scale, it still consisted of six courses, two of which were of pork. One ate lying on the *triclinium*, a sort of divan with room for three, to relax the body after the exercise taken shortly before. The left arm rested on a cushion to support the head, the right was used to take food from the table. The cooking was dull and included many sauces derived from animal fats. However, the Romans had cast-iron stomachs and gave proof of this on the occasion of the banquets which they frequently gave.

These started at four in the afternoon and lasted far into the night if not till morning. The tables were decorated with flowers and the air was perfumed. The servants, in rich liveries, had to be at least twice as numerous as the guests. Only rare and exotic dishes were served. "For the fish course," said Juvenal, "the fish should cost more than the fishermen." Lobster was much sought after and purchasers used to pay up to $96 apiece for them. Vedius Pollio was the first to try to breed them. Oysters and thrushes' breasts were highly esteemed delicacies. Apicius created a social position for himself by inventing a new dish, *pâté de foie gras*, by fattening his geese on figs. He was a curious fellow, this Apicius. He ate up an enormous inheritance worth of dinners, and when he realized that he had eaten himself down to his last million and-a-half dollars, he considered himself penniless and so committed suicide.

The banquets regularly used to develop into orgies, the host would offer precious gifts to his guests, and servants passed from table to table distributing emetics so that everyone could go on eating.

Belching was permissible. It was, in fact, a sign of one's appreciation of the excellence of the food.

XXXIX

The Economy

ROME WAS NOT AN INDUSTRIAL CITY. IT HAD ONLY TWO LARGE factories, a paper mill and a dyeworks. Continuously though, since those ancient times, its real industry had been politics, then as now regarded as more likely than hard work to offer opportunities of getting rich quickly.

The main sources of gain of the Roman gentry were: (*a*)

trafficking in the corridors of the various ministries and (b) plundering the provinces. They spent a good deal of money on getting launched in a career but, once they had achieved senior administrative rank, they repaid themselves well and quickly. They invested the proceeds in agriculture. Junius Columella and Pliny have left us a clear picture of this class of landowner and of the methods they used for exploiting their farms. The small farms that the Gracchi, Caesar, and Augustus had tried to institute with their agrarian laws had not been able to stand up to competition from the big estates. A war or a year of drought was enough to ruin them, to the advantage of the large properties, which were able to survive these misfortunes. Some of them were as vast as kingdoms, says Seneca, and were looked after by slaves who cost nothing, but who had absolutely no regard for the land. They specialized in cattle breeding, which was more profitable than growing wheat. Pastures of 25–50,000 acres with 10–20,000 head of cattle were not uncommon.

Between the reigns of Claudius and Domitian a slow transformation began to take place. The long period of peace and the extension of full citizenship to the provinces had cut down the supply of slaves. These became rarer and consequently more expensive. Improvement in breeding brought on a crisis of overproduction of cattle and it was difficult to obtain enough fodder for them. As a result prices fell. Many cattle breeders found it more profitable to return to agriculture and divided up their properties into smaller lots which they rented to tenants. These were the forerunners of the peasants of today, and if what Pliny says about them is true, the resemblance is striking. They were tenacious, solid, avaricious, suspicious, and conservative. They understood farming and it was in their own interest to make it pay. They immediately adopted the use of fertilizers, the rotation of crops, and the selection of seeds. Fruit growers imported vines, peaches, apricots, and cherries and, after rational experiments, planted vineyards and orchards. Pliny enumerates twenty-nine varieties of figs. Wine was produced in such quantities that Domitian, to avert a crisis, prohibited the planting of new vineyards.

To make their farms more independent, minor industries, on a family and artisan basis, sprang up around them. A farm was considered rich in proportion to its ability to supply its own needs. There was the *abattoir*, where they slaughtered the animals and made sausages. There was the oven for baking bricks. Hides were tanned to make shoes, wool was woven and made into clothes. There was no trace of that specialization which today makes work so dreary and turns the workman into an automaton. The industrious peasant of those days unyoked his oxen from the plow and became a carpenter or set about hammering iron to make hooks or pots. The lives of these farmer-artisans were then much fuller and more varied than our own.

The only industry which was operated more or less according to present-day standards was mining. Theoretically the state owned the mineral rights but they were leased for exploitation on moderate terms to private prospectors. Personal interest led these prospectors to discover sulfur in Sicily, coal in Lombardy, iron on Elba, marble in the Lunigiana, and also the uses to which these raw materials could be put. Production costs were negligible because work in the mines was done exclusively by slaves and convicts, who did not have to be paid or insured against accidents. Judging by the state of the mines, there must have been a number of disasters every week, with thousands of dead. Roman historians, however, fail to mention these episodes, presumably because they were not news. Building was another great industry, with its innumerable specialists ranging from lumberjacks to pump-makers and glaziers. In spite of all this, authentic industrial capitalism could not develop, largely because a hundred slaves cost less than a machine, and mechanization would have created an insoluble unemployment problem.

Even so, many public services were better organized at this time than, say, in eighteenth-century Europe. The empire had over 60,000 miles of highway. Italy alone had about 400 major paved roads along which heavy traffic passed in an orderly manner. They permitted Caesar to cover 900 miles in eight days, and the messenger sent by the senate to Galba to announce the death of Nero only took thirty-six hours to travel 300 miles. The mail was not public although it was called *cursus publicus*. Modelled by Augustus on the Persian system, it was reserved for state correspondence. Private citizens could only avail themselves of it by special permission. Luminous signals flashing lights from hilltop to hilltop took the place of the telegraph, and this system remained substantially unchanged until the time of Napoleon. Private mail was carried by private companies or entrusted to friends or passing travelers. However, some important personages like Lepidus, Apicius, and Pollio had their own private service and were extremely proud of it.

Communications and staging-points were magnificently organized. Every kilometer there was a stone indicating the distance from the nearest town. Every six or seven miles there was a staging-point with a tavern, bedrooms, stables, and fresh horses for hire. Every eighteen or nineteen miles was a hostelry offering the same services, but larger and better equipped. Routes were patrolled by the police, who, however, were never able to make them completely safe. Aristocrats used to travel accompanied by entire trains of wagons in which they used to sleep guarded by their armed servants.

Tourism was almost as flourishing as it is nowadays. Plutarch is very ironical about the globe-trotters who infested the city. As in the case of the young Englishman of the last century, the education of the young Roman was not complete until he had made the Grand Tour. This usually meant Greece. They went there by sea embarking from either Ostia or Puteoli, the two great ports of the time. The poorer ones took one of the numerous cargo boats bound for the orient to pick up freight; the richer used sailing vessels of up to 1,000 tons, 150 feet long, and with luxurious cabins. Under Augustus, piracy had almost completely disappeared, for he had stationed two large permanent fleets in the Mediterranean to stamp it out. So ships also voyaged at night, though they almost always kept near the coast for fear of storms. There were no schedules because everything depended on the winds. Normally ships made five or six knots and the voyage from Ostia to Alexandria took about ten days. But the tickets were not expensive: the voyage on a cargo boat to Athens did not cost more than eight cents. The crews were in good physical shape and not unlike those of today: a quarrelsome, open-minded bunch, with a distinct inclination for bars and bordellos. The masters of such ships were trained mariners who gradually changed their calling into an exact science. Hippalus discovered the periods of the monsoons, and the voyage from Egypt to India, which previously had taken six weeks, now began to take one. The first charts and the first lighthouses began to make their appearance.

All this took place rapidly because the Romans had a passion not only for soldiering and the law but also for engineering. They never carried their mathematical studies to the abstract

heights of the Greeks, but they applied them much more practically. The draining of Lake Fucinus was a real masterpiece
and the roads they built are models even today. The principles
of hydraulics were discovered by the Egyptians, but it was the
Romans who put them into practice with aqueducts and sewers
of colossal proportions. To them we owe the splashing of the
fountains in Rome today. Frontinus laid out the hydraulic system and described it in a manual of great scientific value, com-
paring the Roman public utilities with the complete uselessness
of the Pyramids and so many Greek constructions. His words
sum up the genius of Rome: practical, positive, and at the service of the community instead of the aesthetic whims of individuals.

It is difficult to say how much the economic development
of Rome and the empire was due to private enterprise and how
much to the state. The latter owned all mineral rights, extensive
state lands, and probably some war industries. It guaranteed the
price of grain by buying in bulk, and intervened directly with
great public works to keep down unemployment. It also used
the treasury as a bank and lent money to private citizens against
solid guarantees and at a high rate of interest. Even so, it was
not very rich. Under Vespasian, who increased its revenue and
administered it rigorously, the income did not exceed $160 mil-
lion a year, raised mainly by taxation.

On the whole one can say that the state was more liberal
than socialist. It even left to the initiative of its generals the
right to coin money in the provinces they governed. The complex monetary system which resulted suited the bankers to
perfection and on it they based all their diabolical inventions:
savings books, bills of exchange, checks, and money orders.
They founded credit institutions with branches and agents in
every part of the world. This complicated organization made
booms and crises inevitable.

The Wall Street crash of 1929 had a predecessor in one
which occurred under Augustus. When he returned from Egypt
with the immense treasure of that country, he put it into circulation to promote trade, which was then languishing. This infla-
tionist policy promoted trade all right, but it also stimulated
prices which rose to an astronomical level. Finally Tiberius had
to break this vicious circle by withdrawing currency. Those who
had contracted debts, counting on the continuation of inflation,

found themselves short of ready money and hurried to withdraw it from the savings banks. The houses of Balbus and Ollius had to meet colossal obligations in a single day and were compelled to close. The industries and commercial houses which drew on them could not pay their suppliers and had to close down too. Panic spread like wildfire. Everybody rushed to withdraw his deposits. The banks of Maximus and Vibo (the strongest) were also unable to meet all demands and called on that of Pettius for help. The news spread like lightning and, by presenting their savings books, the clients of Pettius prevented him from rescuing his colleagues. The interdependence of the various provincial and national economies within the framework of the vast empire was shown by the simultaneous runs on the banks of Lyons, Alexandria, Carthage, and Byzantium. It was clear that a wave of distrust in Rome had immediate repercussions to the very fringe of the empire. Even in those days one bankruptcy led to another and there were numerous suicides. Many small farms in debt up to the hilt could not wait until the next harvest and had to be sold at whatever they would fetch, to the advantage of the big estates, which were in condition to hold out. Usury, kept in check by the growth of the banks, flourished again. Prices came toppling down. In the end Tiberius had to reconcile himself to the fact that deflation was as great an evil as inflation. Reluctantly he distributed some $160 million to the banks to be put into circulation but gave orders that they were to be lent for three years free of interest.

The fact that this measure was sufficient to revive the economy, unfreeze credit, and renew confidence shows the enormous importance of the banks, or, in other words, the basically capitalist nature of imperial Rome.

XL

Their Entertainments

WHEN AUGUSTUS CAME TO THE THRONE THE ROMAN CALENDAR contained 76 holidays, more or less the same number as today. When his last successor fell, there were 175—a holiday every other day. They were celebrated by theatrical entertainment and athletic games.

The theater no longer consisted of the pompous and solemn classical dramas that had died out after a short vogue (much more rapidly than they had come in). There is something about the air, not only of Rome, but of all Italy, which makes people indifferent to serious theater. Dramas were still written in this first century of the empire, but only as poetic exercises. In the salons where their authors read them aloud, they had a limited number of listeners, but they were never performed by actors for audiences in the theaters. The uneducated and mainly foreign public knew only elementary Latin, and far preferred pantomime, in which the action is explained by gesture and dancing rather than by the spoken word. The tradition of a certain type of actor dates back to this time. Crude and vulgar, rolling their eyes, grimacing, and gesticulating, favorites like Aesop and Roscius with their risqué sketches and double meanings became the pets of high society, the lovers of prominent aristocratic ladies, and would do anything for publicity. They earned and left staggering sums. There were also women in their companies who because of their profession were officially put on the same footing as prostitutes; have nothing to gain by modesty they contributed brazenly to the obscenity of the performances.

A craving for applause often induced these actors to present scenes full of political allusions in spite of the censors. This is a common phenomenon in tyrannical regimes, where nobody dares say anything but where everybody is delighted by anyone who does. The evening of Vespasian's funeral an actor parodied the corpse sitting up in his coffin and asking the undertakers: "How much is this funeral costing?" "Ten million sesterces." "All right, give me a hundred thousand," said the corpse, "and throw me in the Tiber." Which, it must be admitted, was just the sort of thing the dead emperor might have said. The irreverent actor came to no harm because Vespasian's successor was Titus. But a few years before Caligula had had the author of a much less disrespectful allusion burnt alive.

While the theater degenerated into a variety show, the fortunes of the Circus continued to soar. Large mural posters, like billboards advertising movies, announced forthcoming sporting events. They were the talk of the town, like a World Series, and were discussed eagerly at home, at school, in the

Forum, at the baths, and in the senate. Even the newspaper, *acta diurna,* reported and criticized them. On the day of the contest, crowds of 150–200,000 carrying handkerchiefs with the colors of their favorite team, used to flock to the Circus Maximus, just as they do to the stadium today. High officials had separate boxes with marble seats adorned with bronze. The rest settled themselves on wooden benches, but not until they had poked about in the horses' droppings to see whether they had been properly fed. They then backed their favorites and supplied themselves with sandwiches and cushions, because the show lasted all day. For himself and his family, the emperor actually had an apartment with bedrooms where he could take a nap between contests and of course there was the inevitable bathroom.

As today, horses and jockeys belonged to private stables, each with its own racing colors. The most famous were the Reds and the Greens. Horse races alternated with chariot races, two-, three-, or four-in-hand. The drivers, almost all slaves, used to wear metal helmets and held the reins in one hand and a whip in the other. A knife was hung around their necks with which to cut the traces in case of a fall. Falls were frequent as the races were run without regard for danger, like the *Palio* of Siena today. They had to complete seven laps of the oval arena, avoiding the *metae,* or goal posts, and hugging the bends as closely as possible. The light chariots easily collided with one another and drivers and steeds went rolling over in a heap amid shafts and wheels to be trampled by other oncoming teams: all this to the roars of the public, which terrified the horses.

The most eagerly awaited events were the gladiatorial combats. These were between animal and animal, man and animal, and man and man.

The day Titus inaugurated the Colosseum all Rome gasped in amazement. The arena could be lowered and flooded to form a lake or raised again, transformed by different scenery, to represent part of a desert, for example, or a jungle glade. A marble gallery was reserved for high authorities, and in the center of this towered the imperial box with all its accessories. Here the emperor and empress sat on ivory thrones and anyone could approach him to plead for a pension, a transfer, or mercy for a condemned man. At each corner fountains cast jets of perfumed water into the air, and the back tables were laid for refreshments between the events. Everything was free: entrance, seat, cushion, roast viands, and wine.

The first event was a parade of exotic wild animals, many of which the Romans had never seen before. What with elephants, tigers, lions, leopards, panthers, bears, wolves, crocodiles, hippopotamuses, giraffes, lynxes, and so on, 10,000 wild beasts filed past and many of them were in fancy dress to caricature historic or legendary personages. The arena was then lowered and they reappeared ready for combat: lions against tigers, tigers against bears, leopards against wolves. At the end of this performance only half of these poor beasts were still alive. Again the arena was lowered and reappeared as a *plaza de toros*. The *corrida,* already practiced by the Etruscans, had been imported to Rome by Caesar, who had seen it in Greece. Caesar had a weakness for these spectacles and had been the first to stage a battle between lions for the entertainment of his countrymen. Bullfights had great success with the Romans and were always in demand. The *toreros* did not know the tricks of the trade and thus faced almost certain death. They were, in fact, chosen from among slaves and convicts (like all the other gladiators, for that matter). Many of them did not even fight. They were supposed to represent mythical characters, yet there was nothing mythical about the tragic ends they had to undergo. As propaganda for patriotism one of them was made to appear as Mucius Scaevola and burn his own hand on the coals, another, as Hercules, was cremated alive on a pyre and another, as Orpheus, was torn to shreds as he played the lyre. These were considered such edifying spectacles that the young were admitted to them.

Battles between gladiators came next on the program. These were all men condemned to death for murder, robbery with violence, sacrilege, or mutiny, the crimes punishable by death. However, whenever there was a shortage of gladiators, obliging tribunals used to issue death sentences for much less serious offenses. Rome and its emperors could not do without their ration of human flesh to butcher. Even so, there were some volunteers and not all of them came from the lower orders. They attended special schools before fighting in the arena and these were perhaps the most serious and rigorous schools in Rome. One entered them rather as one enters a seminary, having sworn that one was prepared to be "flogged, burnt, and stabbed." Every time they fought, the gladiators had an even

chance of being killed, but they also had an even chance of becoming popular heroes, to whom poets dedicated their verses,
sculptors their statues, aediles their streets and ladies their
favors. Before the contest they were offered a gigantic banquet
and if they lost they were expected to die with complete indifference. They were called by various names according to the
weapons they used. Every show in the Circus contained numbers
of these duels. They did not always end fatally. If the loser displayed great courage and skill he might even be reprieved by
the crowd which, on these occasions, made the gesture of the
upturned thumb. In one of the shows put on by Augustus (it
lasted eight days), 10,000 gladiators took part. Guards, dressed
as Charon and Mercury, used to prod the fallen with sharp forks
to see whether they were dead and those who feigned death
were beheaded. Negro slaves then piled up the corpses and
brought on fresh sand for the subsequent combats.

Even the strictest moralists raised no objection to this delight in bloodshed. Juvenal, who criticized everything, was mad
about the Circus. Tacitus had moments of doubt but came to
the conclusion that the blood shed in the Circus was "vile" and
justified it by the use of this adjective. Even Pliny, the most
civilized and modern gentleman of the period, found that these
massacres had educational value since they accustomed the
spectator to a stoic contempt for life. Statius and Martial, the
two poets who sang the praises of Domitian, practically lived at
the Circus and drew poetic inspiration from it. Statius was a
former Neapolitan actor who had made himself a name with a
bad poem, *The Thebais*. When he was invited to dinner by the
emperor, so that all Naples should know about it he wrote a
book depicting Domitian as a god and dedicated to him his
Silvae, the only good poems he ever wrote. He died at the age
of thirty-five, when his star had already been eclipsed by that of
Martial, poet laureate of the Circus and the bordello.

Martial was a Spaniard from Bilbao who came to Rome
when he was twenty-four. He was a protégé of his compatriots
Seneca and Lucan; at that time the Spaniards abroad helped
one another just as Sicilians do nowadays. He was not a great
poet but he was a master of the witty comment that bites hard
enough to leave a wound. "My pages bear the imprint of men,"
he used to say, and it was true. His characters are riffraff whom
he chose from among the ignominious company of whores and

gladiators, but precisely because of this they are vivid in their frank vulgarity. He himself was not too noble a character. He fawned on Domitian, slandered his own benefactors, and lived in the underworld squandering his money on wine, dicing, and betting on the races. Fortunately he did not know the meaning of the word rhetoric, and his *Epigrams* remain the most perfect examples of their kind while the account he has left us of Rome is, perhaps, the most lifelike. He finally returned to Bilbao, then only a small town, and lived by sponging on a friend who gave him a villa. He left Rome with only one regret, and that was for the Circus. He was no longer of an age to regret the bordello.

Seneca alone condemns the gladiatorial games, which he says he did not patronize. He visited the Colosseum only once and was appalled. "Man, the most sacred thing to man, is killed here for sport and amusement," he wrote when he got home.

The fact of the matter is that this "sport and amusement" corresponded exactly to the moral level of a Rome which was not yet Christian but no longer truly pagan. Its emperor was the high priest or pope of a state religion which, because it had no religious content, had no objections to such abominations. It continued to celebrate feasts with an increasingly elaborate ritual, to build ever more magnificent temples and to create new idols such as Anna and Fortuna. Only marble capitals supported these temples—certainly not faith. This last was the monopoly of the few hundred (or thousand) Christians, mostly Jews. Instead of going to the Circus to gloat over the butchery of men, they met in their little *ecclesiae* to pray for their souls.

XLI

Nerva and Trajan

DOMITIAN'S KILLERS HAD NOT GIVEN THEIR VICTIM TIME TO NOMI-nate his heir. The senate, which had never officially recognized this right of the emperors but in practice had always accepted it, took advantage of this situation to elect one of its own members as successor.

Marcus Cocceius Nerva was a man of the law whose hobby was poetry, but he was neither afflicted by the quarrelsomeness of the lawyer nor the vanity of the poet. He was a tall, heavy-set man who had never harmed anyone, had never been ambitious, and at the end of his reign could justly say that he had never done anything that might have made his return to private life risky.

Perhaps it was not so much for his good qualities that they elected him but because he was already sixty-six and had a weak stomach, grounds for assuming that his reign would be short. In fact it lasted only two years, yet they were enough for Nerva to right the wrongs of his predecessor. He recalled the proscripts, distributed extensive lands to the poor, exempted the Jews from the tribute that Vespasian had imposed on them, and put the state's finances on a sound basis. This did not prevent the praetorian guards, who did not care for this new master who resisted their arrogant demands, from besieging him in the palace, killing a few of his advisers, and insisting on the handing over of Domitian's executioners. Nerva, in an attempt to save his servants, offered his own head in exchange. When this offer was turned down he tendered his resignation to the senate, who refused it. Nerva never took any decision without consulting the senate and never went contrary to their opinion. On this occasion, too, he yielded. Perhaps he felt that the end was near. He spent the little time that was left in finding an heir who would meet with the senate's approval. Having no sons of his own, and to prevent the praetorian guard from choosing his successor, he adopted one. The choice of Trajan was perhaps the greatest service Nerva ever rendered to the state.

Trajan was a general at that moment commanding an army in Germany. When he learned that he had been proclaimed emperor he received the news with composure. He sent a message to thank the senators for their confidence in him and assured them that he would come and assume power as soon as he could find the time. He did not find it for two years, having first to settle accounts with the Teutons. Born forty years before, in Spain, of a family of Roman functionaries, he had followed the family calling by becoming a kind of soldier-functionary. He was tall, strong, and of spartan habits, brave as a lion but not ostentatiously so. His wife Plotina declared that she was the happiest of spouses, for though he may have deceived her occasionally with some young man he never did so with other women. He passed as a man of culture because he always used to take Dion Chrysostom along with him in his command vehicle. Chrysostom was a famous rhetorician addicted to long discourses on philosophy. One day, however, Trajan confessed that he had never understood a single word of Dion's outpourings, had never even listened to them, in fact, but liked to be lulled by their silvery sound while he thought of other things.

When Trajan finally found the leisure to come and be crowned, Pliny the Younger was assigned the task of addressing a panegyric to him. In this Trajan was courteously reminded that he owed his election to the senators and ought to consult them before making decisions. Trajan listened to this part of the speech with nods of approval to which nobody attached much importance—mistakenly, as it turned out. Power never went to his head and even the threat of conspiracies did not change him into a suspicious and bloody despot. When he discovered Licinius Sura's plot, he went to dinner with him and not only ate everything that was put on his plate, but even had himself shaved by the conspirator's barber.

He was a demonic worker and drove his subordinates hard. Many a slothful senator was sent to inspect and reform the provincial administration and one gets a good idea of his efficiency and energy from the surviving letters he exchanged with these inspectors. His political views were those of an enlightened conservative. He believed more in sound administration than in sweeping reforms. He did not approve of violence, but he knew when to use a firm hand. This was why he did not hesitate to declare war on Dacia (present-day Rumania) when its king, Decebalus, threatened the conquests he had made in Germany. The campaign was brilliant. The beaten Decebalus surrendered but Trajan spared his life and throne and merely imposed vassalage on him. Such clemency, novel in the annals of Roman history, was ill-rewarded. Two years later Decebalus rebelled again. Again Trajan defeated his perfidious enemy, pillaged the Transylvanian gold mines, and with the loot celebrated his victory by an unbroken four months of games involving 10,000 gladiators. The surplus enabled him to carry out a program of public works destined to make his reign one of the most memorable in the history of city planning, engineering, and architecture.

An imposing aqueduct, a new port at Ostia, four great highways, and the amphitheater at Verona were among his major achievements. The most famous, however, is the Forum of Trajan, due to the genius of Apollodorus, a Greek from Damascus. This architect had previously built in only a few days a wonderful bridge over the Danube which had enabled Trajan to overthrow Decebalus. To raise the column which still stands in front of the Basilica Ulpia, eighteen blocks of special marble, weighing fifteen tons each, were brought from Paros: for those times a miracle. Two thousand figures, in a vaguely neorealistic style, were carved on it in bas-relief. The carvings are too crowded to be beautiful, but from the documentary point of view they are very interesting and it is this that must certainly have pleased Trajan.

After six years of peace, during which he was kept busy with his reconstruction work, Trajan began to long for the camp again. Although he was almost sixty he made up his mind to complete the work of Caesar and Antony in the east by advancing the frontiers of the empire to the Indian Ocean. He was successful and marched triumphantly through Mesopotamia, Persia, Syria, and Armenia, all of which were reduced to the status of Roman provinces. He built a Red Sea fleet and certainly regretted being too old to sail away with it and conquer India and the Far East. But leaving garrisons in these countries was not enough to ensure lasting order and before Trajan got home widespread revolts had broken out behind his back. The weary warrior wanted to turn back and stamp them out himself, but he couldn't because of his dropsy. He sent Lusius Quietus and Marcius Turba in his place, and resumed his journey to Rome, hoping to arrive before he died. Paralysis struck him down at Selinus in A.D. 117 in his sixty-fourth year. Only his ashes returned to Rome and these were buried beneath his column.

Nerva and Trajan were certainly two great emperors, but apart from the many real merits for which they are remembered, they also had the extraordinary good luck of earning the gratitude of a historian like Tacitus and a diarist like Pliny. The testimony of these two was to have a decisive effect on the verdict of posterity.

Tacitus, who wrote the lives of so many other people, forgot to tell us anything about himself. We do not know exactly where he was born and we are not even sure that he was the son of the Cornelius Tacitus who was governor of Belgium. His family must have belonged to the wealthy middle classes which later became part of the aristocracy. He was much prouder of his wife's family than his own. She was the daughter of that Agricola, proconsul and governor of Britain, whom Domitian had made the mistake of dismissing. We only know this Agricola from the biography written by his son-in-law, who was a past master in the art. However, since Tacitus had all the gifts of a great writer save that of objectivity, we cannot tell whether this portrait is really an authentic likeness. We only know that Tacitus' admiration for his father-in-law must have been sincere.

Tacitus was a great lawyer. Pliny considered him a greater one than Cicero himself. It is to be feared, however, that he wrote history by the same standards he used when defending his clients, that is by making a case rather than by establishing the truth. His first historical effort dealt with the years between Galba and Domitian, a period of which he had been an eyewitness. His masterly diatribe against tyranny had such success among those aristocrats who had been its chief victims that he then went back to the reigns of Nero, Claudius, Caligula, and Tiberius. Tacitus recognizes quite honestly that in Domitian's time he had bowed to the arbitrary whims of that sovereign and as a senator had condoned his injustices. It is not difficult to infer that his love of liberty must have dated from that period. He wrote fourteen books of history, of which only four still exist, and sixteen *Annals,* of which twelve have survived. He also wrote various other works, such as the *Life of Agricola* and a treatise on the Germans in which, with extraordinary polemical skill, he extols that race's virtues and thus, by inference, denounces the shortcomings of the Romans.

Tacitus should be read judiciously. One should not expect sociological or economic analyses from him. Enough to be satisfied with his great feature stories, perfect in the unfolding of their narratives, complete with thrills and suspense. His pages are peopled with personages who are probably largely invented, but so extraordinarily well drawn in a vigorous style (achieved by no other writer after him) that they remain etched on the memory. His authorities are questionable and he probably never

even bothered to check them. He goes by hearsay, quoting such
sources as suit him, even if untrue, and discarding such as do
not, though they happen to be true. His one aim is to propound
his own doctrines: that freedom is the highest expression of
good, that freedom can only be guaranteed by aristocratic oli-
garchies, that character is more important than brains, and that
reforms are only a step in the wrong direction. All in all, it was
a sin and a shame that Tacitus prided himself on the writing of
history. Had he had the ambition to be a novelist, and fulfilled
it, it would have been better for him and for us.

Less brilliant and colorful, but more circumstantial and
credible, is the picture of the society of that time left us by Pliny
the Younger. Pliny was born with a silver spoon in his mouth.
He had a rich uncle, who left him his name and fortune, an excellent education, a virtuous wife, and a nature which enabled
him to see the brighter side of everything and everybody. He
was, in fact, a "gentleman" in the tradition of Atticus. Born at
Como, he started life as a lawyer. Tacitus offered to share with
him the honor and onus of the prosecution of Marius Priscus, an
official accused of malpractice and cruelty. Pliny accepted, but
instead of arraigning the accused, pronounced a declamatory
praise of his colleague two hours in length. When it came to his
turn, Tacitus returned the compliment (and Priscus in the jail,
wringing his hands the while, feeling he had been completely
forgotten).

Pliny carried out various missions with efficiency and
honesty, particularly in diplomacy, for which Trajan, a good
judge of men, often picked him. His fundamental quality was,
in fact, "tact." It is enough to read the letter he wrote to his old
preceptor, Quintilian, the great jurist, apologizing for being unable to give him more than 50,000 sesterces for his daughter's
dowry: he seems to be asking a favor instead of offering one.
Whenever he was sent on some mission or tour of inspection, he
refused to accept a salary or expenses and filled his baggage
with presents for the wives of the governors, generals, and prefects he would meet on his travels. So as to be able to discuss
literature, he always took somebody along with him at his own
expense, usually Suetonius, for whom he had a weakness. With
his passion for writing letters to all and sundry he kept up his
"contacts" wherever he went and invitations were showered on
him. He always replied in writing: "I accept your invitation to

dinner, my friend, but on condition you let me go home early
and treat me frugally. Let there be philosophic converse at the
table, but let us partake of it in moderation."

Moderation: this sums up his ethics, aesthetics, and diete-
tics. Pliny did everything in moderation, even falling in love.
In his descriptive letters to the emperor, his colleagues, relations,
and clients, he wrote about everything with moderation. These
letters are the best of his writing that remains, and the light
they throw on the society and customs of his time renders them
particularly precious to us.

XLII

Hadrian

IT IS POSSIBLE THAT SO FORTUNATE AN EVENT AS THE ACCESSION OF
the greatest emperor of antiquity was due to a banal coinci-
dence, the somewhat nasty business of adultery. Nevertheless,
Dion Cassius swears that Hadrian had only one qualification for
taking the place of Trajan, who had left no heir: that of being
the lover of Trajan's wife Plotina.

Hearsay should always be treated with a certain amount of
reserve, especially when it concerns extraconjugal relations, but
Plotina certainly did have a hand in getting Hadrian crowned.
It is true they were, though not by blood, aunt and nephew,
though being related never proved an impediment to making
love in ancient Rome. Trajan and Hadrian came from the same
town, both having been born at Italica in Spain. Hadrian was
so called because his family originally came from Hadria (now
Adria). He was twenty-four years younger than Trajan, who, in
his dual capacity as friend of the family and legal guardian, had
brought him to Rome. He was a lively boy, who took a keen
interest in everything—mathematics, music, medicine, philosophy, literature, sculpture, geometry; he studied them all eagerly
and was quick to learn. Trajan gave him his niece, Vivia Sabina,
in marriage. It was an icily respectable marriage which produced neither love nor children. Sabina, as beautiful and cold

as a statue, was heard to mutter that her husband had more
time for his horses and dogs than he had for her. Even so,
Hadrian took her with him on his travels, overwhelmed her
with attentions, and dismissed his own secretary Suetonius for
speaking of her once with scant respect.

Hadrian was barely forty when he came to the throne, and
his first move was to settle speedily the military situation left by
Trajan. He had never approved of his predecessor's warlike
enterprises and as soon as he succeeded him, withdrew the
armies from Persia and Armenia, much to the disgust of their
commanders, to whom a purely defensive policy meant the beginning of the end of the empire as well as their own careers,
honors, and other perquisites. It has never been clear how it
came about that four of the most valorous and influential commanders were shortly afterward put to death without trial.
Hadrian was on the Danube at the time, seeking a permanent
settlement with the Dacians which would exclude further conflict. He hastened to Rome. The senate took full responsibility
for the executions on the grounds that the generals had been
conspiring against the state. Nobody believed in Hadrian's innocence, but the matter was dropped when he distributed a billion
sesterces among the citizens, cancelled their debts to the state,
and entertained them for weeks on end with magnificent dis-
plays at the Circus.

These beginnings caused many Romans to fear a return to
the methods of Nero and their suspicions were confirmed by the
fact that, like Nero, Hadrian used to sing, paint, and compose.
However, it was soon realized that these artistic tendencies had
no taint of the pathological. Hadrian only indulged in them in
his spare time, to rest from his labors as a scrupulous and able
administrator. He was a tall, handsome, elegant man, with curly
hair and a fair beard which all the Romans immediately wanted
to copy, not knowing perhaps that he had only grown it to hide
certain ugly bluish patches on his cheeks. It is not easy to
understand his complex and contradictory character. Usually
he was courteous and good-tempered, but sometimes he was
harsh to the point of cruelty. In private life he was skeptical
and derisive of the gods and oracles. When he performed his
duties as supreme pontiff, however, he would tolerate no signs
of irreverence. Nobody knows what his personal beliefs were.

Perhaps he believed in the stars because every now and

then he dabbled in astrology and was highly superstitious about eclipses and the tides. Nevertheless, he considered religion a mainstay of society and for this reason took the attitude he did toward irreverence in public. After he had had Apollodorus put to death for a scornful refusal to participate in the work, he himself supervised the plans for the new temple to Venus and Roma.

Intellectually he tended to Stoicism and was an admirer of Epictetus, whose works he had carefully studied. However, he never bothered to put his precepts into practice. He took his pleasures wherever he found them, with good taste but without shame or remorse. He had love affairs with either sex without ever losing his head. Though he liked eating well, he hated banquets, preferring intimate dinners with a few companions chosen for their conversational skill. He also founded a university, appointing to its faculty the greatest masters of the time, mostly Greeks. These and their pupils were his usual dinner guests. He used to argue fairly and accepted criticism and contradiction. One day, in fact, he chided Favorinus, a Gaulish intellectual, for giving in to him too often. "A man who bases his arguments on thirty divisions under arms is always right," the young philosopher replied. The emperor was so pleased that he repeated the remark for the amusement of the senate.

His most extraordinary characteristic was that he did not feel indispensable. Indeed he did everything possible to avoid becoming so or being taken for the usual "man of destiny" most absolute monarchs think, and hope others will think, they are. His constant aim was to set up an effective bureaucratic organization which needed only senatorial supervision. He had a talent for orderliness and sought to achieve this by simplifying the laws, by now piled up in an inextricable chaos. In this task, which he entrusted to Julian, he preceded Justinian.

Hadrian also arranged a rational division of duties which would allow the apparatus of the state to function almost automatically. He had purely selfish reasons, since he enjoyed travel and wanted to be able to leave without the worry that in his absence affairs would be mismanaged. He was thus able to make very long tours, lasting as long as five years, and so got to know the empire and its outposts really well. Four years after his coronation he left for a detailed inspection of Gaul. He travelled like any private citizen, with few precautions for his safety, very limited baggage, and a retinue almost entirely composed of technicians. He pounced without warning on governors and generals who had to give an account of their administration down to the last detail. He would then order a new bridge or road and award promotions or reprimands. If opportunity arose, he, the man of peace, would take command of a legion to settle in battle the question of a doubtful frontier. On foot, at the head of his infantry, he was capable of marching up to twenty-five miles a day and never lost even a skirmish.

From Gaul he crossed into Germany, where he reorganized the garrisons and made a profound study of the natives, whose primitive strength filled him with admiration and foreboding. He then sailed down the Rhine and across to Britain, where he ordered the construction of his famous Wall. Returning to Gaul, he went on to Spain where, at Tarragona, he was attacked by a slave. In spite of the man's strength, Hadrian disarmed him and handed him over to the doctors, who pronounced him insane. Hadrian accepted this alibi and pardoned him. From Spain he crossed over to Africa where, at the head of a couple of legions, he stamped out a Moorish revolt before going on to Asia Minor.

In Rome they began to be concerned about their absentee emperor. When they heard that he had boarded a ship going up the Nile with a new guest among his suite, gossip began to take on a malicious tinge. This new guest was an extremely good-looking Greek youth, with curly hair and languid eyes, called Antinous.

It seems to have been fated that from Caesar onward any Roman of high consequence who landed in Egypt should become involved in an unfortunate emotional entanglement. We do not know exactly what the relations were between Hadrian and Antinous. Sabina, who accompanied the emperor, seems to have raised no objection to the youth's presence. The circumstances of his death, however, have never been satisfactorily explained. It appears that he was drowned in the river. This was a terrible blow to Hadrian. "He wept," says Spartianus, "just like a woman." Hadrian had a temple erected in his honor, and around this temple built a city, Antinoopolis, which rose to importance in the time of Byzantium. According to a legend, which perhaps grew up much later than the actual events, Antinous killed himself because he had learned from the oracles that the plans of his protector would only succeed if he himself were dead. Certainly, by disappearing from the scene, the boy rendered one valuable service: he left the succession open to a monarch of the stature of Antoninus. If Antinous had lived, perhaps Rome might have ended up with him on its back as emperor.

The man who returned to Rome after this tragedy was no longer the gay and jovial sovereign who had set out. He had become something of a misanthrope. Whereas before he had abandoned his desk with relief, happy to enjoy his leisure and knowing exactly what to do with it, he now seemed to dread the empty hours and spent them in writing. A grammar, some poems, and an autobiography are the results of this solitude. His main occupation, however, was his building program. He rebuilt the Pantheon, which had originally been built by Agrippa, and destroyed by fire. For this he adopted the Greek style, which he preferred to the Roman, and there is no doubt that it remains the best-preserved monument of antiquity. When Pope Urban VII dismantled the ceiling of the portico, he recovered enough bronze to forge over a hundred cannon as well as the canopy over the main altar in Saint Peter's, which is still there.

Another of his architectural masterpieces was the villa around which Tivoli later sprang up. It contained everything: temples, a hippodrome, libraries, and museums. For two thousand years the armies of the entire world have gone there for loot, and have always found it. But as soon as Hadrian went to live there his health began to fail. His body became swollen and he suffered from copious nosebleeds. Feeling that the end was near, he sent for his friend Lucius Verus, adopted him as his son, and started training him for the monarchy. Unfortunately Verus died soon afterwards.

Hadrian's choice then fell on Antoninus, to whom he gave the title of *Caesar*, keeping that of *Augustus* for himself. From then on the title of *Caesar* was given to all heirs apparent.

Hadrian's sufferings were so atrocious that all he longed for was death. He had one tomb built on the far side of the Tiber, access to which was gained by a special bridge, the Pons Aelius. Today it is that great mausoleum called Castel Sant'Angelo. One day, when the building was already completed, the Stoic philosopher Euphrates came to ask Hadrian's permission to commit suicide. The emperor gave his consent and then discussed with him the uselessness of life. When Euphrates had drunk the hemlock, he ordered some to be brought for himself so that he could follow the philosopher's example, but nobody would bring him any. He commanded his doctor to do so but, in order not to disobey, the doctor killed himself. He begged a servant to get him a sword or a dagger, but the servant fled. "Behold a man," he exclaimed in despair, "who has the power to put to death anyone he pleases except himself."

At the age of sixty-two, after a reign of twenty-one years, he finally closed his eyes. A few days before his death he composed a little poem recalling days gone by, which is, perhaps, one of the most exquisite of Latin lyrics: *Animula vagula, blandula hospes comesque corporis. . . .* "Little soul, wandering, pleasant, guest and companion of the body. . . ."

With him died not only a great emperor, but also one of the most complex, disquieting, and captivating personalities in all history, and perhaps the most modern of all the characters of the ancient world. Like Nerva, on leaving Rome he rendered her a signal service: he designated as his heir the man least likely to cause him to be regretted.

XLIII

Marcus Aurelius

THE TITLE OF *pius* WAS GIVEN POSTHUMOUSLY TO ANTONINUS BY the senate. It also called him *optimus princeps,* the best of princes. His successor, Marcus Aurelius, however, used to call him a "monster of virtue" and when in a difficulty, would say to himself: "Do what Antoninus would have done in this case." This was not as easy as it sounded. The difficulty was knowing what he would have done.

Antoninus was no longer a young man but already over fifty when he came to the throne in A.D. 138. And if one had asked one of the many Romans who acclaimed his succession with joy what they were so happy about, he would have been at a loss for an answer. Up to that time Antoninus had done absolutely nothing worthy of note. He was an excellent lawyer but as he distinctly disliked oratory, he practiced little and for what little he did he took no pay, since he was very rich. His family were bankers who had come from France a couple of generations before. He had received an upper-middle-class education and had studied philosophy, but only superficially; his primary interest was religion. He was reverent but not bigoted. Probably he was one of the last of the Romans to believe sincerely in the gods, or at least to behave as though he did. He was knowledgeable about literature and protected many writers, but treated them somewhat loftily, with indulgent and aristocratic detachment, as though they were purely decorative elements of society, not to be taken too seriously. He was broad shouldered with a placid and serene expression and everybody liked him for his kindliness, his genuine sympathy with the misfortunes of others, and the discretion he showed in hiding his own. Nevertheless, this man so universally liked had one enemy, in his own home, his wife. Faustina was beautiful but, to say the least, a bit too lively. Even if one discounts generously everything said about her she was still enough to drive any husband out of his wits. They had two daughters, one of whom died. The other took after her mother and behaved toward her poor husband, Marcus Aurelius, in much the same manner. Antoninus suffered Faustina in silence. When she died, he erected a temple and created a foundation for the education of poor girls in her honor. He had only reproached her once in his life. This was when she had just become empress and wanted a few luxuries. "Don't you realize," he asked her, "that we have now lost everything we had?"

These were not idle words, because the first thing Antoninus did as emperor was to pour his huge private fortune into the coffers of the state. On his death his personal patrimony was nil, while that of the empire amounted to 2,007,000,000 sesterces, a figure never again to be reached. He achieved this result by judicious but not miserly administration. He revised and reduced Hadrian's reconstruction program, but did not cancel it. For every item of expenditure, even the most trivial, he used to ask the authorization of the senate, and he accounted to them for every last penny. With its approval he also went ahead with the reorganization and liberalization of the laws begun by his predecessor. For the first time the rights and duties of married couples were made equal, torture almost completely abolished, and the killing of a slave proclaimed a crime.

Unlike the restless and inquisitive Hadrian, he was of a sedentary temperament and respected office hours like a perfect bureaucrat. It does not appear that he ever went, even for one day, any farther than Lanuvium, where he had a villa, and where he used to spend the weekend fishing or hunting with his friends. After he became a widower, he took a concubine (much more faithful to him than his wife had ever been), but he kept her secluded and did not let her mix in affairs of state. All he wanted was peace. Perhaps he wanted it a bit too much, that is to say at the expense of the empire's prestige. In Germany, for example, he showed excessive docility, thus encouraging the boldness of the rebels. However, there is no foreign writer of the period who does not praise the order and tranquility which the world enjoyed under him. According to Appianus, Antoninus was literally besieged by ambassadors of various countries begging to be annexed to the empire. Like all happy ones, his reign, although it lasted twenty-three years, produced no history or great events. "The ideal," says Renan, "seemed to have been attained: the world was governed by a father."

At the age of seventy-four Antoninus fell ill. As it was possibly the first time in his life, although the symptom was only a stomach ache, he felt that his time had come. He already had a *Caesar* on hand. The dying Hadrian himself had indicated him in the person of the seventeen-year-old Marcus Aurelius, Antoninus' nephew. He sent for him and said to him in effect: "Now it's up to you." He then ordered his servants to take the gold statue of the goddess Fortuna to Marcus' rooms, gave the duty officer the password for the day, "Equanimity," and said that he wished to be left alone to sleep. He then turned over in bed and actually went to sleep forever.

At this time (A.D. 161) Marcus was forty. He was one of those rare beings who are born lucky and admit it. "I owe a great debt to the gods," he wrote. "They gave me good grandparents, good parents, a good sister, good teachers, and good friends." Among the latter had been Hadrian, who used to visit his house and had taken a great liking to Marcus even as a little boy. The reason for this friendship was their common Spanish origin. The Aurelii also came from Spain where, for their honesty, they had earned the surname of "Verus." When the boy was orphaned at the age of a few months, his grandfather, then consul, had taken care of him. He must have had great faith in this grandson, judging by the number of preceptors he gave him: four for grammar, four for rhetoric, two for jurisprudence, six for philosophy, and one for mathematics, a total of seventeen. How the lad ever managed to learn anything it is difficult to imagine. Cornelius Fronto, the rhetorician, was his favorite among these pedagogues, but he despised the subject he taught. Legal quibbling and verbosity were the traits he admired least in his fellow countrymen. On the other hand, he took a keen interest in philosophy. He preferred Stoicism, and not content with studying it deeply, he even wished to practice it. At the age of twelve he had the bed taken out of his room, slept on the bare floor and went on such a strict diet that his health was affected. But he did not complain. Indeed, he even thanked the gods for having kept him chaste and capable of restraining his sexual impulses until the age of eighteen.

He might have become one of the more puritanical priests of the cult of Stoicism if Antoninus had not made him *Caesar* and taken him in to share in the government while still an adolescent. He adopted him, together with Lucius Verus, son of the man whom Hadrian had nominated as his heir but who had died before him. This Lucius was quite a different type. He was worldly and lecherous, and was not in the least upset when Antoninus later excluded him and designated Marcus as sole *Caesar*. Nevertheless Marcus, mindful of the wishes of Hadrian, called in Lucius to share the throne and gave him his daughter, Lucilla, in marriage. Unfortunately loyalty in politics is not always a wise counselor.

When Marcus was crowned, all the philosophers of the empire rejoiced, expecting to see the triumph of their ideas and the foundation of Utopia. But they had a disappointment in store for them. Marcus was not a great statesman. He knew nothing about economics. For example, he used to get his estimates all wrong and, from time to time, his accounts needed auditing and checking. However, from the apprenticeship he had served under Antoninus, that enlightened and somewhat skeptical conservative, he had learned his lesson about men. Knowing that laws are not enough to reform human nature, when like his two predecessors he set about to reform the legal code, he did so only half-heartedly, as though he did not have much faith in the benefits this would confer. As a moralist he considered a good example more efficacious. He set one by leading an ascetic life which his subjects admired but were never tempted to imitate.

Events did nothing to help him. He had hardly come to the throne when the Britons, the Germans and the Persians, encouraged by Antoninus' docility, began threatening the frontiers of the empire. Marcus sent Lucius east with an army but when he got as far as Antioch he met Panthea and stopped. She was a local Cleopatra and Lucius was another Mark Antony, but without the latter's courage and military genius. As soon as he saw this remarkable woman, he lost his head completely. She is said to have contributed to his irresponsibility by feeding him philters, though if she was really as lovely as they said she could not have had much need for them.

Marcus did not protest against this behavior on the part of Lucius, who continued to linger with Panthea while the Persians overran Syria as they pleased. He discreetly sent an order to Avidius Cassius, his colleague's chief of staff, with instructions to carry it out to the letter. This strategic plan, it is said, revealed great military ability. While Lucius was enjoying himself in Antioch, his army overwhelmingly defeated the Persians. He only resumed command of it to be crowned with laurel on the day of the triumph awarded him. Unfortunately, along with the spoils of the beaten enemy, he brought his fellow citizens an ugly gift, the germs of the plague. This was a terrible scourge which in Rome alone caused the death of over 200,000 people. Galen, the most celebrated physician of the time, reports that its victims were racked with a hacking cough and covered with pustules. Their breath, too, was malodorous. All Italy was infected by this plague and towns and villages were deserted. People crowded the sanctuaries to implore the protection of the gods. All work ceased, and in the wake of the epidemic came famine.

The emperor devoted himself to nursing in the hospital wards. Science at that time could unfortunately offer no remedy. To crown these public calamities came private griefs. Faustina, the daughter Antoninus had given him as a wife, was in every way the image of her mother and bore the same name. She was beautiful, gay, and unfaithful. Her adulteries were not proven, but they were the talk of Rome. It may be that there was some excuse for her. Her husband, ascetically absorbed in his priestly calling of "first servant of the state," could not have afforded much stimulation to so high-spirited a young woman. Marcus, as courteous as his predecessor and father-in-law, surrounded her with attentions and tenderness and never uttered a word of complaint. In his *Meditations,* in fact, he thanked the gods for having given him such a devoted and affectionate wife. Of the four children born of this marriage, one daughter was dead and the other had become the wretched wife of Lucius, whose one kindness to her was to leave her a widow. The other two were twins whose real father (all Rome said) was a gladiator; one of them died at birth and the other, named Commodus, was already renowned at seven for his beauty and his prowess as an athlete. His aversion to study and his unbridled passion for the Circus, in particular combats with wild animals, were already the despair of his tutors. But Marcus adored him.

The mortality rate caused by plague and famine had made Rome a gloomy and despondent city. Prematurely agéd by all these tribulations before he was fifty, and a martyr to insomnia and what may have been a gastric ulcer, Marcus hardly had time to deal with the problems rapidly succeeding one another. The Germanic tribes now started reaching out towards Hungary and Rumania. When Marcus put himself at the head of the legions many smiled. This gaunt and fragile little vegetarian hardly seemed to bear the mark of a great leader. Yet seldom had the legions fought with such dash as they did under his direct command. This peaceful man fought for six long years and defeated one after another the most aggressive of foes, the Quadi, the Langobards, the Marcomanni, and the Sarmatians. Nevertheless, alone in his tent after a day of battle, he opened his book of *Meditations* and wrote: "When a spider catches a fly in his web, he thinks he has done something extraordinary. He who captures a Sarmatian thinks the same. What neither of them realizes is that they are a couple of petty thieves." This consideration did not, however, deflect him on the following day from another attack upon the Sarmatians.

Marcus was in Bohemia, completing a brilliant series of victories, when Avidius Cassius rebelled in Egypt and proclaimed himself emperor. This was the ex-chief of staff of Lucius who, by adopting Marcus' plan, had beaten the Persians. Marcus concluded a rapid and generous peace with his enemies, assembled the troops and told them that, if Rome agreed, he was quite willing to abdicate in favor of his rival. He then returned to Rome, where the senate unanimously declined his offer. While Marcus was advancing toward Cassius, the latter was killed by one of his own officers. Marcus regretted that he had been unable to pardon him. He stopped at Athens for an exchange of views with the local exponents of the various philosophical schools and then returned to Rome. Here he reluctantly submitted to the triumph accorded him and shared it with Commodus who, by now, was famous for his prowess as a gladiator, his cruelty, and his filthy language.

Perhaps it was partly to distract him from these practices that Marcus resumed the war against the Germans, taking the boy with him. He was on the verge of final victory when he fell ill in Vienna. For five days he refused to eat or drink. On the sixth he rose, presented Commodus to the assembled troops as their new emperor, and begged him to carry forward the frontiers of Rome as far as the Elbe. He then went back to bed, covered his face with the sheet, and awaited his death.

His *Meditations,* written in his tent in Greek, have been handed down to us. They are not a great work of literature, but they contain the loftiest moral code left us by the classical world. When the conscience of Rome was flickering out, this emperor was its brilliant, final gleam.

XLIV

The Severi

WHEN PRESENTING COMMODUS TO THE SOLDIERS AS HIS HEIR, Marcus had referred to him as the "rising sun." To the eyes of his putative father he apparently did appear so. The legionaries, too, approved of the foul-mouthed youth with the appetite as well as the strength of a horse, in the belief that he would be more of a soldier than his father. Their dismay can therefore be imagined when, instead of exterminating the enemy caught like rats in a trap, he offered them a hasty and ill-considered peace. Twice these turbulent Germans had been saved by a miracle, miracles for which Rome was later to pay dearly.

Commodus was by no means a coward but the only battles he really loved were those in the arena against gladiators and wild beasts. On rising, he declined breakfast until he had slaughtered his daily tiger. As there were no tigers in Germany he was in a hurry to get back to Rome to those which the governors of the orient had orders to ship back wholesale. This was why, heedless of the empire and its destiny, he signed this disastrous peace which left every problem unsolved.

The senate had renounced its right to elect new emperors in favor of that system of adoption which, from Nerva onward, had worked so well. Now it accepted the restoration of the hereditary principle represented by this new monarch.

As in the cases of Nero and Caligula, even when one discounts most of what his contemporaries have written about him, there is still enough left for us to condemn Commodus as a dangerous character. A gambler, a lecher, and a drunkard, he seems to have had only one real affection, for a certain Marcia. Since she was a Christian, it is rather difficult to understand how she reconciled her austere faith with such a shady lover. Nevertheless, it did probably serve to protect her coreligionists from persecution.

A crisis arose when the informers told Commodus of a plot against him headed by his aunt, his father's sister, Lucilla. Without troubling to seek proof he killed her, and inaugurated a new reign of terror. Cleander, the commander of the praetorian guards, was appointed to carry it out. For the first time since the days of Domitian, Rome cowered before the outrages perpetrated by these troops. Finally the population, more out of fear than courage, besieged them in the palace and demanded Cleander's head. Commodus yielded without hesitation and replaced him by Laetus.

Laetus, a wiser man, realized that once he had accepted the post he was certain either to be killed by the people for trying to please the emperor or by the emperor for trying to please the people. There was only one way out of the dilemma and that was to kill the emperor first. This was the solution he adopted, with the complicity of Marcia. Marcia undertook to give her royal lover a poisoned drink but his constitution was so rugged that the poison had to be supplemented by strangulation. This was the thirty-first of December, A.D. 192. Complete anarchy followed.

The senators, delighted at the death of Commodus, acted as though they themselves had been responsible for it and elected as his successor one of their own number, Pertinax, who accepted most reluctantly. To put the financial situation on a sound basis, he had to economize, and to economize he had to dismiss useless functionaries including the praetorian guard. After two months he was found dead, murdered by members of the guard, who then announced that the throne was up for sale to the highest bidder. Didius Julianus, an immensely wealthy banker, was peacefully having dinner in his palace when his highly ambitious wife and daughter burst into the room, flung his toga around him and hurried him off to the auction. Hesitant but fearing his womenfolk more than the unknown hazards of the throne, Didius offered the praetorians $5,000 a man and emerged the winner.

The senate had sunk pretty low, but not quite so low as to confirm such a transaction. It secretly sent desperate appeals for help to the generals stationed in the provinces. One of these, Septimius Severus, appeared with an offer twice as much as Julian's, which was accepted. The banker was shut up, weeping, in a bathroom and there decapitated.

For the first time an African of Jewish origin ascended the throne. Rome had not chosen him. The senate had, in fact, favored another general, Albinus. However, by the time Septimius had put to death all his opponents and conclusively transformed the empire into a hereditary monarchy of a military character, no further objections were raised. It was monstrous that things should have come to this pass, but once they had—and certainly through no fault of Septimius—he had no other choice. A strong hand was needed to restore control and this Septimius possessed. He was a sturdy, handsome man of about fifty, an excellent strategist and a witty talker who did not mince words. Of a well-to-do family, he had studied philosophy at Athens and law at Rome, but still spoke Latin with a marked Phoenician accent. He certainly did not have the moral fiber of an Antoninus or a Marcus Aurelius nor the intellectual complexity of a Hadrian. He was basically a cynic, but a straightforward and honest one with an acute sense of reality. His one aberration was astrology, and this was responsible for a marriage which boded ill for Rome. When his first wife, a good and simple woman, died, he was in Syria. The widower immediately con-

sulted the stars and learned that a meteorite had fallen in the
neighborhood of Emesa. He went there and found that a temple
had been built over this celestial fragment. The caretakers were
a priest and his daughter, Julia Domna, who, as it happened,
was of a rare beauty. A first encounter was sufficient to convince
Septimius that this was the bride indicated by the stars. She
was an intelligent and cultivated woman who as empress presided over a literary salon, and introduced the customs and
fashions of the orient. Julia frequently deceived her husband,
who was too busy to notice. This misfortune was of a purely
private nature. What was much more serious was the fact that
she gave birth to Caracalla and Geta.

Septimius reigned for seventeen years, only addressing himself to the senate to issue orders, and spent most of them waging
wars. One great, but dangerous novelty which he introduced was
obligatory military service for all citizens, with the exception of
the Italians, to whom it was forbidden. This was official recognition of the irremediable military decadence of the country.
From now on it was to be at the mercy of foreign legions. With
these legions, Septimius fought a series of successful wars, not
merely to reinforce the frontiers but also to keep their garrisons
in training. He was just finishing off the last of them when death
laid him low in Britain in A.D. 211. The same man who had reproached Marcus Aurelius for designating Commodus as his
heir now nominated Caracalla and Geta. Perhaps it was because
he too was a father? Or because, having always been far away
from them, he did not know them, or simply did not care? To
one of his henchmen he once said: "I have got exactly where I
wanted. I now realize that it was not worth the trouble." To his
two heirs he left the advice: "Never be stingy with your soldiers
and everything else will take care of itself."

The advice was unnecessary. Caracalla and Geta cared so
little for anything else, including their father, that they ordered
the doctors to speed his death.

Of the two, Caracalla was the Commodus of the situation
and lost no time in showing it. Discontented with having to
share the throne with his brother, he had him murdered, condemned to death 20,000 citizens suspected of being his followers, and mindful of his father's advice, got on the right side of
the discontented soldiery by filling their pockets with sesterces.
He was not deliberately wicked, just completely amoral. Every

morning, as soon as he woke, he would wrestle with a bear, sit down at the table with a tiger as his companion, and at night sleep between the paws of a lion. He would not receive the senators thronging his antechamber but was affable with the soldiers and heaped favors on them. He extended citizenship to all males in the empire, but only to increase the revenue from death duties. Only citizens were subject to them.

He took little interest in politics, preferring to leave such matters to his mother, who was not without experience but inclined to indulge her personal likes and dislikes. Julia dealt with the correspondence and received in audience ministers and ambassadors while her son studied the career of Alexander the Great and prepared to imitate him. He recruited a "phalanx," equipped it just like those of his hero and marched off to Persia. But in battle he forgot that he was the general. It amused him much more to play the soldier and to challenge the enemy in single combat. Finally the legionaries, bored with a lot of marching in aimless campaigns, producing neither victories nor booty, stabbed him to death.

Julia Domna, having lost everything—husband, throne, and sons—was deported to Antioch, where she died of self-starvation. But she left a sister, Julia Maesa, who was as cunning and ambitious as herself. Maesa had two grandsons, children of two of her daughters. One was called Varius Avitus and, under the pseudonym of Heliogabalus (meaning sun-god), was a priest at Emesa, the place of origin of the empress' family. The other, Alexian, was still a baby. Maesa spread the rumor that Heliogabalus was the natural son of Caracalla, and the legionaries in Syria, who had been converted to the local religion, accorded the fourteen-year-old priest their allegiance as the representative of the Lord. They proclaimed him emperor and, together with his grandmother and mother, brought him in triumph to Rome. In consequence, one fine day in the spring of A.D. 219, the city witnessed the arrival of the strangest of its *Augusti:* a lad dressed completely in red silk, with rouged lips, henna on his eyelashes, a string of pearls around his neck, emerald bracelets and anklets, and a diamond crown on his head. Rome acclaimed him nevertheless. By now even the most fantastic of masquerades had lost the power to scandalize.

But the real emperor was again a woman: Maesa, the sister of Julia. Heliogabalus regarded the throne as a toy and treated it as such. His favorite pastimes seemed innocent enough, harmless pranks, lotteries with unexpected prizes, practical jokes, and card games. But he did enjoy extravagant living and, as he wanted the best of everything, he spent money like water. He never traveled with fewer than 500 wagons in his train and was prepared to spend a fortune on a vial of rare scent. When a seer prophesied that he would die a violent death, he emptied the state coffers to purchase all the most refined instruments of suicide: a gold sword, a whole collection of silk nooses, and diamond-encrusted caskets for hemlock. Occasionally he would remember his religious background and have mystical crises. On one occasion he circumcised himself and on another he tried to emasculate himself. He had the famous meteorite of his maternal great-grandfather sent over from Emesa and built a temple for it. He even offered to recognize the religions of the Jews and Christians as the state religion if they would substitute this big rock of his for Jehovah and Jesus.

Maesa realized that her grandson was a menace to the dynasty so she persuaded him to adopt his young cousin, Alexian, and to designate him *Caesar* under the imposing name of Marcus Aurelius Severus Alexander. Then, with the easy detachment characteristic of the family, she had him murdered together with his mother, her own daughter.

It is odd that such a horrible crime should have resulted in the reign of a saint. Alexander Severus, who was only fourteen, did honor to his name. He studied diligently, slept on a hard couch, ate sparingly, took cold showers even in winter, dressed like anybody else, and had inherited only one trait from his predecessor: impartiality toward all religions, with pronounced sympathy for the moral code of the Jews and Christians. He ordered their precept: "Do unto others as you would have them do unto you" to be graven on many public buildings. He used to discuss religious questions with an open mind in theological circles and in this was encouraged by his mother, Mammaea, who had taken the place of Maesa. She had leanings toward Christianity and a respect for the genius of Origen, an ascetic who had moved by way of Stoicism to the new faith.

While sympathetic to her son's unworldly interests, Mammaea, counseled by Ulpian, Alexander's old tutor, ruled the earth with considerable efficiency. She pursued an intelligent economic policy, reduced the influence of the army, and restored

part of its powers to the senate. She committed only one injustice and this toward her daughter-in-law. Having made her
Alexander's wife, Mammaea became jealous of her and had her
banished. When the Persians began to renew their threats, she
left with her son at the head of the army to drive them back.
Alexander, before joining battle, sent the enemy king a letter in
which he tried to convince him not to insist on fighting. The
latter took this as a sign of weakness, launched his attack, and
was beaten. Later, Alexander, who sincerely hated war, tried to
avoid one with the Germans by meeting their emissaries in
Gaul and offering to pay them an annual tribute if they would
withdraw.

It was perhaps the only mistake he ever made and it cost
him dear. The legions, though no longer thirsting for battle, had
not yet sunk so low as to buy peace. In indignation they rebelled. Alexander, his mother, and all their suite were killed in
their tents. Julius Maximinus, the general commanding the army
in Pannonia, was proclaimed emperor in his stead. The year was
A.D. 235.

XLV

Diocletian

THE ANARCHY WHICH FOLLOWED THE DEATH OF ALEXANDER SEVERUS
lasted fifty years, that is, until the time of Diocletian. This
period is difficult to treat as part of the history of Rome because
of its utter confusion. It even becomes difficult to follow the
succession to the throne, and there is little hope that the most
zealous of readers will remember the names of each one of
those who, after murdering his predecessor, occupied it. A
brief note will suffice.

Maximinus was nearly seven feet tall and broad in proportion. His fingers were so big that he used his wife's bracelets as
rings. Son of a Thracian peasant, he suffered from such a sense
of inferiority because of his general ignorance that during the
three years of his reign he never set foot in Rome, preferring

the company of the soldiers with whom he had grown up. To finance wars, his only amusement, he taxed the rich so heavily that they set up Gordianus, the proconsul of Africa, a cultured and courteous old gentleman of eighty, in opposition to him. Maximinus killed his son in battle and Gordianus committed suicide.

His supporters then turned to Maximus and Balbinus, whom they proclaimed co-emperors. Maximinus was on the point of defeating them both when he was assassinated by his own troops. His rivals were unable to enjoy their advantage since they immediately suffered the same fate at the hands of the praetorian guard, who put their own candidate, another Gordianus, on the throne. The legionaries in turn disposed of this Gordianus III six years afterward as he was leading them against the Persians, and elected Philip the Arab who received the same treatment five years later from Decius at Verona.

Decius succeeded in remaining emperor for two years, a long reign by contemporary standards. He put in hand several radical reforms, including the restoration of the ancient religion in opposition to Christianity, which he wanted to stamp out. He was, however, defeated and killed by the Goths. His place was taken by Gallus, who was assassinated shortly afterward by his own soldiers. These then proclaimed Aemilianus but, a few months later, turned against him as well.

The next on the throne was the sixty-year-old Valerian, who found himself with five simultaneous wars on his hands: against the Goths, the Alemanni, the Franks, the Scythians, and the Persians. He went personally to cope with the eastern enemies, leaving his son, Gallienus, to deal with the western ones. Valerian was taken prisoner and thus Gallienus became sole emperor. He was under forty, and had courage, determination, and brains. In other times he would have made a magnificent sovereign but by now no human power could fend off catastrophe. The Persians were in Syria, the Scythians in Asia Minor, and the Goths in Dalmatia. The Rome of Caesar, not to mention that of Scipio, would have been able to overcome these simultaneous disasters. That of Gallienus was merely a drifting wreck which could be saved only by a miracle.

In the orient something like a miracle did actually occur. Odenathus, who governed Palmyra on behalf of Rome, routed the Persians and proclaimed himself king of Cilicia, Armenia, and Cappadocia. On his death he left the throne to Zenobia, the greatest queen of the east. With the subtle arts of a woman she combined the brains, courage, and steadfastness of a man. Officially she acted in the name of Rome, and as its representative, annexed Egypt; in practice hers was an independent kingdom which had sprung up within the boundaries of the empire. But it acted as a bulwark against the Sarmatian and Scythian hordes now sweeping down from the north after having already overrun Greece. Gallienus, in a close-fought battle, managed to hold them off, only to be killed in due course by his own troops. The barbarians, returning in greater force than before against his successor, Claudius II, launched an attack which, had it been successful, would probably have meant the end of Rome itself. The slaughter was so great that it led to a pestilence from which Claudius himself died in A.D. 270.

At this juncture a truly great general came to the throne. Lucius Domitius Aurelian was the son of a poor Illyrian peasant and was called by his soldiers "Hand on the Hilt." He had always been a soldier, but he also had the qualities of a statesman. Realizing immediately that he could not take on all these enemies at once, he tried winning some of them over by diplomacy. He gave Dacia to the Goths, the most dangerous, to keep them quiet, and then attacked separately the Vandals and Alemanni, who had already invaded Italy and whom he routed in three successive battles. But he was fully aware that these victories merely delayed the ultimate catastrophe. This was why he took a measure which sealed the fate of Rome and marked the beginning of the Middle Ages. He ordered all the cities of the empire to surround themselves with walls and proclaimed that henceforth each was to rely on its own forces. The central power was abdicating.

Yet this realistic assessment of the future did not deter Aurelian from doing his duty to the utmost. Unwilling to acknowledge Zenobia's *de facto* independence he marched against her and defeated her. Having put her adviser and prime minister, Longinus, to death, he took her prisoner in her own capital and brought her to Rome in chains. She was confined in a splendid villa at Tivoli where she grew old in peace and was given a fair measure of freedom. For a moment Rome thought of herself as *caput mundi* again and gave the title of *restitutor* to Aurelian, who now tried to consolidate his work on a political and moral basis. This strange man, who saw everything with such disillusioned clarity, tried to put an end to the religious conflict which tormented the empire by creating a new faith which would reconcile the old deities with the new Christian God. He invented the "God of the Sun," for whom he had a magnificent temple built. Under him, for the first time, the official religion became monotheistic, in other words, it recognized only one god, even if it was the wrong one. In any case, it was a great step forward toward the final triumph of Christianity. Aurelian claimed to have been invested with the supreme power by this unique god and not by the mere mortals of the senate. He thus sanctioned the principle of absolute monarchy which proclaims itself such by divine right—a principle which was to survive and flourish for a great many centuries.

It did not save Aurelian, however, from the fate of so many of his less loftily appointed predecessors. Nor did the senate apparently take it into account when electing in his place Tacitus, a descendent of the illustrious historian, who only accepted because he was already seventy-five and had nothing to lose. In fact he only survived six months and was thus able to die in his bed. After him, in A.D. 276, came Probus, a man of probity by name and nature. Unfortunately for him he was also a dreamer. Having won several minor wars against the Germans, who continued their forays up and down the frontiers, he set his soldiers to reclaiming the land, thinking to settle them on it as peasants. Preferring to live by pillage, they killed him, but immediately repented and raised a monument to his memory.

And so the way was opened for Diocletian, the last real Roman emperor. The son of a Dalmatian freedman, he had grasped the truth that for the seeker after power neither a political nor a military career offered the same advantages as a strategic post in the palace, and it was from the command of the praetorian guard that he ascended the throne. He also grasped the truth that, once crowned, it was best to remove himself from the palace before he met the same violent end as his predecessors, indeed to remove himself from Rome altogether. Almost his first important decision, therefore, was to transfer the capital to Nicomedia in Asia Minor. The Romans were offended, but Diocletian was able to justify the step on the ground of military necessity: the city was no longer at the center of the empire, and the defender of the threatened fron-

tiers had to be near them. The supreme authority itself was
then divided. Diocletian, with the title of *Augustus* and the
bulk of the army, stood guard over the eastern frontiers, as
Valerian had done. To the equivalent duty on the western
frontiers, with headquarters in Milan, he nominated Maximianus, who also bore the title of *Augustus*. Each of the two
Augusti chose his own *Caesar*: Diocletian selected Galerius,
who set up his capital at Mitroviča in what is now Yugoslavia,
and Maximianus appointed Constantius Chlorus (so named
from the pallor of his face) to exercise control from Trier in
Germany. Thus the so-called tetrarchy was formed, in which
Rome had no part, not even a secondary one. She was merely
the largest city in an empire which was becoming less Roman
every day. All that remained were the theaters, the circuses,
the palaces of the great, the gossip, the intellectual salons, and
the presumption. The brain and heart had already migrated
elsewhere.

The two *Augusti* solemnly pledged themselves to abdicate
after twenty years in favor of their respective *Caesars* and, with
this in view, married them off to their own daughters. At the
same time, however, Diocletian completed the transformation
of the state, already begun by Aurelian, into an absolutism
which flatly contradicted the nominal decentralization of power.
It was a socialist experiment which included a planned economy, the nationalization of industry, and the multiplication of
the bureaucracy. Money was attached to a gold standard which
remained unchanged for over a thousand years. The peasants
were bound to the land and thus became "slaves to the soil."
Workmen and artisans were frozen in hereditary corporations,
which none of them could abandon. State supply depots were
set up. The system plainly could not work without strict price
controls, and these were established in 301 A.D. by means of a
famous edict which still remains one of the masterpieces of controlled economy. Everything was foreseen and regulated except
the natural human tendency towards evasion and ingenuity in
contriving it. As a countermeasure Diocletian had to increase
indefinitely the number of government inspectors. "In this empire of ours," grumbled the liberal Lactantius, "out of every
two citizens one is a civil servant." Informers, supervisors and
controllers swarmed everywhere. In spite of this, goods were
withheld from the state depots and sold on the black market.

Desertions from the corporations of arts and crafts became a daily occurrence. Arrests grew so numerous and punishments so heavy that fines drained the fortunes of millionaires down to nothing. Now, for the first time in the history of the city, Roman citizens were seen to cross the limits of the empire (the Iron Curtain of that time) to seek refuge among the "barbarians." Up to then it had been the barbarians who had sought refuge within the empire, regarding its citizenship as the most precious of treasures. It was the beginning of the end.

Nevertheless, constraint was the only remedy that Diocletian could try. His aim was to lace the Roman world in a steel corset to keep it from falling apart. Although ineffective, the policy was imposed by circumstances, and in spite of its many shortcomings, did do some good. Constantius and Galerius, the military chieftains, carried the Roman standards back to Britain and Persia. At home order reigned, even if it resembled the peace of the cemetery. Everything had become sterile and withered. Every trade had become a hereditary caste whose main interest lay in elaborating a complicated and oriental-sounding title for itself. For the first time the emperor had a real court with all the ceremonial trimmings. Diocletian proclaimed himself the reincarnation of Jove (Maximianus, more modestly, that of Hercules). He insisted on being addressed as *Dominus* and by and large behaved just like an emperor of Byzantium some years before the capital was transferred there. But he did not abuse his absolute powers, and being a level-headed man with a sense of humor, perhaps inwardly he laughed at them. He was also a shrewd administrator and an impartial judge and, when his twenty-year term of sovereignty expired, he kept the pledge he had made when he ascended the throne.

In 305 A.D., with a solemn ceremony held simultaneously at Nicomedia and Milan, the two *Augusti* abdicated, each in favor of his own *Caesar* and son-in-law. Diocletian, who was only fifty-five, retired to the beautiful palace he had built for himself at Split on the Dalmatian coast and never left it again. Some years later, when Maximianus asked him to intervene to put an end to the war of succession which had broken out as a result of the new tetrarchy, he replied that such an invitation could have been issued only by someone who had never seen how well the cabbages came up in his kitchen garden, and sent back a refusal.

Although he lived to the age of sixty-three, nobody has ever known his real opinion of the anarchy which set in immediately after his retirement. He had done everything humanly possible. He had delayed it for twenty years.

XLVI

Constantine

FLAVIUS VALERIUS CONSTANTINE WAS THE BASTARD SON OF CON-stantius Chlorus, the *Caesar* of Maximianus, who was now the new *Augustus* of Milan. His mother was Helena, an oriental servant who had been his father's concubine. When Diocletian had made Constantius *Caesar* at Trier, he had insisted on his getting rid of her and marrying Theodora, the daughter of Maximianus. Young Constantine had not had much of an education from his stepmother, but he had received excellent training in the army, which he had joined as a mere boy. Galerius, the *Augustus* of Nicomedia, sent for this brilliant young officer with the intention of holding him as a hostage in case of disagreement with Constantine's father, his colleague in Milan. Constantius was supposed to be his subordinate and, as *Caesar*, Galerius had imposed Severus on him. For himself he had chosen Maximinus Daia. Constantine, uneasy in Galerius' care, crossed the whole of Europe to join his father in Britain. During this campaign he was of valuable assistance to Constantius until the latter died some months later at York. The troops, with whom Constantine was highly popular because of his military prowess, acclaimed him *Augustus*, but Constantine preferred the more modest title of *Caesar*. "It leaves me in command of the legions," he said "without whom my life wouldn't be worth very much." Galerius, the reigning *Augustus*, reluctantly confirmed the appointment.

At Milan meanwhile, two pretenders were disputing the title of *Augustus*. The rightful claimant should have been Severus, who was already *Caesar*. Maxentius, however, the son

of Maximianus, with the support of the praetorian guard, put
forward his own candidature. Fearing that he might not attain
his ends by himself, he appealed to his father for help. Maximianus resumed the title he had abdicated simultaneously with
Diocletian, and father and son together marched against
Severus, who was killed by his soldiers. Galerius, from Nicomedia, tried to settle the dispute by nominating an *Augustus* of
his own, a certain Licinius. This was the cue for Constantine
also to proclaim himself *Augustus*. To add to the general confusion, Maximinus Daia, the *Caesar* of Galerius, did likewise.
Thus Diocletian, peacefully watering his cabbages at Split,
learned that his tetrarchy had become a hexarchy, composed
entirely of *Augusti*, all at war with one another.

The end of all this confusion also marked the end of the
pagan and the beginning of the Christian era. On the twenty-
seventh of October, A.D. 312 the two major contenders for the
throne, Constantine and Maxentius, faced each other with their
armies about twelve miles north of Rome. Constantine, by a
cunning maneuver, had trapped Maxentius with his back to the
Tiber. Constantine looked up at the sky and, as he later told the
historian Eusebius, saw a fiery cross appear with the following
words on it: *In hoc signo vinces,* "Under this sign you shall
conquer."

That night in his sleep a voice echoed in his ears exhorting
him to paint the cross of Christ on the shields of his legionaries.
At dawn he issued the necessary orders, and in place of the
standard, he raised a *labarum* bearing a cross entwined with the
initials of Jesus. The banner flying over the enemy army bore
the symbol of the sun, imposed by Aurelian as the new pagan
god. For the first time in the history of Rome a war was fought
in the name of religion. The cross won, and as the Tiber swept
the teeming corpses of Maxentius and his soldiers out to sea, it
seemed to be sweeping away the last remnants of the ancient
world.

Not everything was settled, for there were still Licinius and
Maximinus to be reckoned with. Constantine met Licinius in
Milan in A.D. 313, and the upshot of their interview was the
division of the empire between the two of them as *Augusti*, and
the compilation of that famous edict which proclaimed the
state's tolerance for all religions alike and restored to the Christians all the property confiscated from them during the recent

persecutions. Maximinus died, Licinius married the sister of Constantine, and for the moment it seemed that the two emperors were ready for a peaceful dyarchy.

One year later they were at war again. Constantine defeated an army of Licinius in Pannonia and the latter retaliated by resuming the persecutions of the oriental Christians. Constantine was not yet officially converted, but the Christians, who by now formed the overwhelming majority if not the totality of his army, regarded him as their champion. This army was 130,000 strong and he personally led it against the 160,000 defenders of paganism under the orders of Licinius. Twice Constantine won the day, first at Adrianople and then at Scutari. Licinius surrendered and for the moment his life was spared. The following year, however, he was strangled. In this manner, the empire was restored in the name of Christ. There was nothing Roman about it except its name.

Well, then, what had happened? When we last saw the Christians in Rome they were in the infancy of their organization. They were at first a few hundred, then a few thousand souls, almost all of them Jews, grouped into small *ecclesiae*, which had little connection with one another. Their doctrine was still in a state of flux. The Gentiles regarded them with indifference rather than hostility. Their scattered and scanty cells were united by the belief that Jesus was the Son of God, that his return to establish the kingdom of Heaven on earth was imminent and that faith in him would be rewarded by paradise. Now, however, wide differences of opinion over the date of his return were beginning to creep in. Some people saw its harbingers in the calamities which were befalling the empire. Tertullian said the second coming was to be expected after the fall of Rome and this seemed to be so imminent that a bishop of Syria, together with his flock, actually set out for the desert, sure of meeting the Lord there. Barnabas, on the other hand, proclaimed that it was not due for another thousand years. Only much later did St. Paul's theory, which transferred the kingdom of God to the life beyond the grave, prevail. Nevertheless, during this early period, enormous impetus was given to the spreading of the faith by the expectation of the imminent establishment of the "kingdom," with the immediate promises this implied.

However, there were other points of doctrine which threatened to give rise to definite heresies. Celsus, one of the most violent anti-Christians, wrote that the new religion was divided into sects and that each individual Christian interpreted it as he saw fit. Irenaeus gives a list of about twenty of these sects. To obtain a final ruling on what was true and what was false, a central authority was necessary.

The first decision to be taken, at the end of a controversy lasting two centuries, was where its capital was to be situated. The new religion had been born in Jerusalem, but in favor of Rome there were the words of Jesus: "Thou art Peter and upon this rock will I build my Church." The fact that the world was governed from Rome and not from Jerusalem carried more weight than mere argument. Tertullian declares that the dying Peter had entrusted the future of the Church to Linus, but the first certain successor is the third, Clement. A letter from him to the other bishops, couched in authoritative terms, still exists.

These bishops used to meet increasingly often in their synods, and these synods were the supreme arbiters of the Christian religion, called Catholic because it was universal. The title of pope became exclusive to the supreme pontiff only four centuries later. Up until then it was given to all bishops alike to emphasize their equality.

This was the first primitive organization which the Church used to fight its war on two fronts: the external one with the state and the internal one with heresy. We do not know which was the more dangerous. We only know that by the end of the second century the Church had begun to perturb the Romans so much that Celsus, one of the most cultivated of men, dedicated his whole life to the study of how it functioned and wrote an accurate and extremely well-informed book about it. He is, however, one-sided and vindictive in the conclusions he draws. These boil down to the assumption that a Christian could not be a good citizen. As long as the state was pagan, there was a certain amount of truth in what he said, but the fact remained that paganism no longer had any supporters. Even those who refused to embrace the new faith had no arguments in defense of the old. Like Marcus Aurelius and Epictetus, Plotinus can only be described as a pagan philosopher insofar as he was never baptized. But as in their case, all his morality is already Christian.

Even when they denied the doctrine of Jesus and the

Apostles, all the great minds of the time pondered deeply over it. Although Tertullian came from Carthage, he had the precise legal mind of the Roman and was a great lawyer. On his conversion he extracted from the Gospel a practical design for living, drawn up with the precision of the test of a law. This vigorous orator, who spoke like Cicero and wrote like Tacitus, was quarrelsome and sarcastic, but invaluable to the Church. After so much Greek theology and metaphysics it needed organizers and codifiers. In his frenzy of zeal Tertullian almost ended by becoming a heretic. In his old age he turned cantankerous and criticized orthodox Christians for being too lukewarm, indulgent, and soft. He embraced the sterner creed of Montanus, a sort of Luther born before his time, who preached the return to a more austere faith.

Another stalwart propagandist was Origen, the author of over 6,000 books and leaflets. When he was only seventeen, his father was condemned to death for being a Christian. The boy begged to be allowed to share his martyrdom, and to prevent this his mother hid his clothes. In his last letter to his father the boy wrote: "Do not, I beg you, renounce your faith for love of us." He led the life of an ascetic, fasting and sleeping naked on the floor, and in the end emasculated himself. As a matter of fact Origen was the classic type of Stoic, and had his own interpretation of Christianity which for a while was accepted, but not by everybody. Demetrius, bishop of Alexandria, considered it incompatible with his cloth, which Origen had meanwhile assumed, and revoked his ordination. With commendable zeal the unfrocked priest continued to preach and to confute the theories of Celsus in a work which has remained famous. When he was put in prison and tortured, he did not deny his faith and died as he had lived, poor and beyond reproach. Some 200 years later his theories were censured by the Church. But by then she had enough authority to do so.

The pope who did most to consolidate the organization of the Church in those first difficult years was Calixtus. Many considered him an adventurer, saying that he had been a slave before his conversion and that he had made money by somewhat dubious methods. They added that, becoming a banker, he had defrauded his clients, had been sentenced to hard labor, and had escaped by subterfuge. The fact that as soon as he became pope he decreed that true repentence was enough to wash away any sin, even a mortal one, may have given credibility to these rumors. Nevertheless he was a great pope and he eradicated the heresy of Hippolytus and definitely asserted the authority of the central power. Decius, an implacable enemy of the Christians, used to say that he would rather have a rival emperor than a pope like Calixtus in Rome. In many ways, under him the papacy really became Roman. From the pagan priests of the city he borrowed the stole, the use of incense, candles on the altar, and the architecture of the basilicas. Not all these acquisitions were of a formal nature. The founders of the Church looked with particular attention at the administrative framework of the empire. They copied it by putting an archbishop by the side of and in opposition to the governor of every province and a bishop by the side of and in opposition to every prefect. As the state began to drift and its political influence waned, the representatives of the Church assumed this influence. By the time Constantine came to the throne, many of the duties of the prefects (who had greatly declined in quality) were carried out by the bishops. It was obvious that the Church was the naturally appointed heir to the crumbling empire. The Jews had given the Church their ethics, and the Greeks their philosophy; Rome was now giving her her language, her practical and methodical spirit, her liturgy and hierarchy.

XLVII

The Triumph of the Christians

THANKS TO A SERIES OF BAD NOVELS AND EVEN WORSE FILMS, MANY people think that Nero is the chief villain when it comes to persecuting Christians. This is a mistake. True, Nero condemned a certain number of Christians to death for the fire of Rome, but with the sole object of turning people's suspicions from himself. It was a purely diversionary maneuver and not based on any serious resentment of the people or state against this religious community. In fact the Christian community was one of the most peaceful, and in common with all the others in Rome it

enjoyed a wide measure of tolerance. The city offered hospitality to the gods of all foreigners who came to live there and so
lived up to her name of *caput mundi*. Over 3,000 of these gods
lived there peacefully together. Even when a foreigner applied
for citizenship there were no religious conditions attached.

Discord first arose when it was laid down that the emperor
had to be recognized as a god and worshipped as such. For the
pagans this offered no difficulty at all. Their Olympus was so
full of gods that one more, whether he was called Caracalla or
Commodus, made no difference. On the other hand, the Jews
and the Christians (the police could never tell the difference
between them) worshipped only one God and were not prepared to compromise about it. As a result, even before Nero, a
law had been passed exempting them from this gesture which
was for them tantamount to abjuration. Nero and his successors had scant regard for the law and this gave rise to the first
misunderstanding, which led to other and deeper differences.
It was not by mere chance that Celsus, the first to make a serious study of the Christians, said that refusal to worship the
emperor was, substantially, a refusal to submit to the state, of
which, in Rome, religion was merely an instrument. He also discovered that the Christians placed Christ above Caesar and that
their moral code was in violent contrast to that of Rome, which
regarded the gods as the foremost servants of the state. Tertullian, in reply, agreed with him, saying that Christianity's superiority lay precisely in this and that his accusations were well-
founded. He went even farther. He declared that it was the duty
of a Christian to disobey a law which he found unjust.

As long as only philosophers were concerned in this debate,
it merely gave rise to wrangling, but when the Christians had increased in numbers and their conduct attracted the attention of
the people, the latter began to distrust them and this feeling
was cunningly played upon by propagandists. The same technique had since been widely used against the Jews. People
began to say that they practiced exorcisms and magic, that they
drank human blood, that they worshipped an ass, and had the
evil eye. A mob spirit was unleashed which soon created the
atmosphere of the pogrom and witch hunt.

After Nero's time aversion toward them developed into a
mounting tide of hate. The law which established the death penalty for professing the new faith was not due merely to the whim

of some emperor but was the result of an upsurge of collective animosity. As a matter of fact, most emperors tried to evade this law or to apply it with indulgence. Trajan wrote to Pliny praising his lenience: "I approve of your methods. An accused man who denies being a Christian and proves it by an act of submission to our gods should most certainly be acquitted." Hadrian, as a good skeptic, went one better. He granted pardon for a simple gesture of formal repentance. Nevertheless, it is difficult to stand up against a wave of popular hatred, especially when it breaks out on the occasion of some calamity, which was interpreted as the indignation of the gods for the tolerance shown toward the irreverent Christians. In Rome the pagan religion was dead, but superstition was still very much alive. The poor Christians were held to account for every earthquake, pestilence, or famine. Even the saintly Marcus Aurelius, whose reign abounded in catastrophes, could not resist these outbursts and was compelled to yield. Attalus, Potheinus, and Polycarp were among the most illustrious of these martyrs.

Persecution began to be systematic under Septimius Severus, who declared baptism a crime. By this time, however, the Christians were strong enough to react, and started a propaganda campaign which defined Rome as the "new Babylon," took a favorable view of its destruction, and proclaimed that military service was incompatible with the new faith. It was an open incitement to defeatism and aroused the ire of those patriots who were unwilling to fight for the fatherland, threatened by external enemies, but who were implacable toward their internal, unarmed adversaries. Decius thought that this wave of indignation could be exploited to reinforce national unity and pandered to it. He organized a great ceremony of homage to the gods and gave solemn warning that the names would be taken of all those who did not attend. Many apostasies were caused by fear, but there were many acts of heroism, rewarded by torture. Tertullian had said: "Do not weep for the martyrs. They are our seed." A terrible and merciless truth. Six years later, under Valerian, the pope himself, Sixtus II, was put to death.

The greatest battle was against Diocletian. It is curious that such a great emperor did not see the uselessness or, rather, what would be the contrary effect of his acts. It appears that a fit of temper was responsible. One day, when he was officiating as supreme pontiff, the Christians around him made the sign of the cross. Irritated, Diocletian ordered all his subjects, civilian and military, to repeat the sacrifice. Whoever refused was to be flogged. The refusals were numerous and the emperor gave orders that all Christian churches be razed to the ground, all their goods confiscated, their books burned, and their members killed.

These orders were still being carried out when he retired to Split. Here he had time to spare for meditating on the results of his persecution, which now seemed to him a confirmation of the Christian message and thus definitely sealed their triumph. The *Acts of the Martyrs,* which describes possibly with some exaggeration the tortures and deaths of the Christians who did not abjure their faith, was a formidable propaganda weapon. It spread the conviction that the Lord rendered insensible to sufferings all those who endured them in his name and flung open to them the gates of the kingdom of Heaven.

We cannot say whether or not Constantine was convinced of this when he had the cross of Christ stamped on his *labarum.* His mother was a Christian, but had not had much say in his education. This the boy had picked up among the soldiers in camp, where he had been surrounded by pagan philosophers and orators. Even after his conversion, he continued to bless the armies and harvests according to the pagan ritual. He rarely went to church, and to a friend who asked him the secret of his success, he replied: "It is Fortune that makes an emperor of a man." He was high-handed in his dealings with priests and gave them a free hand only in theological matters, not because he recognized their authority but because he had not the slightest interest in such questions. According to contemporary Christians like Eusebius, who had the best of motives for being grateful to him, he was little short of a saint. The more objective opinion is that he was a cool, calculating, far-sighted politician with a good deal of common sense. Having personally observed the failure of persecution, he preferred to abandon it.

It is also very probable that this appraisal of the situation was influenced by other and more complex factors. He must have been greatly impressed by the superior morality of the Christians, by the decency of their lives and by the revolution they had brought about in the habits of an empire now devoid of morals. By this time, if one wanted to find a good writer, a reliable lawyer, or an honest and efficient official, one had to look for him among the Christians. One could honestly say that there was no city in which the bishop was not a better man than the prefect. Could not, perhaps, these aged and corrupt bureaucrats be replaced by the irreproachable prelates and could not the latter be made the backbone of a new empire? Revolutions are not successful because of their ideas, but triumph if they manage to produce a ruling class better than that of their predecessors. This was just what Christianity had succeeded in doing.

Constantine began by giving the bishops the powers of judges in their own districts or dioceses. Then he exempted Church property from taxation and recognized the association of the faithful as "juridical bodies." He had his son baptized and gave him a priest as tutor. Finally he revoked the Edict of Milan, which guaranteed complete tolerance to all religions on an equal basis, and gave supremacy to Catholicism, which from that moment onward became the state religion. The decrees of the synod were now binding on all citizens.

Acting more as pope than as monarch, Constantine summoned the first ecumenical (universal) council of the Church to settle the internal dissensions which were rending it. Out of state funds he provided the means for 318 bishops and innumerable lesser prelates to travel to Nicea, near Nicomedia. There were serious problems to be solved. A number of ascetic extremists had seceded from the priesthood because, in their eyes, it was too inclined to compromise and was too attached to worldly goods. They had started a monastic movement.

Almost at the same time Donatus, the bishop of Carthage, had launched a proposal which immediately gained supporters: that priests who during the persecutions had abjured out of fear, and those who had been baptized by them should be dismissed. The proposal was rejected but gave rise to a schism which was to last for centuries. The greatest danger, however, was Arius, a preacher from Alexandria, who attacked the doctrine at its very foundations by denying the consubstantiality of Christ with God. His bishop had excommunicated him, but Arius continued to preach and win proselytes. Constantine had sent for the two litigants and tried to act as mediator between them so as to get them to come to a compromise. This attempt had failed and the rift had widened and deepened. This was the main reason why the council had become necessary.

As Pope Silvester I was too old and ill to attend, Athanasius brought the action against Arius, who replied with courage and honesty. He was a poor, sincere, melancholy man, who erred in good faith. Of the 318 bishops, only two supported him to the end and were excommunicated with him. Constantine was present at all the hearings, but only rarely intervened to exhort the contestants to calm and clear thinking when the argument grew heated. When the verdict confirmed the divinity of Christ, and condemned Arius, he drew up an edict which banished the heretic and his two supporters, ordered his books to be publicly burned and established the death penalty for anybody guilty of concealing them.

Constantine wound up the council by offering a great banquet to the participants and then set about organizing his new capital which with a solemn ceremony he dedicated to the Virgin. He called it "New Rome" but posterity, in his honor, named it Constantinople.

We do not know whether he realized that the transfer of the capital virtually meant the end of the Roman Empire and would give rise to a new one. This would, indeed, continue to call itself Roman, but Italy would be reduced to the status of a province with Rome as its capital.

Constantine was a strange and complex personality. Publicly he made a great display of Christian fervor but in family matters he did not show nearly as much subservience to the teachings of Jesus. True, he sent his mother Helena to Jerusalem to pull down the temple of Aphrodite, which profane Roman governors had built over the tomb of the Redeemer. (Eusebius says the cross on which Christ had died was found there.) Immediately afterward, however, he had his wife, son, and nephew put to death.

He had been married twice: first to Minervina, who had borne him Crispus, a brilliant officer who had covered himself with honors during the campaigns against Licinius, and then to Fausta, the daughter of Maximianus, who had given him three boys and three girls. It appears that Fausta, to get Crispus excluded from the succession, denounced him to the emperor for having tried to seduce her. Hereupon Helena, who had a weakness for Crispus, told Constantine that Fausta had been the one to seduce her stepson. To make quite sure of things, the emperor slaughtered them both. As for his nephew Licinianus,

the son of his sister Constantia and Licinius, Constantine is said
to have put him to death for conspiracy.

One does not read a word of all this in the *Life of Constantine,* written as a panegyric by Eusebius. Logically, he aimed at
extolling the virtues of the man who had raised a persecuted
sect up to be the church of the empire. Constantine was not the
saint his biographer makes him out to be. He may have been a
great general, a wise administrator, and a statesman of vision,
but he too made mistakes.

On Easter Day, A.D. 337, on the thirtieth anniversary of his
coming to the throne, he realized that his end was near. He
asked for a priest and received the sacraments. Then putting off
the imperial purple, he dressed in the white robe worn by those
about to be baptized and calmly awaited death.

XLVIII

Constantine's Heritage

CONSTANTINE WAS THE ONLY SUCCESSOR OF AUGUSTUS TO REMAIN
on the throne for over thirty years but he ruined his great work
of reconstruction by the most absurd of wills. It divided the
empire into five portions which were assigned to his three sons,
Constantine, Constantius and Constans, and his two nephews,
Delmatius and Hannibalian.

This is astonishing, since he must have seen the strife
caused by Diocletian's division and the evils it had provoked.
Even so, once he had made up his mind, he might at least have
taken the precaution of giving his three sons names by which
we might tell them apart a little better.

The garrison regiments of the capital somewhat simplified
the historians' task by weeding out some of the rivals. No sooner
was Constantine's corpse lowered into its grave than they rebelled and let go with a pretty fair massacre in which two of
the five heirs, Delmatius and Hannibalian, perished. They also
killed the half-brothers of the dead man and all their sons except
two. These were Gallus and Julian, who were banished and of

whom we shall hear more presently. An unspecified number of important officials suffered the same fate at the hands of the soldiery. Constantinople had hardly been built when the series of slaughters began which was to punctuate its history.

Did Constantius really give orders for this butchery, as he was later said to have done? It is hard to say. He is known to have been in the city when it took place; he did nothing to prevent it, and he was the one who stood to gain the most from it. He arranged a meeting with his two brothers at Smyrna and with them agreed on a second partition. For himself he kept all the orient, with Constantinople and Thrace; to Constans, the youngest, he gave Italy, Illyria, Africa, Macedonia, and Achaia, but submitted him to a kind of vassalage to Constantine II, whose share was all Gaul.

If Constantius had designed this clause for the purpose of stirring up rivalry between the two so as to remain arbiter of the situation himself, he succeeded only in part. Within three years they were at war. In the first battle Constantine II, who was of an impetuous temperament, incautiously advanced too far, fell into an ambush and was killed. Constans lost no time in annexing all his possessions. Constantius, who was perhaps hoping for a long war which would have exhausted both contenders, was left with only one rival, but now this rival was stronger than he was.

Once again fortune came to his aid in the form of a plot against Constans. Since he was a good general, Constans was winning battle after battle against the rebels in Gaul. As a statesman, however, he was inferior. He oppressed his subjects with taxes, irritated them by his obstinacy, and scandalized them by his habits. Magnentius, a commander of the barbarian militia, murdered him and proclaimed himself emperor. Vetranio, who commanded the troops in Illyria, and Nepotianus, the nephew of the dead man, promptly issued similar proclamations on their own behalf.

Constantius now had a legitimate excuse for intervening in the west to see that justice was done. At this moment he had just concluded an armistice with Sapor, king of Persia, who up till now had been making trouble and had been keeping his armies occupied. However, he was now free to lead them against the usurpers. He accompanied his military initiative with a cunning piece of diplomacy, an art in which he excelled. Vetranio, duped, met and joined forces with him on the plain of Serdica, where he knelt and begged his pardon. This was granted and Vetranio was given promotion and some decorations. The two armies then marched together against Magnentius, defeated him in Hungary, and pursued him into Spain. Here he was driven to commit suicide, together with his brother, Decentius, and the empire was thus reunited under a single ruler.

Unlike his father, Constantius was not a great general. He disliked wars and tried to avoid them. However, when he had to go to war he made a thorough, if cautious, business of it. He risked his life courageously, had a strict sense of duty and performed it regardless of sacrifice and expense. He was a solitary and suspicious man, gloomy and silent. He had no enthusiasm or human warmth, but was neither vicious nor self-indulgent. In many respects he resembled Philip II of Spain and Franz Josef of Austria. Like them, he was pious, but he did not add to his faith the two other theological virtues: hope and charity. He was in fact a pessimist, and incapable of indulgence. He believed that it was very often necessary to burn a body in order to save a soul. He had been married three times, not for love, but because he wanted an heir. None of his three wives had produced one and now he found himself without a successor. His two brothers had also been too busy to see to the matter and the only survivors of the once numerous progeny of Constantine were the two boys who had weathered the massacre of A.D. 337, Gallus and Julian.

They had been leading a dreary, lonesome existence for years in a small Cappadocian town under the tutelage of Eusebius, an Arian bishop, who seems also to have been somewhat deficient in charity. Their mother Basilina was already dead when Gallus, then ten, and Julian, six, witnessed the slaughter of their father, uncles, cousins, and household servants. Both of them learned that directly or indirectly Constantius had been responsible for the massacre, and here he was suddenly taking an interest in them.

Constantius chose Gallus, the elder, who in the course of one day found himself the husband of Constantina, sister to the emperor. He was immediately nominated *Caesar* and enthroned at Antioch with almost absolute powers. Being notoriously of limited mental capacity, he lost his head in this abrupt change in his circumstances. What he had seen as a boy had led him to

believe that murder and treachery were the normal course of
events and in self-defense he took the least suspicion for proven
fact and put all suspects to death. Before Constantius had time
to realize the mistake he had made, Gallus had not only murdered single individuals but entire populations. Fearing that if
he deposed Gallus, he might provoke him to open rebellion, the
emperor pretended to notice nothing; he kept on friendly terms
with him and invited him to Milan, where he happened to be
at the time. Somewhat worried, Gallus first sent Constantina to
discover Constantius' intentions, but she died on the journey.
Gallus then had to go in person, but when he got to Pannonia,
he was arrested by a detachment of soldiers and taken to the
same castle in Pola where Constantine had had his first-born,
Crispus, put to death. A summary trial was held which went
very smoothly, thanks to the well-remunerated evidence of a
court eunuch, and the death sentence was carried out on the
spot.

Constantius, once more without an heir, was getting old.
The day he decided to get rid of Gallus he had also sent Julian
back into confinement, suspecting that he might have been his
brother's accomplice. Still, he was the only one who still had
the blood of Constantine in his veins, and having no other
choice, Constantius after much hesitation sent for him and proclaimed him *Caesar*.

The result at once turned out to be excellent. Julian had the
reputation of being an idler who was only interested in literature and philosophy, but as soon as he was given any responsibility, he discharged it brilliantly. When the emperor handed
over to him the western provinces, then in open rebellion, he
had never seen a barracks. At first Julian let the generals handle
matters, but studied their moves very carefully. Then he took
effective command of the troops, confronted the hordes of
Franks and Alemanni, who had slipped across the Rhine, and
wiped them out. He then subdued the rebellion of the natives
and reestablished imperial authority over Britain. Never had the
title of *Caesar* been given more appropriately.

Unfortunately the Persian king, Sapor, chose this moment
to resume hostilities and, to fend off this threat, Constantius
asked Julian to send him part of his army. Julian, who had taken
a liking to soldiering, obeyed, but with reluctance. We do not
know how much of an effort he made to conceal his ill humor at

being parted from his troops. The fact remains that they were
sure of interpreting his wishes correctly when they refused to
obey and even acclaimed him emperor. Julian hastily wrote to
Constantius disclaiming all responsibility for this disobedience.
When Constantius replied that he would pardon him if he
would renounce the title and make an act of submission to him,
instead of agreeing Julian marched against him at the head of
his army.

The war never took place because Constantius, who had
already marched forth, died on the way. When his will was
opened, everybody was completely dumbfounded to find that he
had nominated as his sole heir the man he had set out to defeat
and whom, had he succeeded, he would probably have killed. As
usual, reasons of state had outweighed sentiment. Realizing that
the ingrate was a great politician, he had made him his successor. Julian returned the compliment by giving him a solemn
funeral, going into mourning and shedding tears over his coffin.

Rivers of ink have flowed on the subject of Julian, as if
those he himself poured out were not more than sufficient. He
could not stop writing and had a mania for proclamations,
panegyrics, and semi-political, semi-philosophical essays. Possibly the importance of this emperor, who only ruled twenty
months, has been overrated.

The reason that such a fuss had always been made about
him is that the intention of replacing Christianity with paganism
has been attributed to him. Already Constantius had had to devote the greater part of his time to religious questions. Apart
from being emperor, he had in fact acted as pope, intervening in
the internal quarrels of the Church between Donatists, Arians,
and Meletians. He was a Christian and a fervent one too. Yet,
more like a pagan than a Christian, he considered the Church an
instrument of the state, and under the excuse of protecting it,
meant to keep it under his control.

The same interest in religion was manifested by Julian, but
his point of view was diametrically opposed to that of Constantius and earned him the title of "Apostate." There is no doubt
that Bishop Eusebius was largely to blame for Julian's dislike
of the new faith. As his tutor, he had not spared the cane during
lessons on the catechism. The only human affection he had felt
during his confinement in Nicomedia was for Mardonius, an old
Scythian servant, who used to read him Homer and the Greek

philosophers. We do not know whether Mardonius was pagan
or Christian. We only know for certain that he was steeped in
the classics and that he transmitted his love of them to his master and pupil. Looking around him, Julian did not find the Christians he saw exemplary. He was doubtless not a profound
thinker. A glance at his writings is enough to convince one of
this. At times his reasoning is quite incoherent. He had an excellent memory, but understood nothing of art, although he
delighted in high-flown quotations. He used to get worked up
about the details of minor philosophical problems and lose sight
of the major ones. It was inevitable that he would confuse the
Church with its second-rate pastors and take an equal dislike to
both. But the project attributed to him, which he may really
have cherished, of a return to paganism, does not redound to
his intelligence as a politician. Any "return" in politics is likely
to prove a mistake.

The famous "apostasy" of Julian was mainly a question of
agnosticism. He took no interest in the heresies which continued
to rend the Church and it is probable that he welcomed them.
He granted freedom of worship to the Jews and permitted them
to rebuild the temple of Solomon. When its framework was
destroyed by an earthquake, Christian writers naturally claimed
that it was the punishment of Heaven. It has been said that he
actually encouraged the celebration of the ancient pagan rites,
but this has never been proved. In any case, he could not have
got much satisfaction out of it because either people did not
cooperate or did so half-heartedly and without enthusiasm. At
Alexandria, Bishop Georgius was killed by the pagans and at
Antioch the temple of Apollo was burned down by the Christians. In neither case did Julian take disciplinary action. He
wanted to be impartial.

It is impossible to say where this reactionary religious policy would have carried him if Sapor had not compelled him to
take up arms again. He prepared for the difficult and dangerous
expedition with his usual care, mustering a huge army and fitting out a fleet of 1,000 ships to sail down the Tigris. The first
encounters went well for him but the city of Ctesiphon, with its
formidable fortifications, held out, and he was eventually forced
to retire. As the ships were unable to sail upstream, Julian gave
orders for them to be burnt. Although it was the only course
open to him, this decision demoralized and angered the soldiers.

The countryside was poor, stony, sun-scorched, and hostile. The Persion cavalry harassed their march and inflicted heavy casualties with their darts. One of these wounded Julian in the liver. The emperor, trying to pluck it out with his hands, enlarged the wound and started a fatal hemorrhage. Realizing that his last hours had come, he called two philosopher friends, Maximus and Priscus, to his bedside and calmly discussed with them the immortality of the soul. They say that at a certain point he put his hand in the wound and, flicking a few drops of blood into the air, angrily exclaimed: "Thou has conquered, O Galilean!" However, it is probably not true.

XLIX

Ambrose and Theodosius

JULIAN'S SUCCESSOR WAS CHOSEN BY THE ARMY FROM AMONG ITS own officers as it continued to retreat. This was natural considering the gravity of the emergency. The man elected was a certain Jovian who was destined to accomplish one action only as emperor. It was a stupid and cowardly one. He concluded a hasty peace which gave Armenia and Mesopotamia to the Persians as fruits of a victory they had not won. Thereupon Jovian fell ill and died before reaching the capital.

Again the army halted to elect a new emperor and this time their choice fell on Valentinian, an excellent general, who was the son of a Pannonian ropemaker. It is said that Julian had previously debarred him because he would not renounce Christianity. Overwhelmed by the load of responsibilities which his accession heaped on his shoulders, he divided them equally with his brother. To Valens he left Constantinople and the eastern provinces, keeping for himself the western ones of which Milan was now the capital. This was in A.D. 364.

Both brothers were immediately faced by two major problems. Valens had to deal with the revolt of Procopius who, as Julian's only relative, put himself at the head of the troops in Cappadocia and had himself proclaimed emperor. Procopius was defeated, taken prisoner, and beheaded. Valentinian had to cope with the Alemanni. They had been afraid of Julian because he had beaten them soundly, but on the news of his death they began invading Gaul again. The emperor encircled them on the Rhine and wiped them out. He then sent his best general, Theodosius, to Britain where he reestablished order by trouncing the Saxons and Scots. This worthy soldier, however, was ill-rewarded for the services he had rendered. On being sent to Africa to put down disorders, he fell victim to the intrigues of certain corrupt and libelous officials. He was accused of treason, condemned to death, and beheaded.

Valentinian, who had been duped, certainly made this mistake in good faith. His mind was not exactly brilliant but he had common sense and a resolute and straightforward character. Unfortunately he was subject to fits of anger, during which he made the two biggest mistakes of his life. Signing Theodosius' death warrant was the first, and the other resulted in his own demise. One day when he flew into a violent rage with the rebellious Quadi he dropped dead from a stroke.

It was now November of A.D. 375, and this time the question of the succession was already settled. Eight years before, Valentinian had appointed as his colleague his son Gratian, whom he had married at the age of fifteen to Constantia, the posthumous daughter of Constantius, whose widow had later married Procopius. Although she was widowed a second time, she had had another child, Valentinian II. To put it more clearly, Valentinian had, apart from his brother Valens, to whom he had given the eastern part of the empire, a son named Gratian. This boy had married Constantia, the daughter of the emperor Constantius. Her mother, Justina, on becoming a widow, had married the usurper Procopius by whom she had a son, Valentinian. This second Valentinian was therefore half-brother to Constantia.

Now Justina was a highly ambitious woman. She had schemed and intrigued so much that she had managed to get Valentinian to appoint as his colleague not only Gratian but also Valentinian II. At the time he was only four years old. Thus, on the death of the emperor, Valens remained at Constantinople while young Gratian ascended the throne of Milan. Gratian was regent for Valentinian II until such time as he was old enough to share in the government.

It was an awkward moment because just then hordes of Huns, the most terrible barbarians of all, were sweeping down from Russia. They had already run up against the Goths, who formed a federation under their king, Hermanric, on the eastern confines of the empire. In terror Hermanric asked Valens to annex them, promising in return to act as his outposts. After much hesitation, Valens accepted, but soon thought better of it when he saw these new subjects, some 200,-300,000 strong, indulging in their customary pillage and brigandage. He had been on the point of renewing the war against the Persians but had to postpone his plans and hasten to Adrianople, which had been occupied by the troublesome Goths. Instead of waiting for his nephew Gratian, who was due to arrive from the north, Valens attacked on his own and lost all his army. He himself was wounded and was burned alive in a hut to which his attendants had taken him.

Gratian did not dare attack alone. Although he was only twenty he had already proved to be a good general. He now showed good sense. He retired cautiously and stationed his forces in defense of Illyria and Italy. Realizing that he could not share the responsibilities of the empire with his infant half-brother-in-law, Valentinian II, he decided to appoint a colleague for the east. He very wisely chose the general Theodosius, son of the one whom Valentinian had unjustly executed in Africa, and entrusted the eastern empire to him.

In the meanwhile another very important personage had appeared on the scene. This was Ambrose, the bishop of Milan, now venerated as a saint by the Italians and the Lombards in particular. Originally he had not been a priest nor had he been educated in a seminary. He was a first-class civil servant and until A.D. 374 had been governor of Liguria and Aemilia. In this capacity he had had to arbitrate in the controversies which had raged between Arians and Catholics in those dioceses. He had done so well that on the death of Bishop Ausentius, an Arian, he was appointed as his successor. At the time he had not even been baptized and the choice appeared highly irregular. Nevertheless Valentinian I, who had a high opinion of him, confirmed it. In the course of a few days Ambrose received the sacraments, Holy Orders, and his miter.

A man of immense ability, had he been born in America he would have become a Ford or a Rockefeller. Gratian, after his father's death, gave him his complete confidence, and in turn Ambrose gave invaluable assistance to his sovereign in carrying on the struggle against paganism and the Arian heresy. This heresy, after the death of Valens who had been ensnared by it, no longer commanded many supporters. Theodosius, who may have owed his appointment largely to Ambrose, was a zealous executor of orders in religious matters. Paganism was more or less exterminated. Within and without the Christian faith Catholicism had triumphed.

Unfortunately, on the strictly political side, things did not go so well. Magnus Maximus, the governor of Britain, contemptuously critical of Gratian as a kind of priest-worshipper and "semi-Christian," rebelled against him. The insurrection had supporters even at the young emperor's court, which at the moment happened to be in Paris. Gratian was stabbed while trying to escape. Maximus hypocritically deplored the incident in a letter to Theodosius, in which he also proposed leaving Italy to Valentinian II under the regency of his mother and Ambrose, and ruling over the western provinces himself.

Theodosius was an honest man but slow in coming to a decision; his enemies said that he could never make up his mind. The death of Gratian, the friend and colleague to whom he owed so much, had angered him. However, under the circumstances in which the empire now found itself, with the Goths giving trouble and the Huns and Persians at the gates, he rejected the idea of a war. Instead he sent a vague and dilatory reply which Maximus took to be favorable. Forgetting the accusations of servility he had made against Gratian, Maximus, to curry favor with Ambrose, displayed great zeal in the struggle against the heretics. Nevertheless, in spite of his pledge to Valentinian II, he coveted Italy. With the excuse of reinforcing the frontier garrisons he managed to send there various military units which were loyal to him. Things would certainly have ended up in another regicide if Justina, in alarm, had not hastened to Theodosius, taking her son with her as well as her daughter Galla, who was already a famous beauty.

Theodosius fell in love with Galla at first sight and was persuaded to punish the usurper, a thing which political calculation had failed to accomplish. The battle was fought in Pannonia and the defeated Maximus was beheaded. Theodosius married Galla and escorted his mother-in-law and young brother-in-law back to Milan. He spent some time with them there, thus setting a sort of precedent for the tutelage of the western empire by that of the east.

In the meantime Ambrose had continued to wage war on heresy. The Arians, who had been put out of action by Theodosius in Constantinople, were protected by Justina in Italy and she had educated Valentinian in accordance with their teachings. She now demanded that at least one church should be granted to them. Ambrose refused and Valentinian sentenced him to banishment. Ambrose did not budge; sanctity proved compatible with obstinacy. Immediately after this, other sensational events took place. The Christians of Callinicus burned down a synagogue. Theodosius, who was still in Milan, ordered it to be rebuilt at the expense of the guilty parties. Ambrose went to demand the annulment of the order, and as he was not received, he resorted to the pen. "I am writing to you so that you may hear me in your palace. Otherwise, I will make you listen to me in my church. . . ."

What had happened to the world that a priest could take the liberty of passing judgment on the supreme head of a state of which, until quite recently, he himself had been no more than an official? Had Theodosius been Valentinian I, he too might have expired of rage. As it was he yielded in silence. Soon afterward he had to take action against the Thessalonians for massacring some guards who had been guilty of arresting a charioteer idolized by the public. True, his treatment was somewhat harsh but this time it was not a question of religion. Nevertheless, even on this occasion, Ambrose denounced the emperor from the pulpit, refused to receive him, and forbade him to enter a church until he had done solemn and humble penance. It was the triumph of spiritual over temporal power, and a special hymn was composed to celebrate it: the *Te Deum laudamus*.

Paganism made one more effort with Arbogast, a Frankish chieftain, who had remained faithful to it and who had rendered signal services to the empire under Gratian. He was now commander of Valentinian's guards but he despised this youth who knelt before Ambrose and kissed his ring. One day the young emperor was found dead in his bed. Arbogast said that he had committed suicide but did not try to take his place. He realized that the Roman Empire, decadent though it was, had not yet reached the point of accepting a barbarian like himself on the throne. Instead he installed Flavius Eugenius, head of the civil service, keeping the command of the army for himself.

Theodosius did not immediately react but waited two years before meting out punishment. During this period Arbogast forced Eugenius to pursue a policy of tolerance and coexistence between the two religions, but in the end he had to conclude that paganism could not be resurrected even by force.

In A.D. 394 the emperor and the usurper went to war. Flavius and Arbogast, who waited for the enemy in Italy, dotted the passes of the eastern Alps with statues of Jove who, armed with golden thunderbolts, thus made his final appearance among men. Theodosius, before setting out, had gone to the desert of Thebais to visit an anchorite who prophesied his victory. Each of the two armies had, so to speak, mobilized its own god. In fact the battle was decided by a sort of meteorological miracle: an extremely violent north wind blew into the faces of the Flavians, almost blinding them. Jove, Arbogast, and Eugenius were all swept away in the ensuing debacle. Though nominally the battle was won by the Roman Emperor Theodosius in the name of Jesus, the real authors of the victory were pagan Goths under the command of Alaric.

The victorious Theodosius entered Milan and died there of dropsy. This Roman emperor was not yet fifty and had never been to Rome, which by now was isolated from major politics. He had been a good sovereign but not a great one; loyal and honest, even though vacillating and timid.

He left two sons: Arcadius aged eighteen, and Honorius aged eleven.

L

The End

THE WESTERN EMPIRE, WHICH FELL TO THE LOT OF YOUNG HON-orius, had already been regarded by Theodosius as a satellite of the eastern empire. A bishop had placed it under the spiritual tutelage of the Church, and for self-preservation it had had to accept pagan barbarian peoples within its own boundaries, peoples who were completely ignorant of the concept of the state and the rights of citizens. Furthermore, it was crumbling internally. No longer garrisoned by the army, which foreign wars drew away to the frontiers, the small towns of the provinces relied increasingly for their defense on minor lordlings who kept their own private armies. These were called *potentes*, and as the central authority became progressively weaker, their independence increased. From Diocletian onward, this trend was facilitated by legislation which divided society into rigid categories. The peasant had become a mere serf, irrevocably bound to the land and his master. Similarly the artisan was bound to his trade. By now everyone was born to an unalterable destiny. Anyone who abandoned farm or workshop was doomed to starvation, because even if he avoided arrest by the police when the hue and cry had been raised, he could not find another job. Even the rich, if they transferred or lost their riches, had to continue paying taxes. Otherwise they ended up in prison.

These laws, grotesque as they may seem, were imposed by circumstances. Crumbling skeletons have to be put in plaster. The plaster does not prevent their decomposition but it retards it. The new dispensation, however, meant the end of Rome, of her civilization, of her juridical order which had made every man the master of his own fate and all men equal in the eyes of the law. It was the end of that Rome whose citizens had been not just subjects, but the principal actors. The Middle Ages had begun. The lordling supplants the state, which he opposes with increasing success, until he splits it up into myriad feudal domains, each headed by its own heavily-armed *seigneur*. Under his rod of iron lives an amorphous mass of defenseless dependents, left to their own devices and deprived of all their rights, even those of changing their jobs or homes.

The eleven-year-old Honorius, heir to this tottering edifice, was upheld by the general Stilicho, a Vandal, a barbarian of German stock, whose appointment shows the level to which the Romans were reduced. Of all the officers in the army only he possessed the necessary loyalty, courage, and shrewdness. And before Theodosius was even cold in his grave, the fight which began between Milan and Constantinople enabled him to give proof of these qualities. Although the late emperor had divided the empire into two, he had omitted to state which provinces were to belong to which half. Arcadius, who had inherited the throne of the east and whose equivalent of Stilicho was a certain Rufinus, regarded Dacia and Macedonia as his own perquisites. A dispute broke out between the two capitals. Alaric who, in spite of promises, had never been rewarded for the help he had given to Theodosius during the war against Arbogast, marched on Constantinople. He would certainly have laid waste to it had not Rufinus persuaded him that Greece was much more worth conquering. The empire, incapable of self-defense, saved its capital at the expense of the provinces.

The only man to be indignant was the barbarian Stilicho. At the request of Arcadius he sent a detachment of troops to Constantinople, but gave orders for their commander, another barbarian named Gaina, to kill Rufinus. These orders were duly carried out and the court chamberlain, Eutropius, an enemy of the dead man, was appointed in his place. It was thus possible for the two imperial brothers Honorius and Arcadius to come to an agreement. Stilicho at once took advantage of this situation to settle with the Goths, who were ravaging the Peloponnese. He had already bottled them up in the Isthmus of Corinth when Constantinople, jealous of a western success, made an alliance with them and ordered the general to withdraw. Stilicho was furious but obeyed. One reason was that just at this moment Africa, with the secret connivance of Arcadius and Eutropius, had revolted, and fresh waves of barbarians were pouring into the Balkans. Furthermore Alaric, the ally of Constantinople, having marched through Albania and Dalmatia, had debouched into the Po Valley itself. The unfortunate Vandal general, the only one who still believed in the empire and served it faithfully, was forced to spend his days in the saddle, galloping from place to place to stop the gaps which were continually opening. He returned to Italy and defeated Alaric but did not destroy his forces. His idea was to make an alliance with him to beat off other more overwhelming enemies. Unable to rely on Milan which was without natural defenses and at anybody's mercy, he transferred the capital to Ravenna, an unimportant town surrounded by malarial marshes which made its siege impossible. This was in A.D. 403.

The transfer was effected just in time to avoid invasion by another race of Goths. These were called Ostrogoths to distinguish them from Alaric's Visigoths. They crossed the Alps and swept down the peninsula, overrunning it as far south as Tuscany. It was the first time since the days of Hannibal that Italy had had to swallow such an affront. Stilicho took a year to muster his troops and only in A.D. 406 did he raise enough of them to surprise and exterminate the Ostrogoths at Faesulae. Simultaneously Vandals, Alani, and Suevi broke through the Roman defenses at Mainz and entered Gaul. A usurper called Constantine also crossed to Gaul from Britain and put the barbarians to flight, but instead of retreating to where they had come from they overran Spain. All the fairest provinces of the west were virtually lost and Italy was isolated.

In this chaos, which was enough to make anybody lose his head, the only man to keep his clear was Stilicho. While negotiating the help of Alaric, he attempted to mobilize the Italians. The latter not only refused to help but accused him of capitulation before the barbarians. Seeing that they refused to supply him with soldiers, he had nothing with which to defend Rome. Honorius, alarmed and quite oblivious of the signal services his faithful captain had rendered him these last ten years, gave orders for his arrest. Stilicho could easily have rebelled since the few troops the empire possessed were loyal to him alone, but he had too much respect for authority to do so. He was murdered in a church in Ravenna. This was perhaps the most stupid, ignoble, and catastrophic crime ever committed in the name of Rome. It not only deprived the empire of its most able servant but made abundantly clear to such of the barbarians as were still faithful to it the depths to which it had sunk. These barbarians were the elite of the army and the civil service and it was they who kept the standards aloft. They believed in the prestige of Rome, and Rome, by the murder of Stilicho, destroyed this prestige with her own hands.

From now on everything went from bad to worse. Instead of coming to Italy as an ally, Alaric came as a conqueror. He offered terms to Honorius, who rejected them with a haughtiness which might have seemed noble had it been accompanied by some act of courage. As things were, it merely seemed ridiculous bravado, coming from a man safely tucked away in his stronghold at Ravenna. Defended by little more than his army of mosquitoes, he abandoned the rest of Italy to the enemy. Alaric marched straight on Rome and laid siege to it. The world held its breath. What next? How dared anyone besiege Rome?

When the city surrendered without striking a blow, Alaric himself seems to have been awe-stricken. He forbade his soldiers to enter and went in alone and unarmed to ask the senate to depose Honorius. The senate, by now only a figurehead, immediately agreed. The following year, however, Alaric returned, and since Honorius had not left the throne, he quartered his whole army on the city. Nevertheless he prevented, or tried to prevent, his troops from pillaging. Amazed and frightened at their own audacity, the barbarians explored the city. In the German forests whence their ancestors had come, Rome had always been looked upon as a fabulous and unattainable mirage. Far from despoiling, they were despoiled by a people who had forgotten how to fight but had learned to steal. Even the victorious Alaric became a prisoner once he had set eyes on Galla Placidia, the beautiful daughter of Theodosius, and sister to Honorius and Arcadius. From that moment the king obeyed by all the Goths was at the beck and call of a queen. He took her with him on his last venture, an expedition to Africa, treating her with all the deference due to her rank. While preparations were being made on the Calabrian coast, he died at Cosentia. His soldiers had a huge magnificent underground tomb built for him. Then, lest anyone should learn the secret and violate it, they massacred all the slaves who had been employed in its construction. His wife's brother, Atawulf, was proclaimed his successor. He was an extremely handsome young man, who for some time had been Galla Placidia's lover.

The violation of Rome in A.D. 410 and the preference of a princess of the blood royal for the unadorned tent of a barbarian chieftain rather than the sophisticated imperial court plunged the whole world into dismay. The pagans attributed it to the vengeance of the gods for the treachery of mankind. The Christians, who had struggled with Rome for four centuries, suddenly felt bereaved by her fall, and saw in it the sign for the coming of the Antichrist. "The source of our tears has dried up," mourned Saint Jerome.

Only Honorius did not seem to care. Hidden away in the marshes of Ravenna, he refused his consent to the marriage of Galla and Atawulf. Heedless of the chaos into which Italy was rapidly falling, he continued to vegetate until A.D. 423, when he died in the flower of his misspent youth. Some time before, Atawulf too had been killed, stabbed to death by a barbarian, and Galla had become a widow again. Honorius forced her to marry Constantius, an elderly general, and having no heir of his own, designated Valentinian III, the son born of this marriage, as his successor.

In Constantinople Arcadius was also dead and had left a small boy, Theodosius II, on the throne. At this juncture it is tragi-comical to see the two halves of the empire, both of them under the threat of the same disaster, indulging in futile quarrels over their boundaries. With the whole empire already in the hands of the barbarians, the two Roman emperors, first cousins, were disputing a theoretical sovereignty over provinces already out of their hands. In Africa alone, Rome gave one final sign of pride and courage. Here Boniface, a general who had already been condemned for high treason, and Bishop Augustine were being besieged by Genseric's Vandals at Hippo. It was at the height of the battle, in which he later died, that the prelate Augustine finished his crowning work: *The City of God.*

The increasing ascendancy of the Germanic over the Roman element is symbolized and summed up by the vicissitudes of the imperial family. Valentinian III was on the throne of Ravenna but the power behind it was Galla Placidia. She had chosen as her right-hand man Aetius, another barbarian and a worthy successor to Stilicho. Having already shown that she had no faith in the Romans as husbands, one can well imagine how little she had in them as generals and statesmen. When Attila appeared on the horizon with his terrible Huns, she made her daughter Honoria do what she herself had done with Atawulf—offer herself to him as a wife. Captive of the barbarians that Rome now was, there remained but one field on which she could still do battle successfully: the bed.

But Attila was not Alaric. Instead of losing his head over Honoria, he demanded the most exorbitant of dowries: all Gaul. This was the finest province of the empire and, although the imperial sovereignty over it was purely theoretical, the court of Ravenna could not give it up. Attila overran it nevertheless, and Aetius was compelled to take up arms against him. To raise the necessary army he had to perform a miracle of diplomacy; he managed to enlist the aid of Theodoric, king of the Visigoths. The titanic battle was fought on the plain of Catalaunicum near

Troyes. The Romans won, but they were Roman in name only. It was merely a defeat of barbarians by barbarians. Even the commander in chief of the victors was a Romanized barbarian. He remained master of the field but did not pursue the enemy, who retired in good order. Was he not strong enough or did he hope to make allies of them as Stilicho had been able to do with the Goths?

In A.D. 452 Attila reappeared. This time, instead of attacking Gaul, he marched on Italy. Valentinian who, on the death of his mother, had taken over the reins of government, did not wish to repeat Honorius' undignified mistake of leaving Rome to its fate. Against the advice of Aetius, who counseled him to escape to the orient (partly in order to get rid of him), he moved to Rome to share its destiny. Here he came to an agreement with Pope Leo I to send a delegation of senators to Attila, by now encamped on the Mincius.

Legend tells us that Attila was intimidated by the threat of excommunication if he dared attack Rome. As he was a pagan it is hard to see what possible effect this could have had on him. The fact remains, however, that, instead of crossing the Apennines, he recrossed the Alps. The following year he died. Of the vast ephemeral empire that he had founded, stretching from Russia to the Po, nothing remained. Not even his people. They were dispersed and rapidly absorbed by the Slav and Germanic populations among whom they had set up their camps as overlords.

For Italy and Europe the end of this dangerous enemy was a great relief. For Aetius, who had remained barricaded in Ravenna and had not collaborated, it was a bitter blow. Valentinian, who had always resented this arrogant servant, took the opportunity of getting rid of him (just as Honorius had gotten rid of Stilicho). One day, during an argument, he ran him through with his sword. It was another fatal mistake. Immediately all the barbarians encamped throughout the provinces arose, and though they had accepted a theoretical vassalage, one of them killed Valentinian himself on the Field of Mars. This was the signal for Genseric, king of the Vandals. The master of Africa now arrived with his army, proclaiming himself the emperor's avenger. What he really wanted was to put his son, Hunneric, in the dead man's place by marrying him to Eudocia, Valentinian's daughter. The wedding actually took place, but while the soldiery were celebrating it by systematically sacking the city (thus giving the word vandal the meaning we all know), in Gaul Theodoric II named a new emperor, a protégé of his named Avitus.

Genseric hastened back to Africa taking with him the spoils of war: a daughter-in-law, her mother (the widow of Valentinian), the latter's other daughter, Placidia, and some thousands of highly-placed Romans, including a few dozen senators. This meant that he now regarded Rome as his own private domain. On arrival home he fitted out a fleet and occupied Sicily, Corsica and southern Italy.

Avitus also had a great general in his service, a barbarian, of course. This was Ricimer, a man of the same caliber as Stilicho and Aetius. Ricimer defeated the enemy in a great naval battle and then deposed Avitus. Avitus took comfort in the faith and had himself consecrated bishop of Placentia. Only four years later, in A.D. 457, did he designate Majorian as his successor.

Avitus only did this in an attempt to discipline the Vandals, the Visigoths, and all the other barbarians who had been taking advantage of the fact that there was no emperor to proclaim themselves formally independent. It did little good. The barbarians continued to do just what they liked. Majorian attempted an expedition against Genseric, who destroyed his fleet by treachery. Ricimer, furious that Majorian wanted to rule in earnest, had him killed, and replaced him with Libius Severus, a more malleable character. Genseric, however, had other views. Having given up the idea of putting his son, Hunneric, the husband of Eudocia, on the throne, he was now supporting the senator Anicius Olybrius who had married Placidia, the sister of Genseric's daughter-in-law. He now began a new war against Rome or, rather, he intensified the one he had been waging against her for years.

To defend himself Ricimer resorted to Constantinople. Severus had died and so, to gain the support of the capital of the east, he offered the throne to her nominee. This was Procopius Anthemius, who came to Italy and was crowned in A.D. 467. Anthemius now fitted out a fleet of 1,000 ships and launched them against the Tunisian coast with 100,000 men under the command of the general Basiliscus. On landing, all Basiliscus did was to offer a five-day truce to Genseric, who profited by it to attack and set fire to his ships. The general has been accused of treachery. Actually the treachery had been on the part of the court of Constantinople which had made a secret alliance with the king of the Vandals. Genseric then went over to the offensive and sacked Rome for the third time. Ricimer accepted Olybrius as emperor but they both died in that same year (A.D. 472).

The Vandals now tried to put Glycerius on the throne but Constantinople refused to recognize him and appointed Julius Nepos in his stead. In order to keep him out of the clutches of Genseric, they bought a disastrous peace from the latter, recognizing his suzerainty not only over all Africa, but also over Sicily, Sardinia, Corsica, and the Balearic Islands. The following year Euricus, king of the Visigoths, obtained Spain in return for his neutrality. Burgundians, Alemanni, and Rugii divided up the rest of Gaul and the western empire was reduced to Italy alone. Nepos ordered the general Orestes to disband the army which he could no longer afford to keep. The barbarians who composed it mutinied. Orestes took command and Nepos fled to join Glycerius in Dalmatia, the same Glycerius he himself had banished after usurping his throne.

Orestes proclaimed his own son, Romulus Augustus, as emperor. By the irony of fate this boy, who was destined to be the last emperor of Rome, had the same name as the first. The triumphant barbarian soldiers now claimed lands in the heart of the peninsula itself. Some wanted the Po Valley, others Aemilia, others Tuscany. Odoacer, one of their officers, headed a rebellion and attacked, defeated, and killed Orestes at Ticinum (Pavia). Romulus Augustus, whom historians have called *Augustulus* or "the little Augustus," to distinguish him from "the Great," was deposed and confined in the Castel dell'Uovo at Naples with a princely allowance. Odoacer then sent the insignia of empire to the eastern emperor, Zeno, saying that from now on he intended to govern Italy as his second-in-command.

This time it really was the end. Even the name had gone. The eagles had flown and the Middle Ages were beginning.

L I

Conclusion

THIS, TOO, IS THE END OF OUR STORY. ROME, LIKE ALL GREAT EM-
pires, was not overthrown by external enemies but undermined
by internal decay. The actual moment of its fall does not date
from the deposition of Romulus Augustulus, but from the adoption of Christianity as the official state religion and the transfer
of the capital to Constantinople. This double event opened a
new chapter for Rome.

Most historians maintain that the catastrophe had two
prime causes: Christianity and the pressure of the barbarians
from north and east. We do not believe this. Christianity destroyed nothing. It merely buried a corpse, the corpse of a religion in which nobody any longer believed. It then filled the
gap so created. A religion is not important just because it builds
temples and performs certain rites, but because of the code of
moral conduct to which it gives rise. Formerly paganism had
supplied this code, but, by the time Christ was born, it had
already become obsolete. Consciously or unconsciously, mankind awaited another. It was not the rise of the new faith which
caused the decline of the old. It was the decline of the old
which favored the rise of the new. The extremely perspicacious
Tertullian said so openly. According to him, the whole pagan
world was already on its deathbed and the sooner it was buried
the better for everybody.

As for enemies, Rome had been accustomed to coping with
them for a thousand years. She had fought them and won. The
Visigoths, Vandals, and Huns were no fiercer nor were they
better warriors than the Cimbri, the Teutons, and Gauls who
crossed the Alps only to be met and destroyed by Caesar and
Marius. There is no reason to believe that Attila was a greater
general than Hannibal, who beat the Romans in ten battles and
still lost the war. Attila merely found himself up against a Roman army composed entirely of Germans, officers included.
(Gallienus had forbidden even senators to serve in the army.)
Rome was already occupied and garrisoned by foreign soldiery.

The so-called invasion was only a changing of the guard between barbarians.

This military crisis was the result of a more complex decadence of a mainly biological nature. It had begun among the upper classes in Rome (in Naples they say "fish always begins to stink at the head") with the loosening of family ties, the spread of birth control, the practice of abortion. The proud old aristocracy had been one of the greatest ruling classes the world has ever seen. For centuries it had set an example of integrity, courage, patriotism, in short, the "Roman character." After the Punic Wars, and more so after Caesar, it began to set an example of self-indulgence and vice. True, the families which composed the aristocracy had been decimated by political persecutions and wars in which their offspring had sacrificed themselves nobly. But the main reason they became extinct was the shortage of children. Great reformers like Caesar and Vespasian tried to replace them with more solid dynasties of country gentlemen from the provinces. These in their turn also became corrupt and the second generation were degenerate dandies of the type who would have been quite recognizable in the twentieth century.

This bad example was quick to spread. Already in the days of Tiberius there were state contributions to peasants to encourage them to have large families. Already, quite apart from plagues and wars, birth control was also practiced in the country, where the population was thinning out. Pertinax offered abandoned farms free to anybody who guaranteed to cultivate them. Foreigners poured into this material void, which was the result of a moral void. They came, especially from the east, in such overwhelming numbers that Rome had no time to absorb and weld them into a new and vital society. The process of assimilation had worked well up to Caesar's time. He had invited the Gauls to participate in the life of the city and had made them citizens, civil servants, officers and even senators. This, however, was impossible with the Germans, refractory as they were to classical civilization. As for the Orientals, they were a disaster. They fitted into the civilization, but only to corrupt it.

Politically, the result of all this was the despotism introduced by Tiberius. Only in a few cases was it "enlightened." It is silly to criticize Tiberius and throw all the blame on him for the catastrophe. Despotism is always an evil but there are situations which render it necessary. Rome was in just such a situation when Caesar initiated it. Brutus, his murderer, if he was not inspired by vulgar ambition, was certainly a poor devil who thought he could cure the dread disease by suppressing the symptoms while leaving the germ. Even the planned socialist experiment of Diocletian was an evil which solved no problem. Circumstances made it necessary as a last desperate resort.

To take a long view of events and to try to explain them, one might say that Rome was created for a mission, that she accomplished it, and died on its completion. This mission was to embody all the civilizations which had preceded her, those of Greece, the orient, Egypt, and Carthage, to fuse them into one and then to spread the resulting amalgam all over Europe and the Mediterranean basin. She did not contribute much in the fields of philosophy, art, or science. She did, however, provide the roads along which they traveled, the armies to defend them, a formidable legal code to ensure their orderly development, and a language to render them universal. Neither did she invent a political system. Monarchies and republics, aristocracies and democracies, liberalism and despotism, had all been tried before. Rome created models of them, and in all of them her practical, systematic genius is clearly to be seen.

When Constantine abdicated, she passed on her administrative structure to Constantinople which lived under it for another thousand years. Even Christianity, in order to triumph throughout the world, had to become Roman. Peter himself was well aware that the missionaries of Jesus could only conquer the earth if they took the Appian, Cassian, Aurelian, and other highways built by Roman engineers and avoided those unreliable tracks which merely led to the desert. His successors called themselves "supreme pontiffs" like those who had presided over the religious affairs of the pagan city. To mitigate the austere Hebrew ritual, they introduced many pagan elements into the new liturgy, such as the splendor and pageantry of certain ceremonies, the Latin tongue, and even a hint of polytheism in the veneration of the saints.

Thus as the hub of Christianity and no longer as the political capital of an empire, Rome prepared to resume her position as *caput mundi*. This she was to remain until the Reformation.

No city in the world has ever lived such a wonderful adventure. Her history is so great that even the gigantic crimes with which it is strewn pale into insignificance. Perhaps one of the troubles with Italy is that it has for its capital a city whose name and past are out of all proportion to the unassuming nature of its present inhabitants. Now when they shout *"Forza Roma!"* they are only cheering for a local soccer team.

Brief Chronological Table

CHAPTERS		
I–VI	753–510 B.C.	Founding of the city of Rome by Romulus. Romulus is succeeded by other kings: Numa Pompilius, Tullus Hostilius, Ancus Martius, and the Tarquins who are finally expelled and the republic established in 510 B.C.
VII–XI	493–264 B.C.	Rome expands over the Italian mainland.
XII–XVIII	264–146 B.C.	The wars against Carthage. Regulus, Fabius, Cato, the Scipios.
XIX–XXII	133–79 B.C.	The Gracchi, Marius, Sulla. The civil wars.
XXIII–XXVIII	70–30 B.C.	The last years of the republic. Pompey, Cicero, Caesar, Mark Antony.
XXIX–XXXVI	30 B.C.–A.D. 68	The Julio-Claudian emperors: Augustus, Tiberius, Caligula, Claudius, Nero. The beginning of Christianity.
XXXVII–XL	A.D. 69–96	The Flavian emperors: Vespasian, Titus, Domitian.

XLI–XLIII	A.D. 96–180	The golden age of the empire. Nerva, Trajan, Hadrian, Antoninus Pius, Marcus Aurelius.
XLIV	A.D. 180–235	Decline of the empire. Commodus, Septimius Severus, Caracalla, Heliogabalus, Alexander Severus.
XLV–XLVII	A.D. 284–337	Diocletian and Constantine. The division of the empire and the establishment of Christianity.
XLVIII–L	A.D. 337–476	Final decline and collapse of the western empire.

1. *Genealogical Tree of the Julian-Claudian Family*

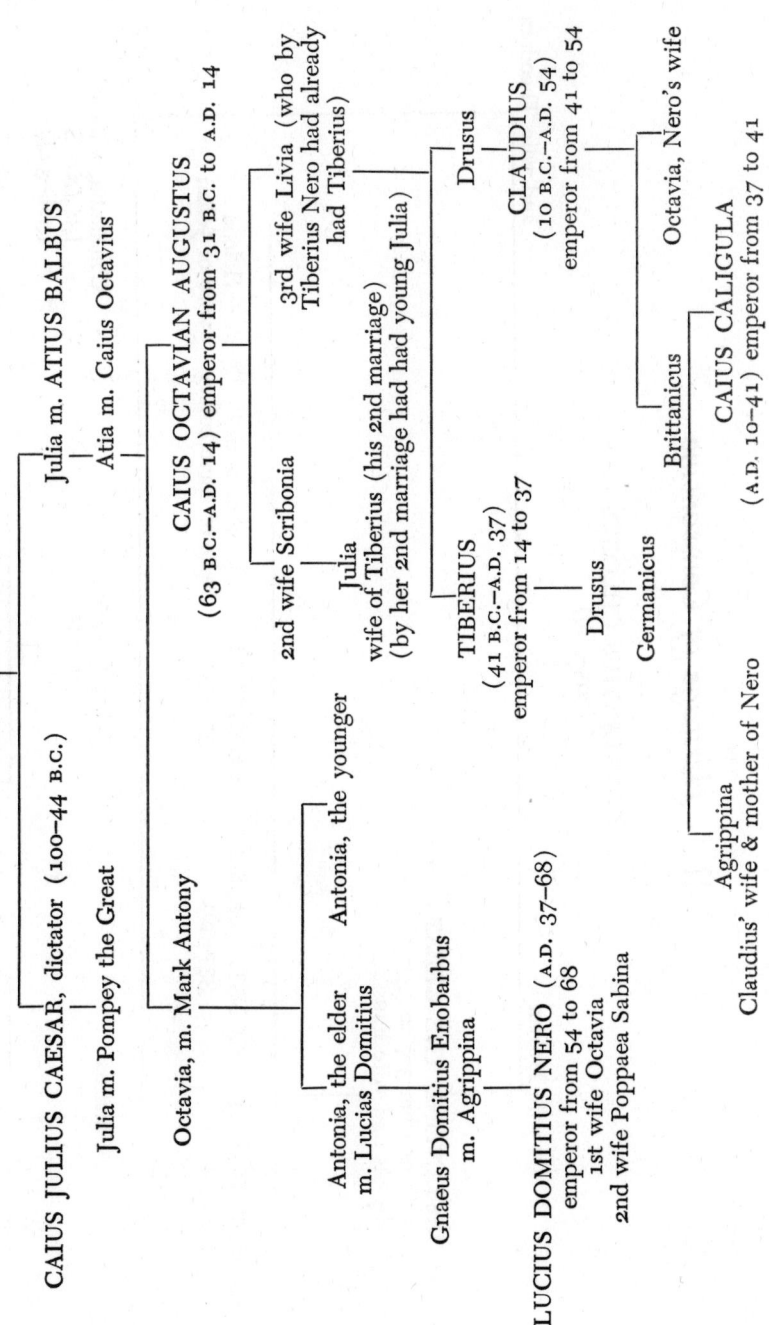

II. *Heritage of Constantine*

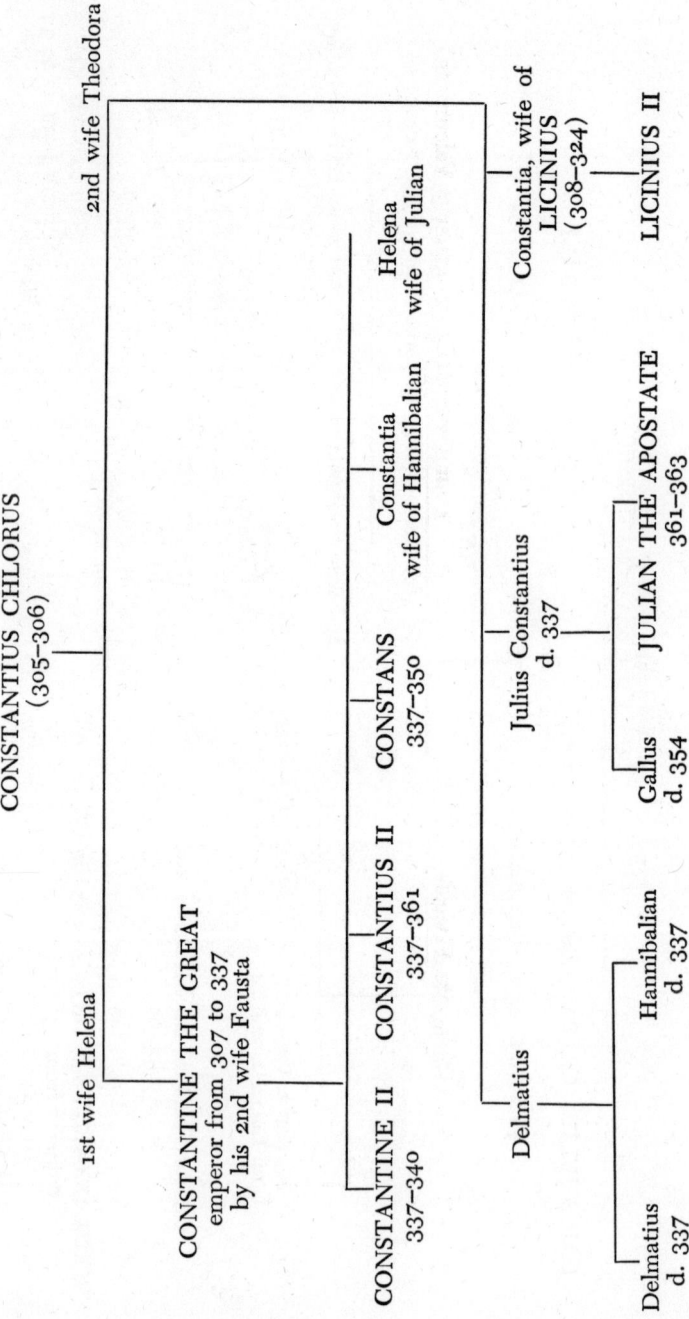

III. Heritage of Theodosius

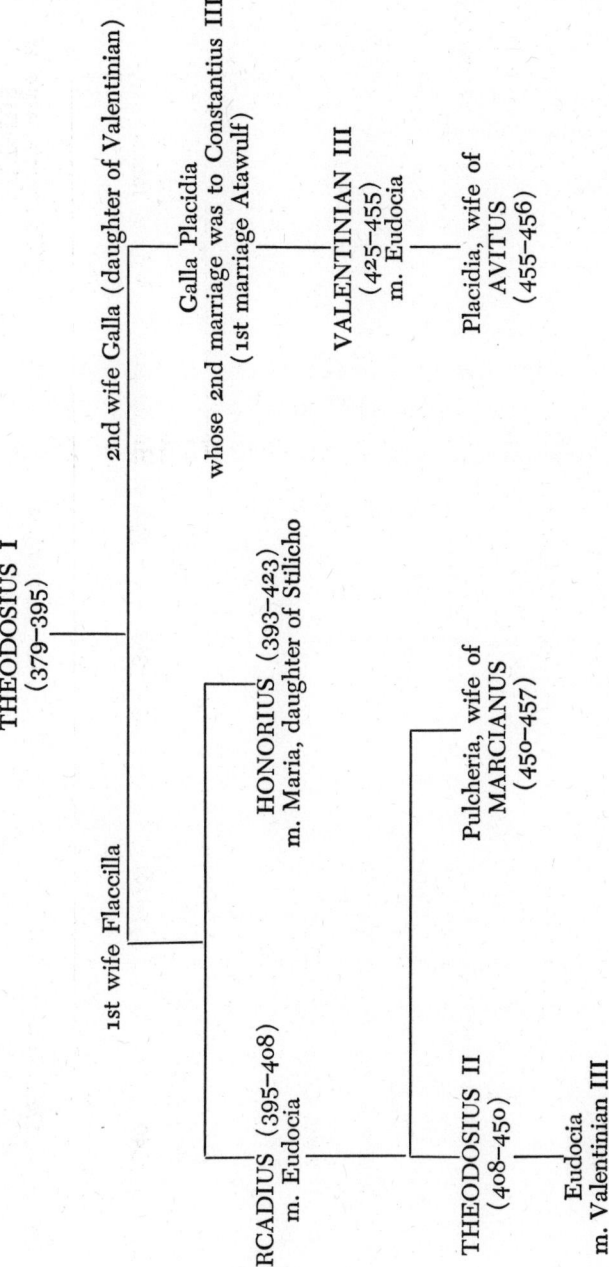

THEODOSIUS I
(379–395)

1st wife Flaccilla

2nd wife Galla (daughter of Valentinian)

ARCADIUS (395–408)
m. Eudocia

HONORIUS (393–423)
m. Maria, daughter of Stilicho

Galla Placidia
whose 2nd marriage was to Constantius III
(1st marriage Atawulf)

THEODOSIUS II
(408–450)

Pulcheria, wife of
MARCIANUS
(450–457)

VALENTINIAN III
(425–455)
m. Eudocia

Eudocia
m. Valentinian III

Placidia, wife of
AVITUS
(455–456)

Index

Senate, 18, 19, 26, 30, 36, 37, 38,
40, 43, 55, 58–59, 61–62, 74,
132–33, 134, 137, 140, 159, 160,
168–70, 175, 182, 188, 189, 270;
Carthaginian, 80
Seneca, 202, 206–8, 209–10, 211,
212, 235, 239, 247–48
Sertorius, Quintus, 149
Servius Tullius, 26–27, 31, 38
Severus, Alexander, 270
Severus, Caracalla, 268–69
Severus, Flavius Valerius, 277
Severus, Geta, 268
Severus, Libius, 306
Severus, Lucius Septimius, 267–68
Severus, Septimius, 284
Sextius, 44
Sicily, 36, 48, 84–85, 87–88, 90, 96,
125, 143, 170, 306, 307
Sidon, 77, 80
Sixtus II, Pope, 284
Spendius, 89
Statius, Caecilius, 118, 231, 235,
247
Stephen, Saint, 223
Stilicho, 300, 301, 302
Suetonius, 155, 174, 179, 202, 253,
255
Sulla, Lucius Cornelius, 131, 135–
141, 144, 145, 150, 157
Syracuse, 86, 90, 97
Syria, 166, 183, 251, 263

Tacitus, 207, 210, 229, 230, 231,
247, 252, 253
Tanaquilla, 12, 26
Tarentum, 47, 48, 49, 50, 173
Tarquin family, 20, 21, 23, 25, 28–
29, 31, 33
Tarquin, the Proud, 16, 28–29, 32,
34, 35, 38
Tarquinia, 11, 13, 14, 15, 25, 32,
33, 216, 217
Tarquin Priscus (Lucius Tarqui-
nius), 20, 24, 37, 75
Terence, 118, 119
Terentia (wife of Cicero), 143, 153
Tertullian, 226, 227, 279, 281, 283,
284, 308
Teutons, 131–32, 136
Thapsus, 175, 177
Theodosius (general), 294–95
Theodosius, Flavius, 296, 297–99,
300

Thessaly, 171, 297
Tiber, river, 5, 14, 15, 34, 278
Tiberius, 186, 189, 190, 191, 192,
194, 198–201, 242, 309
Tinia, 12
Titus, 230–31, 232, 244
Titus Tatius, 8–9, 16
Trajan, 208, 249–51, 254, 284
Tribunes, 60, 62, 140, 150
Tullus Hostilius, 17, 19–20
Tuscany, 8, 9, 89, 90, 216
Tusculum, 144, 153
Twelve Tables of the Decemvirs,
63–64, 120
Tyre, 77, 80
Tyrrhenian Sea, 10, 28

Umbrians, 7, 46
Utica, 172, 175

Valens, 294, 295–96
Valentinian I, 294–95, 297
Valentinian II, 295, 296, 297, 298
Valentinian III, 304, 306
Vandals, 273, 302, 304, 306, 307
Varro, Terentius, 95, 148
Veii, 11, 13, 35, 36, 41, 43
Venus-Aphrodite, 3, 6
Vercingetorix, 165
Verona, 216, 251
Verus, Lucius, 262, 263, 264
Verus, Lucius (father of above),
258
Vespasian, Titus Flavius, 205, 215,
228, 229–31, 234, 236, 242, 244
Vestal virgins, 67
Vindex, Julius, 212–13
Vipsania (wife of Tiberius), 191,
198
Virgil, 193–94, 196
Virginius, Lucius, 43
Vitellius, Aulus, 228–29
Volsci, 39, 40, 41, 43
Volterra, 33, 216

Xanthippus, 87
Xanthus, 184

Zama, 93, 99, 105, 106, 107
Zenobia, 273